Intersecting Environmental Social Governance and AI for Business Sustainability

Cristina Raluca Gh. Popescu
University of Bucharest, Romania & The Bucharest University of Economic Studies, Romania & The National Institute for Research and Development in Environmental Protection, Romania & INCDPM, Bucharest, Romania & National Research and Development Institute for Gas Turbines (COMOTI), Bucharest, Romania

Poshan Yu
Soochow University, China & Australian Studies Centre, Shanghai University, China

A volume in the Advances in Business Information Systems and Analytics (ABISA) Book Series

IGI Global
PUBLISHER of TIMELY KNOWLEDGE

Published in the United States of America by
IGI Global
Business Science Reference (an imprint of IGI Global)
701 E. Chocolate Avenue
Hershey PA, USA 17033
Tel: 717-533-8845
Fax: 717-533-8661
E-mail: cust@igi-global.com
Web site: http://www.igi-global.com

Library of Congress Cataloging-in-Publication Data

Names: Popescu, Cristina Raluca Gh., 1983- editor. | Yu, Poshan, editor.
Title: Intersecting environmental social governance and AI for business sustainability / edited by Cristina Raluca Gh. Popescu, Poshan Yu.
Description: Hershey, PA : Business Science Reference, [2024] | Includes bibliographical references and index. | Summary: "The primary objective of this book is to present a comprehensive overview of how the integration of ESG and AI is reshaping various industries and sectors around the globe"-- Provided by publisher.
Identifiers: LCCN 2023049073 (print) | LCCN 2023049074 (ebook) | ISBN 9798369311516 (hardcover) | ISBN 9798369311523 (ebook)
Subjects: LCSH: Industrial management--Environmental aspects. | Social responsibility of business. | Artificial intelligence.
Classification: LCC HD30.255 .I585 2024 (print) | LCC HD30.255 (ebook) | DDC 658.4/080285--dc23/eng/20240209
LC record available at https://lccn.loc.gov/2023049073
LC ebook record available at https://lccn.loc.gov/2023049074

This book is published in the IGI Global book series Advances in Business Information Systems and Analytics (ABISA) (ISSN: 2327-3275; eISSN: 2327-3283)

British Cataloguing in Publication Data
A Cataloguing in Publication record for this book is available from the British Library.

All work contributed to this book is new, previously-unpublished material.
The views expressed in this book are those of the authors, but not necessarily of the publisher.

For electronic access to this publication, please contact: eresources@igi-global.com.

Advances in Business Information Systems and Analytics (ABISA) Book Series

ISSN:2327-3275
EISSN:2327-3283

Editor-in-Chief: Madjid Tavana, La Salle University, USA

MISSION

The successful development and management of information systems and business analytics is crucial to the success of an organization. New technological developments and methods for data analysis have allowed organizations to not only improve their processes and allow for greater productivity, but have also provided businesses with a venue through which to cut costs, plan for the future, and maintain competitive advantage in the information age.

The **Advances in Business Information Systems and Analytics (ABISA) Book Series** aims to present diverse and timely research in the development, deployment, and management of business information systems and business analytics for continued organizational development and improved business value.

COVERAGE

- Geo-BIS
- Business Systems Engineering
- Strategic Information Systems
- Algorithms
- Data Management
- Business Intelligence
- Business Decision Making
- Data Analytics
- Performance Metrics
- Data Strategy

IGI Global is currently accepting manuscripts for publication within this series. To submit a proposal for a volume in this series, please contact our Acquisition Editors at Acquisitions@igi-global.com or visit: http://www.igi-global.com/publish/.

The Advances in Business Information Systems and Analytics (ABISA) Book Series (ISSN 2327-3275) is published by IGI Global, 701 E. Chocolate Avenue, Hershey, PA 17033-1240, USA, www.igi-global.com. This series is composed of titles available for purchase individually; each title is edited to be contextually exclusive from any other title within the series. For pricing and ordering information please visit http://www.igi-global.com/book-series/advances-business-information-systems-analytics/37155. Postmaster: Send all address changes to above address.

Titles in this Series

For a list of additional titles in this series, please visit:
http://www.igi-global.com/book-series/advances-business-information-systems-analytics/37155

Data-Driven Intelligent Business Sustainability
Sonia Singh (Toss Global Management, UAE) S. Suman Rajest (Dhaanish Ahmed College of Engineering, India) Slim Hadoussa (Brest Business School, France) Ahmed J. Obaid (University of Kufa, Iraq) and R. Regin (SRM Institute of Science and Technology, Ramapuram, India)
Business Science Reference • © 2024 • 320pp • H/C (ISBN: 9798369300497) • US $265.00

Advancement in Business Analytics Tools for Higher Financial Performance
Reza Gharoie Ahangar (Lewis University, USA) and Mark Napier (Lewis University, USA)
Business Science Reference • © 2023 • 321pp • H/C (ISBN: 9781668483862) • US $250.00

Cases on Enhancing Business Sustainability Through Knowledge Management Systems
Meir Russ (University of Wisconsin-Green Bay, USA & Stellenbosch University, South Africa)
Business Science Reference • © 2023 • 366pp • H/C (ISBN: 9781668458594) • US $240.00

Streamlining Organizational Processes Through AI, IoT, Blockchain, and Virtual Environments
Marisol Hernández Hernández (Universidad Autónoma del Estado de México, Mexico)
Business Science Reference • © 2023 • 253pp • H/C (ISBN: 9781668486399) • US $250.00

Data-Driven Approaches for Effective Managerial Decision Making
Anubha (Jaipuria Institute of Management, Ghaziabad, India) and Himanshu Sharma (IILM Institute for Higher Education, New Delhi, India)
Business Science Reference • © 2023 • 336pp • H/C (ISBN: 9781668475683) • US $255.00

Handbook of Research on AI and Machine Learning Applications in Customer Support and Analytics
Md Shamim Hossain (Hajee Mohammad Danesh Science and Technology University, Bangladesh) Ree Chan Ho (Taylor's University, Malaysia) and Goran Trajkovski (Western Governors University, USA)
Business Science Reference • © 2023 • 423pp • H/C (ISBN: 9781668471050) • US $325.00

For an entire list of titles in this series, please visit:
http://www.igi-global.com/book-series/advances-business-information-systems-analytics/37155

IGI Global
PUBLISHER of TIMELY KNOWLEDGE

701 East Chocolate Avenue, Hershey, PA 17033, USA
Tel: 717-533-8845 x100 • Fax: 717-533-8661
E-Mail: cust@igi-global.com • www.igi-global.com

Editorial Advisory Board

Table of Contents

Detailed Table of Contents

Investigating the unprecedented and not yet fully known impact of artificial intelligence (AI) for business sustainability in digital ecosystem implicates acknowledging and reshaping the pivotal role played by the environmental social governance (ESG) framework used to assess efficiency, performance, and international strategies in terms of business practices. What is more, achieving the Sustainable Development Goals (SDGs) by benefiting from guidance from ESG, as well as intelligence demonstrated by computers, may present both opportunities and risks, depending on the perspectives taken into consideration. Furthermore, building a culture of sustainability and developing successful sustainable business models have the amazing power of fostering climate justice, restoring damaged ecosystems, and developing action plans capable of offering immediate responses to climate change. Can individuals' quality of life and standards of living boost the overall well-being of societies when businesses are becoming more sustainable? Are the global living standards moving in the right direction?

Socially conscious investors, especially Gen Z, value ethics over money. ESG reports are as important as financial reports for them. ESG ratings from various sources can puzzle these Gen Z investors, as there is no standardization in ESG data. Firstly, the chapter focuses on the need to integrate AI into ESG reporting by highlighting the limitations of mere frameworks such as GRI, SASB, and ISSB. Secondly, it emphasizes the difference between traditional reporting and AI-integrated ESG reporting. It also points out the challenges of AI integration and ways to overcome these challenges. Lastly, the chapter also proposes the need for a unified framework, making it easier for investors to compare and make decisions.

This research delves into the nexus between corporate social responsibility (CSR) and green innovation performance (GIP) within Spain's wine sector. A novel conceptual framework is posited and empirically tested using a structural equation modelling technique (PLS-SEM), drawing on data from 202 Spanish wineries collated between September 2021 and January 2022. Findings underscore a robust positive correlation between CSR and GIP, with green intellectual capital (GIC) and knowledge management (KM) serving as pivotal mediators in this dynamic. This study augments the academic discourse in three salient ways: it illuminates the interplay between CSR and GIP in Spain's wine realm; pioneers the exploration of GIC and KM as mediatory factors in this relationship, a hitherto uncharted territory; and introduces a theoretical model, marking a significant stride in academic enrichment.

There seems to be a growing demand for companies to disclose information about natural, human, and financial resources used by them and its implications on environment and society. This gives rise to ESG metrics and related corporate reporting in their annual reports. The study aims to examine the relationship between internal and external sources of funds and the environmental, social, and governance score. The study is based on a sample of Nifty 50 companies listed on the National Stock Exchange of India, consisting of 245 observations. The study period was 5 years starting from 2017 to 2021. The variables studied were debt-equity ratio; retained earnings; and environmental, social, and corporate governance performance (ESG score). The study provides evidence of a negative relationship between debt-equity ratio and ESG score. The practical implication of the study is taken from the findings that it is high time for the firms to pay more attention towards improving their ESG score by taking up more sustainable projects through compliance of regulations in their business decisions.

This study centers on an examination of the influence of green intellectual capital (GIC), which encompasses the intangible assets related to sustainability within wineries and their associates, on green innovation performance (GIP). The investigation specifically delves into how GIP is shaped by GIC, with a particular focus on the mediating roles played by two key factors: knowledge management (KM) and corporate social responsibility (CSR). Moreover, the research introduces a conceptual model, which draws from prior research, and subjects it to testing using structural equation modeling (PLS-SEM) based on data collected from 202 wineries in Spain.

This study offers a pioneering exploration into the influence of organizational ambidexterity (OA) on sustainable performance (SP) within the Spanish wine sector. It further delves into the potential catalytic roles of corporate social responsibility (CSR) and knowledge management infrastructure (KMI) on these constructs. Drawing from an extensive literature review, a novel theoretical framework is proposed and empirically tested using structural equation modeling (PLS-SEM) on data sourced from 202 Spanish wineries between September 2021 and January 2022. Findings reveal a robust positive correlation between OA and SP, with OA serving as a partial mediator in the CSR-SP and KMI-SP dynamics. This research not only fills a notable gap in the literature by being the first to probe the OA-SP nexus in the wine milieu but also illuminates the under-researched catalysts of OA, thereby offering a refreshed perspective on enhancing wineries' multifaceted performance.

The objective of this chapter is to study the impact of organisational project management (OPM3) on the project performance (PP). PP performed by the organisations was assessed, based on interviews with project managers. Currently, little evidence is found in the academic literature regarding the impacts of the maturity models (MM) on the PP. The results show that the OPM3 provided a positive contribution to PP. Some of the interviewees stated that the adoption of OPM3 brought improvements at the process level, which made it possible to define in a more appropriate way, the scope, schedule, costs, and goals to perform improvements in the stakeholder's communication.

At a global level, governments are implementing transformation projects and initiatives to respond to a changing society and as part of a drive for efficiency and cost savings. Considering the profile of digital transformation (DT) projects within the context of the Portuguese public administration (PA), the proposal for a framework was developed which contains a set of attributes and criteria to identify the feasibility and adequacy of the projects submitted for evaluation. The study identifies the set of characteristics, critical success factors, challenges, and difficulties of DT projects in this public administration context. A qualitative methodological approach was used, and a single case study strategy was applied. The proposed framework enables a better alignment of strategies, as well as an improved allocation of resources and the consequent improvement of the performance objectives defined by the PA.

Preface

In recent years, the global business landscape has witnessed a remarkable convergence of two critical areas, Environmental Social Governance (ESG) and Artificial Intelligence (AI). As the world grapples with unprecedented challenges, from climate change to social inequities and economic uncertainties, the integration of ESG principles and AI technologies has emerged as a pivotal force in promoting sustainability and responsible business practices.

AI plays a vital role in today's landscape, offering people and organizations the opportunity to analyze all the information surrounding the environmental, the social, and the governance opportunities and risks, thus making all parties accountable for their decisions and actions. In this matter, AI has turned out to be an essential tool capable of assessing and addressing social and environmental issues in the best way possible. What is more, AI systems - through the AI applications - have the power to detect anomalies and prevent unwanted situations, focusing on ensuring transparency in communication and enabling the optimization of government functionalities.

This edited book, *Intersecting Environmental Social Governance and AI for Business Sustainability*, by Cristina Raluca Gh. Popescu and Poshan Yu, aims to explore the current trends and developments in the integration of ESG and AI, shedding light on their potential to drive transformative change in this new era, commonly referred to as the "New Normal." By delving into the multifaceted dimensions of this integration, we seek to provide valuable insights and critical analysis for academics, researchers, policymakers, and practitioners navigating the rapidly evolving landscape of sustainability and AI.

The primary objective of this book is to present a comprehensive overview of how the integration of ESG and AI is reshaping various industries and sectors around the globe. By analyzing case studies, empirical research, and relevant theoretical frameworks, we aim to highlight both the immense opportunities and potential challenges that arise when combining these two powerful domains.

Specifically, this book aims to address the following key themes:

1. ESG Metrics and AI: Exploring how AI can enhance the measurement, monitoring, and reporting of ESG metrics, enabling organizations to effectively assess their environmental and social impact.
2. AI-Driven Sustainable Operations: Investigating how AI-driven technologies can optimize resource allocation, energy efficiency, and waste management, thus fostering sustainable operational practices across different industries.
3. AI and Ethical Considerations: Examining the ethical dilemmas and risks associated with integrating AI and ESG, such as biases, privacy concerns, and potential negative externalities, while proposing strategies to mitigate them.
4. AI-Driven Decision-Making and Governance: Investigating the role of AI in augmenting decision-making processes, facilitating responsible investment decisions, and enhancing stakeholder engagement within an ESG context.
5. Emerging AI-Based Solutions for Sustainable Development: Showcasing innovative AI-powered solutions, such as predictive analytics, smart cities, and precision agriculture, which contribute to sustainable development goals.
6. AI-Based Solutions for Corporate Governance Data: These days, specialists emphasize the role of AI in those cases in which corporate governance data analysis is involved. In this matter, there is a pivotal role played by AI in regard to the analysis of corporate governance data, since the purpose is to be able to assess, on the one hand, the organizations' ESG performance and, on the other hand, to present the aspects that require improvement over time. Sustainability comes to play a determining role in these situations, since organizations are able to identify the ESG tremendous risks as well as the great opportunities due to arise. The accent ought to be put on enhancing the sustainability strategies, in the context in which AI can reduce the harm done by individuals and by companies to the environment.

This book is designed to:

- Clearly articulate the purpose and scope of the study on current trends and developments in the integration of environmental social governance (ESG) and artificial intelligence to promote sustainability in the new normal.
- Provide an insightful analysis of the advancements and shifts in the integration of ESG and artificial intelligence, identifying key trends and developments in this evolving field.
- Present comprehensive research on the practical applications and benefits of integrating ESG and artificial intelligence for sustainability, highlighting successful case studies and their impact.

- Explore the challenges and potential risks associated with the integration of ESG and artificial intelligence, examining ethical considerations and the need for responsible deployment.
- Offer recommendations and insights for businesses, policymakers, and stakeholders to effectively leverage the integration of ESG and artificial intelligence to drive sustainable practices and address pressing environmental and social issues.
- Provide a forward-looking perspective on the future trajectory of the integration of ESG and artificial intelligence, discussing emerging technologies and potential opportunities for further advancement.
- Foster a deeper understanding of the concept of sustainability in the new normal, emphasizing the role and significance of ESG and artificial intelligence in shaping sustainable practices across industries.
- Engage with key stakeholders in the field, including industry experts, academics, and professionals, in order to gather diverse perspectives and enhance the credibility and relevance of the study.
- Establish a framework for continued research and exploration in the field, encouraging further investigation into the integration of ESG and artificial intelligence as a means to promote sustainability in the ever-evolving new normal.
- Contribute to the broader discourse surrounding the intersection of ESG, artificial intelligence, and sustainability, generating new insights and knowledge that can guide businesses and organizations toward responsible and sustainable practices in the future.
- Highlight the impact that AI might have on corporate governance, in the context in which AI techniques are the ones responsible for facilitating both customers and shareholders' interests within different types of organizations.

This book will delve into various aspects of ESG and AI integration, providing readers with a comprehensive understanding of the challenges, opportunities, and ethical considerations surrounding this critical intersection. We will examine the impact of AI on ESG integration for sustainable development in the post-pandemic era, the evolution of ESG practices, and the role of AI in optimizing environmental, social, and governance data collection. We will also explore the potential ethical concerns and challenges, compare different AI-based tools, evaluate the benefits and drawbacks of incorporating AI, and study the role of AI in predicting and mitigating ESG risks.

Furthermore, the book will present case studies highlighting successful AI applications in ESG integration and investigate the barriers to AI adoption in ESG integration. It will also analyze the potential implications of AI in reshaping corporate governance practices and driving positive environmental and social impacts.

As we continue to explore the methods and solutions that AI investments can bring to the identification of ESG impacts and the reduction of harm to the environment, we will also focus on how AI can enhance and optimize individuals' lives, contributing to global sustainable development strategies and emphasizing the improvement of activities between people and businesses.

AI solutions in the context of ESG should be responsible for finding valuable ways to enhance energy efficiency sources, reduce waste, and preserve ecosystems and biodiversity. This book will serve as a guide for those seeking to understand and navigate the dynamic landscape where ESG and AI intersect for the greater goal of sustainability in the new normal. We hope that the insights, research, and discussions within these pages will inspire and inform the next generation of responsible business practices.

CHAPTER OVERVIEW

Chapter 1: Exploring the Synergies Between Environmental Social Governance and AI for Business Sustainability – Tackling Climate Adaptation, Mitigating Climate Change Efforts, and Pursuing Climate Justice

In this chapter, authored by Cristina Raluca Gh. Popescu and Arturo Luque González, we embark on a journey to investigate the significant yet not fully understood impact of Artificial Intelligence (AI) on business sustainability within the digital ecosystem. Our exploration is centered on the pivotal role played by the Environmental Social Governance (ESG) framework in assessing business efficiency, performance, and international strategies. We delve into the possibilities and challenges of harnessing AI and ESG principles to achieve the Sustainable Development Goals (SDGs) from different perspectives. Furthermore, we examine how fostering a culture of sustainability and developing successful sustainable business models can contribute to climate justice, ecosystem restoration, and the formulation of action plans to combat climate change. Our chapter also raises important questions about whether businesses becoming more sustainable can elevate the overall well-being and living standards of societies worldwide.

Chapter 2: Role of AI in Strengthening ESG Governance – Perspective From Industry Experts

This chapter, authored by Jayalakshmi M, Maria A, and Girish S, provides a detailed exploration of how Artificial Intelligence (AI) facilitates the seamless integration of key sustainability reporting frameworks such as the Global Reporting Initiative (GRI), the Sustainability Accounting Standards Board (SASB), and the International Sustainability Standards Board (ISSB). The chapter illuminates the intersection of AI and sustainability by offering a comprehensive perspective on how organizations employ algorithmic systems to enhance their ESG governance. It also delves into the challenges associated with integrating AI, particularly the environmental considerations and the imperative for responsible AI development. Furthermore, the chapter highlights how AI can be effectively incorporated into sustainable development and the alterations required in decision-making processes. Readers will gain insights into how AI can enhance data analysis and reporting and how organizations manage their ESG responsibilities.

Chapter 3: Bridging Corporate Social Responsibility and Green Innovation – A Structural Equation Study of Spain's Wine Industry

Authored by Javier Martínez Falcó, Bartolomé Marco, Eduardo Sánchez-García, Luis A. Millán-Tudela, and Cristina Raluca Gh. Popescu, this research investigates the relationship between Corporate Social Responsibility (CSR) and Green Innovation Performance (GIP) within Spain's wine industry. Using advanced structural equation modeling techniques, the chapter empirically tests a novel conceptual framework and highlights the significant role played by Green Intellectual Capital (GIC) and Knowledge Management (KM) as mediators in this dynamic relationship. This study not only enhances our understanding of CSR and GIP in Spain's wine sector but also introduces a theoretical model, contributing substantially to the academic discourse.

Chapter 4: The Role of Air Pollution in the ESG Model at World Level

Authored by Cosimo Magazzino and Angelo Leogrande, this chapter delves into the role of Air Pollution (AP) within the Environmental, Social, and Governance (ESG) model using data from the World Bank's ESG Database for 193 countries. The chapter employs various statistical methodologies to analyze the relationship between AP and various factors. Additionally, the authors explore machine learning algorithms for predicting future AP levels. The chapter concludes with insights into the expected changes in AP for the analyzed countries. This chapter provides valuable insights into the complex interplay of environmental factors and ESG metrics on a global scale.

Chapter 5: Critical Analysis of Emerging and Disruptive Digital Technologies in an Era of Artificial Intelligence (AI)

In this chapter, authored by José Vargas-Hernandez and Omar Vargas-Gonzàlez, we embark on a critical analysis of emerging and disruptive digital technologies in the era of Artificial Intelligence (AI). The study assesses how these technologies create both opportunities and challenges, impacting individuals, organizations, institutions, and society as a whole. The analysis is based on recent developments reported in scientific literature, and it highlights the need for ethical discussions and leadership to guide digital transformation and address ethical concerns in the near future. Readers will gain a deep understanding of the evolving landscape of digital technologies and AI in a rapidly changing world.

Chapter 6: Capital Structure Decisions Influencing Non-Financial Performance of Companies (ESG)

Authored by Hemalata Radhakrishna and Konyn Lappay, this chapter addresses the growing demand for companies to disclose information about their use of natural, human, and financial resources and their impact on the environment and society. The study examines the relationship between internal and external sources of funds and Environmental, Social, and Corporate Governance (ESG) scores using data from the National Stock Exchange of India. The findings reveal a negative relationship between Debt-Equity ratios and ESG scores, highlighting the need for firms to improve their ESG performance by taking up more sustainable projects. This chapter offers valuable insights into the financial decisions that influence non-financial performance.

Chapter 7: The Interplay of Green Intellectual Capital and Green Innovation Performance – Insights From Spain's Wine Sector

Authored by Javier Martínez Falcó, Bartolomé Marco-Lajara, Eduardo Sánchez-García, Luis A. Millán-Tudela, and Cristina Raluca Gh. Popescu, this chapter examines the influence of Green Intellectual Capital (GIC) on Green Innovation Performance (GIP) within the Spanish wine sector. The study explores the mediating roles of Knowledge Management (KM) and Corporate Social Responsibility (CSR) in shaping

GIP. Using structural equation modeling, the chapter tests a conceptual model based on data from Spanish wineries. This research contributes to our understanding of the impact of GIC on GIP and highlights the dynamic relationship between these factors in the context of sustainability.

Chapter 8: Organizational Ambidexterity and Its Impact on Sustainability – Insights From Spain's Wine Industry

In this chapter, authored by Javier Martínez Falcó, Bartolomé Marco, Eduardo Sánchez-García, Luis A. Millán-Tudela, and Cristina Raluca Gh. Popescu, we explore the influence of Organizational Ambidexterity (OA) on Sustainable Performance (SP) within Spain's wine sector. The study delves into the potential roles of Corporate Social Responsibility (CSR) and Knowledge Management Infrastructure (KMI) in shaping OA and SP. By proposing a theoretical framework and employing structural equation modeling, the chapter offers valuable insights into the dynamic relationship between these factors and their impact on wineries' multifaceted performance. This research advances our understanding of how organizations can enhance their sustainability efforts.

Chapter 9: Project Management Maturity – OPM3 Study

Authored by Jorge Gomes, Mário Romão, and Ilércio Bento, this chapter focuses on the impact of Organisational Project Management (OPM3) on Project Performance (PP). The study assesses the contribution of OPM3 to project performance based on interviews with project managers. The findings indicate a positive contribution of OPM3 to PP, particularly in terms of process improvement and stakeholder communication. This chapter sheds light on the role of project management maturity models in enhancing project performance, offering insights for practitioners and researchers in the field.

Chapter 10: Advancing Sustainability – ESG Evolution and the AI Edge

In this chapter, authored by Nitish Minz and Yash Khattar, we delve into how Artificial Intelligence (AI) can advance corporate sustainability by integrating Environmental, Social, and Governance (ESG) practices. The research investigates the effective integration of AI into ESG initiatives, addresses challenges, and explores ethical considerations. By employing a literature review and case studies, the chapter demonstrates AI's impact on ESG efforts, focusing on data analysis, predictive modeling, and risk assessment. Readers will gain insights into the expanding role of ESG and AI's integration for sustainability in today's business landscape.

Chapter 11: Benefits Management and Balanced Scorecard in Dynamic Environments

Authored by Jorge Gomes and Mário Romão, this chapter examines the limitations of the Balanced Scorecard (BSC) in rapidly changing business environments. The study proposes a complementary approach, benefits management, using a benefits dependency network. By analyzing a case study, the chapter highlights the strengths of benefits management in guiding and supporting benefits achievement related to investments in dynamic business environments. This chapter provides valuable insights into managing business performance and investments in a world characterized by unpredictability and change.

Chapter 12: Digital Transformation in Public Administration

In this chapter, authored by Jorge Gomes and Mário Romão, the focus shifts to digital transformation in public administration, a critical domain undergoing significant change. The authors propose a framework with attributes and criteria for evaluating digital transformation projects in the context of Portuguese public administration. This framework aims to improve strategy alignment, resource allocation, and performance objectives. Through a qualitative case study approach, the chapter identifies the characteristics, critical success factors, challenges, and difficulties associated with digital transformation projects in the public administration context. This chapter offers valuable insights for governments and public organizations striving for efficiency and cost savings in a rapidly evolving society.

These chapters cover a broad spectrum of topics at the intersection of Environmental Social Governance (ESG) and Artificial Intelligence (AI), providing readers with diverse insights into the impact and potential of this dynamic field. From the challenges of tackling climate change and climate justice to the role of AI in ESG governance, and from corporate social responsibility in the wine industry to the impact of air pollution at a global level, this edited book offers a comprehensive exploration of this critical intersection. Each chapter provides a unique perspective, contributing to the ongoing conversation about sustainability and responsible business practices.

IN SUMMARY

In concluding this edited reference book, we find ourselves at the nexus of two transformative domains: Environmental Social Governance (ESG) and Artificial Intelligence (AI). The journey we've undertaken, with the help of our esteemed contributors, has illuminated the immense potential and inherent challenges at the intersection of these fields.

The chapters in this book have explored the multifaceted dimensions of ESG and AI integration, shedding light on the profound impact they have on business sustainability, environmental stewardship, and social justice. We have ventured into uncharted territories, delving into the pivotal role AI plays in redefining the way businesses assess efficiency, performance, and international strategies within the digital ecosystem. Our exploration has revealed opportunities and risks, highlighting the need for a balanced perspective on the utilization of AI for the common good.

We've witnessed how ESG and AI can offer tools and methodologies for addressing critical global challenges, from climate adaptation and mitigating climate change efforts to pursuing climate justice. By harnessing AI's analytical capabilities and integrating ESG principles, organizations have the potential to navigate this ever-evolving landscape responsibly and sustainably.

Through the lens of industry experts, we've examined the practical applications of AI for ESG governance, offering insights into the integration of sustainability reporting frameworks and the potential for improving data analysis and reporting. We've discussed the ethical considerations that must underpin AI development in the ESG context, emphasizing the importance of responsible AI deployment.

Within the context of the wine industry in Spain, we've explored the intricate relationship between Corporate Social Responsibility (CSR) and Green Innovation Performance (GIP). These chapters have unveiled the pivotal role of Green Intellectual Capital (GIC) and Knowledge Management (KM) in shaping this dynamic, providing invaluable insights for businesses striving for sustainability.

The exploration of air pollution's role in the ESG model on a global scale has further broadened our perspective. Our contributors have demonstrated the complexities of this interplay, shedding light on the environmental factors that influence ESG metrics. The use of machine learning algorithms for predicting future air pollution levels has given us a glimpse into the potential of AI in addressing environmental challenges.

Our critical analysis of emerging and disruptive digital technologies in the era of AI has emphasized the importance of ethical leadership and the need to guide the ethical disruption of digital technologies. We've recognized that digital transformation is an unstoppable force that must be directed by humans with a clear understanding of acceptable ethical behaviors.

The relationship between capital structure decisions and non-financial performance, as examined in the Indian context, has highlighted the imperative for companies to pay attention to their ESG scores. By analyzing the impact of Debt-Equity ratios and Retained Earnings on ESG performance, we've underscored the importance of making sustainable choices in business decisions.

The exploration of Green Intellectual Capital (GIC) and its impact on Green Innovation Performance (GIP) within the Spanish wine sector has contributed significantly to our understanding of how sustainability and knowledge management influence innovation. This research lays the foundation for more informed decisions in the quest for sustainability.

Organizational Ambidexterity's influence on Sustainable Performance within the Spanish wine sector has opened new avenues for research. We've uncovered the positive correlation between Organizational Ambidexterity (OA) and Sustainable Performance (SP) and identified key mediators, such as Corporate Social Responsibility (CSR) and Knowledge Management Infrastructure (KMI). This research underscores the complexity of managing multifaceted performance in organizations.

Project Management Maturity, as examined through OPM3, has revealed its positive contribution to Project Performance. The study offers insights into how mature project management practices can enhance project outcomes, improving process efficiency and stakeholder communication.

Our exploration of the evolving role of ESG and AI integration for corporate sustainability emphasizes the importance of data-driven decision-making and innovation. AI offers the potential to revolutionize the way we approach sustainability, fostering a more responsible and efficient business landscape.

Lastly, we've explored the challenges of operating in dynamic business environments and how benefits management can complement the Balanced Scorecard approach to guide and support benefits achievement related to investments. In a world marked by rapid change, this research provides a roadmap for businesses seeking to thrive in uncertainty.

As we conclude this journey, we are left with a profound understanding of the transformative power of ESG and AI. The insights offered in this book have far-reaching implications for businesses, policymakers, researchers, and practitioners navigating the evolving landscape of sustainability. They guide us in our collective quest for responsible and sustainable practices in a world facing unprecedented challenges.

We extend our heartfelt gratitude to our contributors for their invaluable insights and expertise. It is our hope that the knowledge shared in this edited reference book will continue to drive transformative change, fostering a more sustainable and just future.

In the ever-evolving "New Normal," let these chapters serve as a source of inspiration and guidance for the responsible integration of ESG and AI, and the pursuit of a better, more sustainable world.

Warm regards,

Cristina Raluca Gh. Popescu
University of Bucharest, Romania & The Bucharest University of Economic Studies, Romania & The National Institute for Research and Development in Environmental Protection, Romania & INCDPM, Bucharest, Romania & National Research and Development Institute for Gas Turbines (COMOTI), Bucharest, Romania

Poshan Yu
Soochow University, China & Australian Studies Centre, Shanghai University, China

Chapter 1
Exploring the Synergies Between Environmental Social Governance and AI for Business Sustainability:
Tackling Climate Adaptation, Mitigating Climate Change Efforts, and Pursuing Climate Justice

Cristina Raluca Gh. Popescu
https://orcid.org/0000-0002-5876-0550
University of Bucharest, Romania & The Bucharest University of Economic Studies, Romania

Arturo Luque González
Universidad Técnica de Manabí, Ecuador & Observatorio Euromediterráneo de Espacio Público y Democracia, Ecuador

ABSTRACT

Investigating the unprecedented and not yet fully known impact of artificial intelligence (AI) for business sustainability in digital ecosystem implicates acknowledging and reshaping the pivotal role played by the environmental social governance (ESG) framework used to assess efficiency, performance, and international strategies in terms of business practices. What is more, achieving the Sustainable Development Goals (SDGs) by benefiting from guidance from ESG, as well as intelligence demonstrated by computers, may present both opportunities and risks, depending

DOI: 10.4018/979-8-3693-1151-6.ch001

on the perspectives taken into consideration. Furthermore, building a culture of sustainability and developing successful sustainable business models have the amazing power of fostering climate justice, restoring damaged ecosystems, and developing action plans capable of offering immediate responses to climate change. Can individuals' quality of life and standards of living boost the overall well-being of societies when businesses are becoming more sustainable? Are the global living standards moving in the right direction?

INTRODUCTION

Nowadays, more and more specialists at a global level are emphasizing the fact that intersecting Environmental Social Governance (ESG) and Artificial Intelligence (AI) for business sustainability plays a vital role in coping with the latest changes and challenges that the world currently confronts with. In this given context, it seems that ESG is being regarded as far more necessary and far more powerful than any other form of governance, since the accent is put on both the environment and the society – which are both in tremendous need of attention these days. In addition, the society in which all the activities take place and, also, which is responsible for the manner in which these activities are performed by individuals, is becoming more and more aware of the power provided by the use of AI.

Nevertheless, there is already common knowledge that the intensive use of AI may either help individuals, communities, and businesses, or it may as well enhance the problems already existing in today's society by generating more and more controversies regarding sensible, yet highly problematic issues, such as, for example: (a) the fact that, by regularly using AI, there will be less and less needed to implicate individuals in routine tasks, since these tasks will be performed far better and much faster by robots, which will automatically lead to very high employment rates; (b) the fact that, by asking individuals to work together with AI for specific jobs – the purpose being, in essence, to determine individuals to "show" the robots what they have learned so far and what they are capable to accomplish so far with their own knowledge and strength, the AI programs will get the opportunity to become more and more powerful, will gain precious knowledge by performing different tasks and will, ultimately, become indispensable to the employers and users; (c) the fact that, there is a fine line these days between working ethically and making use responsibly of AI in all the jobs in which AI is currently being used in today's society since creating the legal background and frameworks for the use of AI is only at the beginning; and (d) the fact that, although it is being more and more criticized by some categories of professionals and specialists, the use of AI will soon be inevitable in a lot of jobs, for the simple reason that it will implicate, on the medium and long term, less costs for the ones using AI, better performed tasks, faster performed activities, and less stress for business developers and owners that would normally arise when working with people.

Going further with the current analysis, today's society has clearly become more avid and more capable to explore the synergies between ESG and AI for business sustainability, in this manner becoming closer and closer to approaching and to obtaining valuable goals for the preservation and the good health of the Planet, such as, for instance: tackling opportunities for climate adaptation, mitigating climate change efforts, and pursuing climate justice. In consequence, there should be a major concern these days for the well-being of individuals as well as for the health of the Planet, given the fact that, lately, there have been registered so many disasters as a result of humans not managing their lives, their jobs, and the areas, regions, or countries in which they live and work in a sustainable manner (Luque González *et al.*, 2022a). Fortunately, there is an important accent put today on key aspects, such as: (a) the way in which living standards should be interpreted and how should these living standards highlight the reality of today's society (Popescu & Luque González, 2022a); (b) the importance of happiness at a wide level, not only in the case of individuals, but, also, when referring to communities and the environment (Popescu & Luque González, 2022b); (c) the living costs which should be associated with responsible and sustainable ways of performing in the society; (d) the responsible and the sustainable use of computer-controlled robots, so that benefits arise not only for the employers but, also, for the communities and the society as a whole (Popescu & Luque González, 2022c); and (e) the power of creativity and the role of innovation for businesses and for raising quality, enhancing knowledge, yet with a particular accent on the ambitious Sustainable Development Goals (SDGs), Corporate Social Responsibility (CSR), and Global Economic Environment Preservation (Luque González *et al.*, 2022b).

What is more, since there is such an immense pressure put on all countries to comply with the SDGs, it is our firm belief that achieving the SDGs by benefiting from guidance from ESG as well as intelligence demonstrated by computers, may present both opportunities and risks, depending on the perspectives taken into consideration. Hence, according to specialists, everything has to be seen through multiple facets and all aspects need to be considered before taking certain steps and making decisions in this matter. First of all, there ought to be emphasized that the SDGs have not only supporters but also critics. For instance, these aims may not only lead to making the activities more sustainable and the individuals more responsible but, also, they may put more pressure on people, communities, and entities to comply, in a very short time period, with certain rules, regulations, and general targets, which may lead to certain losses both at the level of people and Organizations: (a) some individuals may lose their jobs, in case their work implicates using resources that are not considered sustainable anymore by the governments; (b) some businesses may soon disappear – in those cases in which they are considered by world leaders highly polluting, which may irreversibly affect the lives of the communities, areas, regions, and countries where those activities were located; and (c) some businesses may be closed and replaced with some new ones which, at a certain moment in time, may seem more responsibly and more sustainably oriented, yet over the years may be regarded even more dangerous and polluting than the previous activities. Second of all, the SDGs have numerous supporters at a global level and, generally thinking, their role is vital to the well-being of individuals and to the health of the Planet. Nevertheless, adopting these SGDs ought to be done step by step. The implementation of the SDGs aims and targets needs to be done in a personalized manner, taking into consideration the individuals, the groups of individuals, and the countries under analysis. Indeed, the Global Goals (GG) are regarded as extremely brave but, in order to be successful on the medium and on the long term, they should protect the communities, countries, and environment – without further increasing the gaps between people. In this matter, achieving the SDGs – by benefiting from guidance from ESG as well as intelligence demonstrated by computers, may become essential, not only at present, but, also, for the next decades to come.

Furthermore, on the one hand, building a culture of sustainability and, on the other hand, developing successful Sustainable Business Models (SBM) have the wonderful power of fostering climate justice, restoring the damaged ecosystems, and developing the action plans capable to offer immediate responses to climate change (Popescu & González, 2023). As seen in practice in the last years, the idea of becoming sustainable is not just a present state of mind. It is something that should be built in time, little by little, step by step, yet with significant results due to be expected now and over the next years to come. Also, since sustainability addresses the case of the present generations as well as the situations specific to the future generations, the idea of creating and of building a culture of sustainability becomes pivotal to the existence of mankind.

In this day and age, understanding the implications of people's living standards on the day to day activities as well as on the economy as a whole represents a vital task for visionary country leaders, skilled managers, influential professionals which are activating in the business world, and highly trained specialists belonging to different domains of activity. Hence, specialists are asking themselves: What is the significance of "a better life"? Or, can "a better life" be measured and can specific indicators be attributed to "a better life" in order to have a general accepted concept by all? Based on the most recent studies, on the one hand, it is very challenging for specialists to create an indicator capable to reflect individuals' general image on what does a better life represent for them and, on the other hand, it is highly difficult for professionals to have access to recent data capable to reflect individuals' shared views on what does a better life represent for them in the context in which such indicators are created (OECD (Organization for Economic Co-operation and Development), 2022a). Also, there are major challenges faced by individuals, depending on the social, economic, political, and demographical context, which implicates the fact that people's living standards are hard to evaluate and are even harder to predict on the medium-term and long-term.

Besides all these, the living standards ought to be thoroughly analyzed and carefully addressed while relating them to the importance, role, and meaning of the SDGs (United Nations (UN), 2015; United Nations (UN), 2018). Hence, there are numerous aspects that should be taken into account, as follows: (a) first of all, in the specialists' opinion, the living standards might be successfully reflected with the aid of the general quality of life indicators which have the crucial role of measuring population's well-being in various material and immaterial dimensions, such as, for instance the income, the jobs, and the housing conditions – seen as an integrating part of the material dimension; and the health, the education, the environmental quality, the personal security, the civic engagement, and the work and the life balance – seen as an integrating part of the immaterial dimensions (United Nations (UN), 2015; United Nations (UN), 2018; Federal Statistical Office, 2022); (b) second of all, the living standards might be successfully reflected with the aid of the specific, more targeted quality of life indicators which have the tremendous power to expend the general framework normally attributed to those processes specific to measuring the population's well-being (United Nations (UN), 2015; United Nations (UN), 2018; Federal Statistical Office, 2022).

Interestingly, according to the most recent international researches available on this very important theme, the Swiss Federal Statistical Office expended the quality of life dimensions with new and pivotal factors, such as: the infrastructure and the services, the mobility and the culture and the leisure (Federal Statistical Office, 2022). There could be several explanations for such a brave decision to enlarge the list specific to the quality of life dimensions. In this matter, for instance, the infrastructure and the services have the major power of offering individuals and businesses the opportunity to get to one place to another in a faster way with decent and most necessary means of transportation available these days. In addition, for example, the mobility and the culture and the leisure are responsible for making people's lives more comfortable. Constantly adapting to the newest and more sophisticated trends in terms of transportation may have seemed a luxury a while ago for certain individuals, communities or businesses. Yet, these days, the idea of luxury in this matter has almost disappeared and is little by little replaced by the simple necessity to get from one place to another in order to maintain a decent lifestyle, have a decent job and, in essence, have the possibility to a lead decent existence.

At a general level, the living standards refer to both objective and subjective characteristics, such as, the following ones: (a) first of all, when addressing the objective (tangible) characteristics which belong to the standards of living, one could think about the level of income belonging to the individuals, the material goods possessed, the access to clean water, the quality of the healthcare systems, the existence of the education standards, and the safety of the place where the individuals live (Federal Statistical Office, 2022; Šebestová and Popescu, 2022); and (b) second of all, when addressing the subjective (intangible) characteristics which belong to the standards of living, one could have in mind the degree of comfort perceived by people, the necessities due to be satisfied in different areas and the wealth belonging to certain classes, individuals' personal liberty, the environmental quality, and the aspirations of individuals as members of the society while compared to their family, friends, and the group to which they belong as part of a community (United Nations Geneva, 2022; Organization for Economic Co-operation and Development), 2022b). Hence, it can be concluded that both objective and subjective characteristics of the living standards are highly interesting and are of utmost importance given the times humanity is currently living.

So, what does living a better life mean? Is there a successful recipe for this? How can people have access to this recipe and what do they have to do in order to be happier, more satisfied, and more fulfilled with joy?

Given the fact that individuals are different in every possible way, it is impossible to offer a "success recipe" due to be applied afterwards by people in order to replicate the experiences lived by other in order to be able to generate their own success in life. Besides these, the idea of increasing the living standards of the population – although highly mediatized in the recent years, is very challenging since there are so many gaps and inequalities among people and communities at a worldwide level. What may seem for someone in a true delicacy or a luxury in one part of the world, may be for someone else a common good that may not even be appreciated enough due to its abundance in that certain area. A good example in this case is represented by water. In some parts of the world, water is a rear good to which individuals have limited access (maybe for several hours a day or just a few times during the week) and which is highly cherished and praised by the people, the communities, and the environment. In other parts of the world, water – also, as a rare good, may be very expensive if filtered or if bought in special recipients when transformed in potable water. However, in other parts of the world water may be a common good. In those areas individuals are able to use water abundantly for their day to day activities, without giving any additional thought that the "good" that they are using represents a true treasure for some other group of people in another part of the Planet. So, there is no way to put an equal sign between the manner in which water is perceived in all parts of the world, but access to water may influence the living standards of people. Some individuals may feel excitement, joy, happiness, and fulfillment when having access to water (even potable water, which may require access to money). In opposition, other individuals may not even understand how fortunate they are to have constant and, theoretically (since all resources are limited in one way or another), unlimited access to water resources for themselves, their families, and their communities. In the simple use of water, these individuals may not perceive any excitement, joy, happiness, and fulfillment, since to them it is common to have access to such a resource.

Unfortunately, precisely because certain goods offered by nature were not cherished and praised enough by people, there are dramatic changes at the level of our Planet. As a general consequence, humanity is now required to address the problems related to climate change, while specialists are expected to tackle climate adaptation, mitigate climate change efforts, and pursue climate justice in all the actions that they are taking.

According to the specialists belonging to the Organization for Economic Co-operation and Development (OECD), the creation and the use of the Better Life Index is essential in determining which would be the optimum "recipe for a better life" for each and every individual, based on the fact that these are aspects that require in-depth analysis at a personal level (OECD (Organization for Economic Co-operation and Development), 2022a). In this matter, the Organization for Economic Co-operation and Development (OECD) states that – on the road of determining the living standards and the household welfare, there are far more important aspects to life than "cold numbers" represented by economic statistics and the figures embodied by the Gross Domestic Product (GDP) (Organization for Economic Co-operation and Development), 2022a). Moreover, the Organization for Economic Co-operation and Development (OECD) Regional Well-Being website displays eleven key indicators which are believed to be responsible for showing people's quality of life over specific periods of time as well as focusing on different regions or countries, such as: the housing, the income, the jobs, the community, the education, the environment, the civic engagement, the health, the life satisfaction, the safety, and the work-life balance (Organization for Economic Co-operation and Development), 2022a). Furthermore, according to researchers, there is an essential question which individuals ought to answer in order to be able to share their personalized vision towards the attributes for a better life, namely "What matters most to people around the world?", hence being able to offer responses capable to reflect their preferences and their understanding regarding life, education, work, and other vital components to them (Organization for Economic Co-operation and Development), 2022a).

There are several questions that come to mind under this given context, namely: (Research Question no. 1 – RQ1) What are the benefits and the provocations of intersecting ESG and AI for business sustainability?; (Research Question no. 2 –

RQ2) What are the opportunities and risks of achieving the SDGs by benefiting from guidance from ESG as well as intelligence demonstrated by computers?; (Research Question no. 3 – RQ3) Is the society in which people live ready to build a culture of sustainability as well as develop successful SBM capable to foster climate justice, restore damaged biodiversity and ecosystems, and develop action plans capable to offer immediate responses to climate change?; (Research Question no. 4 – RQ4) Can individuals' quality of life and standards of living boost overall well-being of societies when businesses are becoming more sustainable?; (Research Question no. 5 – RQ5) Are the global living standards moving in the right direction?.

This current book chapter focuses on exploring the synergies between ESG and AI for business sustainability, on the brave, yet more and more explored road of tackling opportunities for climate adaptation, mitigating climate change efforts, and pursuing climate justice. In the same time, this current study tackles an up-to-date and paramount topic in today's general social, economic, and political context, namely the implications of the living standards on individuals' activities and on the countries' Sustainable Development (SD) evolution, providing vital evidence from Ethiopia. What is more, it is of great importance for this paper to address the implications of the living standards on the business environment, especially in today's social, economic, and demographical context which was irreversibly affected by the COVID-19 pandemic and the COVID-19 crisis. Furthermore, in this particular matter, it needs to be mentioned that the living standards are a clear and undeniable reflection of people's desires and needs put into practice, in their day to day lives and activities, although the indicators embody, due to their background, both a subjective and an objective nature.

The country chosen as a case study is Ethiopia, based on the valuable insights and opportunities that this country has to offer in terms of the data sets and findings: (a) first of all, according to most recent data displayed by the World Bank, Ethiopia is the second most populated country in Africa, after Nigeria, which makes it ideal for a case study since it offers unlimited possibilities to obtain statistically significant data and value them with the aid of empirical analysis and statistics (World Bank (WB), 2022a); (a) second of all, according to most recent data promoted by the World Bank, Ethiopia has a mixed and transition economy, where the government is in the process of privatizing the state-owned businesses (since the economy was previously mostly state-owned), in order to accelerate the process of moving toward a market economy (World Bank (WB), 2022b); and (c) third of all, due to the mixed nature of the economy, the services sector started recently making a tremendous contribution to Ethiopia's GDP – being placed on the second position as contribution brought to this valuable country indicator, while compared to the share of agriculture in Ethiopia's GDP – which still positions itself on the top position while addressing the contribution to this valuable country indicator (World Bank (WB), 2022a; World Bank (WB), 2022c; World Bank (WB), 2022d; World Bank (WB), 2022e).

Besides these, our analysis provides valuable insights on the most recent trends and the most recent situation in Ethiopia, thus shedding a new light on the aspects surrounding the evolution and the perspectives of the developed and the less developed countries worldwide. In this matter, the authors utilized data from the following pivotal documents, as follows: Household Income, Consumption and Expenditure Survey 1995-1996 (Central Statistics Agency (CSA) of Ethiopia, 2010a); Revised Report on the 1995-1996 Household Income, Consumption and Expenditure Survey (Central Statistics Agency (CSA) of Ethiopia, 2010b); Household Income, Consumption and Expenditure Survey 1999-2000 (Central Statistics Agency (CSA) of Ethiopia, 2010c); Report on the 1999-2000 Household Income, Consumption and Expenditure Survey (Central Statistics Agency (CSA) of Ethiopia. (2010d); Household Consumption and Expenditure (HCE) Survey 2010/11 (Central Statistics Agency (CSA) of Ethiopia, 2011a); The 2010/11 Ethiopian Households Consumption – Expenditure (HCE). Survey Results For: Country Level (Central Statistics Agency (CSA) of Ethiopia, 2011b); The 2015/16 Ethiopian Household Consumption – Expenditure (HCE) Survey Results For: Country Level (Central Statistics Agency (CSA) of Ethiopia, 2018a); and Statistical Data report on 3rd mission to Ethiopia- June 2018 (Central Statistics Agency (CSA) of Ethiopia, 2018b).

This first section represented by the introductory part to this study is immediately followed by the background – namely, the literature review which tackles the most recent works on the theme chosen for analysis and debate and which represents the second section of this paper. Moreover, the third section displays the main focus of the chapter where the authors provide substantial arguments capable to support the necessity of such a complex and valuable study that focuses on several issues, namely: (a) what are the advantages and the disadvantages of intersecting ESG and AI for business sustainability; (b) what are the opportunities and risks of achieving the SDGs by benefiting from guidance from ESG as well as intelligence demonstrated by computers; (c) what are the implications of building a culture of sustainability as well as developing successful SBM capable to foster climate justice, restore damaged biodiversity and ecosystems, and develop action plans capable to offer immediate responses to climate change; (d) in what manner intersecting ESG and AI for business sustainability can enable the raise of the individuals' quality of life and the boost of the standards of living for the overall well-being of societies when businesses are becoming more sustainable; and (e) the case of Ethiopia. Furthermore, the fourth section brings to the attention the discussion and synthesis of results concerning the synergies between ESG and AI for business sustainability, while accentuating the opportunities derived from the relationship that exists between ESG and AI for business sustainability for climate adaptation, climate change efforts, and climate justice, with a special focus on the case study on Ethiopia. While the fifth, sixth, and seventh sections center on the solutions and recommendations, future research directions, and conclusions that accompany such a vital in-depth investigation on: (a) the relationship between ESG and AI for business sustainability; (b) the importance of identifying the influence of the relationship between ESG and AI for business sustainability, in order to generate new opportunities meant to lead to climate adaptation, climate change efforts, and climate justice; and (c) weather or not the living standards these days are on the right track, with a particular emphasis on the living standards in the case of Ethiopia.

BACKGROUND

It is our strong belief that intersecting ESG and AI for business sustainability came as a natural step in our society in times in which, on the one hand, individuals are becoming more and more dependent on the use of different forms of techniques and technologies and, on the other hand, caring for the well-being of people and the health of the environment is pivotal to the day to day existence, the development, and the survival of people, communities, biodiversity, and ecosystems.

However, no matter how fast the society tends to evolve at one moment or another – depending on the economic, social, demographic, and political circumstances, besides the so called "natural" or "normal" trends that seem to inadvertently accompany its development, there are numerous controversies and, in most case, even real risks, associated with its evolution.

These days, Governance seems to cover, according to specialists, all the aspects concerning the manner in which an area, a region, or a country is being governed, having in mind, in particular, issues such as: the economic policies, the regulatory framework, and the capacity to adhere and to comply with the rule of law (International Monetary Fund (IMF), 2023). Nevertheless, Governance is a notion that has been used by individuals for many years, in different contexts – some of them very common and others more complex and sophisticated (United Cities and Local Governments Asia-Pacific (UCLG ASPAC), 2021). Also, it has been acknowledged that there is no unanimously accepted official definition of Governance, since its meaning may be different from one context to another, depending on several aspects, such as, the following ones (but not solely limited to them): (a) the general context and the intended purpose of defining and explaining the term; (b) the individuals and the entities that are involved in the analysis of the concept; and (c) the socio-political environment that comes to accompany the use of the notion or in which the term comes into discussion (United Cities and Local Governments Asia-Pacific (UCLG ASPAC), 2021). According to the United Nations (UN), Governance seems to cover the aspects specific to "the exercise of political and administrative authority at all levels to manage a country's affairs" (United Nations (UN), 2012, p.3).

Additionally, in the 1990s, the Word Bank (WB) became the first international institution that, on the one hand, brought the term Good Governance to the attention of the general public and that, on the other hand, used the concept of Good Governance in association with constructive and positive arrangements specific to the developing countries (United Cities and Local Governments Asia-Pacific (UCLG ASPAC), 2021). Hence, according to the WB documents, there is a fine line between Good Governance and other forms of Governance which are not generating positive results capable to enhance the well-being of the people and the ensure the health of the environment (Word Bank (WB), 1992).

In continuation, Good Governance seems to be a concept highly praised by specialists nowadays, being focused on the system in which the public affairs are performed with a responsible conduct, while the management of the public resources was done focusing on key principles, such as, for example: principle no. 1 – "participation, representation, fair conduct of elections"; principle no. 2 – "responsiveness"; principle no. 3 – "efficiency and effectiveness"; principle no. 4 – "openness and transparency"; principle no. 5 – "rule of law"; principle no. 6 – "ethical conduct"; principle no. 7 – "competence and capacity"; principle no. 8 – "innovation and openness to change"; principle no. 9 – "sustainability and long term orientation"; principle no. 10 – "sound financial management"; principle no. 11 – "human rights, cultural diversity, and social cohesion"; and, principle no. 12 – "accountability" (Council of Europe, 2023). In addition, besides the twelve principles of the Council of Europe mentioned in the lines above and which are emphasized in the "Strategy on Innovation and Good Governance" at the local level, endorsed by a decision of the Committee of Ministers of the Council of Europe in 2008, there are, also, the "toolkits to assist local authorities" which were formulated by the Centre of Expertise (Council of Europe, 2023). In addition, specialists have pointed out on numerous occasions already that supporting creativity and innovation, investing in human resources, and focusing on the well-being of individuals and the health of the environment will have, in time, a two folded effect: (a) firstly, people will understand that becoming more creative and innovative will essentially prove to be their only solution to compete with the advantages offered by AI – so, this will clearly represent an asset for employees or people seeking employment; and (b) secondly, business owners will acknowledge that the use of AI may be cheaper and may present numerous advantages, yet, on the medium and long term, nothing will be able to replace the input of the creative and innovative human mind in the business processes targeting both the climate justice and the environmental health (United Cities and Local Governments Asia-Pacific (UCLG ASPAC), 2021).

In order to successfully complement the two concepts stressed in the lines above – namely, Governance and Good Governance, the next concept that requires immediate attention from our side is represented by Corporate Governance (CG), which, according to specialists, makes reference to the system by which entities are directed and controlled (The Institute of Chartered Accountants in England and Wales (ICAEW), 2023). Additionally, CG has the purpose of ensuring the companies' success under the conditions in which the management of these entities acts responsibly, effectively, and takes prudent entrepreneurial and managerial decisions (The Institute of Chartered Accountants in England and Wales (ICAEW), 2023). In turn, CG has numerous principles, among which could be mentioned, for instance: accountability, awareness, based on the rule of law, consensus-oriented, good leadership, effectiveness, efficiency, equitable, impartiality, inclusiveness, fairness, participatory, responsibility, risk management, and transparency (The Chartered Governance Institute UK & Ireland, 2022; Copenhagen Business School (CBS), 2023; Organization for Economic Co-operation and Development (OECD), 2023). In essence, CG focuses on the manner in which businesses are supposed to become more concerned with individuals' well-being, in terms of mental and physical health, as well as with the health of the environment (Government Finance Officers Association (GFOA) of the United States and Canada, 2023).

Figure 1. Getting from governance to environmental social governance (ESG) on the road of becoming more responsible and sustainable

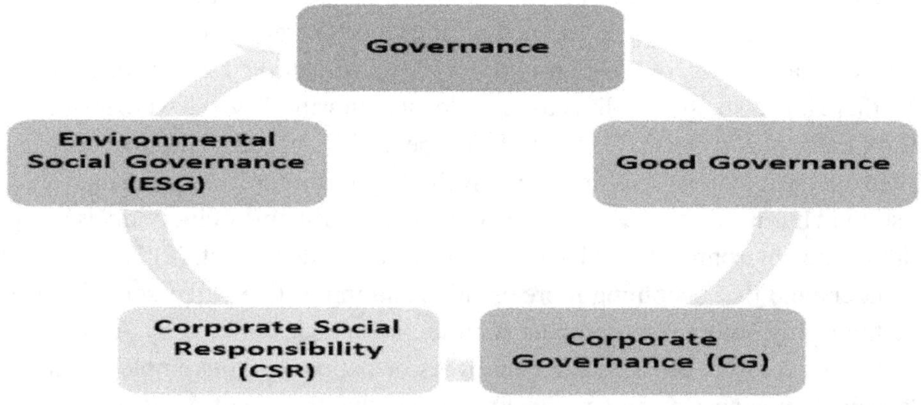

In this given context, AI comes to play a very important role in the society. First of all, AI may be capable to complement the employees' and the employers' daily tasks, by facilitating them access to better solutions capable to transform their work and the businesses in many ways (see, in this matter, Figure 1. Getting from Governance to Environmental Social Governance (ESG) on the Road of Becoming More Responsible and Sustainable). The question that comes to mind is: What is the role of AI in the cases in which businesses are expected to become more sustainable? Second of all, ESG and AI are expected to cooperate together and to find valuable solutions capable to ensure that everyone will be protected in the process of doing business: (a) the businesses should become more centered on using resources in a more sustainable manner, taking great care of the communities and the environment, while finding solutions to mitigate climate change and to support climate regeneration; (b) AI should support the employees' and the employers' and should be integrated in the day to day tasks, without representing a present or a future threat to the workers, to the development of businesses, to the biodiversity, and the ecosystems; and (c) ESG and AI ought to be seen, according to the authors, as two partners who should act together and who should unite their forces in order to ensure and to foster climate justice – in the context in which the Planet is already suffering, for many years already, due to the inappropriate and irresponsible business conduct, while the living standards are, in most cases, a misleading representation of the way in which people and communities are really evolving. So, the question that comes to mind in this context is: Are the living standards the right instrument capable to measure the well-being and the health of individuals? Besides all these, the authors are showing a tremendous concern regarding the way in which AI could be used by different entities in their quest for increased power, more profit, and less costs in identifying the needed resources, in using the work of individuals, and in promoting and selling the products and services.

New and pressing questions come to complement the questions highlighted already in the lines above: Are individuals acting in their own long term benefit, health, well-being, and work-life balance? Or, are people forced to take hasty actions seeking immediate survival and prosperity, while neglecting the real long term implications of their actions? Are these days' living standards a true and a faithful reflection of how people really feel or, in fact, on the quest for having adequate living standards indicators and numerical values people have come to put in danger the manner in which they are really perceiving their lives, their families, their jobs, and their future? Ultimately, the question is: Are people "on the right track" to their balanced lives, strong health, well-being, prosperity, peace of mind, and fulfillment? Or are they moving in the wrong directing justifying their trajectory with the false pretenses that they are in those circumstances due to external factors – even some of them unknown to them, faith, bad judgments, hasty decisions, or misleading forms of advertising fortune, success, and prosperity?

The authors strongly believe that understanding the way in which the relationship between ESG and AI functions it is necessary to address the case of the living standards (see, in this matter, Figure 2. Positive Outcomes Derived from the Relationship Environmental Social Governance (ESG) and Artificial Intelligence (AI) for Sustainability).

Figure 2. Positive outcomes derived from the relationship environmental social governance (ESG) and artificial intelligence (AI) for sustainability

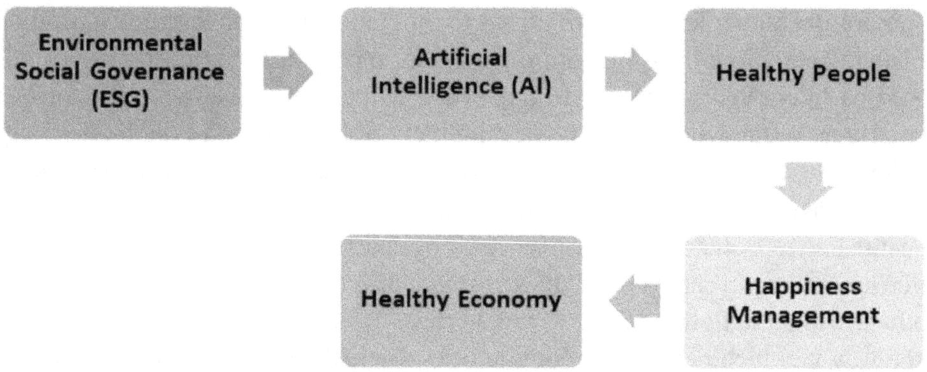

The living standards are regarded by specialists as vital when addressing these days social and economic situation, based on the implications that the quality of life has on people's well-being and individuals' capacity to develop on the medium-term and on the long-term (de Jong, 2015, pp.45-74). In addition, the living standards represent a pivotal barometer of the economy, displaying the most important developments that are taking place in the society in different moments in time as well as the major changes and challenges that the economy is facing over a certain time period (Boarini *et al.*, 2016; Muminov *et al.*, 2020). What is more, improving the living standards represents a constant preoccupation for specialists worldwide, in the attempt, on the one hand, to identify the most recent desires and needs that individuals have and, on the other hand, to discover those actions that are able to lead to putting into practice the people's requirements once they manifest themselves (Majumder and Chakravarty, 1996; Caselli and Michaels, 2013). Furthermore, based on the researchers' most recent and more relevant findings, enhancing the standards of living in the society represents a major instrument capable to measure performance at all levels (Kakwani, 1993; Fleurbaey and Gaulier, 2009; Egger *et al.*, 2021).

The authors strongly believe that performance is a concept having multiple facets, being structured on numerous layers. In the same line with the aforementioned arguments, the authors believe that measuring performance has always represented a challenge for specialists, no matter the field and no matter the circumstances. It has become clear nowadays that performance may have not only an objective nature but, also, a subjective nature. For instance, finding solutions to help the environment and mitigate climate change might represent for some specialists a great accomplishment and a real step forward; hence, it may be associated with performance. Unfortunately, for other individuals performance may be associated with profitability, less costs, less investments in human capital, and more actions taken towards becoming richer and richer every step of the way, despite the damage caused to the environment and to the people or the communities. In which of these cases real performance was truly obtained?

Also, while referring to the living standards, it ought to be noted that the United States Green Building Council (USGBC) promote the life-changing vision according to which: "Healthy people in healthy places equals a healthy economy" (United States Green Building Council (USGBC), 2022). Hence, this message carefully and successfully promoted all around the world has the power to determine leaders, managers, politicians, and individuals, in general, to reimagine and to revise the existing definitions associated to the living standards and to stop deciding between public health and the health of the economy when specific measures are expected to be taken (United States Green Building Council (USGBC), 2022). The reason brought in this matter by the United States Green Building Council (USGBC) is that the public health and a truly healthy economy are interrelated and it is not possible to choose one or the other when targeting important aspects, such as: sustainability, SD, well-being, mental health, and the existence of a healthy economy with positive effects on the environment and the individuals (United States Green Building Council (USGBC), 2022). In other words, "health" should be reflected in all the actions and all the activities that individuals and business perform, displaying, at all times, a clear concern towards the nature, sustainability, and the environment.

The importance of measuring the living standards with the aid of monetary and non-monetary indicators is vital, and the way in which these indicators were selected as well as the measurements models, tools and frameworks has changed over the years (Rao and Min, 2018; Booth, A., 2019; Living Standard, 2022).

Besides all these, the importance of the living standards is recognized all over the world and the indicators on which the measurement of these living standards is done might differ depending on the aspects that need to be accentuated and to be brought to light when performing such investigations (Rao and Min, 2018; Ministry of Social Development, 2022a). In this particular matter, for instance, in the case of New Zeeland, the researchers came to the conclusion that the Material Well-Being Scale had to be modified in order to be able to offer a relevant view capable to consider the whole population (Ministry of Social Development, 2022a). Hence, the specialists were able to create the Economic Living Standard Index (ELSI) which is much more relevant and much more appropriate for New Zeeland population than the previously used scale (Ministry of Social Development, 2022a; Ministry of Social Development, 2022b; Ministry of Social Development, 2022c).

MAIN FOCUS OF THE CHAPTER

The United Nations (UN) members describe the importance of the living standards as well as the population quality of life in the following given context: (a) first of all, there is the need for a "new strategic vision meant" to create "conditions for improving living standards of the country's population" by taking into account "the necessary conditions for sustainable development in various areas of public life" (United Nations (UN), 2017, p.4); (b) second of all, the emphasis should be positioned "on the existing resources in the country, where the accelerator should be certain strategic goals for achieving sustainable development" (United Nations (UN), 2017, p.4); and (c) third of all, "the highest goal of long-term development" that a country might target should be based on improving "the living standards and well-being of the population based on sustainable economic development" (United Nations (UN), 2017, pp.4-5).

In addition, the living standards are very often associated with well-being; hence the creation of well-being frameworks was noted in different regions and countries (ACT Government, 2022). In this case, the specialists show a great concern towards the economy's capacity to offer the population the financial resources in order to live life in a decent manner, harmoniously, and in appropriate conditions (ACT Government, 2022). A very reliable example in this case is provided by the Australian Bureau of Statistics, since the focus of researchers' falls on a broader socio-economic picture by way of comparison with other situations, namely: (a) the living standards have a strong link with the country's financial perspectives and the financial possibilities that an economy has to offer to its population at a certain moment in time; (b) the living standards are reflected by the general well-being status of the population, which is derived from high income levels as well as increased wealth levels; and (c) the living standards and the well-being of individuals is a direct reflection of the evolution of several key indicators that are centered on the Economy, the Health, the Education and the Life-Long Learning, and the Housing and Home (ACT Government, 2022).

In the same line with the aspects pointed out above, the Institute for Fiscal Studies (IFS) concentrates on the analysis of the living standards, the poverty and the inequality in the United Kingdom (UK), being interested in constantly discovering which are the most recent changes and the most vital challenges that have affected individuals' lives while compared to the evolution of the living standards since

1961 (The Institute for Fiscal Studies (IFS), 2022a). According to the most recently published report on the "Living standards, poverty and inequality in the UK: 2022", the most relevant way to determine the population living standards is done by measuring the households' incomes (The Institute for Fiscal Studies (IFS), 2022b).

Although in the developed countries there is already a tradition in measuring the living standards and in finding solutions capable to improve the lives of the inhabitants, in less developed regions and countries these statistics started more recently and mainly as a result of different agreements signed with important International Organizations that are responsible with measuring the progress of the SGDs. In this matter, for instance, a valuable example could be represented by the Pakistan Social and Living Standards Measurement (PSLM) which started on the 1st of July 2015 (Pakistan Bureau of Statistics, 2022). According to the statistical evidence displayed by the Pakistan Bureau of Statistics, the Pakistan Social and Living Standards Measurement (PSLM) mainly focus on major aspects directly related with the SGDs, such as: poverty labor and employment; education; health; housing water and sanitation (Pakistan Bureau of Statistics, 2022). Additionally, in the case of Pakistan for instance, specialists consider that the Pakistan Social and Living Standards Measurement (PSLM) play a crucial role in addressing the achievement of the SGDs at a local level, the result being that 31 indicators of the SGDs are currently successfully being monitored in this way (Pakistan Bureau of Statistics, 2022).

Besides the aforementioned issues, the New Zealand's Secretary to the Treasury, Gabriel Makhlouf delivered on the 4th of September 2018 a highly important speech at Catalyst Trust, in Queenstown, in which a very interesting and plastic comparison was made between the current state of an economy and "Risk and Respectability" (The Treasury of New Zealand, 2018). Additionally, several major links were brought to light while addressing the countries productivity and the individuals' living standards, among which could be mentioned the following ones: (a) the business environment is strongly interlinked with the evolution of the GDP and the business investments (The Treasury of New Zealand, 2018); (b) the power due to be encountered at the level of businesses as well as the Organizations' capacity to develop and to flourish depends mainly on the businesses confidence in the favorable evolution of the marketplace (The Treasury of New Zealand, 2018); (c) there is a fine nuance that ought to be remarked when describing an economy, since it can "either" be seen as "booming or bombing", the difference between the situations described as such being crucial and the target being to increase growth, exports, consumption, production, and productivity (The Treasury of New Zealand, 2018); and (d) the existence of risk is inherent in any situation, but by assuming calculated risks the rewards might be surprising and the rate of development might be an accelerated one, which would lead to an increase in terms of the population quality of life and living standards (The Treasury of New Zealand, 2018).

Hence, official figures showed over the years a tremendous concern towards improving individuals' quality of life, stating that people all around the world ought to have a decent standard of living, making reference to several key solutions able to increase the standard of living, as follows: (a) offering individuals a general framework due to be implemented at a gradual level in order to facilitate the introduction of minimum wages at the countries level, in this matter targeting to impose specific limits in terms of salary in order to prevent Organizations to exploit the poor population in certain regions and countries (Joseph Rowntree Foundation, 2019; United Nations, 2019); (b) introducing smart fiscal policies capable to attract investments especially in affected and less fortunate regions and countries, thus enhancing productivity, performance, and economic growth, while offering new jobs to individuals in need (United Nations, 2019); and (c) centering on creating a more inclusive and a more sustainable environment, more focused on the "populations' health, happiness and overall well-being" (United Nations, 2019; United Nations Development Programme (UNDP), 2022).

According to the United Nations Development Programme (UNDP) chief Achim Steiner the living standards registered, in the last two years, a significant decline due to the most recent problems that the world is facing, namely: (a) to begin with, on top of the agenda the COVID-19 pandemic and the COVID-19 crisis were positioned, due to the irreversible and troublesome implications of the coronavirus in our society; (b) also, the international humanitarian crises were mentioned due to their crucial influence on our society, while the accent was put on different conflicts that tend to escalate among different countries; and (c) in continuation, the severe and most of the times sudden floods, droughts, and wildfires were brought under analysis since these are phenomenon that individuals and entities have generated mainly through their irresponsible activities and actions and without thoroughly analyzing the implications on the environment and the future generations (Deutsche Welle (DW), 2022; United Nations Development Programme (UNDP), 2022).

In the same vein with the aspects highlighted in the lines above, a recently published article illustrates very suggestively the fact that the global living standards are not having the right evolution anymore, pointing out that life in 2022 has become very problematic for individuals due to different international social, political, economic, and financial situations which brought severe changes all over the world (The Economist, 2022). The World Trade Organization (WTO) tackled the current international situation by stressing the fact that in order to increase the living standards a possible solution might be cutting living costs (World Trade Organization (WTO), 2022a). Also, the World Trade Organization (WTO) brought to light the vision according to which protectionism is expensive and leads to an increase while addressing the prices evolution, emphasizing that trade has the power to facilitate the profitable exchange of goods and services through communication, negotiation, and non-discriminatory principles (World Trade Organization (WTO), 2022a). Likewise, the same aforementioned international Organization brought into discussion the dangers that disputes and global conflicts pose on international trade, emphasizing that the trade tensions should be systematically reduced in order to eliminate the existing frictions between regions and countries being able to focus again on the issues that really matter: (a) having tighter relationships between countries based on mutual respect and support, hence facilitating the raise of the living standards (World Trade Organization (WTO), 2022b); (b) creating agreements that are able to confer security and advantage to all involved parties, hence encouraging a competitive economic behavior set to increase sustainability, economic growth, productivity, performance, and trade (World Trade Organization (WTO), 2022c); and (c) offering all nations (developed and less developed countries) the opportunity to reflect on the dangers derived from social, political, and economic conflicts and disputes, while creating a general background capable to support a decent life, well-being, happiness, prosperity, peace, and high living standards (World Trade Organization (WTO), 2022d; World Trade Organization (WTO), 2022e; World Trade Organization (WTO), 2022f).

The United Nations (UN) representatives pointed out in their recent discourses that there is a lot of work to be done at the level of our society in order for "individuals to thrive and societies to flourish", especially in the current global uncertain social, financial and economic situation (United Nations, 2019). In this matter, reference was made several times to "the need to raise living standards above basic subsistence levels", which implicates the fact that the countries leaders have to come to a general agreement regarding "wage policies, collective bargaining, income redistribution and other economic tools" that are capable, once put into practice, to boost happiness, prosperity, performance, and growth (United Nations, 2019).

DISCUSSION AND SYNTHESIS OF RESULTS

When referring to countries that require a specific attention from specialist due to their particular nature in terms of the living standards, it is our strong belief that the focus could be on Ethiopia – an important country positioned in Africa, since this country made significant process over the past decade in terms of government accountability, human development, economic growth, and social engagement (World Bank (WB), 2022e). Nevertheless, our choice concerning the presentation and the analysis of the living standards in Ethiopia was made especially because of the fragile nature of the economy and due to the fact that there is a lot to be accomplished in this matter in order to be able to transform this country into a role model for other economies at a global level (with reference, for instance, to reliable SD frameworks, and Good Governance attributes).

Based on the aspects disclosed in the "Country Partnership Framework for the Federal Democratic Republic of Ethiopia", it has been noted that Ethiopia made significant achievements toward reaching the Millennium Development Goals (MDGs) (World Bank (WB), 2017, p.1). For instance, in this matter, while addressing poverty eradication targets – a major focus according to the United Nation's SDGs, statistics showed a significant decline in terms of the poverty rate's evolution which decreased "from 55.3 per cent in 2000 to 33.5 per cent in 2011" (World Bank (WB), 2017, p.1). Also, as seen above in the study that we successfully presented and analyzed individuals' revenue represents a pivotal indicator when addressing the situation of living standards, at a general level. Hence, "new challenges lie ahead as Ethiopia seeks to attain lower middle-income status by 2025", which displays greater concern from authorities when seeking to address the matters related to improving the living conditions of the population, thus centering on one of "the greatest spatial challenges" belonging to this country (World Bank (WB), 2017, p.1).

Moving on with our in-depth analysis, in the case of living standards in Ethiopia it ought to be emphasized that the Systematic Country Diagnostic (SCD) has shown that there currently exist several binding constraints, as follows: (a) to begin with, extreme poverty is a major concern for governmental authorities especially in the case of developing countries, while boosting shared prosperity is still an aim due to be reached with great effort and with significant involvement from effective, dependable, responsible, and visionary leaders (World Bank (WB), 2017, pp.1-2); (b) also, "the challenges of forging a growth path that is more broadly inclusive and sustainable" implicates the creation and the constant adaptation of "a sustainable financing model for growth" capable to answer to the particularities of a country such as Ethiopia, where the citizens and the governments are expected to become more supportive and more engaged in fostering, in time, the businesses development as well as the environment preservation (World Bank (WB), 2017, pp.1-2); (c) in addition, in order to encourage "strong economic growth" and accelerated SD the major focus ought to be, on the one hand, on "promoting structural and economic transformation through increased productivity" and, on the other hand, on "building resilience and inclusiveness (including gender equality)" (World Bank (WB), 2017, pp.1-2); (d) in continuation, by "fostering faster and more inclusive structural change" a more powerful emphasis needs to be placed on "supporting institutional accountability", while "confronting corruption", in this way being able to obtain more sustainable financial models as well as more adequate feedbacks mechanisms coming from the general population, the entities belonging to the business environment, and other parties strongly anchored in the development and the growth of this country (World

Bank (WB), 2017, pp.1-2); and (e) in the end, the focal point should be on finding viable solutions capable to support increasing competitiveness in Ethiopia, thus being able to raise performance in all the areas part of the business environment (World Bank (WB), 2017, pp.25-26).

Interestingly, according to the 2017 Living Standards Measurement Study (LSMS) Ethiopia confronts itself with "low levels of financial inclusion" and faces major constraints "to boosting productivity and rural livelihoods", which shows us that there is a lot to be done in terms of establishing powerful capital markets in this country (World Bank (WB), 2017, pp.25-26). Additionally, the African Development Bank highlights in the "Ethiopia Economic Outlook" the fact that Ethiopia's economy recorded a decrease to 5.6% growth in 2021 while compared to 6.1% which was the figure registered in 2020, the main explanations being: (a) first of all, the COVID-19 implications in all areas of the economy, but mainly in the transport sector and the hospitability sector; and (b) second of all, the civil conflicts which constantly put at risk the population and generate vulnerabilities and disruptions in all the domains of the economy (African Development Bank, 2022).

The results that the authors successfully managed to obtain are similar with the ones drawn by other studies that centered their attention and their research efforts on addressing the case of countries facing similar problems as well as being provided with similar opportunities. A very good example in this matter is represented by the case of the Republic of Tajikistan, which is a "landlocked country in Central Asia" and which has been thoroughly analyzed by the United Nations (UN) specialists in the document entitled "Improving Living Standards through Mainstreaming of SDGs into the National Development Policy in Tajikistan" (United Nations (UN), 2017, p.1). Among the most crucial findings of the aforementioned research project, could be mentioned the following ones: in order to improve the country's economic growth rate as well as to support the increase at the level of the living standards the focus ought to be on "(1) ensuring energy security and efficient use of electricity; (2) moving out of the communication deadlock and the transformation of the country into a transit country; (3) ensuring food security and access of population to quality nutrition; and (4) expanding productive employment" (United Nations (UN), 2017, p.5).

The aspects that are related with the case of Ethiopia are based on the results displayed in several major sources (mentioned also in the introductory section of this book chapter), namely: Household Income, Consumption and Expenditure Survey 1995-1996 (Central Statistics Agency (CSA) of Ethiopia, 2010a); Revised Report on the 1995-1996 Household Income, Consumption and Expenditure Survey (Central Statistics Agency (CSA) of Ethiopia, 2010b); Household Income, Consumption and Expenditure Survey 1999-2000 (Central Statistics Agency (CSA) of Ethiopia, 2010c); Report on the 1999-2000 Household Income, Consumption and Expenditure Survey

(Central Statistics Agency (CSA) of Ethiopia. (2010d); Household Consumption and Expenditure (HCE) Survey 2010/11 (Central Statistics Agency (CSA) of Ethiopia, 2011a); The 2010/11 Ethiopian Households Consumption – Expenditure (HCE). Survey Results For: Country Level (Central Statistics Agency (CSA) of Ethiopia, 2011b); The 2015/16 Ethiopian Household Consumption – Expenditure (HCE) Survey Results For: Country Level (Central Statistics Agency (CSA) of Ethiopia, 2018a); and Statistical Data report on 3rd mission to Ethiopia- June 2018 (Central Statistics Agency (CSA) of Ethiopia, 2018b).

This current study is seen as vital for these days current social, economic, political, and demographical situation due to the fact that it offers pivotal insights regarding the importance of measuring people's perception on the manner in which they are living. In this matter, it ought to be added that based on the way individuals are living they are able to make valuable decisions regarding their own activities, desires, needs, and future perspective as well as on their family members necessities and opportunities to develop and to prosper.

This paper displays very important attributes that surround the topic of living standards, showing that individuals have different expectations, needs and desires based on the region or the country where they live, the education level they have, the family in which they were raised, the culture and the values in which they were brought up. Although access to education may seem of major importance for individuals living in developed countries, in less developed or emerging countries education may be regarded as less important and may be a real privilege for individuals with high financial possibilities. Hence, in those countries that fall in the category of developing or emerging, possessing transition economies and being on the verge of privatizing their sectors, such as, for instance, Ethiopia, it might be seen that education does not represent an important prerequisite for individuals. As a result, not only adults are expected to work in order to make a decent living, but also children are encouraged to start working at an early age in order to help their family members and offer greater financial support. Going even further with the analysis, people in developed countries automatically perceive their existence linked to the possibility to have access to energy sources and to improved water source, while in less developed regions and countries having access to energy and to clean water sources represents a real problem and may be either simply conditioned by the location of the dwelling or may be restricted by authorities due to the rarity of these resources. In the same vein with the aforementioned aspects, ownership represents an attribute that displays individuals' possessions, possibilities and status in the society. In this matter, the focus might be, for example, on people's capacity to own their dwelling, to own land, and to have in possession other goods that might differentiate them from others and that might provide them higher living standards, better living conditions, and a below average existence. Nevertheless, access to decent work, reliable sources of energy, and clean water represents a desideratum at an international level, based on the United Nations' highly valued and intensely promoted SDGs (United Nations Geneva, 2022). Besides all these, improving individuals' living standards depends on facilitating the access to education, since education enriches people's lives, expends their knowledge and gives them better chances to find better paid jobs. In this particular matter, it ought to be emphasized that education occupies a separate position among the United Nations' SDGs, due to the fact that, on the one hand, it has a specific nature while compared with the rest of the SDGs and, on the other hand, it gives a new meaning to having access to information and to knowledge, while focusing on the paramount role of intellectual capital (IC) and human resources (HR) in a knowledge-based society and economy (United Nations (UN), 2015; United Nations (UN), 2018). In other words, in countries such as Ethiopia, individuals' access to education has the immense power to determine people to develop at an extensive level, in this way accelerating economic growth, SD, and businesses performance.

At this point, it needs to be stressed that the authors utilized data from several sources – as emphasized several times in this book chapter, in order to be able to investigate the living standards in the case of Ethiopia, based on the fact that the information accessed in this way was believed to be vital for the proposed analysis (Central Statistics Agency (CSA) of Ethiopia, 2010a, 2010b, 2010c, 2010d, 2011a, 2011b, 2018a, 2018b). Also, when making reference to the data set used for this study, it should be emphasized that it is considered highly relevant for this scientific work since it is provided by Central Statistics Agency (CSA) of Ethiopia.

SOLUTIONS AND RECOMMENDATIONS

There are numerous recommendations that could be made in order to help the improvement of living standards all over the world. In poor regions and less developed countries it has become clear that there are almost no opportunities for individuals to lead decent lives, to have access to better jobs, and to support through their actions and activities their economy to prosper, which leads to the following general recommendations: (a) firstly, a possible solution in order to offer better chances of SD and economic growth would be to promote economic activities on the entire territory of a country and not only in specific parts, in the bigger cities (World Bank (WB), 2020; World Economic Forum (WEC), 2021; Góngora-Salazar *et al.*, 2022); (b) secondly, another possible solution in order to foster creativity, innovation, and research which lead to SD and economic growth, would be to offer individuals better access to education and training programs and to encourage afterwards people to share their knowledge with their family members and colleagues (World

Bank (WB), 2020; Wu and Pu, 2020; World Economic Forum (WEC), 2021); and (c) thirdly, although specialization offers tremendous benefits to individuals since they become highly skilled in certain domains, due to the spectacular advancement of techniques and technologies all around the globe, there should always be room for improvement and for development in this matter, providing people a chance to change their line of work and their specialization once the activities they recently performed will be taken over by robots and intelligent machines (World Bank (WB), 2020; World Economic Forum (WEC), 2021; Topuz, 2022).

As seen in this paper, the quality of life and the living standards are often associated by specialists with the growth rate of its GDP per capita which may be displayed in two main segments, namely: (a) on the one hand, there is the growth rate of GDP per hour worked, which represents, in essence, a measure of labor productivity that leads in the business environment to an increased business performance level (Federal Reserve Bank of Saint Louis, 2015; Our World in Data (WEC), 2020; Bukowski and Novokmet, 2021); and (b) on the other hand, the growth rate of the number of hours per capita, which represents, in essence, a measure of the way in which labor was utilized while centering on the immeasurable opportunities brought to the economy by intellectual assets (IA), in general, on the road of supporting and promoting sustainability, economic growth, and SD (Federal Reserve Bank of Saint Louis, 2015; Our World in Data (WEC), 2020; Ma *et al.*, 2022; Xiang *et al.*, 2022).

So, given the circumstances, intersecting ESG and AI creates highly promising serious for business sustainability. In like manner, exploring the synergies between ESG and AI for business sustainability has the scope of addressing in a better and in a more complex way the issues surround our Planet, hence, tackling opportunities for climate adaptation, mitigating climate change efforts, and pursuing climate justice.

FUTURE RESEARCH DIRECTIONS

In this particular case, the future research directions are numerous, especially in the context in which the focus is mainly on the relationship that may be encountered between ESG, AI, the SDGs, and business sustainability, while tackling new and vibrant opportunities for climate adaptation, mitigating daring and coherent climate change efforts, and pursuing climate justice.

Although the idea of fostering climate justice may raise certain problems in some areas, regions, and countries, the authors believe that it is never too late to start seriously working in this matter and coherently planning for a better future for all. These are times in which the individuals, the communities, and the environment have been so severely affected in certain parts of the world, that the harm done encompasses the imagination of researchers and specialists. Hence, one possible research direction that may require immediate attention could be on the manner in which those communities and the environment could receive immediate attention and help in order to stop the disasters that have already been produced.

What is more, since the individuals, the communities, and the entities have damaged so greatly certain areas, regions, and countries, the environment was no longer able to cope with the disasters and rebalance itself. That is the reason why in the last years there are so many ecosystems affected, there are numerous species that were already declared extinct or are on the verge of becoming extinct, there are numerous earthquakes, fires, and floods that lead to the death of hundreds and, in some cases, thousands of animals and individuals. It has become clear that the process of the environmental regeneration is no longer possible with the intervention of all involved parties, namely, of the people, the communities, the businesses' managers, the countries' leaders, the official governmental figures, and so on. Hence, a new potential research direction seems to arise in this matter, namely: firstly, choosing a specific area, region or country and analyzing the environmental damage produced so far; secondly, identifying solutions capable to restore the balance between the individuals, the communities, and the businesses, while targeting sustainability; and, thirdly, creating different scenarios capable to address all the identified problems together with all the discovered solutions, while focusing on climate justice, with the aid of the benefits derived from the influence of the relationship existing between ESG and AI.

CONCLUSION

There are several major aspects due to be considered when bringing into analysis the relationship existing between ESG and AI. Firstly, this type of relationship is incipient, which means that this "territory" was not explored enough by researchers, specialists, and practitioners. There are many valuable opportunities that are expected to come up from this relationship, since the focus is on the well-being of communities, the health of the environment, and the sustainable way of doing business. However, there are also worries that come to naturally accompany this relationship, which are mainly derived from the fact that some specialists and practitioners mentioned that AI might, over the years, work against the creators rather than for the creators, due to its capacity to learn and adapt to specific situations far more than people's known capacity so far. Secondly, although this type of relationship has not been explored enough, there are already several proofs that the association between ESG and AI may prove to be very fruitful and extremely successful in the next decades. There are already numerous situations considered by specialists where AI has been of great help to people and to the environment: for example, there are places in which individuals are not able to go and where intelligent robots have absolutely no constraints in operating, such as, radioactive areas or zones that have no oxygen or surfaces which are highly dangerous or polluted; or, for instance, there are jobs that may seem dangerous for individuals and where intelligent machines are not affected or are less affected while performing their tasks, such as, for instance, radioactive zones, areas where extreme climate forms are to be found, and so on; or, another example, there are jobs where people are affected after working for several months or years and where intelligent robots might be of better use, such as, in different forms of therapy, where people are encouraged to present their problems and where the therapy robots might prove to be more helpful by comparison with people, since they have the capacity to find solutions based on algorithms and patterns, while covering more cases from practice than individuals are capable to do.

The changes that the environment currently goes through are somehow expected for a very long time by reputed specialists worldwide. Some of these changes are normal and are expected to take place after a number of years. Others, unfortunately, are of great novelty and are the result of irresponsible and negligent behavior from the individuals, the communities, the businesses, and the government. With the aid of the relationship between ESG and AI our Planet can receive more help from different areas of action. For instance with the help of intelligent technologies and robots, specific areas could be cleaned faster and better from the existing pollutants in order to facilitate the inhabitants a more secure environment to live in from that moment on. In all these cases, it has to be considered, however, that it is going to be a tremendous effort accompanied by great costs, since the use of intelligent technologies and robots is very expensive, while developing the applications that are based on AI have both benefits and disadvantages which makes them vulnerable to cyber tacks. So, the use of such sophisticated technologies implicates that specially trained and equipped professionals will have to monitor them and will have to work together with them in order to ensure great success.

All in all, this current study has several limitations that are displayed in the lines below: (a) first of all, the data sets that accompany the living standards and the quality of live are usually based on the answers (that fall in the categories subjective and objective, depending on the situation and the nature of the question) provided by individuals to different questioners, which might lead to inherent errors coming from those individuals that fill in the documents and that might omit certain aspects during the process; (b) second of all, due to the fact that the living standards and the quality of live contain both subjective and objective attributes, the general results obtained after the data sets were cleaned up, processed, and thoroughly analyzed might also be less objective then expected; (c) the variables that are embodied in the living standards and the quality of live indicators differ depending on the sources used for the data sets, in this case the limitation being by the fact that the data focused only on consumption quintile; rural/urban; ownership of dwelling; access to improved water source; connection to electricity; rental income; received remittance; ownership of land; number of children in household; and number of working age adult in household; and (d) third of all, the analysis done in this paper solely focuses on the case of Ethiopia, which has its own particularities in terms of social, economic, demographical, and political characteristics (Central Statistics Agency (CSA) of Ethiopia, 2010a, 2010b, 2010c, 2010d, 2011a, 2011b, 2018a, 2018b). Nevertheless, it is our pivotal and powerful belief that this current study provides valuable insights regarding the living standards and the quality of live both at a general level as well as in a particular situation, namely the case of Ethiopia. Also, the results that were obtained in this paper might reached for other regions and for other countries that find themselves in similar social, economic, demographical, and political conditions – such as, for example, the case of other regions and countries that have emerging or developing economies, that have transition economies, and where the public sector becomes less and less present at the level of entities, while the private sector becomes more visible and begins to strengthen its influence and its position on the marketplace. In continuation, for instance, one might discover that the characteristics specific to the living standards and the quality of live in Ethiopia might be encountered at the level of numerous other regions and countries in Africa.

In order to conclude, while addressing the standards of living and the quality of live, the modern economic growth imposes certain steps due to be taken in order to increase performance at all levels, as follows: (a) to begin with, overcoming poverty, in order to eliminate hunger and suffering among individuals; (b) also, stopping the decline of the average income, in order to banish starvation and famine all around the Globe, thus fostering increased levels of standards of living for all individuals; (c) in addition, increasing the per capita economic growth while centering on accomplishing SD, in order to improve life expectancy, foster nations' performance and productivity growth; and (d) to end with, promoting economic freedom all around the world as a vital stage part of the economic and the social transformation of our society, in order to ensure well-being, health, mental health, safety, and happiness for all the population on Earth.

So, is humanity moving in the right direction? Are humans on the right sense of the evolution or on the counter-sense (namely, on the opposite track of their evolution)? There are many moments in which it is very difficult to offer an answer in this matter. If prosperity was in the mind of business owners when deciding to make a choice between working responsibly or working for increased profitability, than it was not the case of prosperity for all, it was prosperity for a limited number of individuals and at tremendous costs in terms of sacrificing people's well-being and health, as well as the biodiversity and the ecosystems. Also, if development was on the agenda of country leaders and governmental officials, given some of the natural disasters highly mediatized in the last years, than for sure it was not SD, it was not that development that had to consider the well-being and the heath of the present and the future generations. In these cases, the answer would be that humanity is moving on little by little on the counter-sense, which implicates that the evolution was transformed with involution. Namely, in these situations, some business owners, country leaders, and governmental figures decided in our name to sacrifice the well-being and the health of the present and the future generations, as well as the sustainable future of the environment. The costs with restoring the biodiversity and the ecosystems are, for sure, immense, while offering assistance and help to the people and the communities in need might be, in most cases, regrettably, with no positive results on the medium and long term.

What is more, happiness and happiness management should be regarded by all people as key priorities for the next decades to come. Nevertheless, happiness and happiness management should be seen in a new light, far different than the light in which, most certainly, some individuals or some businesses have come to acknowledge these two concepts in the last years, given the results seen in practice. Hence, happiness and happiness management refer not solely to the benefits and the prosperity that some fortunate people have come across in their lives; true happiness, according to the authors, represents that state of mind in which people are caring, compassionate, and aware of the needs of others, while happiness management may be achieved only in those cases in which individuals are mindful and are seeking for solutions to make good to the communities and to the environment. The idea of being happy may only be true if the happiness is shared with other members of the community.

Furthermore, even though AI has raised lately numerous doubts and questions – like any other major changes that have come to be implemented in the society, there is always place to accept that these changes that will initially shake the very core of our existence, will also be the ones who will, ultimately, lead to efficiency, effectiveness, equity, inclusion, resilience, robustness, and sustainability. There are serious doubts that AI will have the power to help the individuals, communities, and environment, especially when specialists are drawing more attention on the immediate effects of the use of AI in companies that had to give up hundreds and, in some cases, thousands of employees, when deciding to implement new production plans using robotics. However, there is also a solution that has to be considered in this matter, namely that the purpose of AI should be to help people in all of their tasks or almost in all of their tasks, and not replace individuals. For instance, AI is expected to help in the near future people in their houses far more than it has been done until now, which would implicate that individuals will have more free time for themselves, for their families, and for more creative and innovative activities. Or, for example, at the places of work, the burden of repetitive tasks could be taken more and more by robots – especially in those cases in which there is also a danger in performing those activities by people, while the creative and innovative tasks should be performed more thoroughly by the employees based on the fact that they will have more time allocated than before.

In other words, the authors are emphasizing the fact that – even though it is very hard to accept and to adapt to change, novelty will never cease to exist, innovation will never end its capacity to rise new and, apparently, insurmountable challenges, and prosperity will never become an undesirable state of being and of mind for anyone, however the best solutions have to be found in order to cherish all facets that life has to offer. Besides all these, life without a healthy environment is clearly impossible and by trying to break new grounds and to implement new rules the society has always to consider the implications of their activities and actions on others: on the less fortunate people, on the disadvantaged communities, on the restoration of biodiversity, and on the preservation of the ecosystems.

ACKNOWLEDGMENT

This research received no specific grant from any funding agency in the public, commercial, or not-for-profit sectors. Author Contributions: Conceptualization, C.R.G.P. (Cristina Raluca Gh. Popescu) and A.L.G. (Arturo Luque Gonzâlez); methodology, C.R.G.P. and A.L.G.; software, C.R.G.P. and A.L.G.; validation, C.R.G.P. and A.L.G.; formal analysis, C.R.G.P. and A.L.G.; investigation, C.R.G.P. and A.L.G.; resources, C.R.G.P. and A.L.G.; data curation, C.R.G.P. and A.L.G.; writing—original draft preparation, C.R.G.P. and A.L.G.; writing—review and editing, C.R.G.P. and A.L.G.; visualization, C.R.G.P. and A.L.G.; supervision, C.R.G.P. and A.L.G.; project administration, C.R.G.P. and A.L.G.; funding acquisition, C.R.G.P. and A.L.G. All authors have equally contributed to the manuscript. All authors have read and agreed to the published version of the manuscript.

REFERENCES

African Development Bank. (2022). *Ethiopia Economic Outlook*. Available online: https://www.afdb.org/en/countries/east-africa/ethiopia/ethiopia-economic-outlook

Boarini, R., Murtini, F., Schreyeri, P., & Fleurbaey, M. (2016). *Multi-dimensional Living Standards: A Welfare Measure Based on Preferences*. OECD Statistics Working Papers 5. OECD Publishing. doi:10.1787/18152031

Booth, A. (2019). Living Standards in Southeast Asia. Changes over the Long Twentieth Century, 1900-2015. Amsterdam University Press.

Bukowski, P., & Novokmet, F. (2021). Between communism and capitalism: Long-term inequality in Poland, 1892-2015. *Journal of Economic Growth*, *26*(2), 187–239. doi:10.100710887-021-09190-1 PMID:34776755

Caselli, F., & Michaels, G. (2013). Do Oil Windfalls Improve Living Standards? Evidence from Brazil. *American Economic Journal. Applied Economics*, *5*(1), 208–238. doi:10.1257/app.5.1.208

Central Statistics Agency (CSA) of Ethiopia. (2010a). *Household Income, Consumption and Expenditure Survey 1995-1996. Study Documentation.* http://www.csa.gov.et/survey-report/category/72-hice-1995

Central Statistics Agency (CSA) of Ethiopia. (2010b). *Revised Report on the 1995-1996 Household Income, Consumption and Expenditure Survey. Study Documentation. Statistical Bulletin No. 204.* http://www.csa.gov.et/survey-report/category/72-hice-1995

Central Statistics Agency (CSA) of Ethiopia. (2010c). *Household Income, Consumption and Expenditure Survey 1999-2000. Study Documentation. February 2001. Statistical Bulletin No. 258.* http://www.csa.gov.et/survey-report/category/73-hice-2000

Central Statistics Agency (CSA) of Ethiopia. (2010d). *Report on the 1999-2000 Household Income, Consumption and Expenditure Survey. Study Documentation.* http://www.csa.gov.et/survey-report/category/73-hice-2000

Central Statistics Agency (CSA) of Ethiopia. (2011a). *Household Consumption and Expenditure (HCE) Survey 2010/11. Analytical Report. Statistical Bulletin No. 563.* http://www.csa.gov.et/survey-report/category/75-hice-2011

Central Statistics Agency (CSA) of Ethiopia. (2011b). *The 2010/11 Ethiopian Households Consumption – Expenditure (HCE). Survey Results For: Country Level. Statistical Report.* http://www.csa.gov.et/survey-report/category/75-hice-2011

Central Statistics Agency (CSA) of Ethiopia. (2011c). *Ethiopian Data Quality Assessment Framework (EDQAF).* Addis Ababa. http://www.csa.gov.et/component/phocadownload/category/310?Itemid=310

Central Statistics Agency (CSA) of Ethiopia. (2018a). *The 2015/16 Ethiopian Household Consumption – Expenditure (HCE) Survey Results For: Country Level. Statistical Report. Statistical Bulletin No. 585*. http://www.csa.gov.et/survey-report/category/350-hice-2016

Central Statistics Agency (CSA) of Ethiopia. (2018b). *Statistical Data report on 3rd mission to Ethiopia- June 2018*. http://www.csa.gov.et/survey-report/category/350-hice-2016

Copenhagen Business School (CBS). (2023). *Center for Corporate Governance*. https://www.cbs.dk/en/research/departments-and-centres/department-of-accounting/center-corporate-governance

Council of Europe. (2023). *Good Governance. 12 Principles of Good Governance*. https://www.coe.int/en/web/good-governance/12-principles

de Jong, H. (2015). Living Standards in a Modernizing World: A Long-Run Perspective on Material Wellbeing and Human Development. In W Glatzer (ed.), *Global Handbook of Quality of Life: exploration of well-being of nations and continent*. Springer. Available online: https://research.rug.nl/en/publications/living-standards-in-a-modernizing-world-a-long-run-perspective-on

Deutsche Welle (DW). (2022). *Global Issues. Living Standards Declining in 90% of Countries — UN*. Available online: https://www.dw.com/en/un-index-shows-living-standards-declining-in-90-of-countries/a-63052023

Egger, D., Miguel, E., Warren, S. S., Shenoy, A., Collins, E., Karlan, D., Parkerson, D., Mobarak, A. M., Fink, G., Udry, C., Walker, M., Haushofer, J., Larreboure, M., Athey, S., Lopez-Pena, P., Benhachmi, S., Humphreys, M., Lowe, L., Meriggi, N. F., ... Vernot, C. (2021). Falling living standards during the COVID-19 crisis: Quantitative evidence from nine developing countries. *Science Advances*, *7*(6), eabe0997. Advance online publication. doi:10.1126ciadv.abe0997 PMID:33547077

Federal Reserve Bank of Saint Louis. (2015). *What Causes a Country's Standard of Living to Rise?* Available online: https://www.stlouisfed.org/on-the-economy/2015/december/what-causes-countrys-standard-living-rise

Federal Statistical Office. (2022). *Quality of Life Indicators*. Available online: https://www.bfs.admin.ch/bfs/en/home/statistics/cross-sectional-topics/city-statistics/indicators-quality-life.html

Fleurbaey, M., & Gaulier, G. (2009). International Comparisons of Living Standards by Equivalent Incomes. *The Scandinavian Journal of Economics*, *111*(3), 597–624. doi:10.1111/j.1467-9442.2009.01578.x

Góngora-Salazar, P., Casabianca, M. S., & Rodríguez-Lesmes, P. (2022). Income inequality and self-rated health status in Colombia. *International Journal for Equity in Health*, *21*(1), 69. doi:10.118612939-022-01659-8 PMID:35578287

Government, A. C. T. (2022). *ACT Wellbeing Framework. Having the Financial Resources to Live Life Well.* Available online: https://www.act.gov.au/wellbeing/explore-overall-wellbeing/living-standards

Government Finance Officers Association (GFOA) of the United States and Canada. (2023). *Best Practices. "ESG" Best Practice - "G" Governance*. https://www.gfoa.org/materials/esg-best-practice-g-governance

International Development Association (IDA). (2023a). *Governance and Institutions*. https://ida.worldbank.org/en/topics/cross-cutting/governance-and-institutions

International Development Association (IDA). (2023b). *IDA19 Results Measurement System*. https://ida.worldbank.org/en/rms

International Monetary Fund (IMF). (2023). *IMF and Good Governance. Why is good governance important?* https://www.imf.org/en/About/Factsheets/Sheets/2023/The-IMF-and-Good-Governance

Joseph Rowntree Foundation. (2019). *What's the best way to improve living standards?* Available online: https://www.jrf.org.uk/blog/whats-best-way-improve-living-standards

Kakwani, N. (1993). Performance in living standards: An international comparison. *Journal of Development Economics*, *41*(2), 307–336. doi:10.1016/0304-3878(93)90061-Q

Living Standard. (2022). *A New Living Standard.* Available online: https://livingstandard.org/about/

Luque González, A., Guamán, L. K., & Popescu, C. R. G. (2022a). Market Economy and Good Living: Obstacles to Its Achievement in Orellana, Ecuador. In C. Popescu (Ed.), *Frameworks for Sustainable Development Goals to Manage Economic, Social, and Environmental Shocks and Disasters* (pp. 35–56). IGI Global. doi:10.4018/978-1-6684-6750-3.ch003

Luque González, A., Soledispa Ibarra, R. E., & Popescu, C. R. G. (2022b). Analysis of Labor Reform During COVID-19: The Case of Ecuador. In C. Popescu (Ed.), *Handbook of Research on SDGs for Economic Development, Social Development, and Environmental Protection* (pp. 1–25). IGI Global. doi:10.4018/978-1-6684-5113-7.ch001

Ma, N., Cheong, T. S., & Li, J. (2022). Evaluating Global Inequality Using Decomposition Approach. *Front Psychol.* 12:809670. *Frontiers in Psychology, 2022*(Jan), 26. doi:10.3389/fpsyg.2021.809670 PMID:35153930

Majumder, A., & Chakravarty, S. R. (1996). Achievement and improvement in living standards—An empirical analysis. *Social Indicators Research, 37*(3), 269–280. doi:10.1007/BF00286234

Ministry of Social Development. (2022a). *Direct Measurement of Living Standards: The New Zealand ELSI Scale*. Available online: https://www.msd.govt.nz/about-msd-and-our-work/publications-resources/monitoring/living-standards/living-standards-elsi.html

Ministry of Social Development. (2022b). *Living Standards Research*. Available online: https://www.msd.govt.nz/about-msd-and-our-work/publications-resources/monitoring/living-standards/index.html

Ministry of Social Development. (2022c). *Household Incomes in New Zealand: trends in indicators of inequality and hardship 1982 to 2020*. Available online: https://www.msd.govt.nz/about-msd-and-our-work/publications-resources/monitoring/household-incomes/index.html

Muminov, N., Kim, T., Egamberdiyev, F., & Ambartsumyan, A. (2020). The Ways Of Improvement Of Living Standards. *International Journal of Psychosocial Rehabilitation, 24*(4), 1965–1980. doi:10.37200/IJPR/V24I4/PR201305

Organization for Economic Co-operation and Development (OECD). (2022a). *Better Life Index*. Available online: https://www.oecdbetterlifeindex.org/

Organization for Economic Co-operation and Development (OECD). (2022b). *Better Life Index. Definitions and Metadata.* Available online: https://www.oecd.org/wise/OECD-Better-Life-Index-definitions-2021.pdf

Organization for Economic Co-operation and Development (OECD). (2023). *Corporate Governance*. https://www.oecd.org/corporate/

Organization for Security and Co-operation in Europe (OSCE). (2003). *OSCE Strategy Document For The Economic And Environmental Dimension. 2nd day of the Eleventh Meeting MC(11) Journal No. 2, Agenda item 8.* https://www.osce.org/files/f/documents/a/3/20705.pdf

Organization for Security and Co-operation in Europe (OSCE). (2023). *Good Governance*. https://www.osce.org/oceea/446335

Our World in Data (WEC). (2020). *The short history of global living conditions and why it matters that we know it*. Available online: https://ourworldindata.org/a-history-of-global-living-conditions-in-5-charts

Pakistan Bureau of Statistics. (2022). *Pakistan Social and Living Standards Measurement. Brief on PSLM Survey*. Available online: https://www.pbs.gov.pk/content/pakistan-social-and-living-standards-measurement

Popescu, C. R. G., & González, A. L. (2022b). Legendary, Life-Changing, and Memorable Benefits of Digitalization to Restart the Economy: Impact of COVID-19 on Global Economic Environment for Sustainable Development. In C. Popescu (Ed.), *Handbook of Research on Building Inclusive Global Knowledge Societies for Sustainable Development* (pp. 166–184). IGI Global. doi:10.4018/978-1-6684-5109-0.ch008

Popescu, C. R. G., & González, A. L. (2022c). Current High-Powered Challenges and High-Reaching Reforms: Moving to a New Economic Model Based on Green Energy, Digitalization, and Shock Resistance. In C. Popescu (Ed.), *Frameworks for Sustainable Development Goals to Manage Economic, Social, and Environmental Shocks and Disasters* (pp. 133–154). IGI Global. doi:10.4018/978-1-6684-6750-3.ch008

Popescu, C. R. G., & González, A. L. (2023). Digital Transformation Impact on Organizations' Culture and Employees' Motivation: Shaping the "New Normal" and Addressing Sustainable Development Goals. In C. Popescu (Ed.), *Positive and Constructive Contributions for Sustainable Development Goals* (pp. 114–130). IGI Global. doi:10.4018/978-1-6684-7499-0.ch008

Popescu, C. R. G., & Luque González, A. (2022a). Importance and Implications of Influential, Powerful, and Remarkable Economic Policy Mix: Pre-Pandemic and Post-Pandemic Challenges in Building Inclusive Global Knowledge Societies. In C. Popescu (Ed.), *Handbook of Research on SDGs for Economic Development, Social Development, and Environmental Protection* (pp. 46–65). IGI Global. doi:10.4018/978-1-6684-5113-7.ch003

Rao, N. D., & Min, J. (2018). Decent Living Standards: Material Prerequisites for Human Wellbeing. *Social Indicators Research*, *138*(1), 225–244. doi:10.100711205-017-1650-0 PMID:29950752

Šebestová, J. D., & Popescu, C. R. G. (2022). Factors Influencing Investments into Human Resources to Support Company Performance. *J. Risk Financial Manag.*, *15*(1), 19. doi:10.3390/jrfm15010019

The Economist. (2022). *Global living standards are moving in the wrong direction. Climate change and conflict could make things even worse.* Available online: https://www.economist.com/graphic-detail/2022/09/08/global-living-standards-are-moving-in-the-wrong-direction

The Institute of Chartered Accountants in England and Wales (ICAEW). (2023). *What is corporate governance?* https://www.icaew.com/technical/corporate-governance/principles/principles-articles/does-corporate-governance-matter

The Institute for Fiscal Studies (IFS). (2022a). *Living standards, poverty and inequality in the UK.* Available online: https://ifs.org.uk/living-standards-poverty-and-inequality-uk

The Institute for Fiscal Studies (IFS). (2022b). *Report. Living standards, poverty and inequality in the UK: 2022.* Available online: https://ifs.org.uk/publications/living-standards-poverty-and-inequality-uk-2022

The Treasury of New Zealand. (2018). *Improving Living Standards: We Need to Talk About Productivity.* Available online: https://www.treasury.govt.nz/publications/speech/improving-living-standards-we-need-talk-about-productivity

Topuz, S. G. (2022). The Relationship Between Income Inequality and Economic Growth: Are Transmission Channels Effective? *Social Indicators Research, 162*(3), 1177–1231. doi:10.100711205-022-02882-0 PMID:35103032

United Cities and Local Governments Asia-Pacific (UCLG ASPAC). (2021). *Good Governance: Definition and Characteristics.* https://uclg-aspac.org/good-governance-definition-and-characteristics/

United Nations Development Programme (UNDP). (2022). *Human Development Report 2021-22: Uncertain Times, Unsettled Lives: Shaping our Future in a Transforming World.* Available online: https://hdr.undp.org/content/human-development-report-2021-22

United Nations Economic and Social Commission for Asia and the Pacific (UNESCAP). (2023). *What is Good Governance?* https://www.unescap.org/sites/default/files/good-governance.pdf

United Nations Geneva. (2022). *Sustainable Development Goals (SDGs).* Available online: https://www.ungeneva.org/en/topics/sustainable-development-goals

United Nations (UN). (2012). *UN System Task Team on the Post-2015 UN Development Agenda. Governance and Development*. Thematic Think Piece UNDESA, UNDP, UNESCO. https://www.un.org/millenniumgoals/pdf/Think%20 Pieces/7_governance.pdf

United Nations (UN). (2015). *Sustainable Development Goals (SDGs). Do You Know All 17 SDGs?* Available online: https://sdgs.un.org/goals

United Nations (UN). (2018). *The 2030 Agenda and the Sustainable Development Goals: An Opportunity for Latin America and the Caribbean* (LC/G.2681-P/Rev.3). United Nations. Available online: https://repositorio.cepal.org/bitstream/handle/11362/40156/25/S1801140_en.pdf

United Nations (UN). (2019). *Raising Living Standards Boosts Overall Well-Being of Societies, Speakers Say, as Commission for Social Development Continues Session*. Available online: https://press.un.org/en/2019/soc4875.doc.htm

United Nations (UN). (2017). *Improving Living Standards through Mainstreaming of Sustainable Development Goals into the National Development Policy in Tajikistan*. Available online: https://sustainabledevelopment.un.org/content/documents/16021Tajikistan.pdf

United States Green Building Council (USGBC). (2022). *Healthy people in healthy places equals a healthy economy*. Available online: https://www.usgbc.org/resources/healthy-people-healthy-places-equals-healthy-economy

Word Bank (WB). (1992). *Governance and Development*. https://elibrary.worldbank.org/doi/epdf/10.1596/0-8213-2094-7 doi:10.1596/0-8213-2094-7

World Bank (WB). (2017). *World Bank Group Country Partnership Framework for the Democratic Republic of Ethiopia 2018-2022*. Available online: https://documents1.worldbank.org/curated/en/202771504883944180/pdf/119576-revised-Ethiopia-Country-Partnership-Web.pdf

World Bank (WB). (2020). *How can countries support economic growth and improve living standards across all regions?* Available online: https://blogs.worldbank.org/latinamerica/how-can-countries-support-economic-growth-and-improve-living-standards-across-all

World Bank (WB). (2022a). *The World Bank in Ethiopia*. Available online: https://www.worldbank.org/en/country/ethiopia/overview

World Bank (WB). (2022b). *World Bank Group Statement on Current Situation in Ethiopia*. Available online: https://www.worldbank.org/en/news/statement/2021/03/05/world-bank-group-statement-on-current-situation-in-ethiopia

World Bank (WB). (2022c). *World Bank Boosts Pastoral Economies and Climate Action in the Horn of Africa*. Available online: https://www.worldbank.org/en/news/statement/2021/03/05/world-bank-group-statement-on-current-situation-in-ethiopia

World Bank (WB). (2022d). *World Bank Approves $180 Million to Step-Up Support for Refugees and Host Communities in Ethiopia*. Available online: https://www.worldbank.org/en/news/press-release/2022/06/28/world-bank-approves-180-million-to-step-up-support-for-refugees-and-host-communities-in-ethiopia

World Bank (WB). (2022e). *Ethiopia - Country partnership framework for the period FY18 - FY22 (English)*. Available online: https://documents.worldbank.org/en/publication/documents-reports/documentdetail/202771504883944180/ethiopia-country-partnership-framework-for-the-period-fy18-fy22

World Bank (WB). (2023). *Governance*. Available online: https://www.worldbank.org/en/topic/governance/overview

World Economic Forum (WEC). (2021). *Climate Change. 5 surprising ways to increase living standards sustainably*. Available online: https://www.weforum.org/agenda/2021/10/5-surprising-ways-to-increase-living-standards-sustainably/

World Trade Organization. (2022a). *The WTO can ... cut living costs and raise living standards*. Available online: https://www.wto.org/english/thewto_e/whatis_e/10thi_e/10thi01_e.htm

World Trade Organization. (2022b). *The WTO can ... settle disputes and reduce trade tensions*. Available online: https://www.wto.org/english/thewto_e/whatis_e/10thi_e/10thi02_e.htm

World Trade Organization. (2022c). *The WTO can ... stimulate economic growth and employment*. Available online: https://www.wto.org/english/thewto_e/whatis_e/10thi_e/10thi03_e.htm

World Trade Organization. (2022d). *The WTO can ... cut the cost of doing business internationally*. Available online: https://www.wto.org/english/thewto_e/whatis_e/10thi_e/10thi04_e.htm

World Trade Organization. (2022e). *The WTO can ... support the environment and health*. Available online: https://www.wto.org/english/thewto_e/whatis_e/10thi_e/10thi08_e.htm

World Trade Organization. (2022f). *The WTO can ... contribute to peace and stability.* Available online: https://www.wto.org/english/thewto_e/whatis_e/10thi_e/10thi09_e.htm

Wu, J., & Pu, Y. (2020). Air pollution, general government public-health expenditures and income inequality: Empirical analysis based on the spatial Durbin model. *PLoS One*, *15*(10). doi:10.1371/journal.pone.0240053 PMID:33002068

Xiang, G., Liu, J., Zhong, S., & Deng, M. (2022). Comprehensive metrological and content analysis of the income inequality research in health field: A bibliometric analysis. *Frontiers in Public Health*, *10*, 901112. doi:10.3389/fpubh.2022.901112 PMID:36187638

KEY TERMS AND DEFINITIONS

Climate Adaptation, Climate Change Efforts, and Climate Justice: There are important lessons to be learned regarding the way in which human behavior as well as leaders' decisions affected our world, especially in the context in which it has become critical to focus on sustainable growth; in this given context, finding rapid solutions for climate adaptation no longer represent an option, but they have become a must in a society devoured by extreme poverty and imminent climate risks; hence, countries worldwide are called to unite their efforts in terms of ensuring that climate change will stop affecting the present and the future generations, while addressing climate justice in a healthier and more sustainable environment (International Development Association (IDA), 2023a); in this particular matter, the authors draw attention that it is high time to make serious efforts to boost shared prosperity, while building more capable, efficient, resilient, sustainable, inclusive, and accountable communities, businesses, Organizations, and institutions (International Development Association (IDA), 2023b).

Collaboration for Good Governance and Development: In this day and age, everything that seems to surround people's lives is aimed more and more at making them more individualistic and even, in some cases, more focused only on personal and private matters, hence growing to be more immune to the problems of less fortunate ones or the importance of the environment in which people live in; even though this is apparently the general trend, the authors' intention is to make people aware that there are numerous advantages that may be encountered in collaboration, in building economic and social strong connections for a better, safer, and healthier future for all; for example, good governance implicates collaboration between the individuals living in a country and its management, based on the fact that achieving the goals of good governance implicate the fact that the local authorities should receive help and support from the communities (Organization for Security and Co-operation in Europe (OSCE), 2003); in the same line with the aforementioned aspects, another example could be represented by the fact that the well-being of individuals and the good health of the environment strongly depend on building more resilient, robust, and sustainable cities which can only be done with the constant involvement of the people and the authorities (Organization for Security and Co-operation in Europe (OSCE), 2023).

Ethiopian Data Quality Assessment Framework (EDQAF): These days, quality is becoming more and more important, especially when the results derived from the assessment of quality are showing the power of certain entities or countries to enhance effectiveness, efficiency, and performance at a general level (Central Statistics Agency (CSA) of Ethiopia, 2011c, p.7); what is more, the quality assessment process in Ethiopia comes to ensure that all the aspects surrounding the management of quality have been closely addressed and followed, based on standard assessment tools, assessment programs, as well as various other dimensions that accompany quality (Central Statistics Agency (CSA) of Ethiopia, 2011c, p.7). Besides all these, in the case of Ethiopia the EDQAF focuses on major issues, such as: (a) identifying the specific needs of Ethiopia, while taking advantage of the best international practices and tools capable to assess quality, in order to enhance the living standards of people; (b) identifying the quality assessment procedures that are capable, on the long run, to improve the standards of living in the case of Ethiopians, while creating concrete plans capable to support the people, the communities, and the individuals in need of immediate support and attention, hence fostering high quality standards and focusing on sustainable quality improvements; and (c) finding the best solutions to disseminate the results in order to gain visibility, to empower the quality assessment teams to continue their work, and to focus on the positive connections that arise from Environmental Social Governance (ESG) and Artificial Intelligence (AI) for business sustainability (Central Statistics Agency (CSA) of Ethiopia, 2018b, pp.6-9).

Governance and Development: Nowadays, specialists are getting more and more concerned with the idea of governance for development; in this given context, the authors introduce the powerful connection that undeniably exists between governance and development, in order to show that there are at least two sides surrounding this powerful relationship, namely: (a) first of all, governance represents the manner in which countries are managed, mainly, but not exclusively, in terms of their economic and social resources (Word Bank (WB), 1992); while (b) second of all, development may only be regarded as having positive implications in those cases in which the focus is on Sustainable Development (SD), responsibility, equity and inclusiveness, effectiveness and efficiency, as well as accountability (Word Bank

(WB), 1992; United Nations Economic and Social Commission for Asia and the Pacific (UNESCAP), 2023).

Governance Global Practice: Nowadays, the World Bank (WB) researchers and specialists point out that there are three major problems that can be noticed at a global level, namely: (a) the pandemic has seriously weakened the society in which people live, especially due to the fact that everyone might be regarded as profoundly and irreversibly affected by the COVID-19 pandemic and the COVID-19 crisis; (b) the rebellions, the civil wars, and all forms of fights and of wars that are taking place or that recently took place in the society are coming to raise even further the gap between individuals and communities, increasing inequalities and discriminatory behavior as well as economic, social, and political problems; and (c) the climate change represents the result of irresponsible human actions and Organizations' activities, which has come to generate, on a regular basis, disasters at a global level (World Bank (WB), 2023).

Outcomes From Intersecting Environmental Social Governance (ESG) and Artificial Intelligence (AI) for Business Sustainability: Nowadays, two concepts seem to be used more and more due to their surprising results regarding the individuals' mindfulness, people's health, businesses' sustainability, and environmental inclusiveness, resilience, and robustness; these two notions, namely Environmental Social Governance (ESG) and Artificial Intelligence (AI), have proven that they currently have the greatest potential to provide constrictive and positive outcomes to our society in terrible need for climate justice. In this matter, Environmental Social Governance (ESG) and Artificial Intelligence (AI) can develop – with the aid of researchers and with the help of specialists, valuable relationship and synergies, capable to lead to the following desired and expected actions: (a) firstly, the idea of Environmental Social Governance (ESG) encompasses other forms used so far, such as, for instance, Governance, Good Governance, Corporate Social Responsibility, and Corporate Governance, since the accent is out on the environment and on the preservation of biodiversity, ecosystems, and nature as a whole; (b) secondly, the idea of Artificial Intelligence (AI) has more connotations that it might offer at an initial glance, since the priority of the intelligence demonstrated by the computers would be how to restore the natural habitats and to enable the environment to become healthier and more robust; (c) thirdly, the combination between the Environmental Social Governance (ESG) and Artificial Intelligence (AI) for business sustainability may only be considered of true value in those cases in which the ultimate reached results show an increase in the individuals' well-being, the living standards optimization based on environmental regeneration and success stories, and businesses that are capable to produce advantages not only for the employers and the employees, but which are acting in the spirit of Good Governance, with care for people and the environment, dedication for the less fortunate individuals, and support for communities in need.

Sense and Counter-Sense in Sustainable Development (SD) and Evolution: There are so many challenges and temptations these days, which makes it sometimes impossible for some people to make the right choices when it comes to working for doing good or for making profit. Hence, the idea of being on the right track – namely, on the right sense of the development and the evolution, while compared with the idea of stepping on the other side, on the bad track – namely, on the counter-sense of the development and the evolution, arises most naturally as a provocation for individuals, resourceful business owners, prominent country leaders, and renowned governmental officials. There are several questions that come to mind in these particular cases, such as: Can humanity be on the right sense on its development and evolution, if the actions taken are solely focused on making profit? Or, is mankind on the counter-sense when choosing to sacrifice people's well-being and the health of the environment when willing to work for making profit rather than for doing good? In this day and age, the idea of being on the right side in terms of development and evolution should no longer be a mystery for no one, since the answer may be found in the way in which the Sustainable Development Goals (SDGs) are acknowledged and applied in the day to day lives of individuals and businesses. So far, too much damage has been done to our Planet and too many human lives have been affected by irresponsible and irrational behavior, which requires immediate action from the synergies derived from the relationship that exists between the Environmental Social Governance (ESG) and Artificial Intelligence (AI).

Chapter 2
Role of AI in Strengthening ESG Governance:
Perspective From Industry Experts

M. Jayalakshmi
Christ University, India

A. Maria Sneha
Christ University, India

S. Girish
https://orcid.org/0000-0001-8578-7743
Christ University, India

ABSTRACT

Socially conscious investors, especially Gen Z, value ethics over money. ESG reports are as important as financial reports for them. ESG ratings from various sources can puzzle these Gen Z investors, as there is no standardization in ESG data. Firstly, the chapter focuses on the need to integrate AI into ESG reporting by highlighting the limitations of mere frameworks such as GRI, SASB, and ISSB. Secondly, it emphasizes the difference between traditional reporting and AI-integrated ESG reporting. It also points out the challenges of AI integration and ways to overcome these challenges. Lastly, the chapter also proposes the need for a unified framework, making it easier for investors to compare and make decisions.

DOI: 10.4018/979-8-3693-1151-6.ch002

INTRODUCTION

Artificial Intelligence is an eminent technology which can perform tasks similar to humans. With the help of algorithms, AI has the capability to solve complex problems with less time. It is also trained to sense, comprehend, act and learn (Accenture,2022). ESG (Environmental, Social, and Governance) on the other hand has gained prominence and it is used to evaluate the investments of the organizations. Investors who are socially conscious prefer those companies which are concerned towards environment, employees and many other things apart from mere profits. ESG issues have motivated companies to adopt eco-friendly practices which is a concern to most of the Gen Z investors. One such example can be Reliance industry's leading contribution towards CSR. AI in ESG investing for companies like Reliance can help in analysing huge demographics data and let the company know which segment of the society needs more support. Reliance will be able to make data driven decisions if AI is implemented in ESG investing. Artificial Intelligence in general can change the way how business is portrayed in the eyes of stakeholders.

It requires data related to customer history, geographical data, financial auditing, laws and regulations for ensuring businesses are aligned with ESG criteria. If businesses are being serious about ESG it is also time to be serious about AI as there might be many agencies that provide ESG assessments which can compromise on integrity of scoring process (Dressler, n.d.).

In today's world, handling large amount of management data and analysing has become challenging to businesses. Fortunately, AI solutions are changing the industries by implementing automated tasks and improving the efficiency. This automation trend has the capacity to reduce errors and enhance decision making. The data analysis and interpretation of AI outperforms those of human and making it a valuable tool. It is very important to have a balance of both, especially in the situations that requires careful judgement. AI tools have brought significant changes in business sector by automating time consuming processes and does offer great potential for increasing productivity. As the awareness of its benefits have increased, this trend is expected to strengthen. Regulators can enhance their enforcement efforts by utilizing AI, that involves analytical insights to support investigation and enforcement actions. AI mainly focuses on simplifying and clarifying complicated sustainability rules. Additionally, it enables for an easier understanding and communicate effectively in relation to important sustainability concerns (De Villiers et al., 2023a).

When it comes it complex ESG investing decisions, generative AI can be beneficial. Generative AI can break down the complexity of sustainable investment and can easily guide us through what is considered as ethical and sustainable. Identifying sustainable investment for an individual investor can be challenging sometimes mainly because there is no uniform standard that is established. Individuals may relay on the ESG disclosures prepared by the company and most of the time companies hide the material risk associated as per the OECD report (Lack of Standardized ESG Data May Hide Material Risks, OECD Say, n.d.). On the other hand, how ethically can AI be employed is also debatable. A company's reputation will be at trouble if they undermine to consider the likes and preferences of its stakeholders.

ESG ratings have become very important in the business field. They mainly affect how companies make their decisions and the markets view them. Companies sometimes feel restricted as they push themselves to improve their ESG ratings which does results in the downside of stakeholders. The way people view ESG ratings varies, therefore those who indulge in it must make the best use of it for their specific fields. Banks having good ESG ratings can benefit them during tough economic times although the effect of ESG ratings does differ from different businesses. It mainly impacts on how much companies make and borrow. ESG not only focuses on financial assets but also studies about non-financial factors which means focusing on how well a business is able to come with innovative ideas in improving their current position, their contribution towards sustainability and risk management. To truly understand how ESG affect the company's overall performance researchers have looked at factors other than standard financial measures. They consider broader set of indicators to get a complete picture (Wan et al., 2023).

If we observe the ESG ratings in IT industry, HCL Technologies ltd ranks 15 out of 1109 having 11.7 percent of risk when compared to Cognizant Technology Solutions having 14.7 percent of risk ranking 52nd (Company ESG Risk Rating - Sustainalytics, n.d.). Studies found that there is a positive connection between the governance score and financial results. While in some cases, others have a negative relationship. There is no single way on how ESG impacts company's performance. (Aydoğmuş et al., 2022).

REVIEW OF LITERATURE

The three main frameworks that we focus in our study are GRI, SASB and ISSB. These frameworks would function effectively by incorporating artificial intelligence in their processes.

Global Reporting Initiative (GRI)

A popular framework for sustainable reporting is the Global Reporting Initiative which is used across the world. According to the survey conducted by KPMG, 78% of the world's largest 250 companies by revenue (G250) follows GRI (McCalla-

Leacy, 2022). 98.6% of the sustainable reports in Taiwan 2001 was through GRI (GRI - Towards Corporate Transparency in the Greater China Region, n.d.).

Amongst other companies which uses GRI, Tata (Automotive) started to use GRI since 2001 (Telang, 2015). GRI covers various aspects such as social, economic and environmental. This framework aims to give the investors an overall picture of the investments made by the companies in line with sustainability. It covers aspects such as labour practices, workplace diversity and climate change which are usually ignored by other frameworks (GRI - Four-in-five Largest Global Companies Report With GRI, n.d.). The framework is subject to continuous update based on the need of the changing business environment. GRI tries to align modification in line with the SDGs and it has truly gained prominence over time.

When companies use GRI framework for a sustainability reporting they follow structured format to gather important data and evaluate their impact on sustainability, which helps in creating a detailed sustainability report. By discussing openly regarding their sustainability initiatives, efforts and challenges associated, companies become more transparent and accountable. This leads to responsible business environment that enables the increase in corporate responsibility. The GRI framework has gained acceptance across the world but organizations that come under food, retail, cruise and energy face extreme challenges while trying to adopt and implement GRI standards effectively. As GRI covers various aspects in sustainability, it might seem very difficult to adapt it. Understanding and adapting this standard to specific field would be tricky due to these businesses having a shortage of resources both in terms of financials and knowledge and especially acquiring these technologies and analysing will be expensive (Charl, 2022).

On the contrary, Fonseca et al. (2014) discusses real life issue with following GRI. There are instances were mining companies have portrayed their initiatives in an appealing way after harming environment. Many mining companies disclose themselves as sustainable using GRI by carrying out some CSR. GRI lacked to consider the long-term effects of this mining and the impact that their action can cause to the environment. The authors highlight the scope for improvement in GRI such as being futuristic and considering each mining site performance.

Sustainability Accounting Standards Board (SASB)

The Sustainability Accounting Standards Board is an organization in short understood as SASB was established in the year 2011. Being a non- profit organization, the main aim of this standard is to create a clear and consistent standard with regards to sustainability reporting. This way organizations can effectively bridge the gap in communicating their sustainability results to stakeholders. In simple terms, we can describe SASB assists companies in their exhibition to enhance sustainability.

One of the key areas that SASB focuses among its 5 dimensions is diversity (Wilson, 2023). Gender diversity is really important for companies. Gender diversity board (GDB) helps firms to understand how gender dynamics affect their finances, risk and their ESG disclosure. Collective perspectives from all the genders will result to an effective approach that improves company's financial results. In addition, GDB ensures about gender inclusion that companies need to align with ESG principles. This reveals that the company is committed to sustainability. This commitment not only builds a good reputation but also makes stakeholders happy and attracts ethical investors. This process in turn helps the firm grow in a better way.

The GDB acts like a guide in clarifying how gender diversity affects their success. When a company is transparent about its operations and how well it manages ESG issues, financial experts can predict its future earnings more accurately. On the other hand, when a company discusses how they handle environmental issues, it does affect their predictions of future profits significantly. Studies found that having women in higher positions showcases women's participation in boards effectively. Between 2021 and 2023 Fortune 500 companies have grown in inclusivity from 4% to 8.1%. Hong Kong stock exchange proposed on April 2021 to make changes to its corporate governance code in order to enhance gender diversity (*Enhancing Gender Diversity on Boards and in Senior Management of Listed Companies*, n.d.).

It is important to notice that company which functions in a socially responsible manner while communicating their initiatives on sustainability and good governance will eventually perform well when compared to others who don't talk about it. Addressing environmental problems may not have a strong impact on financial performance but will help in long term reputation of the firm (Ahmad et al., 2023). General Motors has its diverse board with 58% of its members being women. The CEO, Mary Barra leads the company and helps in efficient working of the company (The 5 JUST 100 Companies Leading on Gender Board Diversity — JUST Capital, n.d.).

The companies that follow SASB standards focus on variety of ESG related operations. SASB standard ensures that the operations of the business are properly reported so that it can add value to the company. It has a diverse set of metrics which differs from one industry to the other. It gives the advantage to investors for comparing sustainable data which is very essential. Investors who wish to find out what are the risks and opportunities of the business that can affect financial position of the company that they want to invest in, can do it with the help of SASB (SASB - ESG for Investors, 2023).

One of the companies that follow SASB standards are Alibaba Group Holding Limited, China. ESG report of Alibaba 2022 is prepared in accordance with the GRI and SASB standards. Alibaba was able to find out material topics with the help of SASB and GRI. With the help of SASB, it has disclosed how green their operations are, to what extent their consumptions are trust worthy, how responsible they are in creating a sustainable technology (Alibaba Group Holding Limited, 2022).

Additionally using SASB helps companies to implement ISSB. IFRS S1 is very general and doesn't specify what to disclose. So, companies who wish to implement IFRS S1 can follow SASB standards to see what is relevant to be disclosed based on their industry (SASB: Your Pathway to ISSB - SASB, 2023).

International Sustainability Standards Board (ISSB)

The International Sustainability Standards Board (ISSB) is widely used in the world of sustainability reporting. It is an initiative established by the IFRS Foundation, well known for creating global accounting standards. The ISSB aims to contribute how companies report on sustainability by creating a common framework for sustainability disclosures (IFRS - International Sustainability Standards Board, n.d.).

The organization these days, strives to build consistency and comparability by making it easier to understand and help stakeholders make informed decisions about company's sustainability performance and its impact on its long-term value. The ISSB goal is to create standardized sustainability reporting rules similar to financial reporting. All these processes are carried to ultimately make investors and stakeholders rely on this data that includes company's sustainability efforts and their impact on its financial well-being (International Sustainability Standards Board (ISSB), n.d.).

Businesses are observing an increase interest from investors and customers to determine their impact with regards to ESG goals. In March 2022, ISSB releases their initial guidelines which showcased on how companies need to report on sustainability and climate related risks. Genpact and B Team collaborated to make the guidelines in a better way. They included a multi - pronged approach which involved round table discussion with leaders of finance and sustainability. The input was taken from 16 Fortune 500 companies to ensure the guidelines were well informed and clear before finalizing. Five themes were analysed in the discussion which highlighted on greenhouse gas emissions, tracking and reporting of the emissions data and timeliness (Saxena, 2023).

In Australia, the government is thinking of making it mandatory for big companies and financial institutions to share information about climate-related matters following these ISSB Standards. These Standards are likely to be used worldwide to make sure that investors can trust the information provided in sustainability reports (ISSB Standards What They Mean Australian Companies? | FTI, n.d.).

AI and Sustainability

Sustainability has a broader scope when it comes to corporations. Sustainability is how ethical are the companies in managing their resources and can satisfy the demands of current and future generation. This topic of sustainability is becoming the need of the hour may be because of global environmental concerns. Therefore, there is a need for accurate measurement which can evaluate organization's sustainability. Although there is no single definition that can define sustainability, we can say it is reducing doing harm to people and the environment (Moodaley & Telukdarie, 2023). One such example can be Patagonia, a clothing company. They have pledged to spend 1% of their sales towards sustainable practise. To reduce the land fill, they recycle their own cloth materials and they also ensure the materials are ethically sourced (Environmental Responsibility Programs - Patagonia, n.d.).

Sustainability programs have been increasingly high in companies as they observe growth in their firm doing so. When Unilever created dishwashing liquid which required less water, it did work well in the areas where water was scarce. As a result, it did increase sales by 20 percent in the market. Nestle, which started as petroleum refining company now generates its profit from renewable fuels and sustainable products. We can derive an understanding that companies are trying to create a positive edge and flourish well by underlining their products focusing on sustainability. Another aspect that was understood is when companies benefit the society and their employees it in turn makes the happy in their jobs. There was another example quoted where randomly chosen employees received bonuses. This resulted more satisfaction for those employees right away when compared to employees who did not receive the bonus (Five Ways That ESG Creates Value, n.d.).

Customers who are environmental conscious, prefer these companies over the others who don't value sustainability. They will be even ready to pay a higher price for companies which produce environmentally friendly products (Accenture, 2019). The major problem faced by environmental conscious customers are there are many brands which falsely claim they are sustainable. The misleading labels and advertisements make consumer pay green premium wrongly. The trendy phrases like 'Greenwash' and 'Blue wash' may not be true at all for some products. This dishonesty brings us to the need for strict evaluation of sustainable practise. (De Villiers et al., 2023b). ESG scores has come into play to look after this. It helps the consumers to evaluate the company's sustainability. ESG data takes into picture non-financial data which is important for Gen Z investors. 92% of these Gen Z would be ready to switch brand which support ESG ratings (ESG Ratings: Do They Add Value? How to Get Prepared?, n.d-a.). ESG scores quantify the companies on how much sustainable they are and helps to compare which company is doing the best. On the other hand, ESG ratings are not standardised. We have multiple ESG ratings for one company, which is the issue to most of us. Due to this reason, many investors use ESG ratings as base and do their own research before investing.

In the meantime, companies like Infosys, EY and many others are taking initiative and investing in ESG to improve their ratings. They are also trying to find out some ESG aspects that match with their industry since they differ from one industry to the other. Addressing such issues requires a good framework so that issues are selected appropriately and disclosed properly. ESG became extremely popular during COVID-19 when mental health of employees was questioned. After the end of pandemic, people also understood how important ESG ratings are. It is evident that ESG-related funds perform better and gives good return than those non-ESG funds. (Lee et al., 2022). This may be because of the trust and loyalty of investors is higher in ESG related funds.

ESG investing and AI auditing serve distant purposes but they are relative in some cases. AI auditing involves examining individual algorithmic systems to ensure they meet predefined standards. On the other hand, ESG investing takes a comprehensive approach. It assesses company's procedures and practices. ESG investors are interested in understanding how these systems fit into the company's broader sustainability and ethical framework. AI 's impact is just not limited to private businesses but also extends to public and non-profit organizations too. We will have to consider all the different AI systems working together in a company in order to overview the in-depth understanding of how AI is used and processed. This holistic approach helps everyone to gain a better view of AI utilization. ESG investing looks at a broader picture of how a company uses AI in all its processes. While we look into AI auditing, it focuses on monitoring specific algorithms ensuring that they meet certain standards. When investors take the broader view which is offered by ESG, they will gain valuable insights. This way it helps them make more informed assessment of the risks and opportunities associated with the company. This approach would be used for all sorts of organizations, whether they are privately owned, publicly traded, or nonprofit. It emphasizes the need to have a consistent way of understanding how AI works in today's business world (Minkkinen et al., 2022).

ESG investing earlier focused on excluding certain companies from investment portfolios due to their distinctive business practices. However, the focus has been shifted to sustainability and more of a comprehensive view of a company's long-term prospects. The idea of Socially Responsible Investing (SRI) has grabbed the attention widely. Today companies with strong ESG tracks are considered as the best managed, less risky and potential enough to perform better financially in a long run (Syed, 2017).

Also, portfolio managers these days pick those companies which have good ESG ratings to attract investments. ESG ratings are provided by various organizations including Bloomberg, S&P, MSCI and others. ESG related investments are complicated as already discussed in our research mainly because the ratings provided by these organizations can vary. Some organizations like Bloomberg just provide publicly available information. On the other hand, MSCI provide data which is their internal analysis along with the publicly available data (ESG Ratings: Do They Add Value? How to Get Prepared?, n.d.-b).

There is a need for a technology that can help investors in this matter. There is a need for technology which can analyse how relevant was companies' investments towards ESG. AI driven decision making can help to sort out the confusion relating to difference in the ESG scores. With AI we can compare this year's data with the previous year, analyse the impact of any news related to the company on ESG and identify how fair it is to invest in that particular company (Vodenska et al., 2022).

The ideal world comprises of three important factors which are People, Prosperity and Planet. It was the balance between these three which results in sustainable growth. Though Corporate Sustainability Reporting (CSR) has increased but still there is no significant decrease in carbon emissions. Therefore, sustainability reporting still needs room for improvement. Evaluating the accuracy and thoroughness of the data provided is done which helps in investigation on the quality of sustainability reporting. This entails monitoring the full value chain as mentioned in the GRI 101 standard. "Reporting the right thing" helps us understand the fundamental needs of significant stakeholders mainly focusing on people and planet. Surprisingly, only 20% of the 40 Swedish and foreign businesses assessed in Sweden declared their carbon emissions at every stage of the value chain. This results in knowing how difficult it is to constantly recognize and communicate what matters the most in the field of sustainable development. (Ramanathan & Isaksson, 2022).

Businesses these days believe that using AI is really a sustainable thought. Using AI can save energy. Especially smart LED lightings is one simple way through which companies can save energy. There are many companies which have adopted this and reaping benefits. One such example is Infosys. They make use of day time natural light harvesting to automatically dim or increase the brightness. Along with this, entire process of lighting is automated, where lights get adjusted based on the occupancy. They have also claimed because of this automation, they were able to save 60% of energy as compared to 2008 (Limited, n.d.).

AI is also trained to display some behaviours such as cognition, reasoning and problem-solving. Accountants will be benefited if blockchain and AI is combined in preparation of sustainable reports. Although AI is based on human created algorithms, AI can sometimes perform better than humans. Example in terms of speed and accuracy they are much efficient. When AI and blockchain is put together to work, sustainable reports will be much more efficient. They can provide a clear picture of sustainable data to investors. There is also a suggestion to expand the definition on sustainable finance and include much more related to AI such as the model used, systems and how AI in an organization can support them in long term sustainability. (Al-Sartawi et al., 2022). Large amount of data can be analysed and visualised with less time. This also gives the auditors assurance that there was no biased involved in preparation of the reports. To reap this benefit, accountants must be trained to work with AI. We suggest that the accountants must be also aware of the algorithm bias that AI brings in and must be prepared to deal with it and leverage this benefit.

We believe that artificial intelligence would offer a lot to organizations which aims in building a high and effective recruitment processes. In today's world recruiting potential talents and skilled person has become difficult. It is always important for companies to recruit in a way which maintains consistent and high-quality process. AI can be used as an effective tool to automate routine administrative tasks which can lead to improvement in recruitment strategy. New innovations such as chatbots like Tribe Pad's helps to categorize resumes through applicant tracking systems. Sustainability which includes economic, environmental and social components plays a vital role in helping firms achieve their organizational goals. Sustainability offers a wide range of benefits which goes beyond fulfilling corporate social responsibility. It does positively impact the highly competitive business landscape.

For a progressive organization, analysing the relationship between sustainability and human resource is necessary. Ignoring the deeper effects that sustainability has on human resource will have an impact on company's long-term performance by compromising its future anticipation. By embracing sustainability and integrating it to the organization's framework, there can be a balance strived between economic success, environmental responsibility, societal well-being and a flourishing workforce. Additionally, this strategy also contributes to resilience and adaption which helps in enhancing corporate environment and long-term growth in the dynamic world (K & Shanthi, 2020).

Challenges of AI Integration

The risk and drawback that is accompanied with AI needs to be considered and understood. The biggest concern is its adverse environmental impact as shown by the enormous carbon footprint which is approximately 300 tons of CO2 emissions available to a single in-depth NLP programme. Moreover, it is challenging to estimate the total expenses in relation to widely used AI systems. Due to this complexity, it not only includes financial but environmental effects of ai. Eco friendly AI systems should be invented.

By this it becomes very crucial to strike a balance between improving the technology and upholding sustainability. To guarantee that AI would help in being environmentally friendly and inventive this balance must be followed. Act of replacing human in decision making could result as a risk to stakeholders. While we observe certain companies use AI as board members. It not only causes risk to stakeholders but also relying completely on autonomous AI systems may raise ethical and legal questions. Although AI can help in being useful in advising roles, giving it unlimited autonomy is morally not permissible. In order to overcomes these challenges, EU has released recommendations titled as "The expert group's policy and investment recommendation for trustworthy AI", focusing on human agency, technical robustness, privacy, transparency, diversity, social wellbeing and reasonability. These recommendations entail in providing a useful foundation to address the development and application of AI, even though full legislation is still in process of forming. It becomes a growing challenge to market efficiency when AI systems used by companies raise ethical and legal issues. This issue can arise from the use of algorithms intended for market manipulation; this could be made words due to the existing regulations applied in United States are not strong enough to uphold the creators of these AI systems. AI - driven manipulations can have a serious consequence which may disrupt the fair operation. This arises due to improper regulations. It is necessary to have regulations that would closely monitor its use which in turn also helps in ensuring that AI doesn't harm market integrity and stability (McBride et al., 2022).

Amongst many challenges AI could be effectively used by organizations. one such example is Microsoft's vision on healthcare, artificial intelligence, data and ethics. The significant intersection between health and technology has been recognized widely which is prominent in the eyes of policy makers, patients, ethicists and innovators. The company has engaged with both public and private sector clients for discussions who are interested in using technology like cloud computing and AI to enhance human health (Epic, 2019).

viAct is a Con Tech startup which is based in Hong Kong which uses advanced AI technology to help the construction industry in Asia and Europe. Though the company is growing fast, it brings new worries which includes handling risks related to privacy concerns and dealing with cyberattacks. Many construction companies are not ready for cyber threats Therefore it becomes challenging for companies to understand and resolve these issues (Ng et al., 2022)

Transformation in Decision Making for Effective AI Functioning

Deloitte, McKinsey and other consulting firms have started using AI tools for decision making. This will help them to scan the external environment and update them of early signs of big issues. Although humans are excellent in intuitive thinking, AI has surpassed them when it comes to accurate prediction (Jarrahi, 2018).

AI has the ability to identify the cause-and-effect relationship when it comes to complex decision making and helps human to take better decision (Marwala, 2014). It will be necessary to alter the way public decisions are made in order to use AI in decision-making successfully. It has become widely accepted over the past 10 years that minimal modifications to current systems will be able to considerably better our environment. On what exactly needs to change and how these changes should take place, there is disagreement.

Regarding sustainability, some experts think there needs to be a significant change in the way that technology, markets, businesses, cultures, and policies are implemented in areas like energy, transportation, food, and buildings. Another strategy, like the Earth System Governance framework, discusses modifications to the interaction of social, technical, and ecological systems. The whole structure, operation, linkages, and way we perceive these systems would all be impacted by these changes. Good data is crucial, but it's not the only factor influencing how people in general makes judgements. We need to consider how factors like regulations, politics, and conventional ways of doing things can alter if we want AI to aid in making wise decisions for sustainable development. AI should integrate into the changing system of decision-making, taking into account the current priorities and customary procedures (Bolton et al., 2021).

Comparison Between Traditional ESG Reporting and AI Integrated ESG Reporting

There is a growing need for businesses to report ESG activities. ESG reporting done manually with the help of frameworks involve human analysts, collecting data from various sources such as financial reports, sustainability documents and surveys from employees may not be effective.

The major drawback of this process is time consuming, costly and chance for human errors. These errors might lead to inaccurate reports. Another highlighting challenge is the lack of standardized framework for ESG reporting which becomes difficult for companies to compare with other companies on how well they are doing in terms of sustainability. As time is changing adoption of AI in ESG reporting is expected to significantly increase by 2025. This could happen as investors demand for more transparency and accuracy in ESG data (Uhura.Admin, 2023).

According to a report by PWC, 80 percent of senior leaders say that ESG forms as an important aspect in their business strategy. Furthermore, it is seen that 86 percent of investors believe that ESG helps in long - term value (PricewaterhouseCoopers, n.d.).

Machine learning helps in simplifying ESG reporting through automated data collection and forecasting, which results in data accuracy and saves time. BlackRock, a global asset management company which has recently adopted machine learning and natural language processing which helps the investors in identifying climate risks and opportunities in their portfolios. This tool not only enables investors in gaining insights about company's carbon footprint but also exposes to physical risks such as weather events and policy changes (Artificial Intelligence and Machine Learning in Asset Management, n.d.).

OBJECTIVES

To review how AI can enhance sustainability and help in complex decision making
To compare traditional ESG reporting and AI integrated ESG reporting.
To highlight the benefits of integrating AI in ESG reporting
To discuss some of the challenges faced when AI is integrated in ESG reporting
To recommend companies to use a unified framework which makes it easy for the stakeholders to compare.

SCOPE OF THE STUDY

Our study aims to mainly highlight how AI can help ESG reporting with the help of review of literature. It additionally points out the benefits of reporting frameworks such as Global Reporting Initiative (GRI), the Sustainability Accounting Standards Board (SASB), and the International Sustainability Standards Board (ISSB). The real-life issues faced by the companies when using these frameworks are also mentioned with the help of some case studies and practical examples. The chapter has also elaborated how AI can enhance sustainability and the challenges that organizations face in integrating AI in ESG reporting. The advantages of using AI in making complex/ challenging decision is also highlighted. Comparison between traditional reporting and AI integrated ESG reporting is likewise made. An attempt is made to articulate a unified framework which can leverage the benefits of all the frameworks which is also AI integrated. The chapter aims to recommend organizations to integrate AI in preparing their ESG reports to disclose their sustainable initiatives effectively.

METHODOLOGY

The research methodology adopted involves a qualitative approach by gathering insights from industry experts. The main aim is to incur valuable insights and opinions with regards to AI integration to ESG issues. This approach mainly aims to understand how AI is being integrated in ESG factors. We have captured detailed overview of AI in improving ESG ratings. This results in considering a broader context, unique experiences and complex viewpoints that may not be easily quantified. The relationship between AI and ESG has been displayed in such a way which gives deeper insights. Additionally, the chapter includes reviewing academic articles, journals and determining practical examples related to our study. The academic review helps creating a foundation for theoretical understanding and practical examples from the real world offers evidences on how AI is actually making difference in ESG efforts.

RESULTS AND DISCUSSION

AI integration in the above three frameworks would involve effective steps like analysing and leveraging AI tools into the standard. There are numerous ways that we can integrate this process. Primarily, understanding all of these ESG frameworks guidelines is very essential. These recommendations guide us in providing a set of rules and important principles for organizations while they report on their sustainability reports. This gives a clarity on what information to include and ensuring that they meet the standards set by the frameworks. This is important as it enables that the reports are not just meaningful but also reliable which has a long - lasting impact on sustainability.

Automated Data Collection

Automated data collection means involvement of advanced AI tools and technology to gather data that is valuable form different sources in context of sustainability. The sources can be government records, internal corporate databases and publicly available reports (Javaid, 2023).

Let's say for example to understand how a company is Eco-friendly, it entails into looking at aspects like their carbon emission, waste generation, energy consumption and initiatives to support well-being of the employees. Gathering all of these data could be a tedious task, that is when AI comes to picture which can accurately analyse large data which enables the process in a much faster and efficient way. Even if the data is messy and unstructured, AI can extract useful information from it. Automated data collection offers various benefits. It can start from being time effective where instead of having a group of people in deeply gathering the information, AI saves a lot of time by doing this function in fraction of time. One of the main advantages could be reduction in human error. Human could make mistakes while collecting and entering the information which can result in inaccuracies.

On the other hand, AI is highly consistent therefore data collected could be more reliable. Ultimately AI - powered data collection contributes to more informed decisions. When we observe, ESG reporting in Hong Kong nearly takes half a year to prepare it. Automation could be the answer for effectively collecting and preparing the report way more quickly. (Your Guide T O Automating ESG Reporting in Hong Kong, n.d.).

Predictive Analysis

Although the benefits do not end with only data collection, it goes far beyond that. Our second discussion is on how AI is a boon when it comes to forecasting. With the help of algorithms, AI can scan previous year's data and compare it with the current year's data to predict the future. AI is good at identifying the patterns/trends in the data. In order to benefit from this, it is crucial for us make sure we align AI predictions with the ESG frameworks to make better strategies for the future.

Prediction can be done by following steps. Companies need to collect past data on ESG parameters such as climate change, CSR, waste management, etc. This is important process, where an attempt is made to feed AI with the historical trends. After this, AI algorithms will try to learn from the data (learn from the trends). The trends may be related to seasonal changes or link between the company's sustainable initiatives and the increase or decrease in value. With this, AI will predict the future expected events (Božić, 2023).

One such example for this can be related to renewable energy for a logistic company. Assume AI predicts that investments in renewable energy can decrease the carbon emission with the help of cause-and-effect relationship. Likewise, it predicts that investing in renewable energy is also a metrics in framework for logistic industry and can improve ESG scores. With this information, company can plan their future initiatives in this line.

Stakeholder Analysis

Defining an environmental, social and governance strategy could be a little complex but knowing what matters for stakeholders would help the firms manage this complexity. This not only reduces the complexity but helps in creating in strategy that is responsive to stakeholder priorities and concerns.

In stakeholder analysis primarily there needs to be identification of the stakeholders, they can be internal such as employees and board members and external stakeholders such as customers and investors. Secondly prioritizing the stakeholders. Then can be the approach used for these stakeholders (Littenberg, 2022).

According to the recent survey conducted by Bank of New York Mellon, investors primarily raised few questions regarding how the company is working to promote diversity and inclusion and specially issues like gender and ethnicity. Secondly, they questioned with regards to environment, on how the company is addressing the climate change specially in terms of carbon emissions. The rise in these questions gives an understanding how investors are focused on company's responsible and sustainable practices (The Harvard Law School Forum on Corporate Governance, 2020).

AI integration in stakeholder feedback can be categorized and organized to current themes. Certain issues in relation to company's carbon footprint, supply chain ethics are problematic. AI helps in aligning organization's strategies with meeting stakeholders' requirements. AI can also determine whether the stakeholder's information received are positive, negative or neutral. With data analytics organizations would be able to analyse whether the stakeholder expectations are aligning with the ESG criteria.

AI enables monitoring stakeholder sentiment which allows the firms to quickly shift their opinions and ideas. This approach offers a better scope of stakeholder's preferences. For long term this approach would be connective and beneficial which will have a positive impact on society as well. A major growth in the field of ESG reporting is the AI integration. It is very important to acknowledge new stakeholders and address the issues associated with the current ESG ratings. AI is transforming the way we view sustainable investing. There are enormous opportunities, and it is the right time to use AI to create a more inclusive and sustainable future (Tiesset, 2023).

Impact Assessment

From the review of literature conducted, we agree to the fact that AI can help the company in understanding the efficiency of their sustainable initiatives. Quantifying the effects of the initiatives on Environment, Social and Governance factors is one of the important aspects in ESG reporting. Companies can easily analyse the impact with the help of algorithms (Dey, 2022).

For example, AI can analyse how much energy was saved with the help of automated LED lighting. It can do this by simplify comparing two months energy consumption data and quantify to what extent they were sustainable. AI models can also combine data from various sources and produce a complete picture of how an organization's initiatives are aligned with its ESG objectives and helps the company in deciding whether it is right to be disclosed on the ESG reports or not. Along with numbers, AI models can also analyse the impact of initiatives on employee happiness and customer satisfaction. It does this by simply scanning the switching behaviour of the customers and retention ratio of employees. Again, this understanding is important to decide whether it is relevant to disclose that particular initiative or not.

The initiatives with greater positive impact will generally give a good ESG rating to the company. If in case, things do not work according to the plan, organization may re-think about their initiatives in the future. This will make sure that their initiatives have a sustainable impact and is in line with the framework criteria.

Risk Management

In the area of sustainability improving organization's foresight by integrating AI into risk management will be helpful in resolving ESG related issues.

The analysis done by AI enables in tracking historical events. For instance, a company faced a major downfall with relation to environmental regulations, in that case AI could assist in anticipating the regulatory challenges that the company may occur in future. This helps in company taking preventive steps to reduce related risks. It not only helps firms to make informed decisions related to risks but also builds a responsible framework to handle complex challenges.

Using AI integrated platform enables in assessing sustainability of investments and empower business by risk management professionals. Which will give a holistic view and data driven approach in terms of examining ESG strategies. Mitigating reputational risk and maintain trust of shareholders is possible through better understanding and determining the societal impact (Bharathi, n.d.). Any organization who ignores ESG related issues will be at higher risk. As it is going to affect the overall growth of the company. ESG risk management should be part if company's practices Gorley (n.d.).

A Need for Unified Framework and Ethical Consideration

Although all the three frameworks discussed in our study is unique and beneficial, we suggest companies to follow a unified framework. This will benefit the stakeholders to compare ESG disclosures between the companies. A unified framework should include all the metrics that is discussed in three frameworks of GRI, SASB and ISSB. The unified framework will reduce the complexity of selecting the best framework amongst all. It also eliminates the efforts of using multiple frameworks to prepare one ESG report. The unified framework, which is also AI integrated must be free from algorithm bias and ensure it is encrypted. Algorithm must be trained and tested to ensure it is in line with the ethical consideration. This will increase the usability of the framework. The unified framework should also disclose the AI model used for data collection, efficiency of algorithm and any assumptions made during analysis. This will give the stakeholders a complete view of the ethical consideration.

IMPLICATIONS

This chapter aims to imply that AI integrated ESG reporting is the future and companies need to take initiative to adopt AI tools in preparation of their ESG reports. The benefits of AI integrated ESG reports discussed in the chapter such as automated data collection, predictive analysis, stakeholder analysis, impact assessment and risk management will be valuable for the companies who are yet to adopt AI tools in their reporting. Although frameworks from GRI, SASB and ISSB helps in disclosure, companies can make use of unified framework which is a combination of all the standards to maximize the benefit. The chapter also suggests socially conscious investors to act mindfully when making investments choices as there might be bias and errors in reporting if companies use traditional methods of reporting. ESG mutual fund managers are also encouraged to make use of AI tools to make predictive analysis of company's ESG initiatives before investing. This will help fund managers analyse how effective and profitable the initiative is before investing

CONCLUSION

The chapter investigates the transformative areas by integrating AI in ESG. This integration focuses on lending solutions to the issues faced in certain areas. It also helps in improving the accuracy and efficiency of sustainability across many industries. AI has the capacity to completely transform data processing and analysis. It not only enables businesses to build strategies but also help in resulting the standards in line with sustainability. Strengthening the stakeholder's relationship can be attained by AI -driven stakeholder analysis which enables informed decision making. Although there arise issues related to algorithmic biases and privacy issues from AI, it is necessary to strike a proper balance between AI potential and ethical issues. The effective integration of AI into ESG will progress towards sustainable future. Finally, we would like to conclude by determining that the combination of AI and ESG influences how firms can manage their environmental, social and governance responsibilities. By effectively using AI it enables businesses to promote sustainable practices and reducing risks. This also acts in favour for investors, customers and society at a larger view, which generates for a responsible future. This altogether will give an overview on technology coexisting with moral business practices.

REFERENCES

Accenture. (2019, July 12). More than Half of Consumers Would Pay More for Sustainable Products Designed to Be Reused or Recycled Accentu. *Accenture*. https://newsroom.accenture.com/news/more-than-half-of-consumers-would-pay-more-for-sustainable-products-designed-to-be-reused-or-recycled-accenture-survey-finds.htm

Accenture. (2022). N/A. www.accenture.com. https://www.accenture.com/ch-en/insights/artificial-intelligence/what-ai-exactly

Ahmad, H., Yaqub, M., & Lee, S. H. (2023). Environmental-, social-, and governance-related factors for business investment and sustainability: A scientometric review of global trends. *Environment, Development and Sustainability*. Advance online publication. doi:10.100710668-023-02921-x

Al-Sartawi, A. M. M., Hussainey, K., & Razzaque, A. (2022). The role of artificial intelligence in sustainable finance. *Journal of Sustainable Finance & Investment*, 1–6. doi:10.1080/20430795.2022.2057405

Alibaba Group Holding Limited. (2022). *Alibaba Environmental, Social, and Governance Report 2022*. https://data.alibabagroup.com/ecms-files/1452422558/5feb0e46-f04b-4d9c-9568-e4a5912db37e.pdf

Aydoğmuş, M., Gülay, G., & Ergun, K. (2022). Impact of ESG performance on firm value and profitability. *Borsa Istanbul Review*, *22*, S119–S127. doi:10.1016/j.bir.2022.11.006

Bharathi, S. (n.d.). *Data and AI driven approach for managing ESG risks*. https://www.linkedin.com/pulse/data-ai-driven-approach-managing-esg-risks-sudharshana-bharathi

Bolton, M., Raven, R., & Mintrom, M. (2021). Can AI transform public decision-making for sustainable development? An exploration of critical earth system governance questions. *Earth System Governance*, *9*, 100116. doi:10.1016/j.esg.2021.100116

BožićV. (2023). AI and Predictive Analytics. *ResearchGate*. https://doi.org/doi:10.13140/RG.2.2.23798.47682

Charl, D. V. (2022). *The Global Reporting Initiative's (GRI) Past, Present and Future: Critical reflections and a research agenda on sustainability reporting (standard-setting)*. https://papers.ssrn.com/sol3/papers.cfm?abstract_id=4099915

Company ESG Risk Rating - Sustainalytics. (n.d.). sustainalytics.com. https://www.sustainalytics.com/esg-rating/infosys-ltd/1008276252

De Villiers, C., Dimes, R., & Molinari, M. (2023). *How will AI text generation and processing impact sustainability reporting? Critical analysis, a conceptual framework and avenues for future research*. Sustainability Accounting, Management and Policy Journal., doi:10.1108ampj-02-2023-0097

Dey, L. (2022). AI-driven Sustainability Assessment - what, why and how. *TechScape: The Science, Technology and Education Journal of IIT Jodhpur, 03*(01). https://iitj.ac.in/techscape/vol03/issue01/infocus/ai_driven_sustainability_assessment_what_why_and_how/

Dressler, C. (n.d.). *Using AI in ESG Reporting: Where to start and why it's important.* https://www.linkedin.com/pulse/using-ai-esg-reporting-where-start-why-its-important-dressler

Enhancing gender diversity on boards and in senior management of listed companies. (n.d.). https://www.oecd.org/publications/enhancing-gender-diversity-on-boards-and-in-senior-management-of-listed-companies-4f7ca695-en.htm

Environmental Responsibility Programs - Patagonia. (n.d.). https://www.patagonia.com/our-responsibility-programs.html

Epic. (2019, March 4). *Case studies on artificial intelligence - DIGITALEUROPE*. DIGITALEUROPE. https://www.digitaleurope.org/news/case-studies-on-artificial-intelligence/

ESG Ratings: do they add value? How to get prepared? (n.d.). Deloitte. https://www2.deloitte.com/ce/en/pages/about-deloitte/articles/esg-ratings-do-they-add-value.html

Five Ways That ESG Creates Value. (n.d.). https://www.mckinsey.com/~/media/McKinsey/Business%20Functions/Strategy%20and%20Corporate%20Finance/Our%20Insights/Five%20ways%20that%20ESG%20creates%20value/Five-ways-that-ESG-creates-value.ashx

Fonseca, A., McAllister, M. L., & Fitzpatrick, P. (2014). Sustainability reporting among mining corporations: A constructive critique of the GRI approach. *Journal of Cleaner Production*, *84*, 70–83. doi:10.1016/j.jclepro.2012.11.050

Gorley, A. (n.d.). *What is ESG and Why It's Important for Risk Management*. sustainalytics.com. https://www.sustainalytics.com/esg-research/resource/corporate-esg-blog/what-is-esg-why-important-risk-management#:~:text=ESG%20Risk%20Management%20is%20Regular%20Risk%20Management&text=Moreover%2C%20any%20company%20that%20neglects,related%20incidentii%20or%20controversy

GRI - Four-in-five largest global companies report with GRI. (n.d.). https://www.globalreporting.org/news/news-center/four-in-five-largest-global-companies-report-with-gri/

GRI - Towards corporate transparency in the Greater China Region. (n.d.). https://www.globalreporting.org/news/news-center/towards-corporate-transparency-in-the-greater-china-region/

IFRS - International Sustainability Standards Board. (n.d.). https://www.ifrs.org/groups/international-sustainability-standards-board/

ISSB Standards What they mean Australian companies? | FTI. (n.d.). https://www.fticonsulting.com/insights/articles/new-issb-standards-what-they-mean-australian-companies

International Sustainability Standards Board (ISSB). (n.d.). https://www.iasplus.com/en/resources/ifrsf/issb

Jarrahi, M. H. (2018). Artificial intelligence and the future of work: Human-AI symbiosis in organizational decision making. *Business Horizons*, *61*(4), 577–586. doi:10.1016/j.bushor.2018.03.007

Javaid, S. (2023, July 10). Data Collection Automation: Pros, Cons, & 3 [AIMultiple. https://research.aimultiple.com/data-collection-automation/]. *Methods (San Diego, Calif.), 2023.*

K, A., & Shanthi, V. (2020). Artificial Intelligence – A Driving way for Sustainable Organizational Growth. *ResearchGate.* https://www.researchgate.net/publication/344522304_Artificial_Intelligence_-_A_Driving_way_for_Sustainable_Organizational_Growth

Lack of standardized ESG data may hide material risks, OECD says. (n.d.). S&P Global Market Intelligence. https://www.spglobal.com/marketintelligence/en/news-insights/latest-news-headlines/lack-of-standardized-esg-data-may-hide-material-risks-oecd-says-60541261

Lee, O., Joo, H., Choi, H., & Cheon, M. (2022). Proposing an integrated approach to analyzing ESG data via machine learning and deep learning algorithms. *Sustainability*, *14*(14), 8745. doi:10.3390u14148745

Limited, I. (n.d.). *Our lights have intelligence.* https://www.infosys.com/about/esg/environmental/energy/intelligence.html

Littenberg, C. M. M. (2022, October 28). *5 steps to a successful ESG stakeholder assessment*. Crowe LLP. https://www.crowe.com/insights/5-steps-to-a-successful-esg-stakeholder-assessment

Marwala, T. (2014). *Causality, correlation and artificial intelligence for rational decision making*. https://doi.org/ doi:10.1142/9356

McCalla-Leacy, J. (2022, September 8). Big shifts, small steps. *KPMG*. https://kpmg.com/xx/en/home/insights/2022/09/survey-of-sustainability-reporting-2022.html

Minkkinen, M., Niukkanen, A., & Mäntymäki, M. (2022). What about investors? ESG analyses as tools for ethics-based AI auditing. *AI & Society*. Advance online publication. doi:10.100700146-022-01415-0

Moodaley, W., & Telukdarie, A. (2023). Greenwashing, Sustainability Reporting, and Artificial Intelligence: A Systematic Literature review. *Sustainability*, *15*(2), 1481. doi:10.3390u15021481

Ng, G., Cheuk, H., Singh, S., & Sharma, B. (2022). AI and data privacy in ConTech: A case study of viAct's responsible scenario based AI. *ResearchGate*. https://www.researchgate.net/publication/360362065_AI_and_data_privacy_in_ConTech_A_case_study_of_viAct's_responsible_scenario_based_AI

Ramanathan, S., & Isaksson, R. (2022). Sustainability reporting as a 21st century problem statement: Using a quality lens to understand and analyse the challenges. *The TQM Journal*, *35*(5), 1310–1328. doi:10.1108/tqm-01-2022-0035

SASB - ESG for Investors. (2023, June 22). SASB. https://sasb.org/investor-use/

SASB: Your pathway to ISSB - SASB. (2023, August 15). SASB. https://sasb.org/sasb-your-pathway-to-issb/

Syed, A. M. (2017). Environment, social, and governance (ESG) criteria and preference of managers. *Cogent Business & Management*, *4*(1), 1340820. doi:10.1080/23311975.2017.1340820

Telang, S. (2015). GRI based sustainability reporting in India. *Green Clean Guide*. https://greencleanguide.com/gri-based-sustainability-reporting-in-india/

The Harvard Law School Forum on Corporate Governance. (2020, September 14). *The stakeholder model and ESG*. https://corpgov.law.harvard.edu/2020/09/14/the-stakeholder-model-and-esg/

The 5 JUST 100 Companies leading on Gender Board Diversity — JUST Capital. (n.d.). JUST Capital. https://justcapital.com/news/top-companies-for-board-gender-diversity-2022/

Tiesset, A. (2023, June 29). Unveiling the New Stakeholders in ESG: A Transformation in Sustainable Investing. *The future of ESG*. https://www.sesamm.com/blog/unveiling-new-stakeholders-in-esg

Wan, G., Dawod, A. Y., Chanaim, S., & Ramasamy, S. S. (2023). Hotspots and trends of environmental, social and governance (ESG) research: A bibliometric analysis. *Data Science and Management*, *6*(2), 65–75. doi:10.1016/j.dsm.2023.03.001

Wilson, K. O. (2023, June 22). *SASB - ESG Reporting - Diversity and Inclusion - SASB Standards*. SASB. https://sasb.org/blog/exploring-diversity-inclusion-in-the-sasb-standards/

Your Guide to Automating ESG Reporting in Hong Kong. (n.d.). https://www.en-trak.com/wp-content/uploads/2020/07/GUIDE-HOW-TO-AUTOMATE-YOUR-ESG-REPORT.pdf

KEY TERMS AND DEFINITIONS

Artificial Intelligence: Computer Systems that would perform tasks which typically require human intelligence.

GRI: A framework for sustainability reporting which focuses on economic, environmental and social impacts which is internationally recognized.

SASB: A non-profit organisation that performs sustainability accounting standards for particular industries to help businesses disclose significant ESG data.

ISSB: A Framework that develops a high quality and a global baseline of sustainability disclosures.

Socially Responsible Investments: Investments that are socially conscious which helps in creating a positive sustainable impact.

Sustainable Finance: Process of making financial decisions in the aim of attaining longer term sustainability.

ESG ratings: Evaluation of a company's performance in the Environmental, Social and Governance sectors through a rating system.

Data privacy: Protection of sensitive or personal data from unauthorised access

Algorithmic bias: Unfair outcomes that determines repeatable errors

Gender diversity Board: A group within the organisation that studies for gender diversity and balance in strategies and decision making.

Chapter 3
Bridging Corporate Social Responsibility and Green Innovation:
A Structural Equation Study of Spain's Wine Industry

Javier Martínez-Falcó
https://orcid.org/0000-0001-9004-5816
University of Alicante, Spain

Luis A. Millán-Tudela
https://orcid.org/0000-0003-3669-9960
University of Alicante, Spain

Bartolomé Marco-Lajara
https://orcid.org/0000-0001-8811-9118
University of Alicante, Spain

Cristina Raluca Gh. Popescu
https://orcid.org/0000-0002-5876-0550
University of Bucharest, Romania & The Bucharest University of Economic Studies, Romania

Eduardo Sánchez-García
https://orcid.org/0000-0002-8524-4906
University of Alicante, Spain

ABSTRACT

This research delves into the nexus between corporate social responsibility (CSR) and green innovation performance (GIP) within Spain's wine sector. A novel conceptual framework is posited and empirically tested using a structural equation modelling technique (PLS-SEM), drawing on data from 202 Spanish wineries collated between September 2021 and January 2022. Findings underscore a robust positive correlation between CSR and GIP, with green intellectual capital (GIC) and knowledge management (KM) serving as pivotal mediators in this dynamic. This study

DOI: 10.4018/979-8-3693-1151-6.ch003

augments the academic discourse in three salient ways: it illuminates the interplay between CSR and GIP in Spain's wine realm; pioneers the exploration of GIC and KM as mediatory factors in this relationship, a hitherto uncharted territory; and introduces a theoretical model, marking a significant stride in academic enrichment.

INTRODUCTION

Environmental experts, corporate heads, and scholars concur about the influence of corporate actions on our planet. Such activities can exacerbate global warming, elevate air pollutants, drain natural assets, and involve dangerous substances (Soceanu et al., 2021). Given this scenario, businesses ought to prioritize preserving the environment they function within.

The increasing demand for businesses to adopt ecological and societal policies has piqued the curiosity of various scholars, leading them to explore "eco-centric" topics like sustainable HR practices, environmentally-friendly supply chains, reverse logistics, and green innovations (Seman et al., 2019). This research direction recognizes that merely focusing on economic factors isn't sufficient for a competitive edge; addressing the environmental and societal repercussions of business operations is equally crucial. In this study, the emphasis is on Green Innovation Performance (GIP) as the outcome variable, aiming to assess organizational environmental outcomes based on the Green Innovations they introduce, with Corporate Social Responsibility (CSR) as the primary influencing factor. Notably, Green Innovation is seen as a significant determinant of organizational success (Qiu et al., 2020), holding a central position in ensuring sustainable outcomes (Yusliza et al., 2020).

In the contemporary business model, CSR is viewed as a pivotal strategy that seamlessly blends economic, societal, and environmental aspects into strategic planning (Hernández et al., 2020). While past studies on CSR predominantly centered on its connection to economic outcomes (Javed et al., 2020), the rising significance of environmental factors has overshadowed the exploration of the CSR-GIP connection. This study endeavors to bridge this scholarly void by probing into the influence of CSR on GIP, positioning CSR as a driving force for GIP. Moreover, the academic realm has yet to delve into intermediary factors that might elucidate this relationship. In light of this, the current research evaluates Green Intellectual Capital (GIC) and Knowledge Management (KM) as potential intermediaries in the CSR-GIP dynamic, drawing insights from the Intellectual Capital Perspective (ICV) and the Knowledge-Centric Perspective (KBV).

This study is set within the backdrop of Spain's wine sector, recognizing its economic, societal, and ecological significance in the nation (Marco-Lajara et al., 2022a). The wine sector is grappling with escalating demands for heightened sustainability (Gilinsky et al., 2016), given the potential adverse impacts its operations can have on the environment, local communities, and the economy. Such concerns arise from the winemaking procedure, which involves various equipment, leading to emissions that contribute to fossil fuel exhaustion (Goncharuk, 2017). The industry's reliance on cleaning agents, which often contain environmentally detrimental and potentially dangerous chemicals, poses another challenge. When these substances are discarded or drained, they can exacerbate environmental harm (Benedetto, 2013). Additionally, the packaging and distribution stages, involving materials like corks, glass containers, cardboard, and paper, coupled with the resultant rise in CO_2 emissions, further accentuate the environmental concerns (Bonn et al., 2020).

Wineries are confronted with external challenges that jeopardize their continuity, including escalating energy costs, dwindling water resources, heightened environmental consciousness among stakeholders, and the rapid pace of climate change (Annunziata et al., 2018). Given this backdrop, this investigation becomes crucial as it delves into how wineries' CSR initiatives influence their GIP, ensuring the industry's economic viability and its standing within Spanish society. The research seeks to address four central Research Questions (RQs): (RQ1) How does CSR impact GIP? (RQ2) How does GIC act as an intermediary in the CSR-GIP nexus? (RQ3) How does KM influence the CSR-GIP relationship as a mediating factor? and (RQ4) Which CSR strategies can wine businesses employ to enhance their GIP? To address these queries, a theoretical framework is crafted, drawing from existing literature, and is then tested using the structural equation modeling approach. Primary data for this study is gathered through a survey conducted between September 2021 and January 2022.

This investigation offers four significant contributions to scholarly literature. Firstly, it deepens the comprehension of CSR and its association with GIP. Secondly, to our awareness, no prior studies have explored intermediary variables within this relationship. Hence, this study delves into GIC and KM as intermediaries in the CSR-GIP connection. Thirdly, the proposed theoretical framework is novel, marking a noteworthy progression in academic insights. Lastly, there hasn't been any academic work that zeroes in on knowledge management and environmental intangible assets specific to the wine sector. As such, this research stands out by introducing the GIC and KM concepts within the context of the wine industry.

The structure of this paper, aimed at addressing the RQs, is outlined as follows. Following this introductory segment, section 2 delves into existing literature concerning the influence of CSR on GIP, GIC, and KM, subsequently laying out the hypotheses for the proposed framework. Section 3 elucidates the research methodology, detailing the chosen industry for the study, data gathering methods, variable measurements, and the employed statistical approach. Section 4 unveils the primary findings of the investigation. Concluding the article, section 5 offers both theoretical and practical insights derived from the study, while also highlighting its constraints and suggesting avenues for future research.

LITERATURE REVIEW AND HYPOTHESIS DEVELOPMENT

The surge in business strategies prioritizing societal and environmental protection, encapsulated in sustainable competencies like CSR, GIP, KM, and GIC, can be contextualized within the frameworks of the Natural Resource-Based View (NRBV), the ICV, and the KBV. These paradigms are derivatives of the RBV, which posits that a firm's competitive edge is derived from its intrinsic resources and capabilities, emphasizing the internal dynamics of an organization over industry influences (Barney, 1991).

The NRBV contends that organizations can achieve enduring competitive superiority by addressing the environmental expectations of their stakeholders, especially given the potential adverse impacts of their operations (Hart, 1995). This perspective emerged to address the RBV's shortcomings, notably its neglect of the strategic interplay between environmental stewardship and competitive advantage, and its oversight of the dual benefits of environmental capabilities in enhancing performance and reducing costs (Hart and Dowell, 2011).

Under the NRBV lens, CSR-centric research suggests that investments in CSR-related capabilities can bolster organizational outcomes (Singh and Misra, 2021). Such commitments can distinguish a firm from its rivals, elevate its performance, and foster novel organizational proficiencies (Taylor et al., 2018). Consequently, the NRBV offers insights into firms' proactive strategies in harnessing internal competencies related to socio-environmental concerns to reap economic dividends (Oware and Mallikarjunappa, 2019), amplify GIP (Andersén, 2021), refine stakeholder engagement and strategic foresight (Mishra and Yadav, 2021), elevate sustainability leadership (Alnuaimi et al., 2021), and cultivate effective KM practices (Shahzad et al., 2021). In this study, the NRBV elucidates the connections between CSR, GIP, GIC, and KM.

Conversely, the ICV posits that an organization's competitive edge is anchored in its intangible assets, encompassing human, structural, and relational dimensions. This perspective can be perceived as a complement to the KBV, which identifies knowledge as the pivotal intangible asset driving competitive advantage. While both the ICV and KBV underscore the strategic significance of intangible assets, their focal points diverge. The ICV zeroes in on categorizing intangibles and assessing their impact on organizational profitability (Youndt and Snell, 2004), whereas the KBV delves into the determinants that either foster or impede KM, and its ramifications on capability development and performance enhancement (Nonaka and Takeuchi,

1995). Thus, while the KBV elucidates the KM-GIP nexus, the ICV sheds light on the GIC-GIP relationship.

Corporate Social Responsibility and Green Innovation Performance

CSR initiatives enhance the cultivation of a firm's intangible assets, fostering organizational proficiencies that lead to enduring competitive benefits (Bacinello et al., 2021). As highlighted by Mbanyele and colleagues (2022), the inception and propagation of CSR initiatives can catalyze the creation of organizational proficiencies tailored towards environmental conservation and societal betterment. Additionally, CSR facilitates the assimilation of external insights into corporations, broadening their knowledge spectrum (Luo and Du, 2015), sparking innovative thinking (Chopra et al., 2021), and fortifying affiliations with stakeholders (Troise and Camilleri, 2021).

CSR emerges as a pivotal catalyst for organizations in their pursuit of Green Innovations (GIs) (Kraus et al., 2020). Corporate dedication to ecological concerns aligns their operations with societal anticipations, fortifying their business legitimacy (Zhou et al., 2021). Consequently, the embrace of CSR strategies, culminating in enhancements in green methodologies and products, signifies a strategic pivot, underscoring their allegiance to ecological concerns and amplifying their green reputation (Seman et al., 2019). In this vein, Yuan and Cao (2022) emphasize that catering to stakeholders' ecological expectations can steer organizations towards CSR initiatives that champion environmentally-conscious product development.

In contemporary times, the intricacies of CSR initiatives have amplified, given the evolving tools, methodologies, and frameworks that enterprises devise or access in a rapidly changing landscape (Popescu, 2021). Moreover, it's imperative for organizations to recognize the profound influence of their endeavors on individual lives, community welfare, and environmental health (European Commission, 2023). Globally, entities require consistent and clear guidance to evolve into more inclusive, accountable, and sustainable entities (Popescu, 2022; International Labour Organization (ILO), 2023). Additionally, CSR endeavors aim to champion responsible corporate behavior, recognizing that sustainable growth necessitates a harmonious blend of voluntary and obligatory actions, and that corporate strategies and operations should holistically incorporate ethical, societal, economic, and environmental considerations (Popescu, 2023).

Presently, CSR has garnered significant attention across academic circles due to its multifaceted implications, especially as an increasing consumer base seeks eco-friendly products and services. CSR strategies serve as foundational elements to bolster GIs within organizations, addressing evolving consumer preferences

(Kraus et al., 2020). In this milieu, eco-conscious corporations must champion both product and process innovations to elevate energy efficiency, curtail material usage, and minimize CO2 emissions (Bansal and Roth, 2000), thereby enhancing their Green Innovation Performance (GIP) to sustain and elevate their competitive stance. Recent studies by Hong et al. (2020) and Ren et al. (2022) have illuminated the influence of CSR disclosures on the evolution of environmental innovations within Chinese corporate sectors. Similarly, Padilla-Lozano and Collazzo (2021) provided empirical evidence of the positive correlation between CSR initiatives and the evolution of GIs in Ecuadorian manufacturing sectors. Yet, limited scholarly work has delved into CSR as a precursor to GIP (Kraus et al., 2020; Shahzad et al., 2021). This research endeavors to bridge this knowledge chasm by proposing the subsequent hypothesis:

H1. CSR has a positive effect on GIP.

Corporate Social Responsibility, Green Intellectual Capital, and Green Innovation Performance

A plethora of scholarly works substantiates the notion that the advancement of CSR positively impacts a firm's Intellectual Capital (IC), encompassing its human, structural, and relational facets (Wood, 1991; Borger and Kruglianskas, 2006; Jain et al., 2017; Gallardo-Vázquez et al., 2019; Rossi et al., 2021). Contemporary studies further suggest that CSR exerts a positive influence on the triad of Green Intellectual Capital (GIC) dimensions, namely Green Human Capital (GHC), Green Structural Capital (GSC), and Green Relational Capital (GRC) (Yong et al., 2019; Yusliza et al., 2020).

Initially, enterprises emphasizing CSR initiatives can bolster their eco-friendly reputation, thereby enhancing their allure for potential talent (Yong et al., 2019). Such firms, by championing CSR initiatives, can magnetize top-tier professionals, stimulate the assimilation of eco-conscious knowledge among staff, and align with the environmental and social aspirations of their workforce (Cheema and Javed, 2017). Consequently, CSR emerges as a pivotal tool in augmenting GHC metrics. Secondly, Wood (1991) posited that CSR's role in corporations extends beyond strategy formulation to encompass technological innovation enhancement. In a similar vein, Borger and Kruglianskas (2006) contended that a positive correlation exists between CSR and a firm's technological ingenuity and ecological outcomes. Hence, corporations embracing CSR initiatives can effectively cultivate organizational proficiencies, such as eco-centric management and green innovation, thereby amplifying their GSC (Shahzad et al., 2021). Lastly, the ambit of CSR extends beyond appeasing shareholders to encompass a broader stakeholder spectrum, including society, clientele, workforce, vendors, and community entities (Khojastehpour and

Shams, 2020). Firms with pronounced CSR commitments can tailor their offerings to resonate with the eco-centric preferences of their clientele and foster enduring, collaborative ties with their associates and suppliers (Gallardo-Vázquez et al., 2019). Consequently, CSR's role is intrinsically tied to addressing the ecological requisites of a firm's diverse stakeholder base, thereby enhancing its GRC (Kamal, 2021). Drawing from these insights, we postulate the ensuing hypothesis:

H2. CSR has a positive effect on GIC.

Human Capital (HC) stands as a pivotal asset in fostering organizational innovations. The reservoir of knowledge possessed by the workforce is a paramount intangible asset, instrumental in crafting innovations tailored for the contemporary volatile landscape (Fonseca et al., 2019). Consequently, a richer repository of eco-centric knowledge among employees directly correlates with enhanced GIP (Yusoff et al., 2019a). In this paradigm, GHC serves as an accelerator for GIP, equipping entities to invigorate their eco-friendly product and process innovations (Yusoff et al., 2019b). Such eco-conscious intangibles have transitioned into indispensable assets for corporate ecological accomplishments (Ullah et al., 2022). Firms with aspirations of pioneering GIs necessitate a workforce steeped in environmental acumen. Furthermore, GHC can cultivate an organizational milieu that embraces risk, potential setbacks, and ambiguity, thereby nurturing the genesis of inventive solutions geared towards GIs (Singh et al., 2020).

Symbiotic affiliations between personnel and institutional entities expedite innovation trajectories, attributed to the accelerated knowledge dissemination and its optimized application (Onofrei et al., 2020). A growing body of literature underscores the positive ramifications of organizational Relational Capital (RC) on innovation, realized through the dynamic interplay of ideas and knowledge across organizations (Ryu et al., 2021). In an ecological context, the implicit expertise of staff (Mardani et al., 2018), their interpersonal dynamics (Ganguly et al., 2019), coupled with cross-organizational synergies (Singh et al., 2020), converge to pioneer novel technologies, concepts, products, and methodologies. These innovations are geared towards mitigating the environmental footprint of entities, culminating in eco-centric product and process innovations. Consequently, the orchestration of collaborative alliances among enterprises, anchored in Green Relational Capital (GRC), can be a catalyst for GIP enhancement (Dickel et al., 2018).

However, the mere cultivation of GHC and GRC is insufficient if an entity lacks robust environmental governance frameworks and ethos. The bedrock of innovation is often the organizational structure and cultural ethos (Waruwu et al., 2020). Integrating environmental insights within an organization can pave the way for GIs. An entity imbued with a robust environmental ethos stimulates the assimilation of novel green insights by its workforce, culminating in an augmented GIP (Chen et al., 2018). In a similar vein, when such insights are systematized with an environmental stewardship lens, they can be disseminated organization-wide, with the overarching objective of harnessing them for GIs (García-Machado and Martínez-Ávila, 2019). Drawing from these insights, we articulate the ensuing hypothesis:

H3. GIC has a positive effect on GIP.

Considering both previous hypotheses (H2 and H3), the following hypothesis (H4) is proposed, which predicts a mediating effect of the GIC variable as a driver of the effect of CSR on GIP:

H4. GIC mediates the relationship CSR-GIP

Corporate Social Responsibility, Knowledge Management, and Green Innovation Performance

Within scholarly discourse, there exists a discernible nexus between CSR and KM (Ling, 2019). Consequently, when enterprises channel investments into CSR initiatives, the strategic deployment of KM can further optimize resource conservation, enhance resource deployment, and refine operational methodologies (Xu et al., 2019). Concurrently, by championing CSR endeavors, businesses not only cultivate positive perceptions and actions among stakeholders but also fortify the symbiotic relationships binding stakeholders to the institution (Atif, 2019). Moreover, CSR initiatives amplify organizational allegiance (Nguyen et al., 2020), which, in turn, augments the propensity of the workforce to assimilate and disseminate knowledge (Tuan, 2016).

The advent of CSR has catalyzed the systematization of organizational wisdom, thereby bolstering KM proficiency. Pertinently, CSR initiatives facilitate the establishment of a unified set of organizational norms, empowering its constituents to assimilate and propagate them. Indeed, an organization's commitment to securing environmental quality accreditations, aligned with its CSR aspirations, renders knowledge more explicit and thereby more accessible, culminating in enhanced KM efficacy. While empirical studies in this domain remain sparse, there are indications underscoring the positive ramifications of CSR on KM. For instance, research by Guadamillas-Gómez and Donate-Manzanares (2011) unveiled that corporate entities could elevate their KM prowess by championing CSR paradigms. Drawing from these insights, we articulate the subsequent hypothesis:

H5. CSR has a positive effect on KM.

KM encompasses the systematic processes of assimilating, distributing, and adeptly leveraging an organization's knowledge assets (Abbas and Sağsan, 2019). It stands as a pivotal strategy for entities aiming to amplify their GIP and adeptly navigate pathways to sustainable growth (Shahzad et al., 2021). The nexus between KM and GIP crystallizes when leadership channels investments into green-centric resources, thereby harnessing the expertise and skills of their workforce (Pérez-Luño et al., 2019). Consequently, for organizations to realize their GIP aspirations, there must be a harmonious alignment between their overarching corporate strategies and their KM initiatives (Buenechea-Elberdin, 2017; Davenport et al., 2019).

Numerous scholars underscore the significance of knowledge assimilation and dissemination in the genesis of GIs (Shahzad et al., 2020). For instance, Donate and Guadamillas (2010) posit that the act of knowledge dissemination augments an organization's knowledge reservoir, subsequently catalyzing innovative pursuits. Echoing this sentiment, Wong (2013) advocates that knowledge dissemination exerts a profound influence on GIP. Conversely, Madhoushi et al. (2011) contend that harnessing organizational knowledge capacitates entities to manifest their expertise in crafting eco-conscious products and methodologies. Thus, adept utilization of organizational knowledge paves the way for the creation of eco-friendly products and processes (Shahzad et al., 2020). Recent scholarly endeavors have spotlighted the positive reverberations of KM facets on GIP (Mothe et al., 2018; Abbas and Sagsan, 2019; Shahzad et al., 2020; Shahzad et al., 2021), underscoring the burgeoning academic intrigue surrounding the interplay between KM and GIP. Drawing from these insights, we articulate the ensuing hypotheses:

H6. KM has a positive effect on GIP.

Considering both previous hypotheses (H5 and H6), the following one (H7) is proposed, which predicts a mediating effect of the KM variable as a driver of the effect of CSR on GIP:

H7. KM mediates the relationship CSR-GIP

Figure 1 shows graphically the theoretical model proposed with the hypotheses put forward.

Figure 1. Theoretical model

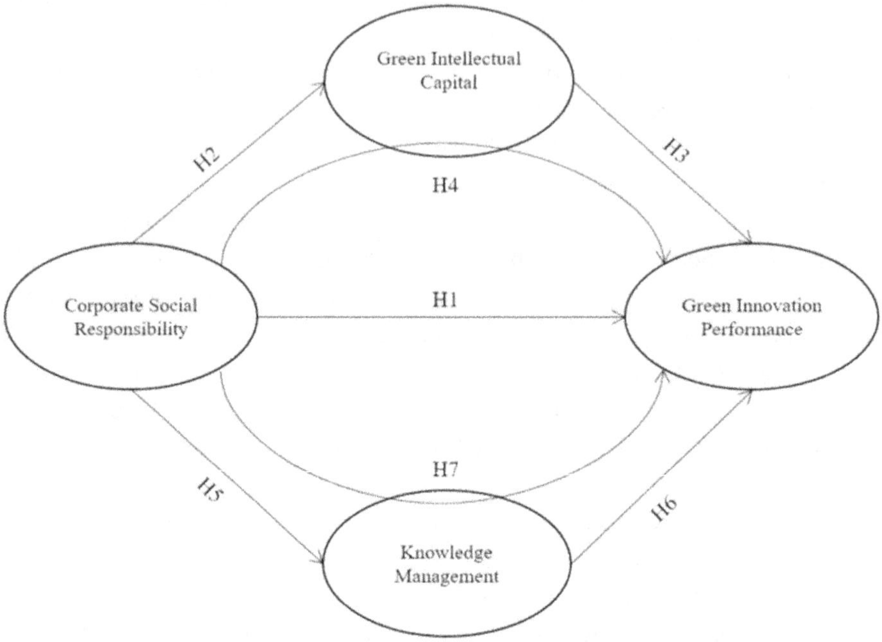

METHODOLOGY

The research methodology for this study is structured into four distinct sections to facilitate comprehension: (1) study backdrop, (2) demographic and sample details, (3) variable definitions, and (4) method of analysis. Each segment is elaborated upon in the subsequent sections.

Study Backdrop

The Spanish wine sector was chosen as the focal point of this research for four primary reasons. Firstly, the wine sector holds significant strategic importance for Spain's economy, contributing over 23.7 billion euros in 2020, accounting for 2.2% of Spain's GVA (AFI, 2020). Beyond its economic significance, the industry also holds cultural, environmental, and societal value. Secondly, the CSR initiatives undertaken by wineries address contemporary environmental and societal demands, as well as stringent environmental regulations, making it a pertinent area of study. Thirdly, in the global wine arena, knowledge has surfaced as a crucial element for sustaining a competitive edge (Agostino and Trivieri, 2014; Muller et al., 2022). Lastly, the proposed theoretical model's relationships have not been previously explored in the context of the wine industry, presenting an avenue for academic advancement.

Demographic and Sample Details

The target demographic for this study encompasses companies classified under the National Code of Economic Activities (CNAE) 1102, which pertains to wine production. As per the Iberian Balance Sheet Analysis System (SABI) database, this code encompasses 4,373 companies. Data was gathered through a literature-based questionnaire, which underwent a pre-test involving environmental and quality managers from wineries to ensure clarity and validity. The online survey, conducted between September 2021 and January 2022, yielded 214 responses. After meticulous scrutiny, 202 responses were deemed suitable for analysis. It's noteworthy that the survey was tailored for top-tier management, specifically winery CEOs.

Variable Definitions

This study employed previously established scales to ensure the variables' reliability, consistency, and validity. CSR was gauged using Salmones et al.'s (2005) scale, viewing CSR as a multi-dimensional construct. GIP was measured using Chen's (2008) scale, which views it as a second-order construct. GIC was assessed using the scale from Zaragoza-Sáez et al. (2020), while KM was gauged using the scale proposed by Pérez-López and Alegre (2012). Additionally, considering the potential influence of individual organizational characteristics on GIP, the age and size of wineries were introduced as control variables. The size was determined based on the OECD's (2005) criteria, while the age was calculated from the company's inception to the study year (2022). All variables were assessed using 7-point Likert scales, with the four primary variables being reflective constructs.

Method of Analysis

Partial least squares structural equation modelling (PLS-SEM) was the chosen analytical technique, executed using the SmartPLS v. 3.3.9 software. This method is adept at examining numerous theoretical relationships between latent or unobservable variables, making it particularly apt for management studies. The decision to employ PLS-SEM was influenced by three primary reasons: its efficacy in analyzing multi-dimensional variables, its ability to handle direct and indirect relationships concurrently, and the suitability of our sample size for this technique (n=202).

RESULTS AND DISCUSSION

In this study, we employed a two-tiered approach grounded in "latent variable scores" due to the multi-faceted nature of most constructs under consideration (Hu and Bentler, 1998). Initially, composite scores were derived, which subsequently served as markers for the second-order constructs. Following Hair et al.'s (2019) guidelines, our model results are bifurcated into: (1) assessment of the measurement model and (2) scrutiny of the structural model.

Prior to delving into the measurement and structural model evaluations, the model's overall fit was ascertained. The model showcases a satisfactory global fit, evidenced by the Standardized Root Mean Squared Residual (SRMSR) being below 0.08 (0.076 < 0.08), suggesting the model's acceptance (Hu and Bentler, 1998). Post the SRMR assessment, both the unweighted least squares discrepancy (d_ULS) and geodesic discrepancy (d_G) metrics were confirmed to lie within the bootstrapped confidence range, specifically beneath HI95 and HI99.

For the measurement model's analysis, we adhered to Hair et al.'s (2019) criteria, encompassing: reliability evaluation of individual indicators, internal consistency reliability assessment, convergent validity verification, and discriminant validity examination.

Firstly, as depicted in Table 1, all variable indicators satisfy the individual item reliability criterion, with their loadings surpassing the 0.707 benchmark set in scholarly literature (Carmines and Zeller, 1979). Post bootstrapping, all loadings were deemed statistically significant, affirming the indicators' robust individual reliability.

Secondly, in terms of internal consistency, all constructs fulfill the criterion, with metrics like Cronbach's alpha, composite reliability (Pc), and the Dijkstra-Henseler (Pa) criterion exceeding 0.8. It's pivotal to recognize that while Cronbach's alpha tends to be conservative, composite reliability might lean towards liberality. The Dijkstra-Henseler criterion is proposed as a middle ground between these extremes in structural equation modeling literature (Dijkstra and Henseler, 2015).

Thirdly, constructs satisfy the convergent validity criterion, with their Average Variance Extracted (AVE) values surpassing 0.5 (Fornell and Larcker, 1981). This implies that each construct elucidates over half of its indicators' variance.

Lastly, Tables 2 and 3 display the discriminant validity assessment based on Fornell and Larcker and Heterotrait-Monotrait (HTMT) criteria. Discriminant validity gauges the distinctiveness of a construct from others (Henseler et al., 2015). For the Fornell and Larcker criterion, the AVE's square root for each construct should surpass its correlations with other constructs. However, the Fornell and Larcker criterion's efficacy has been debated, especially when construct indicators' loadings exhibit minimal variance (Hair et al., 2021). To address this, Henseler et al. (2015)

introduced the HTMT ratio, a measure of inter-construct correlation. As seen in Table 5, the analyzed variables' values are well below 0.85 (Kline, 2011), confirming the uniqueness of each construct. Additionally, 95% confidence intervals for correlations were bootstrapped, ensuring no violation of the discriminant validity criterion.

Table 1. Measurement model analysis: External loadings, construct reliability, and convergent validity

Construct/Items	Outer Loadings	Rho_c (Pc)	Rho_a (Pa)	Cronbach's Alpha	AVE
Corporate Social Responsibility (CSR)		0.882	0.846	0.821	0.691
CSR 1	0.780				
CSR 2	0.848				
CSR 3	0.864				
Green Intellectual Capital (GIC)		0.885	0.884	0.883	0.590
GIC 1	0.778				
GIC 2	0.797				
GIC 3	0.716				
GIC 4	0.833				
GIC 5	0.863				
GIC 6	0.791				
GIC 7	0.797				
Knowledge Management (KM)		0.926	0.917	0.904	0.837
KM 1	0.902				
KM 2	0.928				
KM 3	0.915				
Green Innovation Performance (GIP)		0.924	0.924	0.924	0.929
GIP 1	0.963				
GIP 2	0.965				

Note: The indicators for the second-order variables are: CSR 1= Economic Responsibility; CSR 2= Ethical-legal Responsibility; CSR 3= Philanthropic Responsibility; KM 1= Knowledge Acquisition; KM 2= Knowledge Transfer; KM 3= Knowledge Utilisation; GIP 1= Green Product Innovation Performance; GIP 2= Green Process Innovation Performance.

Source: compiled by authors

Table 2. Discriminant validity analysis based on Fornell-Larcker criterion

	GIC	KM	Age	GIP	CSR	Size
GIC	0.768					
KM	0.477	0.915				
AGE	0.092	0.225	1			
GIP	0.665	0.540	0.104	0.964		
CSR	0.468	0.485	0.211	0.558	0.831	
SIZE	0.006	0.114	-0.135	0.071	0.032	1

Source: compiled by authors

Table 3. Discriminant validity analysis based on the Heterotrait-Monotrait criterion

	AGE	CSR	GIP	KM	SIZE	GIC
AGE						
CSR	0.039					
GIP	0.057	0.264				
KM	0.034	0.021	0.118			
SIZE	0.014	0.039	0.056	0.072		
GIC	0.023	0.298	0.522	0.248	0.112	

Source: compiled by authors

On the other hand, once it was confirmed that the measures of the constructs were reliable and valid, the structural model was evaluated. Based on the indications of Hair et al. (2019), the analysis of the structural model considered: the path coefficients, the R-squared level and the predictive relevance of Q2. The Figure 2 shows the data for the first two indicators (the path coefficients and the R-squared level) based on a bootstrap test with 5,000 subsamples. We tested the direct and indirect effects of CSR on the GIP of the wineries, finding positive and statistically significant effects in all cases. This implies that KM and GIC partially mediate the relationship between CSR and GIP, since both the direct effect (0.253) and the indirect effects (0.211 and 0.100) are positive and significant, with a strong total effect of CSR on GIP of 0.564 ($p<0.000$).

The results of the model, therefore, allow us to verify the seven hypotheses put forward, given that there is a positive and significant effect of CSR on GIP (H1. $\beta=0.253$; $p<0.000$), of CSR on GIC (H2. $\beta=0.468$; $p<0.000$), of GIC on GIP (H3. $\beta=0.452$; $p<0.000$), of CSR on KM (H5. $\beta=0.485$; $p<0.000$), of KM on GIP

(H6. β=0.205; $p<0.000$), GIC mediates the CSR-GIP relationship (H4. β=0.211; $p<0.000$) and KM mediates CSR-GIP relationship (H7. β=0.100; $p<0.002$). The results show that the CSR practices developed by wineries are the strongest predictor of their ability to acquire, transfer and apply knowledge (KM). This may be due to the processes of knowledge creation, transfer and application that occur to ensure the success of the CSR practices developed by the organizations. The strongest predictor of the GIP variable is, on the other hand, the GIC. This may be explained by the importance of firms' stock of green knowledge in developing environmentally friendly product and process innovations. Furthermore, the findings show that the two mediations are partial, since the relationship between CSR and GIP is positive and significant. Therefore, the improvement of GIC can occur not only through the CSR practices developed by the wineries, but also through the improvement of KM and GIC caused by these practices.

Finally, to analyse the quality of the model, the Geisser test (Q2) was performed, which must present estimated values greater than 0 (Q2 > 0). This measure is an indicator of out-of-sample predictive power, such that when a model shows predictive relevance, it accurately predicts data not used in model estimation (Roldán and Cepeda, 2017). Recently, Hair et al. (2019) have proposed as a new rule of thumb that Q2 values greater than 0, 0.25 and 0.50 show respectively situations of small, medium and large predictive relevance. As for the control variables, the results show that winery size has a negative and non-significant impact on GIP (β= -0.033; $p<0.528$) and age presents a positive but non-significant relationship (β=0.034; $p<0.583$). Based on the behaviour of the control variables, it could be interesting to analyse the differences in environmental management between groups of large and small wineries, as well as new and established wineries.

The results of this research suggest that the development of CSR practices in wineries can lead to greater GIP, as these practices favour the development of green product and process innovations. In addition, such organizational capacity can foster the generation of green intangibles (GIC) and new capabilities (KM), which can strengthen the CSR-GIP relationship in the wine industry.

The positive and significant relationship of CSR on GIP is in line with the results obtained by Kraus et al. (2020) and Shahzad et al. (2020), which demonstrate such a relationship for Malaysian and Pakistani manufacturing industry respectively. In addition, CSR acts as a catalyst variable for GIC and KM. On the one hand, through the research of authors Yong et al. (2019) and Yusliza et al. (2020) also point to the existence of a positive relationship between the development of socially responsible practices and the generation of sustainable intangible assets in the organization. On the other hand, the results of Guadamillas-Gómez and Donate-Manzanares (2011) and Shahzad et al. (2021) are in line with the results obtained in the present research, since both studies demonstrate the positive relationship of CSR on KM. Likewise, both GIC and KM positively affect GIP. These relationships are also confirmed by Ullah et al. (2022) and Abbas and Sagsan (2019), given that while the first study demonstrates the capacity of green intangibles on the generation of GIs, the second research addresses the positive relationship between KM and GIP.

The mediating effect of GIC and KM on the CSR-GIP relationship has been unexplored in the academic literature to the best of our knowledge. However, through the NRBV, ICV and KBV approaches, the mediating role that both variables can play has been justified. The results demonstrate that CSR actions not only enhance the development of GIs in the wine industry, but also allow to favour GIC and KM, which in turn support GIP.

Figure 2. Theoretical model with R-squared, path coefficients (β), and significance

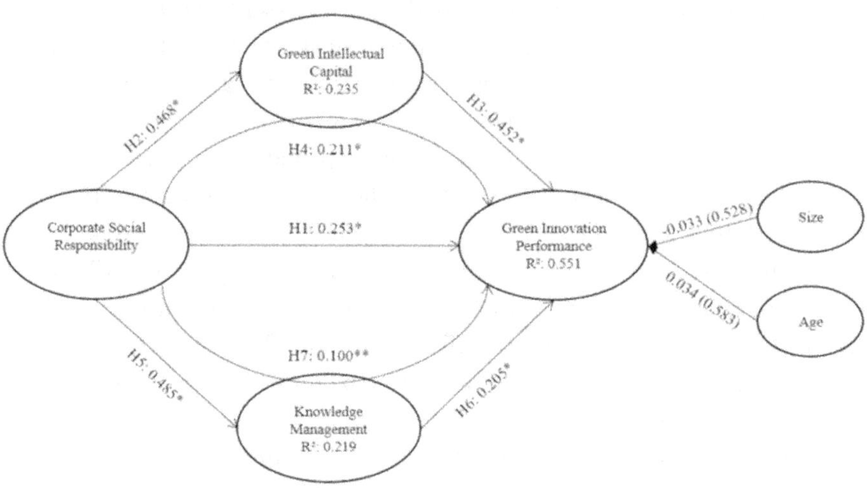

CONCLUSIONS AND IMPLICATIONS

Wineries face mounting challenges to enhance societal and environmental contributions in the coming years. Several imminent challenges, such as escalating global warming, dwindling energy resources, and water shortages, jeopardize the sector's longevity. In this backdrop, the sustainable initiatives undertaken by wineries become paramount. These initiatives not only counteract the detrimental environmental impacts but also pave the way for green product and process innovations, leading to cost savings and distinctiveness for proactive wineries. Thus, this investigation holds significant relevance, shedding light on the influence of sustainable endeavors on wineries, especially given the empirically proven positive correlation between CSR practices and GIP in Spain's wine industry.

Wineries ought to champion sustainability across its three facets (economic, social, and environmental), facilitate knowledge dissemination, invest in training, prioritize human capital, and drive organizational innovation to safeguard the wine industry's future and credibility. Evidently, CSR initiatives by wineries bolster sustainability, foster knowledge exchange among staff, motivate them, and catalyze green innovations. In Spain's wine landscape, numerous CSR endeavors involve forging R&D&I collaborations via the Wine Technology Platform, a pivotal instrument aiding the industry in navigating future challenges and spurring innovation across the wine value chain.

This study offers both theoretical and pragmatic insights. Theoretically, this investigation enriches the scholarly discourse by offering empirical evidence from Spain's wine sector. Specifically, the study empirically validates the positive influence of CSR practices on GIP and the intermediary roles of GIC and KM. While the primary relationship (CSR-GIP) aligns with recent studies like Shahzad et al. (2020) set in the Pakistani manufacturing context, the mediating effects of GIC and KM remain relatively uncharted in literature. Thus, this study serves as a foundational exploration into how organizational capabilities, such as CSR, can cultivate intangible assets and novel competencies, like GIC and KM, to enhance wineries' GIP.

Practically, the study's findings can significantly influence managerial decisions concerning wineries' environmental stewardship. Wineries, from an economic CSR perspective, should bolster regional prosperity, both through direct employment and the ripple effect on ancillary sectors. Ethically and legally, wineries must remain abreast of prevailing regulations, adhere to them, and cultivate an organizational ethos through codes of conduct, environmental best practices, circular economy initiatives, and alignment with prominent wine industry quality standards. Philanthropically, wineries can contribute to societal causes, enhance stakeholder well-being, support local initiatives, and foster community engagement. Such endeavors can amplify GIP, fostering a deeper organizational commitment to societal and environmental betterment.

However, the study isn't without limitations. A broader analysis encompassing other wine-producing nations could offer richer insights. Future research could delve deeper into the CSR-GIP relationship across global wine regions, comparing Old World and New World wine nations. Additionally, the influence of winery size and age warrants deeper exploration. Future studies could also introduce more mediating variables in the CSR-GIP relationship and consider other business attributes beyond age and size, such as export orientation and R&D allocation.

ACKNOWLEDGMENT

Portions of this work have been previously reported in this research: Marco-Lajara, B., Zaragoza-Sáez, P., Falcó, J. M., & Millan-Tudela, L. A. (2022). Corporate Social Responsibility: A Narrative Literature Review. *Frameworks for Sustainable Development Goals to Manage Economic, Social, and Environmental Shocks and Disasters*, 16-34.

REFERENCES

Abbas, J., & Sağsan, M. (2019). Impact of knowledge management practices on green innovation and corporate sustainable development: A structural analysis. *Journal of Cleaner Production*, *229*, 611–620. doi:10.1016/j.jclepro.2019.05.024

AFI. (2020). *Importancia económica y social del sector vitivinícola en España*. Available at: https://www.interprofesionaldelvino.es/publicaciones/informes-importancia-sector/nacional/

Agostino, M., & Trivieri, F. (2014). Geographical indication and wine exports. An empirical investigation considering the major European producers. *Food Policy*, *46*, 22–36. doi:10.1016/j.foodpol.2014.02.002

Alnuaimi, B., Singh, S., & Harney, B. (2021). Unpacking the role of innovation capability: Exploring the impact of leadership style on green procurement via a natural resource-based perspective. *Journal of Business Research*, *134*, 78–88. doi:10.1016/j.jbusres.2021.05.026

Andersén, J. (2021). A relational natural-resource-based view on product innovation: The influence of green product innovation and green suppliers on differentiation advantage in small manufacturing firms. *Technovation*, *104*, 102254. doi:10.1016/j.technovation.2021.102254

Annunziata, E., Pucci, T., Frey, M., & Zanni, L. (2018). The role of organizational capabilities in attaining corporate sustainability practices and economic performance: Evidence from Italian wine industry. *Journal of Cleaner Production*, *171*, 1300–1311. doi:10.1016/j.jclepro.2017.10.035

Atif, M. (2019). (Re)discovering the business purpose: A discursive approach to CSR and stakeholder management. *Society and Business Review*, *14*(4), 401–414. doi:10.1108/SBR-07-2018-0078

Bacinello, E., Tontini, G., & Alberton, A. (2021). Influence of corporate social responsibility on sustainable practices of small and medium-sized enterprises: Implications on business performance. *Corporate Social Responsibility and Environmental Management*, *28*(2), 776–785. doi:10.1002/csr.2087

Barnett, M., & Salomon, R. (2012). Does it pay to be really good? Addressing the shape of the relationship between social and financial performance. *Strategic Management Journal*, *33*(11), 1304–1320. doi:10.1002mj.1980

Barney, J. (1991). Firm resources and sustained competitive advantage. *Journal of Management*, *17*(1), 99–120. doi:10.1177/014920639101700108

Battisti, F., & Siletti, E. (2019). On the Use of Control Variables in PLS-SEM= Sull'Uso Delle Variabili di Controllo Nei PLS-SEM. In Smart Statistics for Smart Applications (pp. 793-798). Pearson.

Benedetto, G. (2013). The environmental impact of a Sardinian wine by partial life cycle assessment. *Wine Economics and Policy*, *2*(1), 33–41. doi:10.1016/j.wep.2013.05.003

Bonn, M., Chang, H., & Cho, M. (2020). The environment and perceptions of wine consumers regarding quality, risk and value: Reputations of regional wines and restaurants. *Journal of Hospitality and Tourism Management*, *45*, 203–212. doi:10.1016/j.jhtm.2020.08.004

Borger, F., & Kruglianskas, I. (2006). Corporate social responsibility and environmental and technological innovation performance: Case studies of Brazilian companies. *International Journal of Technology. Policy and Management*, *6*(4), 399–412.

Buenechea-Elberdin, M., Sáenz, J., & Kianto, A. (2017). Exploring the role of human capital, renewal capital and entrepreneurial capital in innovation performance in high-tech and low-tech firms. *Knowledge Management Research and Practice*, *15*(3), 369–379. doi:10.105741275-017-0069-3

Carmines, E., & Zeller, R. (1979). *Reliability and validity assessment* (Vol. 17). SAGE. doi:10.4135/9781412985642

Cepeda-Carrion, G., Cegarra-Navarro, J., & Cillo, V. (2019). Tips to use partial least squares structural equation modelling (PLS-SEM) in knowledge management. *Journal of Knowledge Management*, *23*(1), 67–89. doi:10.1108/JKM-05-2018-0322

Cheema, S., & Javed, F. (2017). The effects of corporate social responsibility toward green human resource management: The mediating role of sustainable environment. *Cogent Business & Management*, *4*(1), 1310012. doi:10.1080/23311975.2017.1310012

Chen, Y. (2008). The driver of green innovation and green image-green core competence. *Journal of Business Ethics*, *81*(3), 531–543. doi:10.100710551-007-9522-1

Chen, Z., Huang, S., Liu, C., Min, M., & Zhou, L. (2018). Fit between organizational culture and innovation strategy: Implications for innovation performance. *Sustainability (Basel)*, *10*(10), 3378. doi:10.3390u10103378

Chopra, M., Saini, N., Kumar, S., Varma, A., Mangla, S., & Lim, W. (2021). Past, present, and future of knowledge management for business sustainability. *Journal of Cleaner Production*, *328*, 129592. doi:10.1016/j.jclepro.2021.129592

Davenport, M., Delport, M., Blignaut, J., Hichert, T., & Van der Burgh, G. (2019). Combining theory and wisdom in pragmatic, scenario-based decision support for sustainable development. *Journal of Environmental Planning and Management*, *62*(4), 692–716. doi:10.1080/09640568.2018.1428185

Dickel, P., Hörisch, J., & Ritter, T. (2018). Networking for the environment: The impact of environmental orientation on start-ups' networking frequency and network size. *Journal of Cleaner Production*, *179*, 308–316. doi:10.1016/j.jclepro.2018.01.058

Dijkstra, T., & Henseler, J. (2015). Consistent partial least squares path modeling. *Management Information Systems Quarterly*, *39*(2), 297–316. doi:10.25300/MISQ/2015/39.2.02

Dogru, A., & Peyrefitte, J. (2022). Investigation of innovation in wine industry via meta-analysis. *Wine Business Journal*, *5*(1), 44–76. doi:10.26813/001c.31627

Donate, M., & Guadamillas, F. (2010). The effect of organizational culture on knowledge management practices and innovation. *Knowledge and Process Management*, *17*(2), 82–94. doi:10.1002/kpm.344

European Commission. (2023). *Corporate Sustainability and Responsibility*. https://single-market-economy.ec.europa.eu/industry/sustainability/corporate-sustainability-and-responsibility_en

Fonseca, T., De Faria, P., & Lima, F. (2019). Human capital and innovation: The importance of the optimal organizational task structure. *Research Policy*, *48*(3), 616–627. doi:10.1016/j.respol.2018.10.010

Fornell, C., & Larcker, D. (1981). Evaluating structural equation models with unobservable variables and measurement error. *JMR, Journal of Marketing Research*, *18*(1), 39–50. doi:10.1177/002224378101800104

Gallardo-Vázquez, D., Valdez-Juárez, L., & Lizcano-Álvarez, J. (2019). Corporate Social Responsibility and Intellectual Capital: Sources of competitiveness and legitimacy in organizations' management practices. *Sustainability (Basel)*, *11*(20), 5843. doi:10.3390u11205843

Ganguly, A., Talukdar, A., & Chatterjee, D. (2019). Evaluating the role of social capital, tacit knowledge sharing, knowledge quality and reciprocity in determining innovation capability of an organization. *Journal of Knowledge Management*, *23*(6), 1105–1135. doi:10.1108/JKM-03-2018-0190

García-Machado, J., & Martínez-Ávila, M. (2019). Environmental performance and green culture: The mediating effect of green innovation. An application to the automotive industry. *Sustainability (Basel)*, *11*(18), 4874. doi:10.3390u11184874

Gilinsky, A. Jr, Newton, S., & Vega, R. (2016). Sustainability in the global wine industry: Concepts and cases. *Agriculture and Agricultural Science Procedia*, *8*, 37–49. doi:10.1016/j.aaspro.2016.02.006

Goncharuk, A. (2017). Wine value chains: Challenges and prospects. *Journal of Applied Management and Investments*, *6*(1), 11–27.

Guadamillas-Gómez, F., & Donate-Manzanares, M. (2011). Ethics and corporate social responsibility integrated into knowledge management and innovation technology: A case study. *Journal of Management Development*, *30*(6), 569–581. doi:10.1108/02621711111135170

Guerrero-Villegas, J., Sierra-García, L., & Palacios-Florencio, B. (2018). The role of sustainable development and innovation on firm performance. *Corporate Social Responsibility and Environmental Management*, *25*(6), 1350–1362. doi:10.1002/csr.1644

Hair, Hult, Ringle, Sarstedt, Danks, & Ray. (2021). *Partial least squares structural equation modeling (PLS-SEM) using R: A workbook*. Springer.

Hair, J., Sarstedt, M., & Ringle, C. (2019). Rethinking some of the rethinking of partial least squares. *European Journal of Marketing*, *53*(4), 566–584. doi:10.1108/EJM-10-2018-0665

Hart, O. (1995). Corporate governance: Some theory and implications. *Economic Journal (London)*, *105*(430), 678–689. doi:10.2307/2235027

Hart, S., & Dowell, G. (2011). A natural-resource-based view of the firm: Fifteen years after. *Journal of Management*, *37*(5), 1464–1479. doi:10.1177/0149206310390219

Henseler, J., Hubona, G., & Ray, P. (2016). Using PLS path modeling in new technology research: Updated guidelines. *Industrial Management & Data Systems*, *116*(1), 2–20. doi:10.1108/IMDS-09-2015-0382

Henseler, J., Ringle, C., & Sarstedt, M. (2015). A new criterion for assessing discriminant validity in variance-based structural equation modeling. *Journal of the Academy of Marketing Science*, *43*(1), 115–135. doi:10.100711747-014-0403-8

Hernández, J., Yañez-Araque, B., & Moreno-García, J. (2020). Moderating effect of firm size on the influence of corporate social responsibility in the economic performance of micro-, small-and medium-sized enterprises. *Technological Forecasting and Social Change*, *151*, 119774. doi:10.1016/j.techfore.2019.119774

Hong, M., Drakeford, B., & Zhang, K. (2020). The impact of mandatory CSR disclosure on green innovation: Evidence from China. *Green Finance*, *2*(3), 302–322. doi:10.3934/GF.2020017

Hu, L., & Bentler, P. (1998). Fit indices in covariance structure modeling: Sensitivity to underparameterized model misspecification. *Psychological Methods*, *3*(4), 424–453. doi:10.1037/1082-989X.3.4.424

International Labour Organization (ILO). (2023). *Tripartite declaration of principles concerning multinational enterprises and social policy (MNE Declaration)*. https://www.ilo.org/empent/Publications/WCMS_094386/lang--en/index.htm

Jain, P., Vyas, V., & Roy, A. (2017). Exploring the mediating role of intellectual capital and competitive advantage on the relation between CSR and financial performance in SMEs. *Social Responsibility Journal*, *13*(1), 1–23. doi:10.1108/SRJ-04-2015-0048

Javed, M., Rashid, M., Hussain, G., & Ali, H. (2020). The effects of corporate social responsibility on corporate reputation and firm financial performance: Moderating role of responsible leadership. *Corporate Social Responsibility and Environmental Management*, *27*(3), 1395–1409. doi:10.1002/csr.1892

Kamal, Y. (2021). Stakeholders expectations for CSR-related corporate governance disclosure: Evidence from a developing country. *Asian Review of Accounting*, *29*(2), 97–127. doi:10.1108/ARA-04-2020-0052

Khojastehpour, M., & Shams, S. (2020). Addressing the complexity of stakeholder management in international ecological setting: A CSR approach. *Journal of Business Research, 119*, 302–309. doi:10.1016/j.jbusres.2019.05.012

Kline, R. (2011). *Principles and practice of structural equation modelling*. Guilford Press.

Kraus, S., Rehman, S., & García, F. (2020). Corporate social responsibility and environmental performance: The mediating role of environmental strategy and green innovation. *Technological Forecasting and Social Change, 160*, 120262. doi:10.1016/j.techfore.2020.120262

Ling, Y. (2019). Influence of corporate social responsibility on organizational performance: Knowledge management as moderator. *VINE Journal of Information and Knowledge Management Systems, 49*(3), 327–352. doi:10.1108/VJIKMS-11-2018-0096

Luo, X., & Du, S. (2015). Exploring the relationship between corporate social responsibility and firm innovation. *Marketing Letters, 26*(4), 703–714. doi:10.100711002-014-9302-5

Madhoushi, M., Sadati, A., Delavari, H., Mehdivand, M., & Mihandost, R. (2011). Entrepreneurial orientation and innovation performance: The mediating role of knowledge management. *Asian Journal of Business Management, 3*(4), 310–316.

Marco-Lajara, Zaragoza-Sáez, Martínez-Falcó, & Sánchez-García. (2022). Does green intellectual capital affect green innovation performance? Evidence from the Spanish wine industry. *British Food Journal*. doi:10.1108/BFJ-03-2022-0298

Marco-Lajara, B., Zaragoza-Sáez, P., Martínez-Falcó, J., & Ruiz-Fernández, L. (2022). The Effect of Green Intellectual Capital on Green Performance in the Spanish Wine Industry: A Structural Equation Modeling Approach. *Complexity, 6024077*, 1–17. Advance online publication. doi:10.1155/2022/6024077

Marco-Lajara, B., Zaragoza-Sáez, P., Martínez-Falcó, J., & Sánchez-García, E. (2022). Green Intellectual Capital in the Spanish Wine Industry. In Innovative Economic, Social, and Environmental Practices for Progressing Future Sustainability (pp. 102-120). IGI Global. doi:10.4018/978-1-7998-9590-9.ch006

Mardani, A., Nikoosokhan, S., Moradi, M., & Doustar, M. (2018). The relationship between knowledge management and innovation performance. *The Journal of High Technology Management Research, 29*(1), 12–26. doi:10.1016/j.hitech.2018.04.002

Mbanyele, W., Huang, H., Li, Y., Muchenje, L., & Wang, F. (2022). Corporate social responsibility and green innovation: Evidence from mandatory CSR disclosure laws. *Economics Letters*, *212*, 110322. doi:10.1016/j.econlet.2022.110322

Mishra, P., & Yadav, M. (2021). Environmental capabilities, proactive environmental strategy and competitive advantage: A natural-resource-based view of firms operating in India. *Journal of Cleaner Production*, *291*, 125249. doi:10.1016/j.jclepro.2020.125249

Mothe, C., Nguyen-Thi, U., & Triguero, Á. (2018). Innovative products and services with environmental benefits: Design of search strategies for external knowledge and absorptive capacity. *Journal of Environmental Planning and Management*, *61*(11), 1934–1954. doi:10.1080/09640568.2017.1372275

Muller, C., Canale, F., & Cruz, A. (2022). Green innovation in the Latin American agri-food industry: understanding the influence of family involvement and business practices. British Food Journal. doi:10.1108/BFJ-09-2021-0994

Nguyen, T., Pham, T., Le, Q., & Bui, T. (2020). Impact of corporate social responsibility on organizational commitment through organizational trust and organizational identification. *Management Science Letters*, *10*(14), 3453–3462. doi:10.5267/j.msl.2020.5.032

Nonaka, I., & Takeuchi, H. (1995). *The knowledge-creating company: How Japanese companies create the dynamics of innovation*. Oxford University Press.

OECD. (2005). *Manual de Oslo: Guía para la recogida e interpretación de datos sobre innovación.* Retrieved from: http://www.itq.edu.mx/convocatorias/manualdeoslo.pdf

Onofrei, G., Nguyen, H., Zhang, M., & Fynes, B. (2020). Building supply chain relational capital: The impact of supplier and customer leveraging on innovation performance. *Business Strategy and the Environment*, *29*(8), 3422–3434. doi:10.1002/bse.2586

Oware, K., & Mallikarjunappa, T. (2019). Corporate social responsibility investment, third-party assurance and firm performance in India: The moderating effect of financial leverage. *South Asian Journal of Business Studies*, *8*(3), 303–324. doi:10.1108/SAJBS-08-2018-0091

Padilla-Lozano, C., & Collazzo, P. (2021). Corporate social responsibility, green innovation and competitiveness–causality in manufacturing. *Competitiveness Review*, *32*(7), 21–39. doi:10.1108/CR-12-2020-0160

Pérez-López, S., & Alegre, J. (2012). Information technology competency, knowledge processes and firm performance. *Industrial Management & Data Systems*, *112*(4), 644–662. doi:10.1108/02635571211225521

Pérez-Luño, A., Alegre, J., & Valle-Cabrera, R. (2019). The role of tacit knowledge in connecting knowledge exchange and combination with innovation. *Technology Analysis and Strategic Management*, *31*(2), 186–198. doi:10.1080/09537325.2018.1492712

Popescu, C. R. G. (2021). Impact of Innovative Capital on the Global Performance of the European Union: Implications on Sustainability Assessment. In C. Popescu (Ed.), *Handbook of Research on Novel Practices and Current Successes in Achieving the Sustainable Development Goals* (pp. 90–124). IGI Global. doi:10.4018/978-1-7998-8426-2.ch005

Popescu, C. R. G. (2022). Mindfulness at Work, a Sound Business Investment: Focusing on the Employee Well-Being While Increasing Creativity and Innovation. In C. Popescu (Ed.), *Handbook of Research on Changing Dynamics in Responsible and Sustainable Business in the Post-COVID-19 Era* (pp. 1–34). IGI Global. doi:10.4018/978-1-6684-2523-7.ch001

Popescu, C. R. G. (2023). Artificial Intelligence and Sustainability in a Game-Changing Post-COVID-19 Era: Key Drivers for Economic Development, Social Development, and Environmental Protection. In C. Popescu (Ed.), *Positive and Constructive Contributions for Sustainable Development Goals* (pp. 1–20). IGI Global. doi:10.4018/978-1-6684-7499-0.ch001

Qiu, L., Jie, X., Wang, Y., & Zhao, M. (2020). Green product innovation, green dynamic capability, and competitive advantage: Evidence from Chinese manufacturing enterprises. *Corporate Social Responsibility and Environmental Management*, *27*(1), 146–165. doi:10.1002/csr.1780

Reinartz, W., Haenlein, M., & Henseler, J. (2009). An empirical comparison of the efficacy of covariance-based and variance-based SEM. *International Journal of Research in Marketing*, *26*(4), 332–344. doi:10.1016/j.ijresmar.2009.08.001

Ren, Huang, Liu, & Yan. (2022). Understanding the Impact of Mandatory CSR Disclosure on Green Innovation: Evidence from Chinese Listed Firms. *British Journal of Management*. doi:10.1111/1467-8551.12609

Roldan, J., & Cepeda, G. (2017). Modelos de Ecuaciones basados en la Varianza: Partial Least Squares (PLS) para Investigadores en Ciencias Sociales (4a ed.). Universidad de Sevilla.

Rossi, M., Festa, G., Chouaibi, S., Fait, M., & Papa, A. (2021). The effects of business ethics and corporate social responsibility on intellectual capital voluntary disclosure. *Journal of Intellectual Capital*, *8*(3), 303–324. doi:10.1108/JIC-08-2020-0287

Ryu, D., Baek, K., & Yoon, J. (2021). Open Innovation with relational capital, technological innovation capital, and international performance in SMEs. *Sustainability (Basel)*, *13*(6), 3418. doi:10.3390u13063418

Salmones, M., Crespo, A., & Bosque, I. (2005). Influence of corporate social responsibility on loyalty and valuation of services. *Journal of Business Ethics*, *61*(4), 369–385. doi:10.100710551-005-5841-2

Sanchez-Famoso, V., Cano-Rubio, M., & Fuentes-Lombardo, G. (2019). The role of cooperation agreements in the internationalization of Spanish winery and olive oil family firms. *International Journal of Wine Business Research*, *31*(4), 555–577. doi:10.1108/IJWBR-08-2018-0042

Sarstedt, M., Hair, J. Jr, Cheah, J., Becker, J., & Ringle, C. M. (2019). How to specify, estimate, and validate higher-order constructs in PLS-SEM. *Australasian Marketing Journal*, *27*(3), 197–211. doi:10.1016/j.ausmj.2019.05.003

Seman, N., Govindan, K., Mardani, A., Zakuan, N., Saman, M., Hooker, R., & Ozkul, S. (2019). The mediating effect of green innovation on the relationship between green supply chain management and environmental performance. *Journal of Cleaner Production*, *229*, 115–127. doi:10.1016/j.jclepro.2019.03.211

Shahzad, M., Qu, Y., Javed, S., Zafar, A., & Rehman, S. (2020). Relation of environment sustainability to CSR and green innovation: A case of Pakistani manufacturing industry. *Journal of Cleaner Production*, *253*, 119938. doi:10.1016/j.jclepro.2019.119938

Shahzad, M., Qu, Y., Zafar, A., & Appolloni, A. (2021). Does the interaction between the knowledge management process and sustainable development practices boost corporate green innovation? *Business Strategy and the Environment*, *30*(8), 4206–4222. doi:10.1002/bse.2865

Singh, K., & Misra, M. (2021). Linking corporate social responsibility (CSR) and organizational performance: The moderating effect of corporate reputation. *European Research on Management and Business Economics*, *27*(1), 100139. doi:10.1016/j.iedeen.2020.100139

Singh, S., Del Giudice, M., Chierici, R., & Graziano, D. (2020). Green innovation and environmental performance: The role of green transformational leadership and green human resource management. *Technological Forecasting and Social Change*, *150*, 119762. doi:10.1016/j.techfore.2019.119762

Soceanu, A., Dobrinas, S., Sirbu, A., Manea, N., & Popescu, V. (2021). Economic aspects of waste recovery in the wine industry. A multidisciplinary approach. *The Science of the Total Environment*, *759*, 143543. doi:10.1016/j.scitotenv.2020.143543 PMID:33199012

Taylor, J., Vithayathil, J., & Yim, D. (2018). Are corporate social responsibility (CSR) initiatives such as sustainable development and environmental policies value enhancing or window dressing? *Corporate Social Responsibility and Environmental Management*, *25*(5), 971–980. doi:10.1002/csr.1513

Troise, C., & Camilleri, M. (2021). The use of digital media for marketing, CSR communication and stakeholder engagement. In *Strategic corporate communication in the digital age*. Emerald Publishing Limited. doi:10.1108/978-1-80071-264-520211010

Tuan, L. (2016). The chain effect from human resource-based clinical governance through emotional intelligence and CSR to knowledge sharing. *Knowledge Management Research and Practice*, *14*(1), 126–143. doi:10.1057/kmrp.2014.23

Ullah, H., Wang, Z., Mohsin, M., Jiang, W., & Abbas, H. (2022). Multidimensional perspective of green financial innovation between green intellectual capital on sustainable business: The case of Pakistan. *Environmental Science and Pollution Research International*, *29*(4), 5552–5568. doi:10.100711356-021-15919-7 PMID:34424468

Waruwu, H., Asbari, M., Purwanto, A., Nugroho, Y., Fikri, M., Fauji, A., & Dewi, W. (2020). The role of transformational leadership, organizational learning and structure on innovation capacity: Evidence from Indonesia private schools. *Journal of Education, Psychology and Counseling*, *2*(1), 378–397.

Wong, S. (2013). Environmental requirements, knowledge sharing and green innovation: Empirical evidence from the electronics industry in China. *Business Strategy and the Environment*, *22*(5), 321–338. doi:10.1002/bse.1746

Wood, D. (1991). Corporate social performance revisited. *Academy of Management Review*, *16*(4), 691–718. doi:10.2307/258977

Xu, J., Wei, J., & Lu, L. (2019). Strategic stakeholder management, environmental corporate social responsibility engagement, and financial performance of stigmatized firms derived from Chinese special environmental policy. *Business Strategy and the Environment*, *28*(6), 1027–1044. doi:10.1002/bse.2299

Yong, J., Yusliza, M., Ramayah, T., & Fawehinmi, O. (2019). Nexus between green intellectual capital and green human resource management. *Journal of Cleaner Production*, *215*, 364–374. doi:10.1016/j.jclepro.2018.12.306

Youndt, M., Subramaniam, M., & Snell, S. (2004). Intellectual capital profiles: An examination of investments and returns. *Journal of Management Studies*, *41*(2), 335–361. doi:10.1111/j.1467-6486.2004.00435.x

Yuan, B., & Cao, X. (2022). Do corporate social responsibility practices contribute to green innovation? The mediating role of green dynamic capability. *Technology in Society*, *68*, 101868. doi:10.1016/j.techsoc.2022.101868

Yusliza, M., Yong, J., Tanveer, M., Ramayah, T., Faezah, J., & Muhammad, Z. (2020). A structural model of the impact of green intellectual capital on sustainable performance. *Journal of Cleaner Production*, *249*, 119334. doi:10.1016/j.jclepro.2019.119334

Yusoff, Y., Omar, M., & Zaman, M. (2019a). Practice of green intellectual capital. Evidence from Malaysian manufacturing sector. *IOP Conference Series. Materials Science and Engineering*, *469*(1), 012008. doi:10.1088/1757-899X/469/1/012008

Yusoff, Y., Omar, M., Zaman, M., & Samad, S. (2019b). Do all elements of green intellectual capital contribute toward business sustainability? Evidence from the Malaysian context using the Partial Least Squares method. *Journal of Cleaner Production*, *234*, 626–637. doi:10.1016/j.jclepro.2019.06.153

Zaragoza-Sáez, P., Claver-Cortés, E., Marco-Lajara, B., & Úbeda-García, M. (2020). Corporate social responsibility and strategic knowledge management as mediators between sustainable intangible capital and hotel performance. *Journal of Sustainable Tourism*, 1–23. doi:10.1080/09669582.2020.1811289

Zhou, M., Govindan, K., Xie, X., & Yan, L. (2021). How to drive green innovation in China's mining enterprises? Under the perspective of environmental legitimacy and green absorptive capacity. *Resources Policy*, *72*, 102038. doi:10.1016/j.resourpol.2021.102038

Chapter 4
The Role of Air Pollution in the ESG Model at the World Level

Cosimo Magazzino
https://orcid.org/0000-0002-3176-9838
Roma Tre University, Italy

Angelo Leogrande
Lum University, Italy

ABSTRACT

In the following chapter, the authors analyse the role of air pollution (AP) in the context of ESG (environmental, social, and governance) model. They use data from the World Banks' ESG Database for 193 countries during the period 2011-2020. They perform panel data with random effects, panel data with fixed effects, pooled OLS, and WLS. Results show that the level of PA is positively associated, among others, to "cooling degree days," "CO2 emissions," and "agriculture, forestry, and fishing, value added," and negatively associated, among others, to "terrestrial and marine protected areas," "proportion of seats held by women in national parliaments," and "mammal species threatened." Furthermore, they confront eight different machine learning algorithms for the prediction of the future value of AP. Polynomial regression is the best predictive algorithm in the sense either maximization of R-squared either minimization of MAE, MSR, and RMSE. The future value of AP is expected to reduce on average of -0,060% for the analysed countries.

DOI: 10.4018/979-8-3693-1151-6.ch004

1. INTRODUCTION: RESEARCH QUESTION

In the following article we address the issue of the impact of air pollution calculated as Pm 2.5 in the context of the variable system of the ESG-Environmental, Social and Governance model. We used data from the World Bank for 2011-2020 for 193 countries. The issue of air pollution is particularly relevant in the context of the fight against climate change and the application of ESG models. Air pollution shows the presence of an old industrial system, i.e. lacking the ability to invest effectively in green technological innovations. Furthermore, air pollution also derives from deforestation and the presence of a set of polluting sectors such as, for example, those connected to the extraction and processing of oil.

One of the most important problems is the difficulty of modifying production structures especially in countries with a low-middle per capita income. Paradoxically, countries with medium-high per capita incomes have a more sustainable system from the point of view of air emissions. Conversely, countries with low per capita incomes do not have the regulatory or technological power to be sustainable in the reduction of air emissions.

Furthermore, there are several elements that can prevent also countries that are growing in terms of GDP from accessing a more sustainable production system in terms of emissions. In fact, countries that have high levels of air pollution also have low values of human and social capital. And since the change in production systems also requires the formation of a green conscience in the population, it follows that in the absence of adequate human and social capital it is not possible to introduce green innovations or green regulations even in the presence of high levels of industrial air pollution. Finally, even in countries that have anti-pollution legislation with investment in green technology, it is possible that there is a low level of reduction of air pollution due to the lack of adequate metrics for evaluating emissions. It is therefore also necessary to intervene through adequate metrics to identify efficiency gains and losses in the fight against air pollution.

The article continues as follows: the second section analyzes the scientific literature, the third section presents the econometric model, the fourth section compares eight machine learning algorithms for predicting the future value of AP, the fifth section concludes.

2. LITERATURE REVIEW

In the following analysis we present an introduction to the vast literature on the socio-economic and environmental effects of air pollution. The analysis is not exhaustive and serves only to guide the reader to topics related to air pollution.

AP and Labour Force Participation Rate. It should be noted that many of the countries that have high levels of PA also have high levels of labor force participation rates. In fact, many of the countries that have low per capita incomes also have high levels of pollution with high labor force participation. There is a positive relationship between AP and the labour force partecipation rate i.e. countries that have a greater level of labour force partecipation rate also have greater air pollution in a set of 193 countries in the period 2011-2020 (Leogrande & Costantiello, 2023).

AP and ESG Legislation. Legislative interventions are particularly relevant to allow countries to reduce the value of AP. However, it must be considered that the strength of environmental legislation tends to be negatively associated with the level of pollution at the country level. In fact, countries that are more environmentally sensitive also tend to have a more effective environmental regulatory framework. Polluting countries, on the other hand, also lack adequate environmental legislation. Firms that have higher AP levels operate in regions with lower environmental protection in China (Shen, Lyu, & Zhu, 2022). The legislative objectives that the European legislation is oriented to achieve, also in terms of AP can be better measured with the usage of satellite images and ESG metrics (Yang & Broby, 2020).

AP and Banking and Finance. The banking and financial system find it very difficult to evaluate companies based on their environmental sustainability. In fact, banks are not used to evaluating customers based on their ability to be sustainable. Furthermore, many large companies that are historical customers of banks have high levels of polluting emissions. The issue becomes much more serious in the case of finance due to the presence of greenwashing. Information asymmetries, lack of adequate reporting, and green-oriented financial frauds risk to impede the efficient allocation of credit in the ESG context even in countries with high per capita income. Banks either tend to over-estimate firms that are green oriented either continue their to have relationships with pollutant borrowers (Giannetti, Jasova, Loumioti, & Mendicino, 2023). The increase in the level of AP augments the attractiveness of green bonds in China (He, Xu, & Shi, 2023).

AP and Human Capital. Countries that have a high level of air pollutant emissions also tend to have low social capital and low human capital. In fact, the population living in polluted areas often lacks adequate education, schools, and learning opportunities. A pollution trap therefore arises. Pollution is both the cause and the consequence of an insufficient social capital which generates a depletion of human capital. However, the lack of human capital and social capital prevent the reduction of pollution due to the lack of an environmental awareness that can inspire green-oriented economic policies. There is a negative relationship between the level of AP and the level of human capital in China (Xue, Zhang, & Zhao, 2021). AP is negatively associated to human capital (Hospido, Sanz, & Villanueva, 2023). The probability of CEO turnover is greater in high pollutant firms in China because of the application of the Public Environmental Concern-PEC (Gu, Ho, Yan, & Gozgor, 2021).

AP and Firm Performance. The impact of environmental pollution on corporate performance is counterfactual. In fact, polluting companies appear to be very efficient from a financial and profit point of view. Furthermore, companies that are polluting tend to pay greater attention to green-oriented investments. However, the economic and productive areas characterized by the presence of polluting companies are also characterized by greater financial risk. In fact, the possible imposition of green investments by the authorities can create significant financial difficulties for manufacturing companies. There is a positive relationship between AP and firm performance in high-polluted countries. In high-polluted countries, firms tend not to reduce their emission levels not to reduce firm performance (Song, 2023). There is a positive relationship between AP and green investment (Barabanov, Basnet, Walker, Yuan, & Wendt, 2021). AP increases financial risks in Asian countries (Park, Park, Yoo, Yue, & Yu, 2022).

AP, R&D and Green Innovation. Furthermore, companies that have significant levels of environmental pollution also have reduced investment values in research and development. In fact, companies that are highly polluting have no sensitivity towards green innovation. For polluting companies to invest more in green innovation, it is necessary to determine regulatory interventions that require companies to replace polluting technologies with sustainable technologies. However, from a financial point of view, it is very unlikely that polluting companies alone will be able to support the investment in green innovation. It follows that the possibility for the polluting company to invest in green innovation is connected to the existence of economic policies that can offer tax and financial incentives to firms. There is a negative relationship between AP and the expenditures in research and development (Costantiello & Leogrande, The Impact of Research and Development Expenditures on ESG Model in the Global Economy, 2023). Green innovation is negatively associated to AP (Fiorillo, Meles, Mustilli, & Salerno, 2022).

Miscellaneous. Finally, AP also has a range of impacts on people's happiness, health, tourism, and governance. The empirical dimensions of the impact of AP at an economic and social level are very broad and go beyond the ESG dimension. AP also has impact on health and psychological well-being aspects of the population. There is a positive relationship between AP and happiness in China thanks to the application of ESG inspired legislation (Lu, Hamori, & Tian, 2023). Covid 19 had a positive role in reduction AP (Francová, Korhonen, & Kovačević, 2022). The cruise sector significantly increases the level of AP at Barcelona (Ruiz-Guerra, Molina-Moreno, Cortés-García, & Núñez-Cacho, 2019). There is a negative relationship between AP and political stability in a set of 193 countries in the period 2011-2020 (Costantiello & Leogrande, The Role of Political Stability in the Context of ESG Models at World Level, 2023). There is a positive relationship between AP and CO_2 emissions (Costantiello & and Leogrande, The Determinants of CO**2** Emissions in the Context of ESG, 2023). AP is positively associated to renewable energy in a set of 193 countries in the period 2011-2020 (Laureti, Costantiello, & Leogrande, 2022).

3. THE ECONOMETRIC MODEL FOR THE ESTIMATION OF THE VALUE OF PA IN EACH OF THE ESG COMPONENT

In the following analysis, we use a set of econometric techniques to estimate the role of the PA within each component of the ESG model. The data used refer to the World Bank-ESG database for 193 countries in the period 2011-2020. To test the econometric relationships we used the following models i.e. Panel Data with Fixed Effects, Panel Data with Variable Effects, Pooled OLS and WLS.

Below, estimate the value of AP within the variables of the E component of the ESG model (Table 1).

Table 1. Statistical results for the estimation of AP within the e-component in the ESG model

Statistical Results for the Estimation of AP Within the E-Component in the ESG Model										
Variables	**ABB**	**Pooled OLS**		**Fixed-Effects**		**Random-Effects**		**WLS**		**Average**
		Coefficient	**P-Values**	**Coefficient**	**P-Values**	**Coefficient**	**P-Values**	**Coefficient**	**P-Values**	
Coefficient		-2,30375	***	-1,7834	*	-1,49099		-1,10653	***	-1,6712
Agricultural land (% of land area)	AL	0,0400168	**	0,0704061	**	0,0647116	***	0,0239226	***	0,04976
Agriculture, forestry, and fishing, value added (% of GDP)	AFF	0,375263	***	0,25465	***	0,244652	***	0,294988	***	0,29239
Annual freshwater withdrawals, total (% of internal resources)	AFW	0,0106897	***	0,00519773	***	0,00564136	***	0,0113419	***	0,00822
CO2 emissions (metric tons per capita)	CO2E	0,937639	***	0,897408	***	0,882367	***	0,764026	***	0,87036
Cooling Degree Days New	CDD	32,8943	***	55,0262	***	34,8229	***	33,1256	***	38,9673
Energy imports, net (% of energy use)	EIN	-0,0305596	***	-0,0113634	***	-0,0134555	***	-0,025064	***	-0,0201
Energy use (kg of oil equivalent per capita)	EUS	-0,0014008	***	-0,00042926	**	-0,00052662	**	-0,001441	***	-0,0009
Food production index (2014-2016 = 100)	FPI	0,126751	***	0,0966959	***	0,104492	***	0,109133	***	0,10927
Fossil fuel energy consumption (% of total)	FFEC	0,0987711	***	0,0638697	***	0,0673515	***	0,0959427	***	0,08148
Mammal species, threatened	MST	-0,475137	***	-0,548959	***	-0,540342	***	-0,541232	***	-0,5264
Renewable energy consumption (% of total final energy consumption)	REC	0,142862	***	0,232542	***	0,215752	***	0,156132	***	0,18682
Terrestrial and marine protected areas (% of total territorial area)	TMPA	-0,183417	***	-0,147397	***	-0,152541	***	-0,146109	***	-0,1574

Specifically, we estimated the following equation:

$$AP_{it} = \pm_{it} + {}^{2}{}_{1}(AL)_{it} + {}^{2}{}_{2}(AFF)_{it} + {}^{2}{}_{3}(AFW)_{it} + {}^{2}{}_{4}(CO2E)_{it} + {}^{2}{}_{5}(CDD)_{it} + {}^{2}{}_{6}(EIN)_{it} + {}^{2}{}_{7}(EUS)_{it} + {}^{2}{}_{8}(FPI)_{it} + {}^{2}{}_{9}(FFEC)_{it} + {}^{2}{}_{10}(MST)_{it} + {}^{2}{}_{11}(REC)_{it} + {}^{2}{}_{12}(TMPA)_{it}$$

Where $i = 193$ and $t = [2010; 2019]$.

We found that AP is positively associated to:

- *CDD:* It is a measurement designed to quantify the energy demand needed to cool buildings. In particular, it calculates the number of days in which the temperature is above 18 degrees. There is therefore a positive relationship between the CDD value and the AP value. This relationship depends on the fact that if the temperature rises above 18 degrees then the demand for energy to cool buildings tends to grow. That is, the level of pollution tends to grow. Therefore, the level of air pollution is growing. The increase in the value of CDD tends to be a phenomenon connected to "*global warming*". In fact, more and more countries, even countries that generally have harsh climates in terms of temperatures, tend more and more to experience positive series of days with heat above 18 degrees. It follows that the level of air pollution can also increase in the mountains, or in areas generally considered safe from an environmental point of view.
- *CO2E*: are those deriving from the combustion of fossil fuels and the production of cement. They include carbon dioxide produced during the burning of solid, liquid and gaseous fuels and gas flaring. There is a positive relationship between the value of CO_2 Emissions and the value of AP. In fact, the growth in the value of AP tends to be positively associated with the presence of CO_2 emissions. For example, if we take into consideration the top ten countries by CO2E value we can see that these countries also have high levels of PA (WB, CO2 emissions (metric tons per capita), 2023). In particular, considering 2019 we can note that Qatar is in first place for CO2E value with a value of 31.88 followed by PA with an amount of 76.05, Bahrain is in second place with a CO2E value equal to 22.06% and a PA value equal to 59.22, Kuwait in third place with an amount equal to 21.14% and a PA value equal to 60.97, the UAE ranks third with CO2E value of 20.15 and AP value of 43.67%, Oman ranks fifth with CO2E value of 16.46% and AP amount of 44.57%, Brunei Darussalam with CO2E value of 16.11% and AP value of 7.68%, Australia ranks seventh with CO2E value E equal to 15.60% and an amount of App equal to 6.75%, followed by Luxembourg with an amount of CO_2 equal to 15.60% and a value of AP equal to 10.07, Canada

with a value of CO2E equal to 15.05% and an amount of AP equal to 7.10, Saudi Arabia with a value of CO2E equal to 14.70% and a value of AP equal to 61, 51%.

- *AFF*: it is the percentage of GDP that is product from agriculture, forestry and fishering (WB, Agriculture, forestry, and fishing, value added (% of G, 2023). There is a positive relationship between the AFF value and the AP value. In fact, we are generally led to imagine that air pollution is connected with the performance of manufacturing and industrial activities, and that on the contrary the agriculture, fishing and forestry sector is more sustainable from an environmental point of view. The data in this sense is counterfeit. Agriculture pollutes with the use of chemical products. However, even the activity of extracting economic value from forests tends to be polluting because forests are often burned to make room for new crops. Notoriously, in fact, agriculture pollutes with the use of chemical products. However, even the activity of extracting economic value from forests tends to be polluting because forests are often burned to make room for new crops (Figure 1).

Figure 1. Relationship between AP and AFF

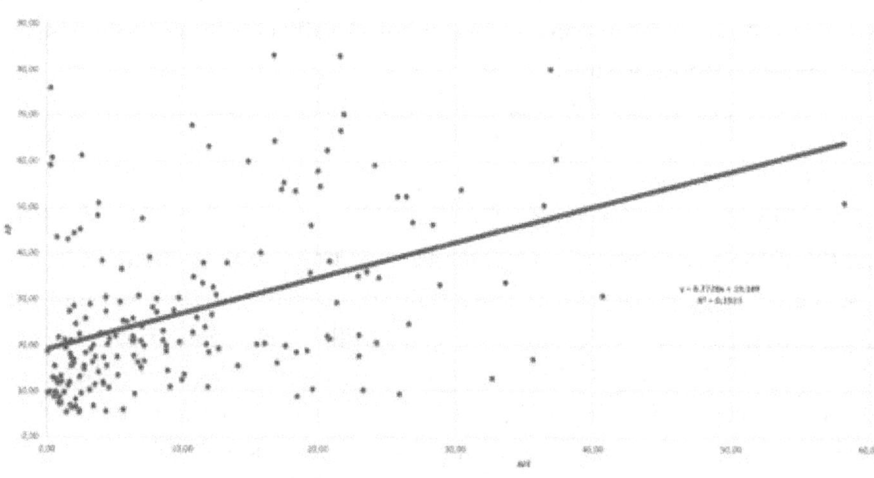

- *REC*: is the share of renewable energy in the total final energy consumption (WB, Renewable energy consumption (% of total final energy consumption), 2023). There is a positive relationship between the REC value and the AP value. The positive relationship tends to be counterfactual. In fact, alternative forms of energy should be used precisely to reduce the value of pollution and improve the quality of the air and the environment in general. On the contrary, we can see that the countries that use renewable energy the most are also the countries that have the worst levels in terms of air pollution. In fact, we may notice that countries that have low REC values also have high PA values. For example, if we consider the year 2019 we notice that Congo Dem. Rep. has a REC value of 96.29 and an AP value of 35.86, Somalia has a REC value of 95.03 and an AP value of 30.36, Uganda has a REC value of 91.62% and an AP value of 35.22%, the Central African Republic has a REC value of 91.26 and an AP value of 46.38%, Gabon with a REC value of 89.78% and an AP value of 36.75%, Liberia with a REC amount of 89.71% and an AP value of 50.6%, Ethiopia with a REC value of 89.5% and an AP value of 33.78%, Guinea Bissau with a value of REC equal to 86.2% and an AP value equal to 54.07%, Burundi with a REC value equal to 84.84% and an AP value equal to 33.28%, Tanzania with a REC value equal to 83.54% and an AP value equal to 24.84%. It therefore follows that many Western countries that have low REC levels still have a higher PA level than the low per capita income countries that have high REC levels (Figure 2).

Figure 2. Relationship between PA and REC in 2019

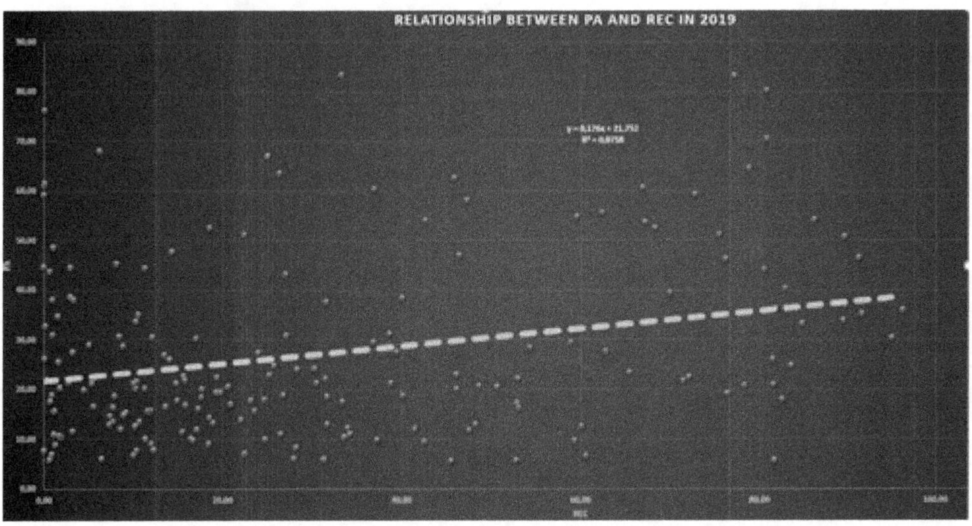

- *FPI*: covers food crops that are considered edible and contain nutrients. Coffee and tea are excluded because, although edible, they have no nutritional value (WB, Food production index (2014-2016 = 100), 2023). There is a positive relationship between the FPI value and the AP value. Countries that have high levels of Food Production Index are also countries that have high levels of air pollution. The reason could be because these countries are often countries that experience wild deforestation produced through the fires of green areas, or they are also oil exporters. In fact, if we take the ranking of the top 10 countries by FPI value in 2019, we can see that these countries also have high levels in terms of PA, i.e.: Senegal with FPI of 152.20 and PA of 60.21, Tajikistan with FPI of 138.70 and PA of 38.32, Saudi Arabia with FPI of 137.09 and PA of 61.51, Djibouti with FPI of 136.75 and PA of 43.17, Qatar with FPI of 136.75% and PA of 76, 05%, Burundi with FPI equal to 135.10 and PA equal to 33.28, Mozambique with FPI equal to 135.03% and PA equal to 20.77, Mongolia with 131.33% and PA equal to 38.06%, Malawi with FPI equal to 130.68% and PA equal to 22.35%, Bahrain with FPI with 129.86% and PA equal to 59.22% (Figure 3).

Figure 3. Relationship between PAP and FPI in 2019

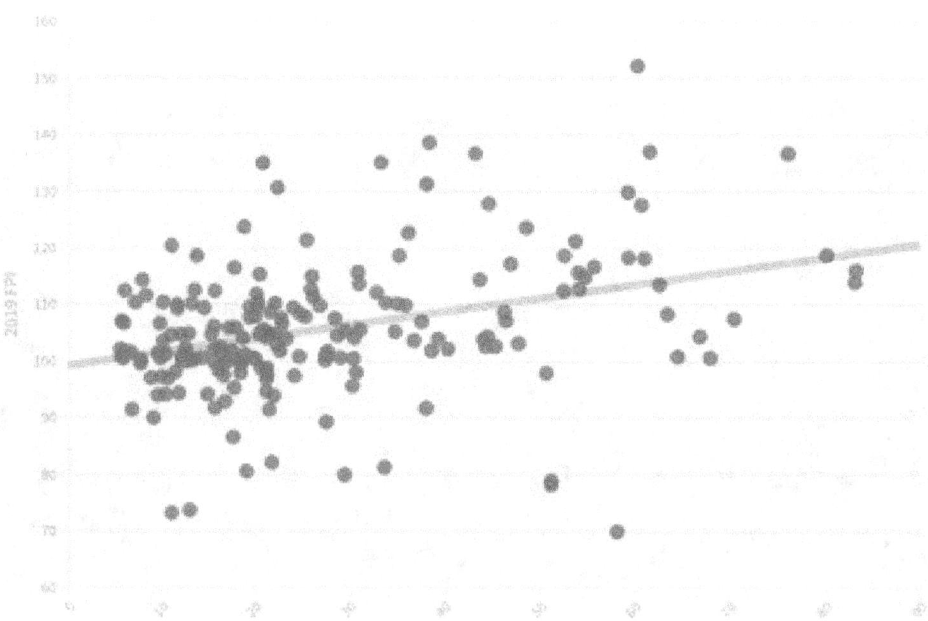

- *FFEC*: includes coal, oil, petroleum and natural gas based products (WB, Fossil fuel energy consumption (% of total), 2023). There is a positive relationship between the FFEC value and the AP value. The countries that consume the most fossil energy are obviously also the ones that emit the most pollution. Especially in the case of coal-fired, power plants, as well as in the case of oil-fired plants. Emissions related to the consumption of fossil energy are very harmful to health and actively contribute to air pollution.

- *AL*: refers to the share of arable land, with permanent crops and permanent pastures. Arable land includes land defined by FAO as land under temporary crops (double harvested areas are counted once), temporary grassland for mowing or grazing, land under market or market gardens and land temporarily fallow (WB, Agricultural land (% of land area), 2023) . Land abandoned due to cultivation shifts is excluded. There is a relationship between AL and AP. In fact, if we consider the first 10 countries by AL value, we can see that 9 have high levels in terms of AP, namely: Saudi Arabia with an AL value equal to 80.75% and an AP value equal to 61.51%, Saudi Arabia with an AL value equal to 80.75% and a PA value equal to 61.51%, South Africa with an AL value equal to 79.42% and an AP value equal to amount of 28.67%, Kazakhstan with an AL value equal to 79.26 and an AP value equal to 20.29%, Burundi with an AL value equal to 79.17% and a PA value equal to 33.28%, Nigeria with an AL value equal to 76.07% and a PA value equal to 70.40%, Syrian Arab Republic with an AL value equal to 75.81% and a PA value equal to an amount of 30.95%, Bangladesh with a PA value equal to 75.63% and a PA value equal to 63.43%, Rwanda with an AL value equal to 73.44% and a PA value equal to 36.18%, and Djibouti with an AL value equal to 73.43% and a PA value equal to a value of 43.17% (Figure 4).

Figure 4. Relationship between AP and AL in 2019

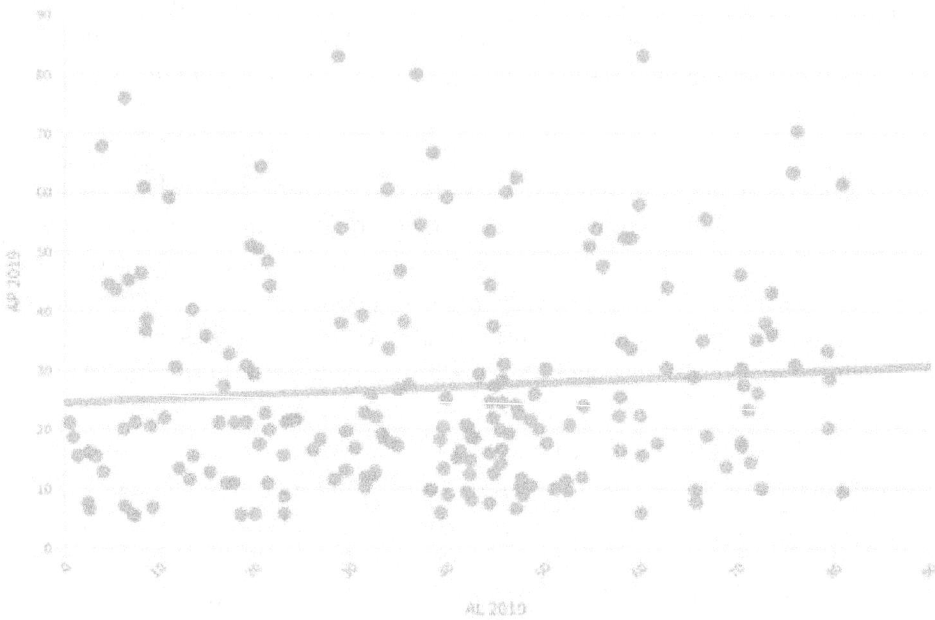

- *AFW*: refers to the total water withdrawals, without counting the losses due to evaporation from the accumulation basins. Withdrawals also include water from desalination plants in countries where it is a significant source (WB, Annual freshwater withdrawals, total (% of internal resources), 2023). Generally, there is a positive relationship between the AFW value and the AP value. The countries that use the most supplies of water are also the countries that have the environmental pollution. The reasons that push countries to increase the use of their water reserves for industrial and agricultural purposes are also the same that lead countries lacking attention to environmental pollution issues. If we consider, for example, the countries that have high AWF values, we can see that they also have high values in terms of PA, namely: Egypt with AWF equal to 7750.00 and PA equal to 67.89, Bahrain with AWF equal to 3877.50 and PA equal to 59.22, Turkmenistan with AWF equal to 1972.11 and PA equal to 26.20, United Arab Emirates with AWF equal to 16 28.67 and PA equal to 43.67, Saudi Arabia with AWF equal to 974.17 and PA equal to 61.51, Libya with an AWF value equal to 817.14 units and 38.59 with PA, Sudan with AWF equal to 673.38 and PA equal to 54.68,

Qatar with AWF equal to 446.43 and PA equal to 76.05 units, Uzbekistan with a value of AWF equal to 360.49 and PA equal to 34.79, Mauritania with AWF equal to 337.05 and PA equal to 66.81 (Figure 5).

Figure 5. Relationship between AP and AWF in 2019

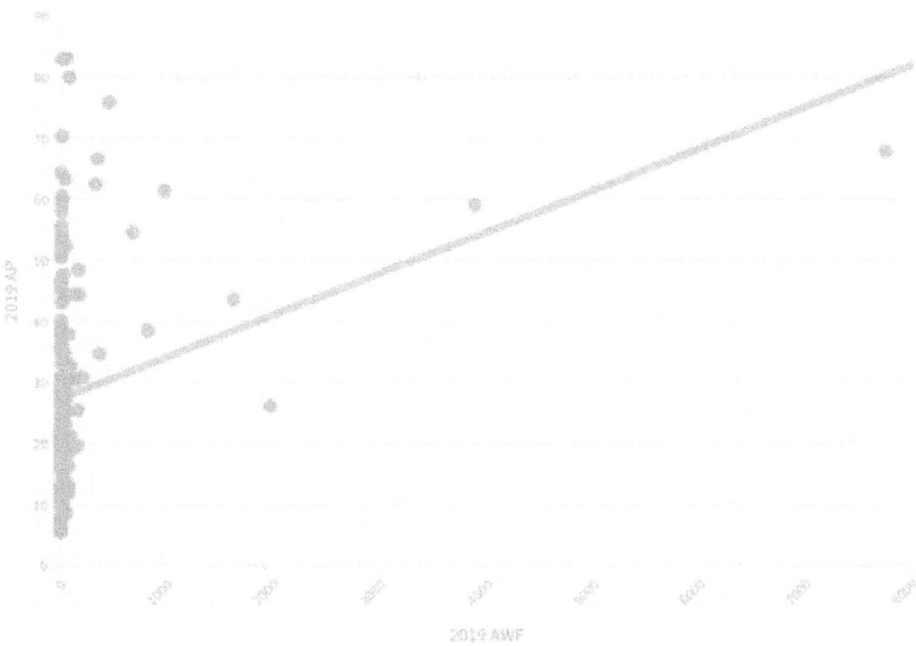

We also find that the level of AP is negatively associated to:

- *EUS*: refers to the use of primary energy before transformation into other end-use fuels, equal to domestic production plus imports and inventory changes, minus exports and fuels supplied to ships and aircraft engaged in international transportation (WB, Energy use (kg of oil equivalent per capita), 2023). There is a negative relationship between the EUS value and the AP value. Specifically, countries that have high EUS values also have low PA values. Considering the EUS top ten it turns out that many have reduced AP values such as for example Iceland with an EU value equal to 17916.12 and an AP amount equal to 5.94, Brunei Darussalam with an EUS equal to 8529.73 and a AP value equal to 7.75, Canada with an EUS value equal to 7897.86 and a AP value equal to 7.49, United States with EUS equal to 6.

960.68 and AP equal to 8.43, Luxembourg with a value of EUS equal to 6861.11 and AP equal to 10.15.

- EIN: are estimated as energy consumption minus production, both measured in oil equivalents. A negative value indicates that the country is a net exporter (WB, Energy imports, net (% of energy use), 2023). Energy consumption refers to the use of primary energy before transformation into other end-use fuels, equal to domestic production plus imports and inventory changes, minus exports and fuels supplied to ships and aircraft engaged in international transportation. There is a negative relationship between the EIN value and the AP value. The countries that import the most energy are also the ones that have the least levels of air pollution. In fact, if we consider the top ten countries by EIN value we can see that many of them have low values in terms of AP such as for example Malta with an EIN amount of 98.38 and an AP value of 13.76, Singapore with an EIN value equal to 97.68 and an AP amount equal to an amount of 17.73, Luxembourg with an EIN value equal to 96.00 and an AP value equal to 10.1 5, Cyprus with an EIN value of 94.03 and an AP value of 16.41, Japan with an EIN value of 93.98 and an AP value of 13.71, Moldova with an EIN value of 90.01 and an AP value of 16.42, Belarus with an EIN value of 86.78 and an AP value of 20.22.
- *TMPA*: are fully or partially protected areas of at least 1,000 hectares which are designated by national authorities as scientific reserves with limited public access, national parks, natural monuments, nature reserves or wildlife sanctuaries, protected landscapes and areas managed primarily for sustainable use (WB, Terrestrial and marine protected areas (% of total territorial area), 2023). There is a negative relationship between the TMPA value and the AP value. The countries that have a significant endowment of TMPA are also those with lower values in terms of AP. For example, in the top ten countries by TMPA value there are many countries that have a low AP value, such as Palau which has a TMPA value of 99.96 and AP of 6.87, Monaco with a TMPA value of 99.38 and AP of 11.67, Slovenia with a TMPA value of 54.09 and AP of 16.97, Luxembourg with a TMPA value of 51, 18 and AP equal to 10.07, Germany with 38.47 TMPA and AP equal to 11.81.
- *MST*: are mammals excluding whales and porpoises. Threatened species are the number of species classified by the IUCN as threatened, vulnerable, rare, undetermined, endangered or insufficiently known (WB, Mammal species, threatened, 2023). There is a negative relationship between the MST value and the AP value. Specifically, the countries where there is the greatest risk of extinction of mammals are also the countries where there is the highest level of PA. In fact, if we consider the top ten countries by MST value, we can see that among these countries there are some that also have low levels of

AP, namely: Indonesia with MST equal to 191 and AP value equal to 19.11, Madagascar with a MST value equal to 121.00 and a AP value equal to 18.27, Mexico with MST equal to 96.00 and AP equal to 20.39, Brazil with an MST value of 80 and AP equal to 11.63, Malaysia with MST equal to 71.00 and AP equal to 16.46, Australia with MST equal to 63.00 and AP equal to 6.74, Colombia with MST equal to 58.00 and AP equal to 22.12.

The S-component. Below we consider the relationship between the impacts of AP within a set of variables that refer to the S dimension of the ESG model (Table 2).

Table 2. Statistical results for the estimation of AP within the s-component in the ESG model

Statistical Results for the Estimation of AP Within the S-Component in the ESG Model										
		WLS		Pooled OLS		Fixed-Effects		Random-Effects		Average
		Coefficient	P-Values	Coefficient	P-Values	Coefficient	P-Values	Coefficient	P-Values	
Coefficient		4,85148	***	5,94313	***	14,0481	***	5,86046	***	7,675793
Access to electricity (% of population)	AE	-0,116504	***	-0,128266	***	-0,172859	***	-0,163159	***	-0,1452
Cause of death, by communicable diseases and maternal, prenatal and nutrition conditions (% of total)	CD	-0,13509	***	-0,122112	***	-0,183907	***	-0,184552	***	-0,15642
Children in employment, total (% of children ages 7-14)	CE	0,18156	***	0,277667	***	0,132854	**	0,143939	***	0,184005
Labor force participation rate, total (% of total population ages 15-64) (modeled ILO estimate)	LFPR	0,0465654	***	0,0763904	***	0,175866	***	0,152452	***	0,112818
Life expectancy at birth, total (years)	LEB	0,188465	***	0,20006	***	0,181906	***	0,192321	***	0,190688
People using safely managed sanitation services (% of population)	PUS	-0,067558	***	-0,050127	***	-0,348715	***	-0,120678	***	-0,14677
Prevalence of overweight (% of adults)	PO	0,23817	***	0,23339	***	0,295571	***	0,297745	***	0,266219
Prevalence of undernourishment (% of population)	PU	0,235685	***	0,233614	***	0,227397	***	0,224081	***	0,230194

Specifically we have estimated the following equation:

$$AP_{it} = \pm_{it} + {}^{2}{}_{1}(AE)_{it} + {}^{2}{}_{2}(CD)_{it} + {}^{2}{}_{3}(CE)_{it} + {}^{2}{}_{4}(LFPR)_{it} + {}^{2}{}_{5}(PUS)_{it} + {}^{2}{}_{6}(PO)_{it} + {}^{2}{}_{7}(PU)_{it}$$

Where $i = 193$ and $t = [2010; 2019]$.

We found that AP is positively associated to:

- *LFPR:* is the percentage of the population aged 15-64 who are economically active: all people who provide work for the production of goods and services during a given period (WB, Labor force participation rate, total (% of total population ages 15-64) (modeled ILO estimate), 2023). There is a positive relationship between the LFPR value and the AP value. If we look at the top ten countries by LFPR value, it turns out that many of these countries have high levels of PA. For example, Qatar has an LFPR value of 88.19 and an AP value of 76.95, Iceland with an LFPR value of 86.81 and an AP value of 17.86, Tanzania with an LFPR value of 85.13 and an AP value equal to 24.74, United Arab Emirates with a LFPR equal to 83.38 and an AP equal to 43.67, Ethiopia with a level of LFPR equal to 82.34 and a AP level equal to 33.78, Korea Dem. Rep. with an LFPR value of 81.56 and an AP level of 44.33.
- *CE:* are children engaged in economic activities for at least one hour in the reference week of the survey. There is a positive relationship between the CE value and the AP value (WB, Children in employment, total (% of children ages 7-14), 2023). Specifically, it should be considered that countries that have high levels of PA tend to also be countries where the protection of human rights for children is not respected. In fact, in the top ten countries by value of AP we find India, Nepal, Niger, Qatar, Nigeria, Egypt, Mauritania, Cameroon, Bangladesh, and Pakistan.
- *LEB:* indicates the number of years a newborn would live if the prevailing patterns of mortality at the time of its birth remained the same throughout life (WB, Life expectancy at birth, total (years), 2023). There is a positive relationship between the LEB value and the AP value. Specifically, the value of LEB tends to be high in countries that also have a high level of PA. Considering that in 2019 the average LEB value was equal to an amount of 72.23, it turns out that 8 of the 10 countries that have the highest levels of PA also have LEB values above the average, i.e.: Nepal with LEB equal to 82, 11, Qatar with LEB of 75.61, Nigeria with 76.60, Egypt with 72.56, Mauritania with 74.24, Cameroon with 82.23, Bangladesh with 77.26 and Saudi Arabia with 68.53.

- *PU:* is the percentage of the population whose usual food consumption is insufficient to supply the dietary energy levels necessary to maintain a normal, active and healthy life (WB, Prevalence of undernourishment (% of population), 2023). Data shown as 2.5 may indicate an undernourishment prevalence of less than 2.5%. There is a positive relationship between the PU value and the AP value. Malnutrition is very high in countries with high AP. Considering the top 10 countries by value of PA in 2019, we can see that 4 of these have an above-average PU value, i.e.: India with a value of 14.60, Nigeria with 12.00, Bangladesh with 11, and Pakistan with 14.10.
- *PO*: is the percentage of adults aged 18 years and older whose body mass index (BMI) is greater than 25 kg/m2. Body mass index (BMI) is a simple index of weight times height, i.e. weight in kilograms divided by height in meters squared (WB, Prevalence of overweight (% of adults), 2023). There is a positive relationship between the PO value and the PA value. The countries that pollute the most are, on average, also the countries that have a greater presence of PAs.

We found that AP is negatively associated to:

- *CD*: Cause of death refers to the share of all deaths for all ages from underlying causes. Communicable diseases and maternal, prenatal, and nutritional conditions include infectious and parasitic diseases, respiratory infections, and nutritional deficiencies such as underweight and stunting (WB, Cause of death, by communicable diseases and maternal, prenatal and nutrition conditions (% of total), 2023). There is a positive relationship between the CD value and the PA value. Countries that have a high PA value also tend to have a high CD value.
- *PUS*: is the percentage of people using improved sanitation facilities that are not shared with other households and where excreta is safely disposed of on-site or transported and processed off-site. Improved sanitation includes flush/flush of piped sewer systems, septic tanks, or pit latrines: vented improved pit latrines, composite toilets, or slab pit latrines (WB, People using safely managed sanitation services (% of population), 2023). There is a negative relationship between the PUS value and the PA value. The countries that have a higher PUS value also have a lower PA value.
- *AE*: is a variable that represents the value of access to electricity is the percentage of the population that has access to electricity. Electrification data is collected from industry, national surveys and international sources (WB, Access to electricity (% of population), 2023). Specifically, the value of AE is

negatively connected to the value of PA. In particular, the countries that have a higher value of AE also have a lower value of PA.

The G-component. Below we consider the relationship between the impacts of AP within a set of variables that refer to the G-Governance dimension of the ESG model (Table 3).

Table 3. The estimation of AP within the G-component in the context of the ESG model

The Estimation of AP Within the G-Component in the Context of the ESG Model										
		Pooled OLS		Fixed-Effects		Random-Effects		WLS		Average
		Coefficient	P-Values	Coefficient	P-Values	Coefficient	P-Values	Coefficient	P-Values	
Coefficient		19,992	***	16,6448	***	16,2928	***	13,6786	***	16,6521
Individuals using the Internet (% of population)	IUI	-0,10456	***	-0,060044	***	-0,068593	***	-0,1127	***	-0,0865
Net migration	NM	-5,67E-06	***	-2,60E-06	**	-2,91E-06	**	-2,52E-06	**	-3E-06
Proportion of seats held by women in national parliaments (%)	PSW	-0,22236	***	-0,495357	***	-0,413895	***	-0,13687	***	-0,3171
Ratio of female to male labor force participation rate (%) (modeled ILO estimate)	RFTM	0,130608	***	0,251008	***	0,23511	***	0,146595	***	0,19083
Scientific and technical journal articles	STJA	3,38E-05	***	4,71E-05	***	4,24E-05	***	2,13E-05	**	3,6E-05

Specifically we have estimated the following equation:

$$AP_{it} = \alpha_{it} + \beta_1 (IUI)_{it} + \beta_2 (NM)_{it} + \beta_3 (PSW)_{it} + \beta_4 (RFTM)_{it} + \beta_5 (STJA)_{it}$$

Where $i = 193$ and $t = [2010; 2019]$.

We found that AP is positively associated to:

- *RFTM*: is the percentage of the population aged 15 and over who are economically active: all people who provide work for the production of goods and services during a given period. The ratio of female to male labour force participation rates is calculated by dividing the female labour force participation rate by the male labour force participation rate and multiplying by 100 (WB, Ratio of female to male labor force participation rate (%) (modeled ILO estimate), 2023). There is a positive relationship between the RFTM value and the PA. The countries that have higher level of RFTM also have higher levels of PA. There are many countries that show high levels of PA in connection with high levels of RFTM such as for example Niger with an RFTM value of 73.49, Nigeria with an RFTM value of 79.34, and Cameron with an RFTM value of 87.76.

- *STJA*: Scientific and technical journal articles refers to the number of scientific and engineering articles published in the following fields: physics, biology, chemistry, mathematics, clinical medicine, biomedical research, engineering and technology, earth and space sciences (WB, Scientific and technical journal articles, 2023). There is a positive relationship between the STJA value and the PA value. There is a positive relationship between the STJA value and the PA value. Specifically many of the countries that have a high PA value also have above average STJA value such as India with a value of 129.549, Nepal with an amount of 1.003, Qatar with a value of 1.785, Nigeria with a value of 6.476 .13, Egypt with an amount of 15,216, Bangladesh with a value of 5,012.04, and Pakistan with a value of 14,627.

We also found that AP is negatively associated to:

- *NM*: is the number of immigrants minus the number of emigrants, including citizens and non-citizens. There is a negative relationship between the NM value and the PA value (WB, Net Migration, 2023). Specifically, countries that have a high value of NM have a low value of PA and vice versa. For example, 9 of the 10 countries in the top ten for PA value have a negative NM value, i.e.: India with a value of -593495, Nepal with -70597, Niger with -15787, Nigeria with -103989, Egypt with a value of -59715, Mauritania with -3018, Cameroon with -12254 Bangladesh with -344054, Pakistan with -1177218 (Figure 6).

Figure 6. Relationship between PA and NM in 2019

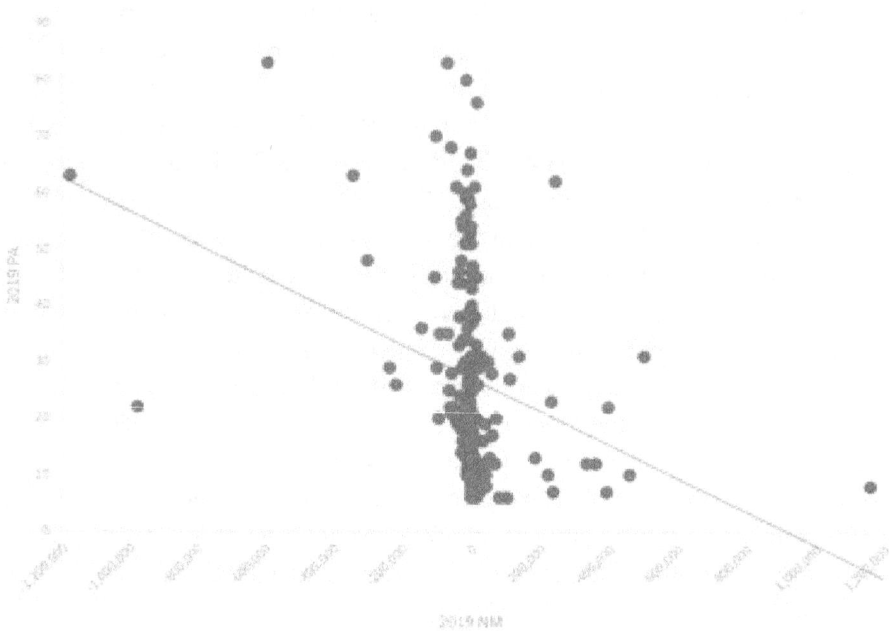

- *IUI*: are individuals who have used the Internet (from anywhere) in the last 3 months. The Internet can be used through a computer, mobile phone, personal digital assistant, gaming machine, digital TV, etc (WB, Individuals using the Internet (% of population), 2023). There is a negative relationship between the IUI value and the BP value. Specifically, countries that have a high level of PA also have a low value of IUI. Considering 2019, about 9 of the 10 countries in the top ten by PA value also have a lower than average IUI value, i.e.: India with an IUI value of 29.52, Nepal with an IUI of 34.81, Niger with IUI 16.61, Nigeria 45.03, Egypt IUI 57.28, Mauritania IUI 42.43, Cameroon IUI 36.54, Bangladesh IUI 27.76, Pakistan with IUI equal to 17.07 (Figure 7).

Figure 7. Relationship between AP and IUI in 2019

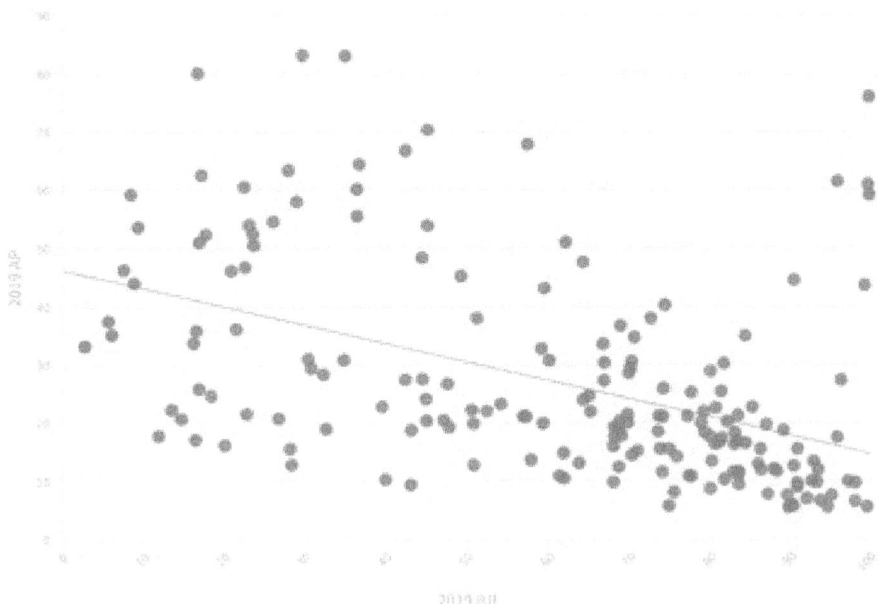

- *PSW*: the percentage of parliamentary seats in a single or lower house held by women. There is a negative relationship between the PWS value and the PA value (WB, Proportion of seats held by women in national parliaments (%), 2023). Specifically, it may be noted that countries that have a high PA value also have a low PWS value. For example, if we look at the top ten countries by PA value in 2019, we can see that many of these countries have a lower PWS value than the industry average. Specifically, the following countries have a lower PWS value despite having a high PA value, i.e. India with a value of 14.39, Niger with 16.95, Qatar with 9.75, Nigeria with 3.3, Egypt with 14, 93, Mauritania with 20.26, Bangladesh with 20.6, Pakistan with 20.2 (Figure 8).

Figure 8. Relationship between PA and PWS

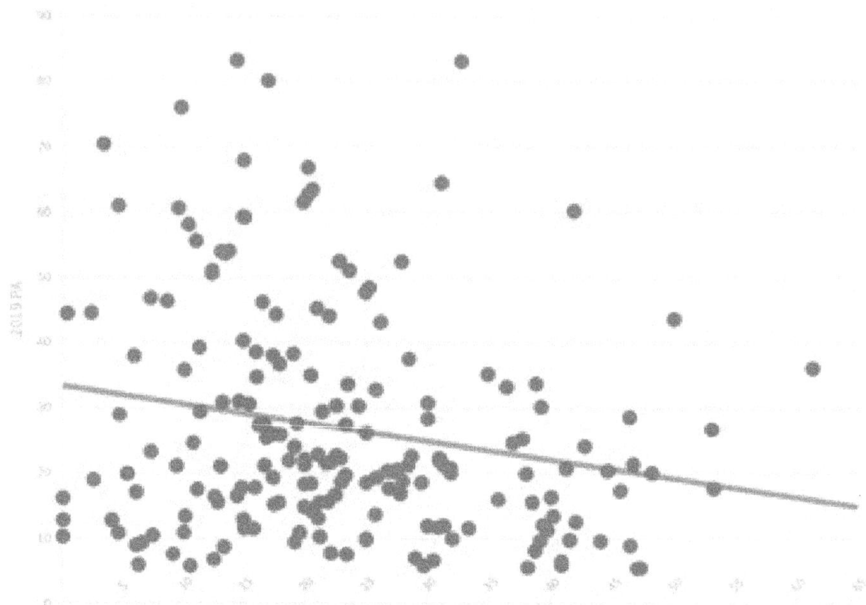

4. MACHINE LEARNING FOR THE PREDICTION OF THE FUTURE VALUE OF AP

In the following analysis, we compare eight different machine-learning algorithms for predicting the future value of the AP value. The algorithms are analysed because of their predictive capacity measured in terms of reduction of statistical errors i.e. MAE, MSE and RMSE and maximization of the R-squared value. Specifically we have estimated the following statistical indicators:

- $$R^2 = 1 - \frac{SumSquaredRegression}{TotalSumOfSquares} = 1 - \frac{\sum(y_i - \hat{y}_i)^2}{\sum(y_i - \bar{y}_i)(y_i - \bar{y}_i)}$$
- $$MAE = \frac{\sum_{i=1}^{n}|y_i - x_i|}{n} = \frac{\sum_{i=1}^{n}|e_i|}{n}$$
- $$MSE = \frac{1}{n}\sum_{i=1}^{n}\left(Y_i - \widehat{Y}_i\right)\left(Y_i - \widehat{Y}_i\right)$$
- $$RMSE = \sqrt{\frac{1}{N}\sum_{i=1}^{N}\left(\widehat{y}_i - y_i\right)\left(\widehat{y}_i - y_i\right)}$$

Each algorithm is assigned a ranking for each ranking analysed. The rankings are then added together. The algorithm that has the lowest total ranking is considered as the best predictor algorithm. To find the best predictor algorithm we have estimated the following formula:

$$\boldsymbol{BestPredictor} = \boldsymbol{Rank}_{min(MSE)} + \boldsymbol{Rank}_{min(RMSE)} + \boldsymbol{Rank}_{min(MAE)} + \boldsymbol{Rank}_{max(R^2)}$$

The algorithms were trained with 70% of the available data while the remaining 30% was used for the actual prediction. The following ordering of the algorithms is found (Figure 9):

- *Polynomial Regression* with a payoff equal to 5;
- *Linear Regression* with a payoff equal to 7;
- *Gradient Boosted Trees* with a payoff value of 12;
- *Random Forest* with a payoff value of 16;
- *Tree Ensemble* with a payoff value of 20;
- *PNN-Probabilistic Neural Network* with a payoff value of 24;
- *ANN-Artificial Neural Network* with a payoff value of 29;
- *Simple Regression Tree* with a payoff value of 31.

Figure 9. Ranking of algorithms for the value of their predictive performance

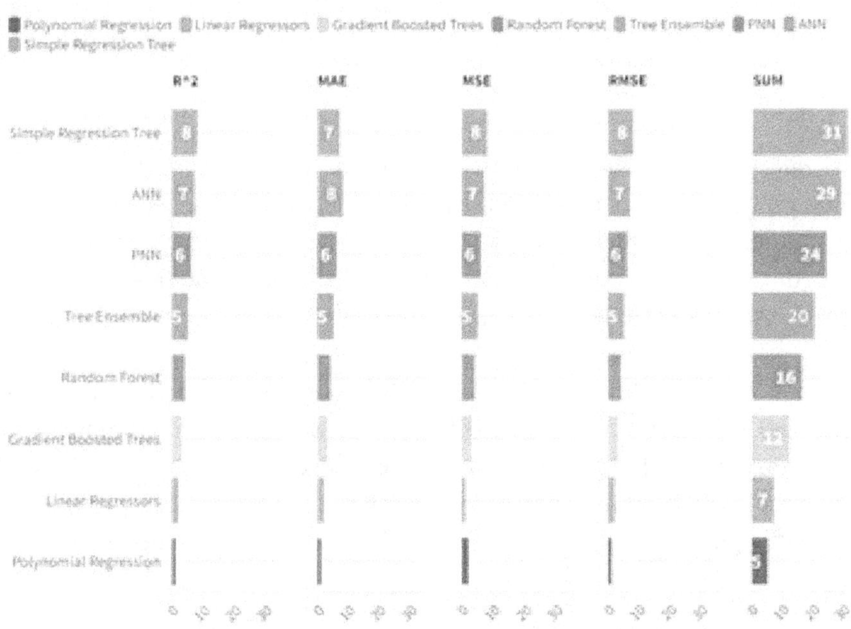

As we can see from the comparative analysis of the algorithms, it results that the best predictor algorithm is Polynomial Regression. Therefore, it is possible to use the Polynomial Regression algorithm to predict the future value of AP. It is therefore possible to identify two different types of countries, namely the winning countries and the losing countries. The winning countries are those countries for which the reduction in the value of AP is predicted. Losing countries are the countries for which growth in the value of AP is predicted (Figure 10).

Figure 10. Statistical errors of algorithms applied to predict the future value of PA

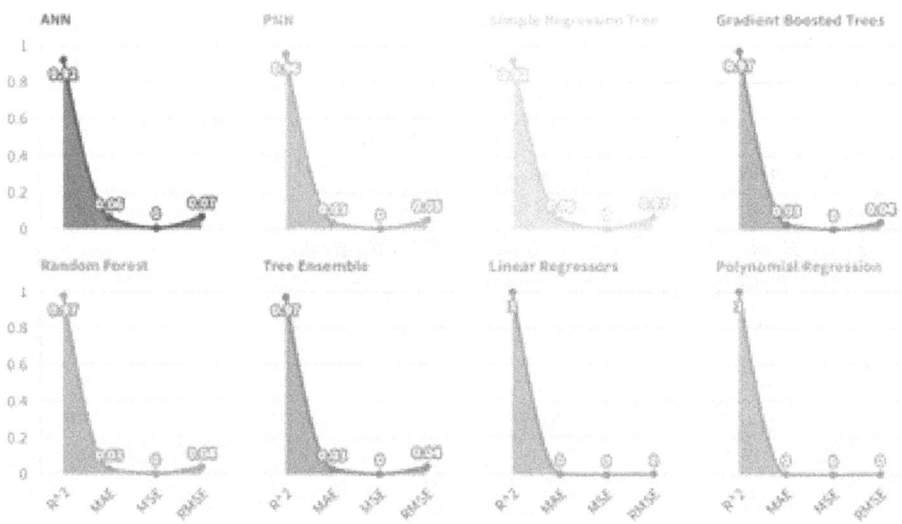

Losing countries. Through the application of the Polynomial Regression algorithm, the following countries are identified which are considered losers because the algorithm predicts a reduction in the value of AP. The countries for which the value of AP is predicted to grow, i.e.: Lesotho with +2.13%, Serbia with +0.9%, Egypt with +0.81%, Angola with +0.74%, Jamaica with +0, 68%, Iraq and Papua New Guinea with +0.49%, Bosnia and Herzegovina with +0.46%, Samoa with +0.44%, Grenada with +0.33%, China with +0.30%, Barbados with +0.28%, Equatorial Guinea with +0.17%, Dominica with +0.15%, Niger with 0.07%. We can note that all the countries for which a growth in the value of PA is predicted have values of reduced per capita income. Furthermore, the value of AP grows also because of the presence of significant oil extraction activities such as, for example, in the case of Iraq in some countries. For example, countries like Lesotho that are landlocked can have high levels of air pollution (Figure 11).

Figure 11. List of losing countries i.e. countries for which is predicted an increase in the level of PA

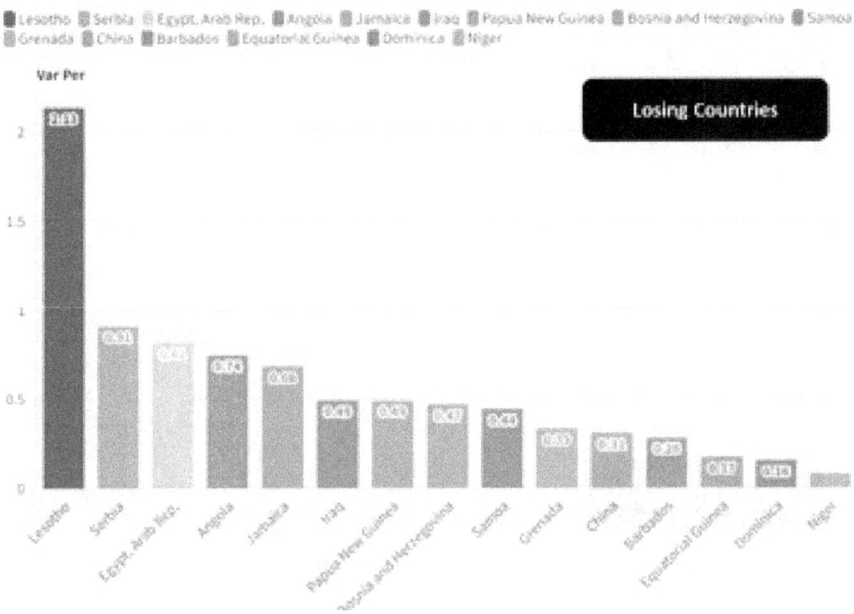

Winning countries. Through the application of the Polynomial Regression algorithm it is possible to identify a set of countries that are winning countries or countries for which a reduction in the value of AP is predicted. Reductions in the value of AP are predicted for the following countries: Yemen with -0.009%, Liberia with -0.13%, Chad with -0.17%, Palau with -0.20%, Turkmenistan with -0.22%, Mauritania with -0.30%, Bhutan with -0.35%, Kuwait with -0.36%, Senegal with -0.41%, Ghana with -0.42%, Cameroon with -0.45%, Costa Rica with -0.46%, Finland with -0.46%, Marshall Islands with -0.488%, Kyrgyz Republic with -0.54%, Brunei Darussalam with -0.54%, Israel with -0.59%, United Kingdom with -0.73%, Thailand with -0.91%, Lao with -0.92%, Norway with -1.21%, Maldives with -1.24%, Sao Tome and Principe with -1.53%, Portugal with -1.68%. We can note that many of the countries for which a reduction in the value of AP is predicted are high per capita income countries such as Finland, Israel, United Kingdom, Norway, Portugal, and Kuwait. This condition could suggest the application of the empirical rule of the Environmental Kutznets Curve-EKC. However, among the countries for which a reduction in the value of PA is predicted, there are also countries with medium-low per capita incomes such as Cameroon, Liberia, Turkmenistan, Senegal, Mauritania. It follows that the reduction of PA emissions must not simply be an option for middle-upper income countries, it can also be an opportunity for countries with low per capita incomes, in line with historical environmental trends (Figure 12).

Figure 12. List of winning countries i.e. countries for which it is predicted an increase in the level of PA

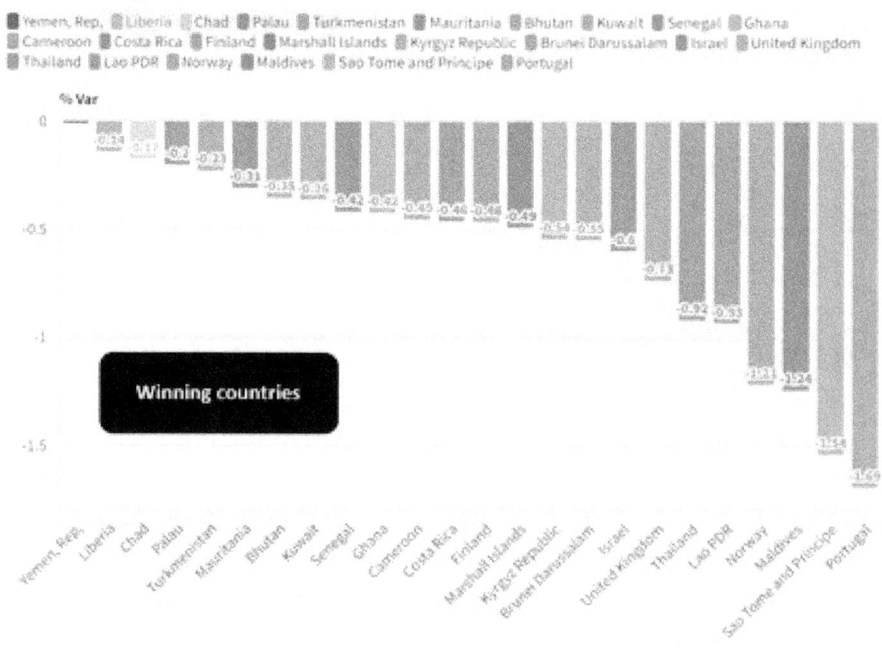

5. CONCLUSION

In the following article, we analyze the role of Air Pollution-AP in the context of ESG-Environmental, Social and Governance model. We analysed data from the World Bank's ESG database for a set of 193 countries over the period 2011-2020. We evaluated the impact of AP on each of the three dimensions of the ESG model: E-Environment, S-Social and G-Governance. We found that AP is negatively associated to each of the three elements of the ESG level at aggregate level. In absolute level is positively associated, among others, to "*Cooling Degree Days*", "*CO_2 Emissions*", and "*Agriculture, forestry, and fishing, value added*" and negatively associated, among others, to "*Terrestrial and Marine Protected Areas*", "*Proportion* *of seats held by women in national parliaments*". We also compared eight different machine learning algorithms for predicting the future value of AP. The best performing algorithm is Polynomial Regression. On average, the value of AP is predicted to grow for the countries analysed. From the point of view of economic policies, it is necessary to consider that countries that have high levels of air pollution tend to have difficulties both in implementing green innovations and in promoting green legislations. It follows that the investment in the education of human and social capital is necessary to create a "*green conscience*" capable of supporting legislative and technological interventions that can reduce polluting emissions even in countries with low per capita income.

6. DECLARATIONS

Data Availability Statement. The data presented in this study are available on request from the corresponding author.

Funding. The authors received no financial support for the research, authorship, and/or publication of this article.

Declaration of Competing Interest. The authors declare that there is no conflict of interests regarding the publication of this manuscript. In addition, the ethical issues, including plagiarism, informed consent, misconduct, data fabrication and/ or falsification, double publication.

Software. The authors have used the following software: Gretl for the econometric models, Orange for clusterization and network analysis, and KNIME for machine learning and predictions. They are all free version without licenses.

Acknowledgements. We are grateful to the teaching staff of the LUM University "Giuseppe Degennaro" and to the management of the LUM Enterprise s.r.l. for the constant inspiration to continue our scientific research work undeterred.

REFERENCES

Barabanov, S. S., Basnet, A., Walker, T. J., Yuan, W., & Wendt, S. (2021). Firm-and country-level determinants of green investments: An empirical analysis. *Managerial Finance*, *47*(11), 1672–1692. doi:10.1108/MF-06-2020-0311

Costantiello, A., & and Leogrande, A. (2023). *The Determinants of CO2 Emissions in the Context of ESG*. Academic Press.

CostantielloA.LeograndeA. (2023). The Impact of Research and Development Expenditures on ESG Model in the Global Economy. SSRN(4414232). doi:10.2139/ssrn.4414232

CostantielloA.LeograndeA. (2023). The Role of Political Stability in the Context of ESG Models at World Level. SSRN (4406997). doi:10.2139/ssrn.4406997

Fiorillo, P., Meles, A., Mustilli, M., & Salerno, D. (2022). How does the financial market influence firms' Green innovation? The role of equity analysts. *Journal of International Financial Management & Accounting*, *33*(3), 428–458. doi:10.1111/jifm.12152

Francová, O., Korhonen, K., & Kovačević, D. (2022). *How programme evaluations can benefit from quality of life considerations*. European Stability Mechanism.

Giannetti, M., Jasova, M., Loumioti, M., & Mendicino, C. (2023). *"Glossy Green" Banks: The Disconnect Between Environmental Disclosures and Lending Activities*. Academic Press.

Gu, Y., Ho, K. C., Yan, C., & Gozgor, G. (2021). Public environmental concern, CEO turnover, and green investment: Evidence from a quasi-natural experiment in China. *Energy Economics*, *100*(105379), 100. doi:10.1016/j.eneco.2021.105379

HeX.XuZ.ShiJ. (2023). The Impact of Air Pollution Levels on Chinese Green Bond Market during COVID-19: A Green Preference Perspective. SSRN (4329551). doi:10.2139/ssrn.4329551

Hospido, L., Sanz, C., & Villanueva, E. (2023). Air pollution: a review of its economic effects and policies to mitigate them. *Banco de Espana Occasionally Paper*(2301).

Laureti, L., Costantiello, A., & Leogrande, A. (2022). *The Role of Renewable Energy Consumption in Promoting Sustainability and Circular Economy. A Data-Driven Analys*. Academic Press.

LeograndeA.CostantielloA. (2023). The Labor Force Participation Rate in the Context of ESG Models at World Level. SSRN (4466452). doi:10.2139/ssrn.4466452

Lu, P., Hamori, S., & Tian, S. (2023). Can ESG investments and new environmental law improve social happiness in China? *Frontiers in Environmental Science*, *11*(1089486), 1089486. doi:10.3389/fenvs.2023.1089486

Park, J., Park, Y., Yoo, J. L., Yue, G., & Yu, J. (2022). Can the perceived risk of particulate matter change people's desires and behavior intentions? *Frontiers in Public Health*, *10*(1035174), 1035174. doi:10.3389/fpubh.2022.1035174 PMID:36466525

Ruiz-Guerra, I., Molina-Moreno, V., Cortés-García, F. J., & Núñez-Cacho, P. (2019). Prediction of the impact on air quality of the cities receiving cruise tourism: The case of the Port of Barcelona. *Heliyon*, *5*(2), e01280. doi:10.1016/j.heliyon.2019.e01280 PMID:30923758

Shen, Y., Lyu, M., & Zhu, J. (2022). Air pollution and corporate green financial constraints: Evidence from China's listed companies. *International Journal of Environmental Research and Public Health*, *22*(15034), 19. doi:10.3390/ijerph192215034 PMID:36429753

Song, J. M. (2023). *Air pollution, regulations on emission and firms' social responsibility*. Singapore Management University.

WB. (2023a). *Access to electricity (% of population)*. https://data.worldbank.org/indicator/EG.ELC.ACCS.ZS

WB. (2023b). *Agricultural land (% of land area)*. https://data.worldbank.org/indicator/AG.LND.AGRI.ZS

WB. (2023c). *Agriculture, forestry, and fishing, value added (% of G)*. https://data.worldbank.org/indicator/NV.AGR.TOTL.ZS

WB. (2023d). *Annual freshwater withdrawals, total (% of internal resources)*. https://data.worldbank.org/indicator/ER.H2O.FWTL.ZS

WB. (2023e). *Cause of death, by communicable diseases and maternal, prenatal and nutrition conditions (% of total)*. https://data.worldbank.org/indicator/SH.DTH.COMM.ZS

WB. (2023)f. *Children in employment, total (% of children ages 7-14)*. 27, 2023 da https://data.worldbank.org/indicator/SL.TLF.0714.ZS

WB. (2023g). *CO2 emissions (metric tons per capita)*. https://data.worldbank.org/indicator/EN.ATM.CO2E.PC

WB. (2023h). *Energy imports, net (% of energy use)*. https://data.worldbank.org/indicator/EG.IMP.CONS.ZS

WB. (2023i). *Energy use (kg of oil equivalent per capita)*. https://data.worldbank.org/indicator/EG.USE.PCAP.KG.OE

WB. (2023j). *Food production index (2014-2016 = 100)*. https://data.worldbank.org/indicator/AG.PRD.FOOD.XD

WB. (2023k). *Fossil fuel energy consumption (% of total)*. https://data.worldbank.org/indicator/EG.USE.COMM.FO.ZS

WB. (2023l). *Individuals using the Internet (% of population).* https://data.worldbank.org/indicator/IT.NET.USER.ZS

WB. (2023m). *Labor force participation rate, total (% of total population ages 15-64) (modeled ILO estimate).* World Bank.

WB. (2023n). *Life expectancy at birth, total (years).* https://data.worldbank.org/indicator/SP.DYN.LE00.IN

WB. (2023o). *Mammal species, threatened.* https://data.worldbank.org/indicator/EN.MAM.THRD.NO

WB. (2023p). *Net Migration.* https://data.worldbank.org/indicator/SM.POP.NETM

WB. (20231). *People using safely managed sanitation services (% of population).* https://data.worldbank.org/indicator/SH.STA.SMSS.ZS

WB. (2023r). *Prevalence of overweight (% of adults).* https://genderdata.worldbank.org/indicators/sh-sta-owad-zs/

WB. (2023s). *Prevalence of undernourishment (% of population).* https://data.worldbank.org/indicator/SN.ITK.DEFC.ZS

WB. (2023t). *Proportion of seats held by women in national parliaments (%).*https://data.worldbank.org/indicator/SG.GEN.PARL.ZS

WB. (2023u). *Ratio of female to male labor force participation rate (%) (modeled ILO estimate).* https://data.worldbank.org/indicator/SL.TLF.CACT.FM.ZS

WB. (2023v). *Renewable energy consumption (% of total final energy consumption).* https://data.worldbank.org/indicator/EG.FEC.RNEW.ZS

WB. (2023w). *Scientific and technical journal articles.* https://data.worldbank.org/indicator/IP.JRN.ARTC.SC

WB. (2023x). *Terrestrial and marine protected areas (% of total territorial area).* https://data.worldbank.org/indicator/ER.PTD.TOTL.ZS

Xue, S., Zhang, B., & Zhao, X. (2021). Brain drain: The impact of air pollution on firm performance. *Journal of Environmental Economics and Management, 110*(102546), 102546. doi:10.1016/j.jeem.2021.102546

Yang, Z., & Broby, D. (2020). *Sustainable Finance: AI Applications in Satellite Imagery and Data.* Financail Technology Paper.

Chapter 5
Critical Analysis of Emerging and Disruptive Digital Technologies in an Era of Artificial Intelligence

José G. Vargas-Hernandez
Budapest Centre for Long-term Sustainability, Hungary

Omar C. Vargas-Gonzàlez
https://orcid.org/0000-0002-6089-956X
Instituto Tecnològico Nacional de Mèxico, Ciudad Guzmàn, Mexico

ABSTRACT

This study aims to analyze the emergent and disruptive digital technologies in an era of artificial intelligence. It departs from the assumption that the emerging technologies create both opportunities and challenges with an impact on individuals, organizations, institutions, and society at large in terms of bias, surveillance, hacking, etc. The method employed is the critical analysis based on the recent developments reported in scientific literature. It is concluded that control over the ethical disruption of digital technologies and more specifically artificial strategy must require a digital conversation and leadership about acceptable ethical behaviors, under the assumption that digital transformation cannot be interrupted and must be guided by humans in in following years of the near future.

DOI: 10.4018/979-8-3693-1151-6.ch005

1. INTRODUCTION

A. I Can Do Everything for You!

Human development in recent decades has been accompanied by emergent and rapid disruptive technological changes leading to a growing proliferation of digitized devices and services. Emergent and disruptive digital technologies have become intrinsic to our current way for life and will be part of our future lifestyle, from mundane routines and activities to improvement of productive, contributing to manage the requirements of an economic growth in a more competitive and dynamic environment, and evaluating the balance of power for a more collective security.

Artificial intelligence (AI) has a significant impact on individuals, organizations, and societies by offering systematic capabilities of learning and reasoning based on inputs and the differences with the expected outputs, predicting and adapting to changes in the socio-ecosystems from its received external environment stimulus. Artificial intelligence is a digital transformation lead using emerging technologies that have broken into all areas and sectors worldwide leading to get benefits in terms of agility, efficiency, transparency, and social welfare, so it can be affirmed that the emerging and disruptive digital technologies play a preponderant role in our environment and can do everything for us!

B. Smart Life on Everything

Artificial intelligence (AI), internet of things (IoT), blockchain and Chat GPT, among others, are emergent and disruptive digital technologies that aid human beings and societies in quick and efficient way to increase economic productivity, support the social wellbeing by providing a more educated, productive and healthier lifestyle of individuals, anticipate and prevent responses to crisis and disasters, absorbing shocks, etc. (Sharifi, Khavarian-Garmsir, & Kummitha, 2021). An increased level of research in chatbots designed to respond to queries of the user by mapping the best possible response in real time feedback, are based on adopted language models and deep learning to address natural language processes (NLP) (Lokman & Ameedeen, 2018; Kushwaha & Kar, 2021).

2. TRANSFORMATIVE EFFECTS OF IOT, BLOCKCHAIN, ARTIFICIAL INTELLIGENCE, AND CHAT GPT ON CLOUD COMPUTING: EVOLUTION, VISION, TRENDS, AND OPEN CHALLENGES

The pace of change is likely to accelerate because of the "frontier technologies" that are redefining our world, taking advantage of digitization and connectivity, include artificial intelligence (AI), big data, blockchain, the Internet of Things (IoT), 3D printing, robotics, drones, biotechnology, and nanotechnology. Emerging and disruptive technologies evolution has become the buzzword of the current economic and productivity growth, geopolitical landscape, and security architecture, to build resilience leading to conclude that there is a strong link between them. The design of future digital technologies is bound to change the technological socio-ecosystem and the society at large.

Organizations and states remain the major actors in technological innovation designing and implementing policies, strategies, tactics, and instruments, although the leading technological edge is currently and will be lead in the future by private firms, university research centers and academia while extending the possibility to involve the whole of society approach in operations.

The emerging technologies create both opportunities and challenges with an impact on individuals, organizations, institutions, and society at large in terms of bias, surveillance, hacking, etc. Digital technologies enhance economic, societal, and socio-ecological resilience in terms of health, education, connectivity, communication, etc.

Innovation and competition are the drivers of an emerging and disruptive digital technologies raising challenges and threats based on dynamic and organic processes that require creative destruction of established technologies and industries that takes considerable time in revealing its true features and ultimate effects (Schumpeter, 1949, 1994). Thus, the organic process of creative destruction applies to a new cycle of emerging and disrupting digital technologies that will win the competition leading to the entire transformation of the technological socio-ecosystem.

A positive impact of these technologies is the promotion of resilience with the identification of maintenance needs by inspecting critical infrastructure leading to respond to the emergencies with assistance of recovery efforts in crises and disasters, for example.

3. WHY IS THE DIGITAL ERA GOING WRONG? WHO CONTROLS THE FUTURE?

Any emergent technological outcome is a neutral tool before receiving connotations depending on how is being used. However, in this era of emerging and disruptive digital technologies we are witnessing heated debates on legal frameworks, standards, recommendations, methods, practices, problems, etc., marked by lack of agreement among the main actors due to divergent interests for control without a clear how to provide solutions.

Emerging, and disruptive digital technologies such as big data, biotechnologies, quantum, autonomous systems require separate international standardization principles of responsible use, which may require various regulatory levels in the space domains. However, the debate on whether ChatGPT's use must be restricted, legislated, and regulated is split. Technological innovation must be stalled by global standards to ensure performance and interoperability between the different emerging technological socio-ecosystems. In the elaboration of this standards must be driven by global governance mechanisms with the participation of other sectors such as private sector and academia.

Obviously, it is difficult to know how far human evil can go, incapacity and stupidity. Suffice it to remember that the largest sources of profit are related to death: war and drugs. Thus, the human being does not seem very trustworthy, as stated by Marín (2023).

A. Artificial Intelligence Focuses on Automation Not on Creating Jobs and Not on the Impact of Creating the Greatest Value

The focus of emerging and disruptive digital technologies has been on automation and not in creating jobs must be amended. Artificial intelligence has been focused on automation and this focus should be changed to the net increase of jobs and job creation. The focus of long term artificial intelligence directions must have an impact on the greatest value of implementation by augmenting people in the jobs, enrichment of jobs and tasks, reimagine and redefine old tasks to create new job activities and transform culture to adapt artificial intelligence threats into new opportunities.

Warnings of job losses confuse artificial intelligence with automation overshadowing the augmentation benefit of a combination and complementation of human and artificial intelligence, where both combine and complement each other. Artificial intelligence has already a negative impact on the workplace by applying to highly repeatable routine tasks requiring copious quantities of data observations and decisions to be analyzed searching for patterns.

Applying artificial intelligence to less-routine with low repeatability and more varied tasks is yielding higher benefits in job creation and greater value. Using auto-generative artificial intelligence have different impacts depending on the industry sector such as to select data or curing diseases. The retailing industry sector is already expanding digital technology, artificial intelligence and human operation activities aimed to improve productivity the in-store check-out process while creating greater value. Applying artificial intelligence to nonroutine tasks tends to combine and complement humans and machines each other to perform more efficiently than either human experts or AI-driven devices and machines working alone.

Investments in artificial intelligence-enable technologies must evaluate the jobs lost, job creation and transformation of co-working collaboration and decision making processes between workers and digital technologies. Technological innovations are associated with a transition period of job loss followed by a recovery. Affected jobs by artificial intelligence varies according to the industry sector with manufacturing and services such as education and healthcare hit the hardest by eliminating middle- and low-level positions, but also creating more new positions of highly skilled, management, the entry-level and low-skilled variety.

Research suggests consumers still prefer the interaction with a knowledgeable human salesperson than using artificial intelligence in more specialized areas who make a significant impact on customer satisfaction. These efforts of applying artificial intelligence and robotics in retailing to replace human tasks prove not be successful to eliminate this job at all despite that operational activities are disrupted, reducing labor, making labor savings, and prompting to reinvest on training to enhance customer experience and satisfaction, creating higher value.

The impact of artificial intelligence and digital technologies in outsourcing are pressured to fundamental changes aimed to reinvent and invest on business models with the symbiosis of human activities instead of only automating practices to create new business opportunities. Improvement of nonroutine work by applying artificial intelligence and robotics must concentrate on leveraging knowledge of digital technologies about general purpose tools to be incorporated into work processes leading to develop a competitive relationship of intelligent employee-robot automation processes to identify and optimize labor-intensive and repetitive activities currently performed by humans.

This improvement resulting from expanding digital technologies, applying artificial intelligence and robotics combined and complemented with humans increment elevated levels of productivity, reducing labor costs and the most important, crate higher levels of value with the creation of new jobs. The entire decision process based on the interaction between human and machines driven by artificial intelligence and other digital technologies must be redesigned to have the advantage of combining and complementing strengths each other to increase agility and optimize the value creation.

Automation, robotics, artificial intelligence, and other digital technologies have a multiplier effect which requires to redefine and create more jobs to create higher value than displacing and killing them, to the extent that should augment the workforce, increasing the productivity and quality of their work, freeing up time to be employed on more strategic priorities. Artificial intelligence, robotics and other digital technologies improves the productivity of many jobs that already has become a positive motivator. Artificial intelligence, robotics, and automation in manufacturing as in any other sectors rather than removing humans from task processes, contribute to augment customer experiences of workers leading to improve productivity by reducing costs, reducing frictions in value chains, optimizing supply chains, and creating higher value opportunities.

B. ChatGPT Could Make These Jobs Obsolete: "The Wolf Is at the Door"

The subtitle of this section is taken from Mitchell (2023) on a recent article of analysis, which I borrowed because it is very illustrative of the situation. Concerned with the emergence of a disruptive tool ChatGPT capabilities, surprising intelligent chat bot upended from and based on artificial intelligence, which since its release on the 30th of November 2022, proving to be a tool with capabilities to perform complex tasks and simplify them (Sagarikabiswas, 2023). Higher education, finance and banking, hospitality and tourism, and information technology industries are sectors in which artificial intelligence and its most recent tool ChatGPT are enhancing business management and marketing activities, among others (Yogesh, et al. (2023).

A competing battle is taking place between artificial intelligence chatbots already released such as ChatGPT, BARD powered by Google, Microsoft-powered Bing, ChatSonic and Ernie powered by China's Baidu App, which are leading to employees and workers to dreadful feelings of losing or getting replaced on their jobs.

OpenAI-powered ChatGPT and released GPT-4 fueling fear among the informational technology due to the replacement of programmers and other informational technology professionals by current ongoing massive layoffs (Sagarikabiswas, 2023). OpenAI's ChatGPT extends the capabilities through the integration of natural language models and deep learning based on a Generative Pre-training Transformer (GPT) architecture (Radford et al., 2018) of neural networks aimed to predict the sequence of words in human interactions through generative and discriminative algorithms (Vaswani et al., 2017) used to generate responses to queries that resembles a human expert.

The ChatGPT system is designed on a huge data set and continually improves itself using a simple text prompt to generate the ability to work through any problem and answer to any question with certain varying accuracy depending on its task Experts and analysts are warning that the improvement of these and other capabilities of the ChatGPT tool could spell doom for numerous job fields in industry.

According to the analysis of (Sagarikabiswas, 2023) by April of 2023, 503 technological companies worldwide have laid off 1,39,165 employees in 2023, in part due to the release of the artificial intelligence chatbot. However, other analysts such as Goldman Sachs, are more pessimistic concluding that at least three hundred million jobs are getting obsolete and replaced. Technology engineering and software design has undergone massive staff layoffs at the Silicon Valley (figure 1). Large firms like Microsoft have announced a large investment in the revolutionary technology of artificial intelligence replacing a substantial portion of its global well-paid white-collar workforce while leaving many employees and industries currently vulnerable, from the financial, health care and publishing sectors. Microsoft has already laid off thousands of workers (Mitchell, 2023).

Large firms, such as Microsoft left out of work ten thousand employees while at the same time investing on partnership with OpenAI to accelerate artificial intelligence breakthroughs in abroad set of products aimed to drive growth (Potter, 2023). Other technological firms going through the layoff of white collar employees to achieve cost-cutting measures, includes Amazon, Facebook, Apple, and Meta (Figure 1)

Figure 1. The job losses across the Silicon Valley (Potter, 2023)

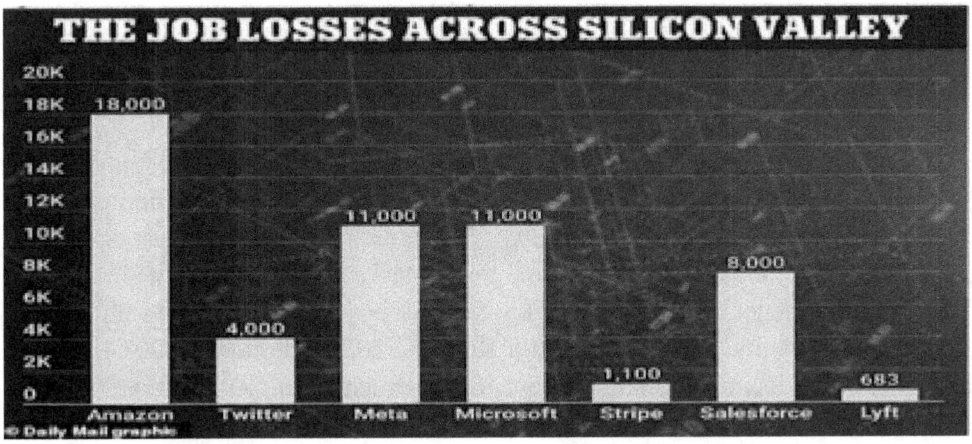

Technology analysts and experts are warning that the artificial intelligence tool ChatGPT are making white collar jobs obsolete and putting millions of people out of work (Potter, 2023). Humans must learn how to harness ChatGPT as a mind-blowing tool of the artificial intelligence technology which is rocking practices on the academia and social media, and leading to the risk that jobs in certain sectors can be supplemented and even replaced such as high education, financial services, journalism, software design engineering and graphics, etc, just to mention some of the affected sectors.

However, the efficient performance of ChatGPT in finding answers to complex questions and solutions to difficult problems in many working tasks and diverse roles of professional fields, there are some tasks and jobs requiring human interaction and empathy, critical thinking, and creativity that artificial intelligence cannot replace. Artificial intelligence cannot replace humans before it has consciousness, autonomy, the ability to act with intent, creativity.

There are some job roles that artificial intelligence is not able to replace in the current and future scenarios. Some of these jobs analyzed by Sagarikabiswas (2023) are programming, hardware technology, network engineering, cyber security analysis, risk analysis, project management and information technology training, among others.

Using ChatGPT is transforming the nature of work, in terms of knowledge, capabilities, competencies and roles of employees. Due to the disruptions already created ChatGPT as it stands today has been already banned or blocked the access in some schools concerned over cheating actions.

C. Consequences of Automation for Jobs, Wages, and Inequality

Automation reduces human intervention in job performance by creating machines capable of replacing human attributes in the execution of more complex and repetitive operations with more certainty and security to work more efficiently by reproducing human tasks and leading to fully substitute workers in some cases.

Regarding research on the effects of automation, many studies forecast that in the following next years there will be a huge job destruction, reduction of wages and thus an increasing level of inequality. (See figures 2 and 3). Automation is often associated with job destruction. Automation of tasks will change with advances in artificial intelligence (Acemoglu, Hazell, & Restrepo (2022). Following automation is a decline in routine jobs (Acemoglu & Restrepo 2020; Humlum, 2020). Research on automation documents that is easier to implement it in routine tasks (Levy & Murnane, 2003) (Figure 2 and 3).

Figure 2. Existing jobs at potential risk of automation (PwC estimates based on OECD PIAAC data median values for 29 countries)

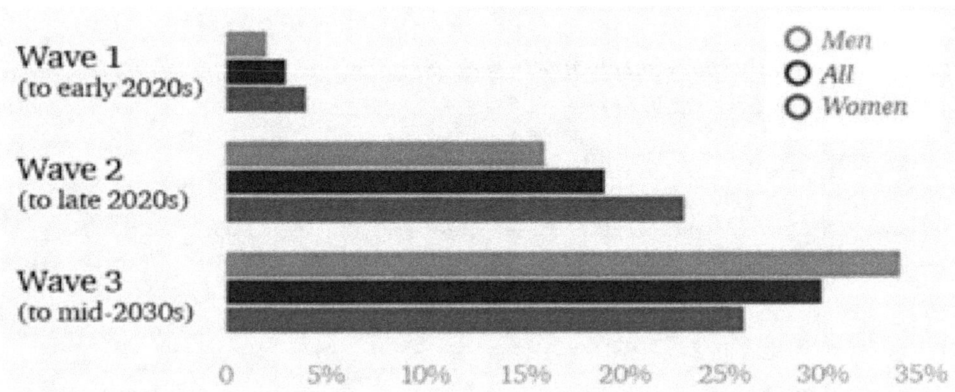

Figure 3. Existing jobs at potential risk of automation (PwC estimates based on OECD PIAAC data median values for 29 countries)

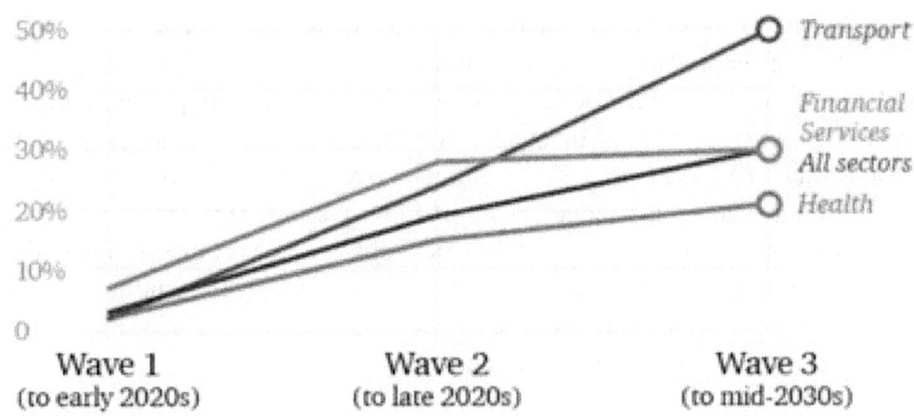

Digital automation technologies tend to expand the tasks performed by the efficient capital, while displacing jobs of certain worker groups for which they have comparative advantage or by reducing the relative, and real, wages of workers specialized in routine tasks in manufacturing industries undergoing digital automation, such as the blue-collar jobs and clerical workers. In contrast, workers with post-graduate studies not displaced from their jobs have wage gains. Wage inequality is rising sharply among the worker groups specialized in routine tasks in routine tasks of industries in economies experiencing rapid automation over the last decades (Acemoglu & Restrepo, 2022) (Figure 4).

Figure 4. Cumulative per cent change in real annual wages, by wage group in United States (Mishel & Bivens, 2021)

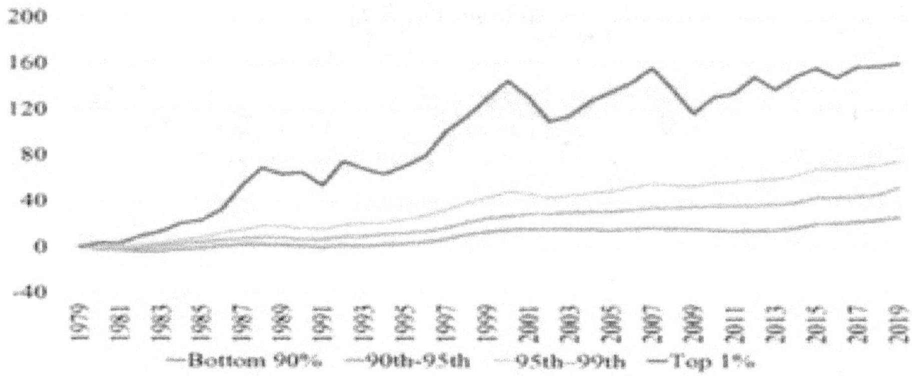

Wage inequality is the result of task displacement, rather than productivity growth and overall capital intensity. According to Acemoglu & Restrepo (2022) task displacement of workers driven by automation from employment opportunities has a defined role in the surge of wage inequality over the last decades. A model designed and developed by Brito & Curl, (2020) with data from 1984 to 2016 demonstrates that the most important consequence of automation is to lower the share of workers in real wages of medium-skilled and low-skilled jobs in domestic production which has steadily declined. Task allocation to diverse types of capital, labor and automation technologies expands tasks performance of capital at the expense of workers. Tax displacement leads to increase in wage inequality.

D. Generative AI Can Reverse Long-Term Trends on Inequality, Worker Power, and Productivity Growth

Artificial intelligence may reverse the trends of slowing global productivity, increasing the gap of inequality, and diminishing the worker power, undermining advancement of living standards. The living standards of people determines the wealth of nations which can be raised by lifting productivity, as the amount of output produced per worker.

Productivity is barely growing and will continue for some years due to economic and geopolitical uncertainty and the rising capital costs leading to holdback increases in economic growth and wages while widening the gap of inequality. Workplace shifts due to pandemic and investments into generative artificial intelligence eventually will produce compelling results unleashing an era of productivity growth despite that will take more than a decade to reap the benefits. There is an optimism on the use of digital technologies for the creation and development of new business models and workers switching tasks and jobs to yield better results in increasing productivity, augmenting wages, and reducing the inequality wage gap.

The implementation of the diverse tools of artificial intelligence in the productivity revolution will take a long-term period to pay off (Strauss, June 4, 2023)

Artificial intelligence tools like ChatGPT are easy to adopt ensuring integration with other everyday use apps, which can amplify inequality of resource access leading to asymmetric use and marginalizing groups that will not have represented data (Chen and Wellman, 2004; Weissglass, 2022).

Gopinath (Jun 5, 2023) from the International Monetary Fund foresees a boost of economic growth and benefits workers raising productivity by automating cognitive tasks and giving rise to new higher-productivity tasks to perform with machines taking care of routine and repetitive tasks. Humans could spend more time on being creative innovators and analytical people. Artificial Intelligence can spread the knowledge of experienced and productive workers. (Figure 5)

Figure 5. The trend of productivity growth has been lower since fiscal crisis (The Conference Board)

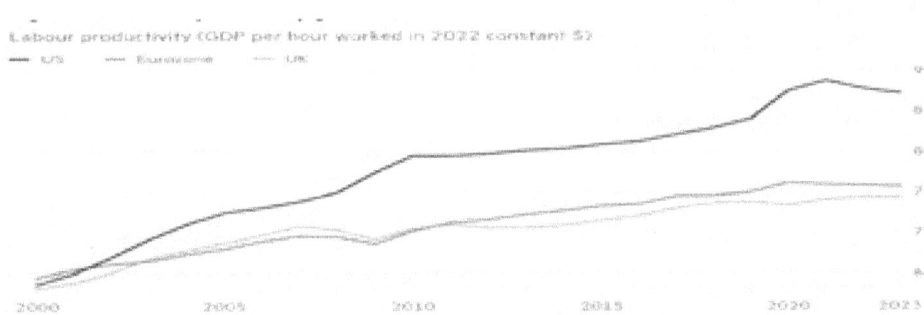

The potential of generative artificial intelligence as more tools are developed, brings about sweeping changes to the global economy, driving about 7%, or almost $7 trillion increase in global GDP lifting productivity growth by about 1.5 percentage points over a 10-year period. Generative AI tools could enhance productivity at office, sales, design building, manufacturing parts, improving healthcare in patient diagnosis, cyber fraud detection, etc. benefiting the global economy. (Figure 6).

Figure 6. AI's impact on labor productivity on its capability and adoption timeline. Effect of AI adoption on annual labor productivity growth, 10-year adoption period (Sacks, 2023)

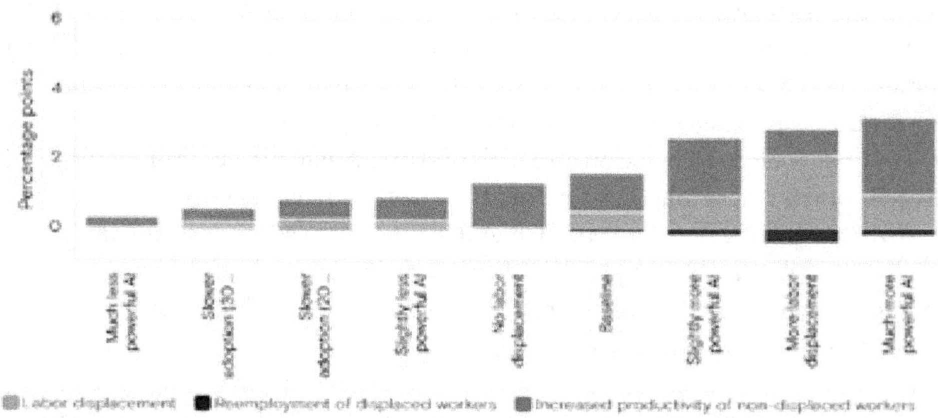

E. Surveillance intensifies

A negative impact of the emerging technologies may be the empowerment of malicious actions and the erosion of individual privacy.

4. ACTIONS TO REDIRECT TECHNOLOGICAL INNOVATION AND CHANGE

A. Change the Narrative

At international level, the discussion on the standardization in the present of future digital technologies exists between communities considering that the measures must be evolutive and most of the times the narratives collide leaving space to black swan scenarios and uncertainties lurking back.

Some of the issues that should be considered in changing the narratives are the optimism instead of realism on strategies for technological supremacy among nations, governance, regulations, and standards, competing and cooperation values, congruent coordination of planning, patterns of interactions between governments, technological firms, start-ups, academic and scientific researchers, global market demand, inadequate protocols, revenues, etc., to address operational needs, solve challenges, create benefits for the actors involved and significant impact for the society at large.

B. Focus on Machine Learning and Intelligence Instead of on Machine Usefulness!

Artificial intelligence systems are characterized as machine-based systems with certain varying levels of autonomy which give support to humans in their objectives and tasks, making predictions, recommendations, decisions, etc., using data analytics also referred as big data based on a massive amount of alternative data sources. Artificial intelligence and machine learning in several industries build applications to take advantage of connections between artificial intelligence and machine learning, helping the companies to transform their processes and products. Machine learning models are techniques of artificial intelligence increasingly deployed in the use experience in big data automatically to learn and improve predictability in performance without being programmed by humans (OECD, 2021). Artificial intelligence and machine learning today are being used in a wide range of applications.

Artificial intelligence and machine learning are used to optimize inventories of retailers, in health organizations in image processing for improved cancer detection; in banking and finance are used for detecting fraud, predicting risk, and proactive financial advice; in sales and marketing for sales forecasting, campaign optimization, sentiment analysis, etc.; in cyber security protect organizations and their clients by detecting anomalies; in customer services, the use of chatbots and cognitive search to gauge customer intent, virtual assistance and answer questions; in transportation improve the efficiency of routs, predictive analysis, traffic forecasting, etc.; in manufacturing, artificial intelligence are used for predictive maintenance and efficiency of operations, etc.

Behind the scenes, the engine of machine learning attempts to reinforce known patterns in the member's behavior and adjusting accordingly when the member change patterns (Burns, 2023). The "Chat Generative Pre-Trained Transformer" (ChatGPT) is a tool of artificial intelligence, with usefulness as machine to overcome resistance to change resulting from the implementation process of digital innovations. As with most tools of artificial intelligence, ChatGPT sometimes works great and simply fine becoming an especially useful learning machine to provide support to human tasks.

An artificial intelligence chatbot performs some cognitive functions, like analysis and interpretation, better than human brains, with more efficiency, effectiveness, and quality, discerning some patterns that elude the human mind to become more useful in contributions to knowledge. Is in this sense, that from a more cheerful outlook, it is required to move from machine learning to machine usefulness.

C. Enhance Human Capabilities

The relationship between humans and the artificial intelligence ecosystem is one of enhancement of human capabilities and not replacement. Artificial intelligence can be leveraged to enhance cognitive functions and human behavior in the analysis, interpretation, and decision-making. However, the digital traces of artificial intelligence require a knowing subject to interpret, analyze, and validate the outcomes.

Humans are uniquely adapted to constantly create becoming good at it, but when it comes to analyzing, interpreting, and understanding data, the larger the data set becomes, the worse humans perform (Williams, 2023). Humans visualizing data miss the smaller trends that have been averaged out besides that are innately biased through past experiences and preexisting assumptions such as spotting correlations to assume causations. While artificial intelligence takes care of the details data analysis and interpretation, humans can concentrate on creating what he-she does best, making best decisions and empowering to implement them, driving behavior change, improving the abilities to inspire, create habits and true accountability. It is difficult to hold accountability in artificial intelligence systems for any errors and problems with generated content because they lack awareness and consciousness as humans have.

Humans have a limited ability to scale only focusing on one item at a time while in comparison, artificial intelligence does not have limitations regarding scalability processing thousands of tasks in a fraction of a second. Thus, humans can have on artificial intelligence scalability as a trait.

D. Create Countervailing Powers

The future of edge digital technologies from artificial intelligence to quantum information science have not clear definition which complicates the standardization and regulation because the global competition of major players to gain the largest global market share (Neaher, *et al.* 2021).

The new standards and regulations for the emerging and disruptive digital technologies must rise from a creative destruction of outdated advances leading to an overall scientific revolution to fully occur to instate no longer emergent the emerging technologies. This argument is supported by Kuhn (1962: 11) who stated that men whose research is based on shared paradigms are committed to the same rules and standards for scientific practice. That commitment and the apparent consensus it creates are prerequisites for normal science.

A new model of cooperation in partnerships between governments and firms sharing both risks and responsibilities, will enable to deliver more value in the digital technologies field by creating more benefits for the involved partners by ensuring proper alignment of interest involving the society at large. Private public partnership cooperation becomes the new structure and a tool for creating economic growth, social development, and socio-ecological resilience, while providing opportunities to balance the advantages for all the involved actors and the society at large.

Convergence of stakeholders in emerging and disruptive digital technology brings new conceptualizations and types of instrumentation of end products and services that will enable major changes in productivity and lifestyles for the wellbeing of the whole society.

5. ALIGNMENT ETHICS

It is difficult to imagine how far the evil and stupidity of the human being can go. The rise of ChatGPT and their effects on individuals and society is an opportunity to discuss ethical issues when using these and other similar tools. In the field of artificial intelligence (AI) alignment ethics aims to steer artificial intelligence systems towards ethical principles based on humans' intended goals and preferences. An artificial intelligence system is considered ethically aligned if it advances the intended objectives of human development. Preceded debates are conducted with moral and ethical considerations on specific technologies, as for example, the Ethics of Artificial Intelligence Recommendation of UNESCO.

Artificial intelligence is a digital technology different from all previous technologies including neural networks, dep learning through algorithms and automatic learning, which have presented new and different risks and ethical concerns (Blackman, 2020) considering that humans have control over the machines, turning on and turning off. Humans need to make decisions on what is an acceptable behavior in the use of digital technologies and more precisely on the tools of artificial intelligence, to design, enact and enforce policies.

Avoiding biases on data and models of AI. Artificial intelligence is already here to stay forever and from ethical alignment to be used responsible which requires the commitment to act and behave ethically at every turn. The increasing use of artificial intelligence is risen significant ethical alignment concerns sparking debates regarding issues from human data privacy to the use of algorithms in chat bots and chatGPT that not only perpetuates but tend to emphasize religious, ethnic, racial, gender and other bias. The ethics of responsible artificial intelligence has an orientation from utilitarianism to justify some threats posed by tools such as the ChatGPT, and similar chat bots that include black- box algorithms to validate copyright, infringement discrimination and biases, vulgarity, plagiarism, fake media, fabricated unauthentic textual content, etc., among others.

These ethical issues are being already reported by academics, organizations, and institutions worried with these developments and some measures are being proposed to deal with them. Among other measures to put into place and enforce to mitigate the negative effects, are the claims of disclosing data collected and transparency of what is done with that data, to establish committees dedicated to overseeing the use of artificial intelligence, to identify intelligent agents and chatbots as non-human entities, etc. (Carufel, Dec. 18, 2019).

Ways to conduct additional training. Academic, institutional, and organizational leaders are worried and concerned about the effect of artificial intelligence replacing the workforce and the ways to conduct additional training to employees that are rightly worried about being displaced from their jobs. Organizations adopting artificial intelligence must understand, analyze, manage, assess, and mitigate risks, monitor, and evaluate ethical reviews and bias screening considering the evolution of algorithms in nature which require training on the heterogeneous algorithm models that possess high velocity and variability. The diverse ways to conduct additional training is an issue that raises ethical concerns.

Permission to use millions of words and material on artificial intelligence training. Reputation and legal risks of artificial intelligence using copyrighted or offensive content, loss of privacy, spreading false information, fraudulent transactions, lack of transparence, misuse, bias, etc. Regarding the integrity issues, to identify the actual scriptwriter by comparing the text created by ChatGPT is still elusive now. There many legal concerns and issues around copyright and ownership of content generated by artificial intelligence.

Laws and regulations are concerned with these ethical issues dealing with the content created by learning machines which create legal disputes over the ownership of rights to use and profit from the generated content. However, generative artificial intelligence content poses an elevated risk for intellectual property rights and copyright protection, which has serious implications for research to avoid potential infringement caused by the use. OpenAI has already declared that it does not take any responsibility for any infringement that may occur.

Long term implications of artificial intelligence are not clear. Artificial intelligence risk management frameworks must consolidate in the long-term the ethical theory to integrate socially responsible judgments leading to ensure reasoned, purposeful, cautious, and ethical leverage alignment to generative artificial intelligence models. Identification of artificial intelligence and management risks lead to design and implement ethical models to be used long-term to determine a path (Ashok et al., 2022). Utilitarism is an ethical approach used to decision making based on the positive and negative impact of actions that does best good and least harm to individuals, organizations, environment (B˙ohm et al., 2022).

Control over the ethical disruption of digital technologies and more specifically artificial strategy must require a digital conversation and leadership about acceptable ethical behaviors, under the assumption that digital transformation cannot be interrupted and must be guided by humans in in following years of the near future.

CONCLUSION

Machine learning in artificial intelligence tools, such as the chat GPT can offer prompt responses with an unforeseen combination of innovative and valuable texts produced from digital traces, with the likelihood of an exceptionally low selection subject to quality of data sources and training. These traces require a knowing subject to interpret, analyze, and validate the outcomes. As a stochastic and algorithm parrot, most of the tools of artificial intelligence are unconscious and not be able to produce self-knowledge, which by themselves do not constitute meaningful, valid, and legitimated scientific knowledge.

The development of ethical codes, law, and regulations for the governance of generative artificial intelligence systems is required aimed to minimize ethical concerns such as discrimination, false data and information, plagiarism, copyright infringement, etc. Further, questions regarding the copyright ownership, intellectual property rights, regulations for acceptable use norms, etc., are issues that must be raised, discussed, analyzed, and addressed.

Research and practice must be extended to explore innovative approaches for using artificial intelligence tools and other digital disruptive and breakthrough technologies for finding solution to all ills leading to potential enhancement of human development, creating social and environmental benefits, increasing productivity. These opportunities to conduct future research calls for more transdisciplinary approaches with implications in educational programs that must be challenged using an ethical perspective of digital technologies and artificial intelligence tools aimed to benefit humanity.

REFERENCES

Acemoglu, D., Hazell, J., & Restrepo, P. (2022). Artificial Intelligence and Jobs: Evidence from Online Vacancies. *Journal of Labor Economics*, *40*(S1), S293–S340. doi:10.1086/718327

Acemoglu, D., Lelarge, C., & Restrepo, P. (2020). Competing With Robots: Firm-Level Evidence from France. *AEA Papers and Proceedings. American Economic Association*, *110*, 383–388. doi:10.1257/pandp.20201003

Acemoglu, D., & Restrepo, P. (2022). Tasks, automation, and the rise in U.S. wage inequality. *Econometrica*, *90*(5), 1973–2016. doi:10.3982/ECTA19815

Ashok, M., Madan, R., Joha, A., & Sivarajah, U. (2022). Ethical framework for Artificial Intelligence and Digital technologies. *International Journal of Information Management*, *62*, 102433. doi:10.1016/j.ijinfomgt.2021.102433

Blackman, R. (2020, October 15). *A Practical Guide to Building Ethical AI*. Retrieved from https://hbr.org/2020/10/a-practical-guide-to-building-ethical-ai

Bohm, S., Carrington, M., Cornelius, N., de Bruin, B., Greenwood, M., Hassan, L., & Shaw, D. (2022). Ethics at the centre of global and local challenges: Thoughts on the future of business ethics. *Journal of Business Ethics*, *180*(3), 835–861.

Brito, D., & Curl, R. F. (2020). *Automation Does Not Kill Jobs. It Increases Inequality*. Baker Institute Report no. 11.06.20. Rice University's Baker Institute for Public Policy.

Burns, E. (2023). Machine Learning. *TechTarget network*. https://www.techtarget.com/searchenterpriseai/definition/machine-learning-ML

Carufel, R. (2019). *Companies embrace AI, but execs cite challenges on alignment, ethics*. Agility, PR Solutions. Retrieved from: https://www.agilitypr.com/pr-news/public-relations/companies-embrace-ai-but-execs-

Chen, W., & Wellman, B. (2004). The global digital divide–within and between countries. *ITandSociety*, *1*(7), 39–45.

Gopinath, G. (2023). *The Power and Perils of the "Artificial Hand": Considering AI Through the Ideas of Adam Smith Speech to commemorate 300th anniversary of Adam Smith's birth University of Glasgow*. International Monetary Fund. Retrieved from https://www.imf.org/en/News/Articles/2023/06/05/sp060523-fdmd-ai-adamsmith?cid=em-COM-123-46688

Humlum, A. (2020). *Robot Adoption and Labor Market Dynamics*. Working paper, University of Chicago.

Kuhn, T. (1962). *The structure of scientific revolutions*. University of Chicago Press.

Kushwaha, A. K., & Kar, A. K. (2021). *MarkBot – A Language Model-Driven Chatbot for Interactive Marketing in Post-Modern World.* Information Systems Frontiers. . doi:10.1007/s10796-021-10184-y

Levy, D. H. F., & Murnane, R. J. (2003). The Skill Content of Recent Technological Change: An Empirical Exploration. *The Quarterly Journal of Economics, 118*(4), 1279–1333. doi:10.1162/003355303322552801

Lokman, A. S., & Ameedeen, M. A. (2018). Modern chatbot systems: A technical review. In *Proceedings of the Future Technologies Conference* (pp. 1012–1023). Springer. 10.1007/978-3-030-02683-7_75

Marín, F. M. (2023). *De las humanidades digitales a la Inteligencia Artificial General.* University of Texas at San Antonio.

Mishel, L., & Bivens, J. (2021). The Productivity-Median Compensation Gap in the United States: The Contribution of Increased Wage Inequality and the Role of Policy Choices. *International Productivity Monitor*, (41), 61. https://link.gale.com/apps/doc/A689169156/AONE?u=anon~10ba8f08&sid=googleScholar&xid=5119dfa8

Mitchell, A. (2023). ChatGPT could make these jobs obsolete: 'The wolf is at the door.' *New York Post.* Retrieved from https://nypost.com/2023/01/25/chat-gpt-could-make-these-jobs-obsolete/

Neaher, G., Bray, D., Mueller-Kaler, J. & Schatz, B. (2021). *Standardizing the future: How can the United States navigate the geopolitics of international technology standards?* Atlantic Council Report.

OECD. (2021). *Artificial Intelligence, Machine Learning and Big Data in Finance: Opportunities, Challenges, and Implications for Policy Makers,* https://www.oecd.org/finance/artificial-intelligence-machine-learning-big-data-in-finance.htm

Potter, W. (2023). *'This is not crying wolf... the wolf is at the door': Fears AI could make white collar jobs obsolete as Microsoft pumps multibillion-dollar investment into ChatGPT after laying off 10,000 workers.* Dailymail.com. Retrieved from https://www.dailymail.co.uk/news/article-11683901/ChatGPT-make-white-collar-jobs-obsolete-Microsoft-pumps-billions-AI.html

Radford, A., Narasimhan, K., Salimans, T., & Sutskever, I. (2018). *Improving Language Understanding with Unsupervised Learning.* Technical Report, OpenAI.

Sacks, G. (2023). *Generative AI could raise global GDP by 7% Artificial Intelligence.* Retrieved from https://www.goldmansachs.com/intelligence/pages/generative-ai-could-raise-global-gdp-by-7-percent.html

Sagarikabiswas. (2023). *ChatGPT: 7 IT Jobs That AI Can't Replace*. Retrieved from https://www.geeksforgeeks.org/chatgpt-7-it-jobs-that-ai-cant-replace/

Schumpeter, J. (1949). *The Theory of Economic Development, An Inquiry into Profits, Capital, Credit, Interest and the Business Cycle*. Harvard University Press.

Schumpeter, J. (1994). *Capitalism, Socialism and democracy*. Routledge.

Sharifi, A., Khavarian-Garmsir, A. R., & Kummitha, R. K. R. (2021). Contributions of smart city solutions and technologies to resilience against the COVID-19 pandemic: A literature review. *Sustainability (Basel)*, *13*(14), 1–28. doi:10.3390u13148018

Strauss, D. (2023). Generative AI's 'productivity revolution' will take time to pay off. *Financial Times*. Retrieved from https://www.ft.com/content/21384711-3506-4901-830c-7ecc3ae6b32a

Vaswani, A., Shazeer, N., Parmar, N., Uszkoreit, J., Jones, L., Gomez, A. N., & Polosukhin, I. (2017). *Attention is all you need. Advances in neural information processing systems*. 31st Conference on Neural Information Processing Systems. https://proceedings.neurips.cc/paper/2017/file/ 3f5ee243547dee91fbd053c1c4a845aa-Paper.pdf

Weissglass, D. E. (2022). Contextual bias, the democratization of healthcare, and medical artificial intelligence in low- and middle-income countries. *Bioethics*, *36*(2), 201–209. doi:10.1111/bioe.12927 PMID:34460977

Williams, J. (2023). How AI Will Enhance Human Capabilities. *Forbes*. Retrieved from https://www.forbes.com/sites/forbescommunicationscouncil/2018/03/19/how-ai-will-enhance-human-capabilities/?sh=1d37cd1e366f

Yogesh, K. (2023). "So, what if ChatGPT wrote it?" Multidisciplinary perspectives on opportunities, challenges, and implications of generative conversational AI for research, practice, and policy. *International Journal of Information Management*, *71*, 102642. doi:10.1016/j.ijinfomgt.2023.102642

Chapter 6
Capital Structure Decisions Influencing Non-Financial Performance of Companies (ESG)

Hemalata Radhakrishna
https://orcid.org/0000-0002-5862-7039
REVA University, India

Konyn Tuba Lappay
REVA University, India

ABSTRACT

There seems to be a growing demand for companies to disclose information about natural, human, and financial resources used by them and its implications on environment and society. This gives rise to ESG metrics and related corporate reporting in their annual reports. The study aims to examine the relationship between internal and external sources of funds and the environmental, social, and governance score. The study is based on a sample of Nifty 50 companies listed on the National Stock Exchange of India, consisting of 245 observations. The study period was 5 years starting from 2017 to 2021. The variables studied were debt-equity ratio; retained earnings; and environmental, social, and corporate governance performance (ESG score). The study provides evidence of a negative relationship between debt-equity ratio and ESG score. The practical implication of the study is taken from the findings that it is high time for the firms to pay more attention towards improving their ESG score by taking up more sustainable projects through compliance of regulations in their business decisions.

DOI: 10.4018/979-8-3693-1151-6.ch006

INTRODUCTION

The concept of sustainability, initially introduced within the environmental context during United Nations Conferences in the 1970s and 1980s, has proliferated in significance within the realms of Economic and Financial Literature (Tiwari, 2022). Looking ahead, it is increasingly probable that both governmental and private investment decisions regarding industrial projects will take into account their environmental impacts, emphasizing the enduring ecological sustainability of such endeavors. Consequently, sustainable finance is poised to become an integral facet of the financial industry's modus operandi (Wilson, 2010).

In the domain of finance, it is imperative to broaden the perspective beyond profitability. Environmental and social challenges must be accorded due consideration. Hence, the paradigm of sustainable finance seamlessly integrates environmental, social, and governance (ESG) criteria into financial decision-making processes (Saidane & Ben Abdallah, 2021). Sustainable finance, a comprehensive term, encompasses various other concepts such as green financing and responsible investment, which fundamentally hinge on the bedrock of Corporate Social Responsibility. Extensive research has already been conducted on green financing and responsible investment. Thus, this research endeavors to pivot the spotlight squarely onto the environmental, social, and governance parameters that constitute the bedrock of sustainable finance.

In tandem with this shift, there has been a discernible uptick in the demand for companies to divulge comprehensive information pertaining to the natural, human, and financial resources they harness, as well as the ensuing implications for both the environment and society at large. This burgeoning necessity has given rise to the formulation of ESG metrics and their subsequent incorporation into corporate reporting practices within annual reports. However, the imperative goes beyond mere disclosure; it becomes incumbent upon companies, investors, stock exchanges, and other stakeholders to pivot towards meaningful, standardized disclosures. This shift is aimed at instilling transparency, reliability, and integrity within the domain of corporate reporting (Kotsantonis & Serafeim, 2019).

The significance of ESG scores in influencing a company's valuation cannot be overstated. Favorable ESG scores can wield a positive impact on a firm's value, culminating in an augmented overall valuation. Conversely, low ESG scores have the potential to yield adverse effects, leading to a diminution in the firm's value (Melinda & Wardhani, 2020). Thus, the value of a firm is inevitably intertwined with its ESG score. For companies charting a course toward sustainable growth and enduring success, it is imperative to accord this metric the seriousness it merits. It is worth noting, however, that while ESG scores manifest a positive impact on a firm's value, the inverse holds true in the case of profitability. A study suggests that an augmentation in ESG scores may potentially lead to a reduction in profitability (Shaista Wasiuzzaman, Salihu Aramide, Ibrahim, Farahiyah Kawi, 2022).

This study embarks upon a nuanced exploration of the interplay between capital structure decisions and the non-financial performance of companies, with a particular emphasis on ESG parameters. By dissecting the intricate web of relationships between financial structures, sustainable practices, and organizational performance, this research endeavors to shed light on the underlying mechanisms that underpin the broader shift towards sustainable finance and responsible investment. Through a meticulous examination of empirical data and rigorous analytical frameworks, this study seeks to equip industry stakeholders, policy makers, and academics with the insights necessary to navigate the evolving landscape of financial decision-making in an increasingly sustainability-conscious world.

BACKGROUND OF THE STUDY

There seems to be a vital relationship between social responsibilities of firm and their performance (Williams, 1999). Therefore, if firms are not being ethical or expressing any unethical activities in their business activity, then this can affect their reputation in the society and when businesses engage in unethical behavior in society, this behavior inevitably eliminates the businesses from society (Deegan 2002). Thus, the political economy theory plays a pivotal role as government intervention can help in eliminating the disorder caused due to unethical activities of business which is having an impact on society (Oliver, 1992).

Another theory, Legitimacy theory, is an extension of Political economy theory where it emphasizes that companies have a the right to use the factors of production in such a way that it maximizes shareholder's wealth and also brings well-being in the interest of society (Dowling and Pfeffer, 1975).

Stakeholder theory states that businesses engage in CSR initiatives and make financial and non-financial information public in order to preserve positive relationships with influential stakeholders (Chu et al, 2013).

The expression "stakeholder" was first used by Stanford Research Institute in 1963 (Strand and Freeman, 2015). The essence of stakeholder theory is derived from the political economy theory, which emphasizes that corporations provide financial and nonfinancial information due to the achievement of the good relationship with persuasive stakeholders. As a result, this term has become widely used in the corporate arena (Chu et al, 2013).

According to Stakeholder's theory, there are three approaches that is descriptive, instrumental and normative approach. The descriptive approach would emphasize on how the companies need to communicate to their shareholders about their financial and non-financial information which can be a motivating factor for the stakeholders for their long-term association with the firm (Freeman, 1999). The instrumental theory focuses on significance of shareholder's interest that without knowing their expectation, It is difficult for any firm to maximize shareholder's wealth and optimize profitability of the firm (Donaldson and Preston, 1995; Freeman, 1999). According to normative theory, every stakeholder has the right to own property and thus managers need to make sure that their demand is given importance in order to run their business and focus on societal growth (Freeman and Phillips, 2002).

Agency theory states that it is important for one to know the difference between managers and owners as both are not the same, managers are usually coined as agent and owners are referred as principal, Agent is someone who works for the company, who uses the resources of the principal and makes decisions. Whereas principal is the owner of the resources and does not involve into day-to-day activities of firm and has entrusted the agent to make decisions but ultimately the risk or profit is gained by the principal (Fama, 1980). There is also an agency problem which arises which is contradictory to shareholder's theory in which mangers who are responsible to take decision for the societal well-being may fail to meet the expectations of shareholders and this can create managers or agents to work unfavourably to owners or principals (Hill and Jones, 1992).

There isn't a single, widely accepted definition of what constitutes a valuable resource, which is a highly common phenomenon under the notion of resource reliance. Research on CSR reporting methods has extensively employed resource dependency theory, with a focus on the board of directors as possible resources for firms (Kiel et al., 2007). According to this theory, corporate and inter-corporate behaviour depends on the organisational environment they exist. Such environment will have three crucial concepts in social context such as corporate autonomy, interest and power. Therefore, such concepts become necessary for the firm especially managers or board to conduct their business activities in society (Davis and Adam-Cobb, 2010).

On the other hand, a theory name Resource based view describes the relationship between corporate resources and sustained competitive advantage which was developed by Wernerfelt (1984). According to this theory, there are companies with heterogeneous strategic resources. These resources are spread across the companies and such resources will have features of worth, individuality, imitability and substitutability and it forms the important base for the firm to involve in CSR activities and gain competitive advantage over others (Barney, 1991).

The institutional theory gives more attention on companies to uphold their social responsibilities. The corporate effective performance and efficient operations are provided by three elements, such as cultural-cognitive, normative, and regulative approaches, and are in line with the needs of stakeholders which is emphasized by Institutional theory (Scott, 2005).

Therefore, such theories focuse on bringing corporate sustainability through companies giving more importance towards social activities and compliance to governance which is crucial for long term survival and sustainability of firms.

THEORETICAL FRAMEWORK

To support the intentions to conduct this study, the researchers have focused on developing a model which states the relationship between Capital structure decisions (Equity, Debt & Retained Earnings) and Non-Financial Disclosures (Environmental, Social & Corporate Governance) leading to Corporate Sustainability.

Figure 1. Proposed model

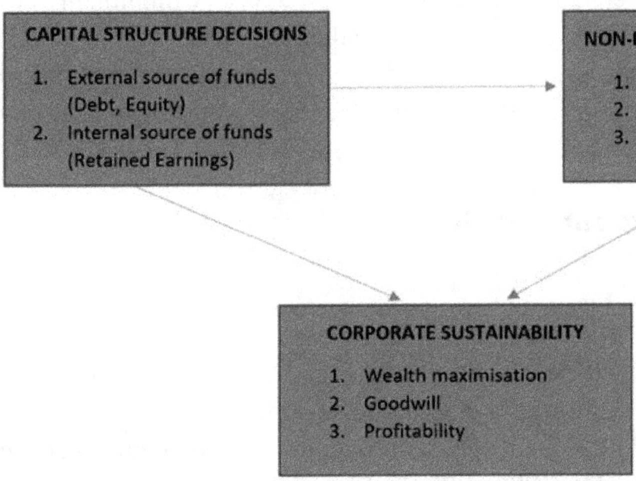

Source: Authors

Capital Structure Decisions

Capital decisions in a business context revolve around identifying sources of funding to support profitable ventures. It is imperative that these financial choices incorporate non-financial objectives, paving the way for sustained long-term growth in the enterprise (Cantino et al., 2017).

The exploration of capital structure has been a focal point for scholars in market research, leading to the development of various theories that aim to guide the selection of optimal capital components and understand the variables influencing this decision. Noteworthy among these are the trade-off theory, pecking order theory, agency theory, signalling theory, and market timing theory (Muhammad, M., Yet, C. E., Tahir, M., & Nasir, A. M., 2020).

The composition of a company's capital structure holds paramount importance as it profoundly impacts key financial metrics, including the cost of capital, earnings per share, net profit, liquidity position, and dividend payout ratio. These metrics, in turn, play a pivotal role in determining the overall value of the firm (Dhankar, R.S., & Boora, A. S., 1996). Consequently, the strategic decision-making process related to capital structure stands as one of the most influential contributors to a firm's valuation.

In the wake of the COVID-19 crisis, the significance of this subject matter has surged. Companies, grappling with serious financial challenges, are compelled to adeptly manage their cost of capital and adapt their financing strategies to sustain their financial performance (OuldDaoudEllili, N., 2020).

In aligning with the objective of maximizing firm value while minimizing overall capital costs, companies are tasked with making judicious choices between debt and equity financing (Chadha S, Sharma AK, 2015). It is imperative that both financial and non-financial considerations be factored into the decision-making process, given the multifaceted nature of capital structure (Desai, J., & Desai, R., 2019).

Non-Financial Disclosures (ESG)

- **Environment**

The foundation of Corporate Social Responsibility (CSR) theory finds its roots in the realms of business ethics and environmental philosophy. Companies that embrace ethical responsibilities demonstrate a heightened inclination towards eco-conscious initiatives (DesJardins, 1998). By voluntarily incorporating environmentally responsible practices, a firm not only cultivates a distinct competitive edge but also propels these endeavors through affiliations with 'green' or 'sustainable' strategies, all of which coalesce to enhance overall quality standards (Forsyth, 1997).

- **Corporate Social Responsibility**

While numerous studies advocate for corporations to prioritize Corporate Social Responsibility (CSR) as a pivotal strategy for enhancing financial performance, a study conducted in Rajasthan focusing on Small and Medium Scale Enterprises (Jain et al., 2016) presents an intriguing perspective. It reveals that many enterprises in this category do not view CSR activities primarily as a means to augment sales or revenue. Instead, they undertake such initiatives driven by religious beliefs and moral values. Consequently, this study suggests a nuanced and potentially weak positive relationship between CSR activities and financial performance.

In contrast, a study analyzing 100 firms listed in the Bombay Stock Exchange (BSE) offers a counterpoint. It suggests that the historical performance of companies may exert influence on subsequent year's CSR activities. This implies that financially stable companies may choose to allocate resources towards socially responsible initiatives, aiming to bolster their market value and reputation (Ray & Mitra, 2018).

Recognizing the strategic significance of CSR, companies are advised to incorporate initiatives in order to gain a competitive edge (Ratnawati et al., 2018). Existing literature underscores that Small and Medium Scale Enterprises (SMEs) engaged in CSR activities that foster innovation and a culture of continuous learning can indeed yield a competitive advantage. This advantage manifests through improvements in product quality, heightened operational efficiency, reduced costs, and ultimately, enhanced profitability.

- **Corporate Governance**

As globalization gains momentum and emerging markets assert increasing economic influence, researchers are showing a heightened interest in the study of corporate governance within developing nations (Che Haat, M.H., Abdul Rahman, R. and Mahenthiran, S., 2008 & Ponnu, C.H., 2008). It's important to note that attempting to directly compare governance systems between well-established and developing markets can be misleading due to variations in corporate governance standards across different nations (Bhatt, P.R. and Bhatt, R.R., 2017).

Rapidly expanding companies often require greater external funding, which may necessitate an enhancement of their governance practices (Durnev, A. and Kim, E. 2005). However, it's worth emphasizing that while improved corporate governance is undeniably valuable, it may not always directly translate to superior organizational performance, particularly if the costs associated with implementing more robust governance processes outweigh their benefits (Roy, A. 2016).

For stakeholders such as shareholders, creditors, debtors, and investors, a comprehensive understanding of corporate governance and its pivotal role within an organization is crucial for making informed investment decisions (Buallay, A., Hamdan, A., & Zureigat, Q. 2017). The adoption of robust corporate governance policies and procedures not only instills confidence in both investors and businesses but also fosters an environment where the investing community feels secure in making future investments (Bhatt, P.R. and Bhatt, R.R., 2017).

The synergy between effective corporate governance and sound capital structure is fundamental in driving firm success. This is evidenced by the heightened financial inflows stemming from improved managerial oversight and control, a stronger alignment with the interests of stakeholders, and an overall enhancement in performance (Mansour, M., Al Amosh, H., Alodat, A. Y., Khatib, S. F. A., & Saleh, M. W. A., 2022). By juxtaposing various corporate governance mechanisms against the performance metrics of individual organizations, one can gauge the efficacy of these governance practices. Both financial and non-financial evaluation techniques are instrumental in assessing a company's performance (Malik, M. S., & Makhdoom, D. D., 2016).

Corporate Sustainability

Corporate sustainability is a strategic approach that places emphasis on the productivity of the company in addition to effectiveness and efficiency, and these factors come from the environmental, economic, and social dimensions which further contribute towards competitiveness (Kocmanová, A., Hřebíček, J., & Dočekalová, M., 2011). Notably, the social and environmental aspects of sustainability exert a profound influence on the trajectory of sustainable business growth. A pivotal strategy lies in bolstering ESG (Environmental, Social, and Corporate Governance) social management, which, in turn, fosters sustainable business expansion (Oprean-Stan, C., Oncioiu, I., Iuga, I. C., & Stan, S., 2020).

However, a critical impediment to fostering sustainable corporate behavior lies in the diverse landscape of corporate reporting. Regrettably, this framework offers scant incentives for companies to adopt more sustainable practices. The prevailing approach, aiming to please all stakeholders, ultimately falls short, failing to satisfy any particular group (Tsagas, G., & Villiers, C., 2020).

Capital Structure Decisions and Non-Financial Disclosures

As we explore the impact of capital structure on sustainability, it's crucial to consider the influence of Capital Structure Decisions (Cost of equity and Cost of debt) on non-financial disclosures.

- **Cost of Equity & ESG**

Incorporating nonfinancial metrics, such as a company's social stance, exerts a notable influence on the cost of equity, which embodies the expected return from an investment contingent on its associated level of risk (Chouaibi, Y., Rossi, M., & Zouari, G. 2021). Notably, enterprises that consistently prioritize employee well-being and environmental preservation demonstrate a remarkable advantage in terms of cost of equity within the realm of Corporate Social Responsibility (CSR) (El Ghoul, S.; Guedhami, O.; Kwok, C.; Mishra, D., 2011). Moreover, companies boasting superior ESG (Environmental, Social, and Governance) scores find themselves in a more advantageous position when procuring equity financing. Noteworthy metrics encompassing Higher Controversies Score, Workforce Score, Product Responsibility Score, and CSR Strategy Score exhibit an inverse relationship with the Cost of Equity. This intricate relationship takes on a U-shaped structure rather than following a linear trajectory. This infers that affording heightened attention to ESG considerations proves advantageous for businesses until a certain scale, delineated by total assets, is attained. Beyond this inflection point, the relationship undergoes a shift towards a positive correlation (Pellegrini, C. B., Caruso, R., & Mehmeti, N. 2019). Conversely, companies operating in sectors classified as "sin" industries, such as nuclear energy or cigarettes, observe an escalation in their cost of equity capital due to the adverse social and environmental implications associated with these industries (Chouaibi, Y., Rossi, M., & Zouari, G. 2021). Notably, within the context of developing economies like India, a noteworthy correlation emerges between the Cost of Equity and CSR disclosures (ESG ratings). Intriguingly, data indicates that investors in India exhibit a reluctance to favor companies deeply engaged in CSR practices. This departure from earlier studies, primarily conducted in the USA, can be attributed to variations in geographical, cultural, religious, socioeconomic, legal, and institutional frameworks (Dahiya, M. and Singh, S. (2021).

- **Cost of Debt & ESG**

While ESG considerations significantly affect the cost of equity, it's equally imperative to examine how these factors intertwine with the cost of debt.

Although the demarcation between ESG (Environmental, Social, and Corporate Governance) sustainability and equity financing remains clear, the contours of the relationship between ESG sustainability and debt financing remain veiled in uncertainty (Cantino, V., Devalle, A., & Fiandrino, S., 2017). In alignment with stakeholder theory, businesses are urged to address sustainability-related concerns of their stakeholders, a practice that can yield lower interest rates on their debts. Additionally, scholars posit that the sustainability performance of the nation in which a firm operates may significantly influence its cost of debt (Sze, A., Tang, I., Li, W., & Yu, I. W., 2021). This connection underscores the intricate interplay between a company's environmental and social commitments and its financial obligations. Companies find themselves at an advantageous position when they exhibit enhanced transparency in transmitting ESG information. This transparency not only facilitates easier access to third-party financial resources but also secures more favorable terms (Raimo, N., Caragnano, A., Zito, M., Vitolla, F., & Mariani, M., 2021). However, firms characterized by low ESG scores may face heightened default risks due to their exposure to environmental, social, and corporate responsibilities. This perceived riskiness underscores the importance of integrating ESG considerations into financing decisions (Apergis, N., Poufinas, T., & Antonopoulos, A., 2022). Among the various ESG dimensions, environmental factors wield the most significant influence on the cost of borrowing as recognized by lending institutions (Eliwa, Y., Aboud, A., & Saleh, A., 2021). Notably, ESG metrics also offer valuable insights into credit risk, exerting a direct impact on loan pricing. Proponents of ESG contend that it extends beyond traditional financial metrics to encompass regulatory concerns, litigation risks, and agency frictions, making it a potent predictor of debt repayment likelihood (Zhang, R. L., 2021).

Capital Structure Decisions and Corporate Sustainability

A well-structured capital foundation not only provides the necessary funding but also fosters enduring success for projects. This extends its positive impact beyond the company, influencing the industry, community, and society at large (Du, J., Wu, H., & Zhao, X, 2018). Irrespective of industry affiliation or geographical location, fledgling enterprises, including startups and young businesses, rely on external financing for their operations. Particularly in their nascent stages, debt emerges as a crucial cornerstone for initial business activities and often stands as the primary choice. As enterprises mature, a pivotal transformation occurs in their capital composition, progressively transitioning from reliance on internal capital to an increased incorporation of debt (La Rocca, M., La Rocca, T., & Cariola, A., 2011). Notably, empirical studies underline the paramount importance of capital structure in prognosticating the financial sustainability of enterprises. This underscores the notion that an escalation in a firm's financial sustainability corresponds with a proportional augmentation in the various facets of its capital structure (Wu, N., Zhao, J., Musah, M., Ma, Z., Zhang, L., Zhou, Y., ... & Li, K., 2023). Hence, prudent financial management often advocates for a strategic emphasis on bolstering internal funding mechanisms, heralding it as a secure alternative to external options. This strategic preference extends to corporations, as internal funding minimizes the potential encumbrance of additional expenses that might jeopardize their viability.

RESEARCH METHODOLOGY

Major question this research intends to study is to know whether the Capital structure ratio of firms can have positive impact on ESG scores of firms (Al Amosh et al., 2022)

Based on the above discussions the following hypothesis is framed:

H1. Capital Structure decisions have a significant positive impact on Environmental, Social & Governance performance. (Al Amosh et al., 2022)

H1a. Debt-equity finance has a significant positive impact on Environmental, Social & Governance performance.

H1b. Retained Earnings have a significant positive impact on Environmental, Social & Governance performance.

Data Collection and Sampling

The study is based on a sample of Nifty 50 companies listed on the National Stock Exchange, India consisting of 250 observations (the final data consisted of 245 observations with available data throughout the year). The study period is of 5 years starting from 2017 to 2021. The variables studied were Debt-equity ratio (D/E ratio), Retained earnings ratio (RE ratio) & Environmental, Social & Governance performance (ESG Score).

The data for financial ratios, Debt to Equity ratio & Retained Earnings ratio was collected from the annual reports of Nifty 50 firms and ESG Score for the respective companies was obtained from S&P Global.

Variables Descriptions

Dependent Variable: The dependent variable in this study is ESG performance which is measured as ESG Score obtained from S&P Global.

Independent Variable: The independent variables in this study are capital structure ratios that is Debt-equity ratio & Retained earnings ratio.

In one of the previous research (Al Amosh et al., 2022), the impact of debt and equity on ESG score was studied with reference to Jordon Companies.

In the current study the authors have measured the impact of Debt, Equity and Retained Earning on ESG performance of Nifty 50 companies in India.

Research Models

$$ESG = \beta_0 + \beta_1 D.E + \beta_2 R.E$$

RESULTS AND DISCUSSIONS

Table 1. Table showing descriptive statistics

Variables	Obs.	Mean	Std. Dev.	Min	Max	Skewness	Kurtosis
D_E_RATIO	245	1.813714	8.647335	0.000000	84.76000	6.958101	54.93993
R_E_RATIO	245	47.12653	119.0075	-1161.74	1153.760	-1.337305	75.75982
ESG_SCORE	245	0.361347	0.239971	0.000000	0.850000	0.388732	1.833210

Note: ESG is ESG Score, D.E is debt & Equity ratio and R.E is Retained Earnings Ratio

Table 2. Table showing unit root test

Variables	Level		1st Difference	
	C	C & T	C	C&T
ESG	**0.000**	**0.000**	**0.000**	**0.000**
D.E	**0.0005**	**0.0033**	**0.000**	**0.000**
R.E	**0.000**	**0.000**	**0.000**	**0.000**

Note: c refers to intercept & C&T refers to trend and intercept

The sample consists of 245 observations drawn from Top 50 companies listed NSE for the past 5 years. From the above table it could be inferred that the average for Debt Equity ratio (2%) is comparatively lower than Retained earnings ratio (47%). Sufficient amount of deviation from mean could be observed which is captured by standard deviation and the direction of variation is measured by skewness which is equal to zero in case of ESG score, which means that distribution is symmetrical. The extent to which the distribution is flat or peak is measured through kurtosis. For ESG the distribution follows a platykurtic curve (flat) as the value is less than 3, whereas for the D.E ratio & R.E ratio is not normally distributed as the standard deviation is slightly greater than mean & also skewness is more than 0 and kurtosis is not equal to 3.

It could be generalized that most of the firms prefer retained earnings over debt or equity as a source of finance for funding their projects.

Table 3. Table showing correlation test

	D_E_RATIO	R_E_RATIO	ESG_SCORE
D_E_RATIO	1	-0.011811162	-0.081246643
R_E_RATIO	-0.011811162	1	-0.038429221
ESG_SCORE	-0.081246643	-0.038429221	1

From the above Table No.3, it could be inferred that there seems to be a low negative relationship of ESG score with Debt-equity ratio & Retained earnings ratio, which indicates that increase in ESG score can result in decrease in debt-equity ratio. This implies that firms which are able to raise debt to finance their projects will not be in a position to meet their commitments towards Environmental, Social & Governance compliance as they will have a fixed obligation towards cost of debt. This in turn contradicts with the study (Gholami et al., 2022) which stated that companies with better ESG scores will be able to attract more debt and thus result in cheaper cost of debt.

The possible reason for the inverse relationship between ESG Score & Capital Structure ratios could be that the Indian retail investors prefer corporate governance over environmental and social factors while investing in the Stock market. Therefore, while a company is raising funds through debt or equity from the Stock Market, ESG Score would not be the significant factor influencing investment decisions of investors. Thus, ESG scores may have a low negative impact on Debt-equity ratio. (Sood et al., 2022)

Table 4. Regression test showing the impact of capital structure ratios on ESG

Dependent Variable: ESG				
Method: Least Squares				
Sample: 1 250				
Included observations: 245				
Variable	**Coefficient**	**Std. Error**	**t-Statistic**	**Prob.**
C	0.369203	0.01682	21.94995	0
D_E_RATIO	-0.002268	0.001777	-1.276264	0.2031
R_E_RATIO	-7.94E-05	0.000129	-0.615303	0.5389
R-squared	0.008153	Mean dependent var		0.361347
Adjusted R-squared	-0.000044	S.D. dependent var		0.239971
S.E. of regression	0.239977	Akaike info criterion		-0.00438
Sum squared resid	13.9365	Schwarz criterion		0.038493
Log likelihood	3.536545	Hannan-Quinn criter.		0.012885
F-statistic	0.994587	Durbin-Watson stat		0.663688
Prob(F-statistic)	0.371383			

Regression Test helps in prediction of value of dependent variable for the given Independent variable and also explains the type of relationship between the dependent and independent variable which this study intends to describe. The Method of Least square is used as it is a more reliable method for finding line of best fit (Lindkvist, L., & Saric, O. 2020).

Regression Model: ESG $=\beta_0 + \beta_1$ D.E $+\beta_2$ R.E

The result shows that Econometric Model ESG $=\beta_0 + \beta_1$ D.E $+\beta_2$ R.E developed to determine impact of capital structure ratios on ESG is not good enough for prediction as the T-statistic value for Debt to Equity ratio (1.27) & Retained Earning Ratio (0.615) is less than 2 and the significant value at 5% is more than 0.05 therefore, it may not be able to predict that increase in D.E ratio by 0.002 (0.2%) with decrease ESG score of companies with the same percentage. Similarly, an increase in RE ratio by 7.94 (79%) may decrease in ESG score with the same percentage. Adjusted R-Square also does not explain variations in dependent variable and probability value of F- statistics (0.31) which is more than 0.05. Therefore, the model is not good for prediction. The Durbin-Watson statistics value is not in the range of 1.7 to 2.2. If the value falls within this range then there is no auto-correlation. But here the variables experience auto-correlation as the value falls below the range and this should be the possible reason for weak prediction as there is presence of Multicollinearity.

CONCLUSION

The study provides evidence that the empirical model framework is not good for predicting the impact of Debt Equity and Retained earnings ratio on ESG Score. This is due to the variables experiencing low negative correlation. The reason for low negative correlation is that the Indian companies do not consider ESG as an important factor in making financial decisions. The Indian Companies Act, 2013 also does not make it mandatory for the companies to disclose ESG score in their annual reports. However, post 2021-22 the Companies Act, 2013 has made it mandatory for the top 1,000 companies (based on market capitalisation) listed on the Indian stock exchanges to undertake mandatory reporting through a business responsibility and sustainability report.

In India, the majority of the companies, while raising funds, are more concerned about cost of capital rather than its impact on ESG disclosure. The inverse relationship between ESG scores and capital structure could be the Indian firms' focus on earning profits and meeting the cost of capital rather than investing on sustainable projects. Indian Investors would prefer regular and fixed income and ESG score would not be the primary parameter for investment. The current study has been undertaken for 5 years i.e., from 2017 to 2021, when ESG disclosures were not yet mandatory for companies listed in the Nifty 50 Index in India. In the year 2021, the Securities and Exchange Board of India (SEBI) issued a circular implementing new sustainability-related reporting requirements for the top 1,000 listed companies by market capitalization. New disclosure is in the format of the Business Responsibility and Sustainability Report (BRSR) containing ESG-related disclosures.

The legal framework governing ESG compliance in India is in its infancy stage. The regulatory framework in India governing ESG issues is not codified under consolidated legislation. Instead, a plethora of laws address ESG-related matters that apply to the operations of corporate entities in India. The ESG framework is a mix of hard law and codes of governance, which in some cases remain voluntary. Compliance with the ESG framework is mandatory for some entities, with the extent of the obligations under the framework depending on the size of the relevant entity.

However, this situation may change in the not-too-distant future. The MCA is contemplating making such reporting mandatory for all companies, whether listed or unlisted. It may also consider formulating standardised ESG ratings for the securities of all Indian companies, which will assist investors in identifying sustainable investments.

Hence, through this study an attempt has been made to make companies realise that they may face higher costs in the short term as they invest in ESG initiatives, but these costs are usually outweighed by the long-term benefits of improved reputation and financial performance.

Scope for Further Research

Further research can be focused on studying the impact of Capital structure decisions on ESG Score by undertaking a comparative study between developing and developed economies. A comparative study of ESG scores and performance of companies within a particular sector or companies from different sectors can be considered. A study on the Impact of capital structure & ESG on corporate sustainability can also be considered. Further research on exploring the employees' perception and role in engaging with the ESG score can be undertaken.

REFERENCES

Al Amosh, H., Khatib, S. F. A., Alkurdi, A., & Bazhair, A. H. (2022). Capital structure decisions and environmental, social and governance performance: Insights from Jordan. *Journal of Financial Reporting and Accounting*. doi:10.1108/JFRA-12-2021-0453

Alareeni, B. A., & Hamdan, A. (n.d.). *ESG impact on performance of US S&P 500-listed firms*. Academic Press.

Apergis, N., Poufinas, T., & Antonopoulos, A. (2022). ESG scores and cost of debt. *Energy Economics*, *112*, 106186. doi:10.1016/j.eneco.2022.106186

Barney, J. B. (1991). Firm resources and sustained competitive advantage. *Journal of Management*, *17*(1), 99–120. doi:10.1177/014920639101700108

Bhatt, P. R., & Bhatt, R. R. (2017). Corporate governance and firm performance in Malaysia. *Corporate Governance (Bradford)*, *17*(5), 896–912. doi:10.1108/CG-03-2016-0054

Buallay, A., Hamdan, A., & Zureigat, Q. (2017). Corporate governance and firm performance: Evidence from Saudi Arabia. Australasian Accounting. *Business and Finance Journal*, *11*(1), 78–98.

Cantino, V., Devalle, A., & Fiandrino, S. (2017). *ESG Sustainability and Financial Capital Structure: Where they Stand Nowadays*. Academic Press.

Chadha, S., & Sharma, A. K. (2015). Capital Structure and Firm Performance: Empirical Evidence from India. *Vision, 19*(4), 295-302. doi:10.1177/0972262915610852

Che Haat, M. H., Abdul Rahman, R., & Mahenthiran, S. (2008). Corporate Governance, transparency and performance of Malaysian companies. *Managerial Auditing Journal*, *23*(8), 744–778. doi:10.1108/02686900810899518

Chouaibi, Y., Rossi, M., & Zouari, G. (2021). The Effect of Corporate Social Responsibility and the Executive Compensation on Implicit Cost of Equity: Evidence from French ESG Data. *Sustainability (Basel)*, *13*(20), 11510. doi:10.3390u132011510

Chu, C. I., Chatterjee, B., & Brown, A. (2013). The current status of greenhouse gas reporting by Chinese companies: A test of legitimacy theory. *Managerial Auditing Journal*, *28*(2), 114–139.

Dahiya, M., & Singh, S. (2020). The linkage between CSR and cost of equity: An Indian perspective. Sustainability Accounting. *Management and Policy Journal*, *12*(3), 499–52.

Dahiya, M., & Singh, S. (2021). The linkage between CSR and cost of equity: An Indian perspective. *Sustainability Accounting, Management and Policy Journal*, *12*(3), 499–521. doi:10.1108/SAMPJ-10-2019-0379

Davis, G. F., & Adam-Cobb, J. (2010). Resource dependence theory: Past and future. *Research in the Sociology of Organizations*, *28*, 21–42. doi:10.1108/S0733-558X(2010)0000028006

Deegan, C. (2002). Introduction. *Accounting, Auditing & Accountability Journal*, *15*(3), 282–311. doi:10.1108/09513570210435852

DesJardins, J. (1998). Corporate environmental responsibility. *Journal of Business Ethics*, *17*(8), 825–838. doi:10.1023/A:1005719707880

Devalle, A., Fiandrino, S., & Cantino, V. (2017). ESG Sustainability and Financial Capital Structure: Where they Stand Nowadays. *International Journal of Business and Social Science*, *8*(5).

Dhankar, R. S., & Boora, A. S. (1996). Cost of capital, optimal capital structure, and value of firm: An empirical study of Indian companies. *Vikalpa*, *21*(3), 29–36. doi:10.1177/0256090919960303

Dimri, V. (2020). A study on the weak form efficiency of chemicals sector in BSE. *International Research Journal of Management Sociology & Humanity*, *11*(1), 64–73.

Donaldson, T., & Preston, L. E. (1995). The stakeholder theory of the corporation: Concepts, evidence, and implications. *Academy of Management Review, 20*(1), 65–91. doi:10.2307/258887

Dowling, J., & Pfeffer, J. (1975). Organizational legitimacy: Social values and organizational behavior. *Pacific Sociological Review, 18*(1), 122–136. doi:10.2307/1388226

Durnev, A., & Kim, E. (2005). To steal or not to steal: Firm attributes, legal environment, and valuation. *The Journal of Finance, 60*(3), 1461–1493. doi:10.1111/j.1540-6261.2005.00767.x

El Ghoul, S., Guedhami, O., Kwok, C., & Mishra, D. (2011). Does corporate social responsibility affect the cost of capital? *Journal of Banking & Finance, 35*(9), 2388–2406. doi:10.1016/j.jbankfin.2011.02.007

Eliwa, Y., Aboud, A., & Saleh, A. (2021). ESG practices and the cost of debt: Evidence from EU countries. *Critical Perspectives on Accounting, 79*, 102097. doi:10.1016/j.cpa.2019.102097

Fama, E. F. (1980). Agency problems and the theory of the firm. *Journal of Political Economy, 88*(2), 288–307. doi:10.1086/260866

Forsyth, T. (1997). Environmental responsibility and business regulation: The case of sustainable tourism. *The Geographical Journal, 163*(3), 270–280. doi:10.2307/3059723

Freeman, R. E. (1999). Divergent stakeholder theory. *Academy of Management Review, 24*(2), 233–236.

Freeman, R. E., & Phillips, R. A. (2002). Stakeholder theory: A libertarian defense. *Business Ethics Quarterly, 12*(3), 331–349. doi:10.2307/3858020

Gholami, A., Sands, J., & Shams, S. (2022). *Corporates' sustainability disclosures impact on cost of capital and idiosyncratic risk.* Meditari Accountancy Research., doi:10.1108/MEDAR-06-2020-0926

Hill, C. W., & Jones, T. M. (1992). Stakeholder-agency theory. *Journal of Management Studies, 29*(2), 131–154. doi:10.1111/j.1467-6486.1992.tb00657.x

Jain, P., Vyas, V., & Chalasani, D. P. S. (2016). Corporate Social Responsibility and Financial Performance in SMEs: A Structural Equation Modelling Approach. *Global Business Review, 17*(3), 630–653. doi:10.1177/0972150916630827

Kiel, G. C., Nicholson, G. J., & Kiel, G. C. (2007). Can directors impact performance? A case based test of three theories of corporate governance. *Corporate Governance, 15*(4), 585–609. doi:10.1111/j.1467-8683.2007.00590.x

Kocmanová, A., Hřebíček, J., & Dočekalová, M. (2011). Corporate governance and sustainability. *Economics & Management, 16.*

Kotsantonis, S., & Serafeim, G. (2019). Four Things No One Will Tell You About ESG Data. *The Bank of America Journal of Applied Corporate Finance, 31*(2), 50–58. doi:10.1111/jacf.12346

Lindkvist, L., & Saric, O. (2020). *Sustainability Performance and Capital Structure: An analysis of the relationship between ESG rating and debt ratio.* Academic Press.

Malik, M. S., & Makhdoom, D. D. (2016). Does corporate governance beget firm performance in fortune global 500 companies? *Corporate Governance (Bradford), 16*(4), 747–764. doi:10.1108/CG-12-2015-0156

Mansour, M., Al Amosh, H., Alodat, A. Y., Khatib, S. F. A., & Saleh, M. W. A. (2022). The Relationship between Corporate Governance Quality and Firm Performance: The Moderating Role of Capital Structure. *Sustainability, 14*(17), 10525. doi:10.3390/su141710525

Melinda, A., & Wardhani, R. (2020). The Effect of Environmental, Social, Governance, and Controversies on Firms' Value: Evidence from Asia. In W. A. Barnett & B. S. Sergi (Eds.), *International Symposia in Economic Theory and Econometrics* (pp. 147–173). Emerald Publishing Limited. doi:10.1108/S1571-038620200000027011

Muhammad, M., Yet, C. E., Tahir, M., & Nasir, A. M. (2020). Capital structure of family firms: The effect of debt and equity market timing. *Journal of Family Business Management, 11*(1), 1–18. doi:10.1108/JFBM-09-2019-0059

Oliver, C. (1992). The antecedents of deinstitutionalization. *Organization Studies, 13*(4), 563–588. doi:10.1177/017084069201300403

Oprean-Stan, C., Oncioiu, I., Iuga, I. C., & Stan, S. (2020). Impact of sustainability reporting and inadequate management of ESG factors on corporate performance and sustainable growth. *Sustainability (Basel), 12*(20), 8536. doi:10.3390u12208536

Ould Daoud Ellili, N. (2020). Environmental, social, and governance disclosure, ownership structure and cost of capital: Evidence from the UAE. *Sustainability (Basel), 12*(18), 7706. doi:10.3390u12187706

Pellegrini, C. B., Caruso, R., & Mehmeti, N. (2019). The impact of ESG scores on cost of equity and firm's profitability. New Challenges in Corporate Governance. *Theory into Practice*, 38–40.

Ponnu, C. H. (2008). Corporate governance structures and the performance of Malaysian public listed companies. *International Review of Business Research Papers*, *4*(2), 217–230.

Raimo, N., Caragnano, A., Zito, M., Vitolla, F., & Mariani, M. (2021). Extending the benefits of ESG disclosure: The effect on the cost of debt financing. *Corporate Social Responsibility and Environmental Management*, *28*(4), 1412–1421. doi:10.1002/csr.2134

Ray, K. K., & Mitra, S. K. (2018). Firm's Financial Performance and Sustainability Efforts: Application of Classifier Models. *Global Business Review*, *19*(3), 722–736. doi:10.1177/0972150917713859

Roy, A. (2016). Corporate governance and firm performance: A study of Indian listed firms. *Metamorphosis*, *15*(1), 31–46. doi:10.1177/0972622516629032

Saidane, D., & Ben Abdallah, S. (2021). Sustainable Finance: Concepts, Analyses and Perspectives. In D. Bourghelle, R. Pérez, & P. Rozin (Eds.), *Critical Studies on Corporate Responsibility, Governance and Sustainability* (pp. 181–192). Emerald Publishing Limited. doi:10.1108/S2043-905920210000015028

Scott, W. R. (2005). Institutional theory: Contributing to a theoretical research program institutional theory. *Great Minds in Management: The Process of Theory Development*, *37*, 460–484.

Sood, K., Pathak, P., Jain, J., & Gupta, S. (2022). How does an investor prioritize ESG factors in India? An assessment based on fuzzy AHP. *Managerial Finance*. Advance online publication. doi:10.1108/MF-04-2022-0162

Strand, R., & Freeman, R. E. (2015). Scandinavian cooperative advantage: The theory and practice of stakeholder engagement in Scandinavia. *Journal of Business Ethics*, *127*(1), 65–85. doi:10.100710551-013-1792-1

Sze, A., Tang, I., Li, W., & Yu, I. W. (2021). *Is the Cost of Corporate Debt Influenced by ESG Factors?* Evidence from the EMEAP Region.

Tiwari, A. K. (2022). Guest editorial: Green and sustainable corporate finance: past, present and future. *International Journal of Managerial Finance*, *18*(4), 613–616. doi:10.1108/IJMF-08-2022-636

Tsagas, G., & Villiers, C. (2020). Why "less is more" in non-financial reporting initiatives: Concrete steps towards supporting sustainability. Accounting, Economics, and Law. *Convivium, 10*(2).

Williams, L. (1999). *Hard Core: Power, Pleasure, and the" Frenzy of the Visible.* Univ of CA Press.

Wilson, C. (2010). Why should sustainable finance be given priority?: Lessons from pollution and biodiversity degradation. *Accounting Research Journal, 23*(3), 267–280. doi:10.1108/10309611011092592

Zhang, R. L. (2021). *ESG and Cost of Debt.* Stanford University.

KEY TERMS AND DEFINITIONS

Capital Structure: Specific mix of debt and equity used to finance a company's assets and operations.

Corporate Sustainability: A strategy where a business delivers its services and goods to facilitate economic and sustainable growth.

Debt-Equity Ratio: A measure of the relative contribution of the creditors and shareholders or owners in the capital employed in business.

ESG: Environmental, Social, and Governance.

Retained Earnings: The amount of profit a company has left over after paying all its direct costs, indirect costs, income taxes and its dividends to shareholders.

Chapter 7
The Interplay of Green Intellectual Capital and Green Innovation Performance:
Insights From Spain's Wine Sector

Javier Martínez-Falcó
https://orcid.org/0000-0001-9004-5816
University of Alicante, Spain

Bartolomé Marco-Lajara
https://orcid.org/0000-0001-8811-9118
University of Alicante, Spain

Eduardo Sánchez-García
https://orcid.org/0000-0002-8524-4906
University of Alicante, Spain

Luis A. Millán-Tudela
https://orcid.org/0000-0003-3669-9960
University of Alicante, Spain

Cristina Raluca Gh. Popescu
https://orcid.org/0000-0002-5876-0550
University of Bucharest, Romania & The Bucharest University of Economic Studies, Romania

ABSTRACT

This study centers on an examination of the influence of green intellectual capital (GIC), which encompasses the intangible assets related to sustainability within wineries and their associates, on green innovation performance (GIP). The investigation specifically delves into how GIP is shaped by GIC, with a particular focus on the mediating roles played by two key factors: knowledge management (KM) and corporate social responsibility (CSR). Moreover, the research introduces a conceptual model, which draws from prior research, and subjects it to testing using structural equation modeling (PLS-SEM) based on data collected from 202 wineries in Spain.

DOI: 10.4018/979-8-3693-1151-6.ch007

INTRODUCTION

In the contemporary business landscape, organizations find themselves compelled to continually conceive and sustain competitive advantages to secure their existence. Industrial dynamics are marked by an accelerating rate of change, precipitating concomitant reductions in product life cycles. Moreover, companies confront mounting pressures to bolster their environmental stewardship initiatives. On one hand, discerning consumers exhibit an increasing cognizance of the formidable environmental predicaments facing the planet, thereby manifesting a heightened proclivity for eco-conscious products. On the other hand, the regulatory framework pertaining to environmental compliance is growing progressively stringent, necessitating that organizations adapt their operational paradigms to align with extant legislation within each jurisdiction (Tan et al., 2021). Consequently, notwithstanding the ongoing discourse surrounding the alignment of environmental considerations with economic imperatives, corporations have come to acknowledge the imperative of orchestrating a judicious equilibrium between environmental management and economic performance (Calza et al., 2021).

What is more, according to specialists, finding the optimum balance between environmental management and economic performance represents a must in today's context, especially when addressing the influence of intangible assets – such as, for instance, human capital and intellectual capital, which are a real challenge to measure (United Nations Economic Commission for Europe, 2016). Furthermore, in the context of sustainable development and sustainability, understanding and quantifying green intellectual capital and green innovation performance became necessary, in particular, for policymakers all over the world (Popescu, C. R. Gh., 2021; The Lisbon Council, 2023). Hence, there is the vital need to discover and value, in an optimum way, all the drivers of economic growth, while addressing the benefits of the labor market (Popescu & Popescu, 2019). Nevertheless, finding the instruments capable to assess the regions and the countries medium-term and long-term sustainability in order to measure the outcomes of human capital use and productivity performance have the purpose of ensuring that the sustainable development path will be reached (European Union Monitor, 2016; Popescu, 2020).

Within the context of the wine sector, the meticulous environmental governance of wineries assumes paramount significance for two principal rationales. Firstly, the industry grapples with an array of climatic vicissitudes that portend potential threats to its sustainability, encompassing challenges posed by climate variability and issues such as water and energy scarcity (Cordano et al., 2010; Gilinsky et al., 2016). Secondly, astute environmental stewardship within wineries can bestow a distinct competitive edge, thereby affording opportunities for market share augmentation emanating from heightened differentiation strategies, exemplified by the production of organic, natural, and biodynamic wines (Flores, 2018). In fact, antecedent scholarly investigations suggest that consumers exhibit a propensity to select organic wines, even in the absence of a comprehensive understanding of the nuanced implications of such choices (Schäufele and Hamm, 2017).

In light of the burgeoning environmental pressures exerted by customers, societies, and governmental entities, environmental management has garnered increasing attention from scholars across diverse academic disciplines. Within this context, the Green Intellectual Capital (GIC) construct, introduced by Chen (2008a) just over a decade ago, has enjoyed widespread development and scholarly stimulation as a means to foster corporate environmentalism. GIC, as articulated by Chang and Chen (2012), pertains to the reservoir of intangible assets and knowledge intrinsically associated with environmental conservation. Notably, recent work by Marco-Lajara et al. (2022a) has undertaken an examination of GIC within the context of the Spanish wine industry, characterizing it as the ensemble of environmental intangibles unique to wineries, endowing them with a differentiating edge vis-à-vis competitors and enabling the accrual of competitive advantages. Moreover, their inquiry extended to an exploration of the nexus between these green intangibles within wineries and the alignment of Spanish wineries with the Sustainable Development Goals (SDGs) (Marco-Lajara et al., 2022b).

However, a pair of fundamental lacunae is discernible within the extant body of research addressing this construct. On one hand, notwithstanding its prominence, the scholarship pertaining to GIC remains relatively limited, particularly in terms of comprehending its interplay with mediating variables. To redress this conspicuous knowledge gap, the current research endeavors to ascertain whether Corporate Social Responsibility (CSR) and Knowledge Management (KM) act as mediators in the relationship between GIC and Green Innovation Performance (GIP). On the other hand, extant literature reveals a divergent spectrum of effects emanating from GIC on competitive advantage (Chaudhry et al., 2016). Consequently, there exists a clear imperative for additional investigations aimed at elucidating the ramifications of this environmental intangibles set.

Simultaneously, given the escalating import of green innovations (GIs), an array of studies has sought to explicate the multifaceted factors, both internal and external, that impinge upon Green Innovation Performance (GIP) (e.g., Arfi et al., 2018). GIP, delineated as organizational enhancements in the sphere of product and/or process innovations designed to ameliorate the adverse externalities generated by business activities on the environment within which they operate (Singh et al., 2020), has elicited scholarly attention concerning its external determinants (e.g., Li, 2014) as well as its internal drivers (e.g., Marin and Lotti, 2017). Within the latter strand of inquiry, GIC has emerged as a pivotal resource instrumental in realizing GIP objectives (e.g., Wang and Jou, 2021). Nevertheless, scant attention has been accorded to the mechanistic underpinnings through which GIC engenders GIP. Hence, the present research aspires to bridge this void in the scholarly landscape by firstly contributing to the ongoing discourse on the nexus between GIC and GIP, and secondly, by scrutinizing the mediating influences exerted by CSR and KM to elucidate this intricate relationship.

The present research contributes to the existing body of literature in several significant ways. Firstly, this study serves as a catalyst for advancing the comprehension of GIC and its intricate interconnection with GIP. Secondly, it endeavors to address an evident void within the scholarly discourse by scrutinizing CSR and KM as pivotal mediating variables within the GIC-GIP linkage. Thirdly, to the best of our knowledge, the model proffered herein has hitherto remained unexplored within the annals of academic literature, thereby representing a noteworthy progression in the domain of scientific knowledge. Fourthly, the research embarks on a pioneering endeavor by exploring the realm of environmental intangibles within the wine industry, a sector increasingly characterized by its knowledge-intensive nature.

Of particular significance is the contextualization of this research within the domain of the Spanish wine industry. Consequently, this study undertakes the elucidation of four fundamental research inquiries: (1) Does GIC exert a positive influence on GIP? (2) To what extent does CSR serve as a mediator in the GIC-GIP relationship? (3) In what capacity does KM function as a mediator in the GIC-GIP relationship? and (4) What actionable measures can winery managers undertake to enhance their GIP?

To address these salient research questions, this article unfolds in the ensuing manner. Subsequent to this introductory exposition, Section 2 conducts an exhaustive review of the extant literature, delving into the impact of GIC on CSR, KM, and GIP, thereby formulating the hypotheses intrinsic to the proposed model. Section 3 meticulously delineates the research methodology employed to accomplish the stipulated research objectives, accentuating facets associated with the industry context, data acquisition, measurement criteria, and the statistical methodology deployed. Section 4 furnishes a comprehensive presentation of the principal findings engendered by the study. Lastly, Section 5 affords insights into the paramount theoretical and practical implications emanating from the research, whilst also acknowledging its inherent limitations and proffering directions for future research endeavors.

LITERATURE REVIEW AND HYPOTHESIS DEVELOPMENT

The prevailing trend within organizational realms, marked by an inclination towards the cultivation of environmentally sustainable business practices and the cultivation of intangible assets alongside enduring capabilities, namely GIC, GIP,

KM, and CSR, can be comprehensively contextualized within the paradigms of the Natural Resource-Based View (NRBV), Intellectual Capital-Based View (ICV), and Knowledge-Based View (KBV). These three theoretical frameworks are regarded as outgrowths of the broader Resource-Based View (RBV), which hinges upon the primacy of internal resources as strategic determinants, as postulated by Barney (1991), wherein the adept management of these resources engenders the potential for competitive advantages.

The NRBV perspective posits that competencies linked to investments in CSR can yield economic dividends for organizations, as posited by Hart and Dowell (2011). CSR investments, under this purview, assume the guise of justified investments, furnishing firms with a means of differentiation from competitors and the enhancement of organizational performance. Consequently, the RBV framework facilitates a nuanced comprehension of corporate initiatives designed to harness internal capabilities, pertinently related to social and environmental aspects, for the purposes of conferring economic advantages. Within the scope of the present research, NRBV elucidates the interconnection between CSR and GIP.

In contrast, ICV assumes a role as a supplementary perspective to KBV, although both theories (KBV and ICV) advocate for the value inherent in intangible assets as generators of competitive advantage, their approaches diverge markedly. Whereas KBV predominantly centers on the assessment of the efficacy of tools that either facilitate or impede Knowledge Management within organizations, encompassing technological systems and organizational culture, as articulated by Nonaka (1994), ICV pivots towards the categorization of knowledge and the examination of its influence upon the cultivation of organizational capabilities, as propounded by Youndt and Snell (2004). Thus, while the linkage between Knowledge Management and Green Innovation Performance finds elucidation within the KBV framework, the connection between GIC and the two pivotal organizational capabilities integral to the generation of environmental intangible assets, namely CSR and KM, derives explication through the ICV paradigm.

Moreover, ICV proffers theoretical elucidation for the intricate nexus encompassing the tripartite elements of Intellectual Capital (IC), spanning the human, social, and organizational facets, with a firm's competitive advantage, as expounded by Reed et al. (2006). Within the extant literature, empirical evidence underscores the positive correlation between Green Innovation and a firm's competitive advantage. Consequently, Green Innovation Performance emerges as a pivotal determinant of a firm's competitive edge, in accordance with findings posited by Zameer et al. (2020). In this vein of reasoning, firms stand to secure a competitive advantage, thereby enhancing their performance metrics, through the adoption of environmentally conscious practices via Green Innovation. Within the ambit of this study, ICV theory serves as the foundational framework for elucidating the intricate relationship GIC

GIP. Subsequent sections delineate the inherent relationships that have materialized within this theoretical construct.

Green Intellectual Capital and Green Innovation Performance

Human capital (HC) stands as the wellspring from which organizational innovation derives its origins, given that the skills, competencies, and experiential reservoirs inherent within organizational members constitute fundamental elements underpinning the capacity for innovation itself, as expounded by Dost et al. (2016). The extant body of academic literature underscores the imperative for employees to acquire a heightened level of environmental knowledge and skills, essential prerequisites for the cultivation of ecological process and product innovations within the organizational milieu (e.g., Dost and Badir, 2018). Consequently, organizations endowed with a robust Human Capital are well-poised to witness heightened contributions from their workforce towards environmental conservation, as posited by Singh et al. (2020). Thus, to foster the development of Green Innovations (GIs), firms must cultivate their Human Capital, as this augmentation engenders the generation of creative ideas and novel opportunities, a premise articulated by Chang (2016).

The realm of GIs in organizations extends beyond the purview of HC to encompass the realm of green organizational resources, which exert a potent influence in augmenting innovations aligned with environmental objectives, as underscored by Jardon and Dasilva (2017). Within this context, various constituents constituting the Green Organizational Resource Spectrum (GSC), including but not limited to organizational structure, organizational culture, and databases, engender a direct amplification of the efficacy of HC, thereby conferring an elevated capacity for the development and implementation of GIs, a perspective articulated by Cinquini et al. (2012). Additionally, organizations fortified with a robust GSC experience a heightened organizational learning capacity, which, in turn, augments their Green Innovation Performance (GIP), as illuminated by Hsu and Fang (2009). Consequently, those entities that enhance their GSC witness a significant elevation in their innovation performance metrics, in accordance with findings posited by Albort-Morant et al. (2018).

In the contemporary knowledge society paradigm, GI is conceptualized as a social process, transcending individual confines. The strategic affiliations fostered by an organization, including strategic alliances and collaborative relationships with customers and suppliers, stand as pivotal determinants in the realization of planned Green Innovation outcomes, as advanced by Badir and O'Connor (2015). The close nexus between an organization and its clientele furnishes the former with insights into the environmental product and process innovation needs of the latter, as elucidated by Wimalachandra et al. (2014). Ergo, the synergistic collaboration between an organization and its environmentally conscious stakeholders contributes substantively to waste reduction, energy conservation, and a concomitant enhancement of GIP.

Within the context of the wine industry, the tripartite dimensions of GIC have been demonstrated to wield a pivotal role in elevating GIP. Firstly, as delineated by Galbreath (2019) in the context of the Australian wine industry, HC assumes a paramount role in catalyzing the development of GIs, emerging as one of the principal drivers of such innovations. Secondly, Leenders & Chandra (2013), based on their study contextualized within New World wine-producing countries, elucidate the influence of technological systems and environmental programs in facilitating the seamless implementation of GIs, underscoring the pivotal role of the GSC in amplifying GIP. Thirdly, Fernandez-Olmos et al. (2020) illuminate the intrinsic connection between RC and organizational innovation within the Spanish wine industry. In light of the aforementioned arguments, we posit the following hypothesis:

H1. GIC has a positive effect on GIP.

Green Intellectual Capital, Knowledge Management, and Green Innovation Performance

The linkage between GIC and KM finds its theoretical foundation within the KBV, which postulates knowledge as the quintessential wellspring underpinning organizational competitiveness and posits a symbiotic relationship between knowledge and its management. This relationship exhibits a dual nature. Firstly, knowledge operates as the bedrock upon which KM processes are predicated. For instance, the synergistic integration of diverse knowledge types augments the reservoir of knowledge embedded within an organization, rendering it a formidable challenge for competitors to replicate the organization's distinct and unique elements, an assertion articulated by Grant (1996). Secondly, KM endeavors, in turn, serve to reinforce and enhance knowledge resources. For instance, the knowledge creation processes propounded by Nonaka and Takeuchi (1995), encompassing four modes of knowledge conversion, can engender learning spirals across individual, group, and organizational echelons. Consequently, this research delves into the analysis of the influence of existing knowledge within an organization upon its capacity to acquire, disseminate, and apply novel knowledge.

HC assumes a pivotal role in fostering KM processes, given that individuals within the organization can spearhead the development of requisite and efficacious KM mechanisms, as articulated by Argote et al. (2003). Additionally, they can harness their knowledge reservoirs to refine these processes, a premise underscored by Nonaka and Takeuchi (1995). Consequently, the environmental intangibles endowed upon employees facilitate the adept development of Knowledge Management (KM) processes, as posited by Agyabeng-Mensah and Tang (2021). Structural Capital

(SC) similarly lends impetus to KM, as diverse forms of organizational capital, including transactional memory systems, organizational structure, and information technologies, can be harnessed to craft and fortify KM mechanisms, a perspective expounded by Olivera et al. (2008). In parallel, the Green Organizational Resource Spectrum (GSC) emerges as an enabler of Knowledge Management (KM) processes, incorporating elements such as environmental organizational culture, decentralized organizational structure, and circular economy programs, as elucidated by Amores-Salvadó et al. (2014). RC emerges as a catalyst for Knowledge Management (KM), as interpersonal interactions facilitate knowledge integration (Grant, 1996), knowledge sharing (Nahapiet and Ghoshal, 1998), knowledge transfer (Chen et al., 2009), and the generation of new knowledge (Nonaka, 1994). Similarly, Green Relational Capital (GRC) plays a facilitative role in KM processes by enabling the integration of environmental knowledge, its seamless transmission within the firm, and its pragmatic application, a perspective substantiated by Yu et al. (2021). Within the context of the wine industry, recent empirical evidence, as demonstrated by Marco-Lajara et al. (2022a), underscores how GIC fosters the acquisition, dissemination, and application of knowledge within Spanish wineries. Grounded in the foregoing rationales, we postulate the following hypothesis:

H2. GIC has a positive effect on KM.

KM represents a multifaceted process encompassing the acquisition, dissemination, and effective utilization of knowledge resources, thereby endowing enterprises with the capacity to augment the extent of their GI development and explore novel avenues to attain sustainable performance, as affirmed by Lim et al. (2017). Consequently, companies can enhance their GIP by adeptly managing their knowledge assets, a proposition substantiated by Kianto et al. (2017).

The nexus between KM and GIP materializes when senior management invests in environmentally sustainable resources to foster the cultivation of Green Innovations (GIs), harnessing the knowledge and competencies of their employees in the process, as elucidated by Pérez-Luño et al. (2019). In this milieu, organizations emphasize the alignment of corporate strategies with Knowledge Management (KM) strategies, thereby facilitating the realization of predefined Green Innovation (GI) objectives, an imperative underscored by Abbas and Sağsan (2019). Several scholars accentuate the pivotal role played by knowledge acquisition and transfer in the pursuit of such Green Innovations (GIs), as delineated by Shahzad et al. (2019). On one hand, Lim et al. (2017) posit that knowledge sharing augments the reservoir of organizational knowledge resources, thereby exerting a consequential influence upon innovative organizational capabilities. Moreover, the sharing of tacit knowledge is also found to exert a substantial impact on innovativeness, as asserted by Ganguly et al. (2019). In a similar vein, Wong (2013) contends that knowledge sharing significantly influences Green Innovation Performance (GIP). Conversely, Madhoushi et al. (2011) underscore the capacity of organizational knowledge utilization in effecting the transformation of a firm's competencies and knowledge into the development of environmentally sustainable products and processes. Furthermore, Ferraris et al. (2017) provide empirical substantiation of the positive ramifications of Knowledge Management (KM) practices on innovative performance. Consequently, the effective utilization of organizational knowledge enables companies to engender the production of sustainable products, in line with the assertions of Shahzad et al. (2020).

Recent scholarly endeavors have undertaken the examination of the affirmative impact of Knowledge Management (KM) dimensions on Green Innovation (GI), exemplified by studies conducted by Lim et al. (2017), Abbas and Sağsan (2019), and Shahzad et al. (2020). In fact, Giacomarra et al. (2021) corroborate the pivotal role of knowledge acquisition and transfer in the innovative intensity observed within Italian family wineries. Hence, the academic literature manifests a discernible interest among researchers in deciphering the mechanisms through which Knowledge Management (KM) facilitates the attainment of Green Innovation Performance (GIP). Grounded in the aforementioned rationale, we advance the following hypothesis:

H3. KM has a positive effect on GIP.

Considering the two previous hypotheses (H2 and H3), the following hypothesis (H4) is proposed, which predicts a mediating effect of the KM variable as a driver of the effect of GIC on GIP.

H4. KM mediates the relationship between GIC and GIP.

Green Intellectual Capital, Corporate Social Responsibility, and Green Innovation Performance

The role of IC has assumed growing importance in the pursuit of organizational objectives encompassing economic, social, and environmental dimensions, as articulated by Paoloni et al. (2021). Indeed, an array of studies has illuminated the existence of a robust and affirmative relationship between the organization's intangible assets and its Corporate Social Responsibility (CSR) activities, exemplified by the work of Nirino et al. (2020).

Sumita (2005) posits that Intellectual Capital (IC) and the Corporate Social Responsibility (CSR) initiatives of companies can be regarded as two sides of the same coin, given that the aspects related to the management and sustenance of IC within a company align harmoniously with its CSR undertakings. This synergy between IC and CSR reporting was further elucidated by Frey et al. (2008), who corroborated a positive and significant association between these two variables. In the contemporary landscape, managers are cognizant that a company's competitive edge hinges predominantly upon its adept utilization of the company's knowledge assets to navigate the challenges posed by sustainable development, a standpoint underscored by Martins et al. (2019). Consequently, the efficacy in executing CSR initiatives is contingent upon the effective management of IC. In this context, as noted by Asmawanti and Wijayanti (2017), companies that cultivate higher levels of IC are better positioned to implement CSR policies within their organizations. Ergo, the development of IC linked to environmental enhancement, i.e., GIC, emerges as a pivotal catalyst in the evolution of CSR practices.

The implementation of CSR necessitates the unwavering commitment of top management and the board of directors, the active involvement of staff, and the provision of requisite skills, tools, and incentives. It is manifestly clear that staff engagement and their alignment with the company's CSR aspirations represent pivotal factors determining its success, as articulated by Freeman and Velamuri (2021). In this context, the dimensions of IC, with HC standing out prominently, are poised to foster the seamless integration of CSR into the company, in accordance with the insights of Aslam et al. (2018). Consequently, it is conceivable that the dimensions of Green Intellectual Capital (GIC) exert a discernible influence on CSR practices. This bears profound implications for the industry, given that the panoply of intangible environmental assets within a company can play a pivotal role in the realization of CSR practices, thereby advancing the trajectory toward a green economy that safeguards the longevity of the wine industry, as posited by Bresciani et al. (2017). To the best of our knowledge, this intricate relationship has not been previously addressed in extant literature. Therefore, to bridge this discernible lacuna and in light of the paramount importance of this relationship in the industry under scrutiny, we posit the following hypothesis:

H5. GIC exerts a positive influence on CSR.

From an empirical standpoint, the academic literature has veritably affirmed the affirmative impact of CSR on GI, as exemplified by the research of Guerrero-Villegas et al. (2018), notwithstanding the challenges in delineating a coherent theory that explicates this linkage, as highlighted by Ratajczak and Szutowski (2016). In consonance with the perspectives of Gallego-Alvarez et al. (2011) and Luo and Du (2015), the relationship between CSR and GI can be elucidated through the synthesis of the Resource-Based View (RBV) and Knowledge-Based View (KBV) paradigms. RBV conceives of the firm as an amalgamation of resources and capabilities that engender competitive advantages and foster organizational performance, as proposed by Barney (1991). In this vein, CSR practices nurture the development of the firm's intangible assets, paving the path for the cultivation of organizational capabilities culminating in sustainable competitive advantages, as expounded by Gallego-Alvarez et al. (2011). CSR further facilitates the infusion of external knowledge into companies, augmenting their knowledge reservoirs (Luo and Du, 2015), thus fostering the generation of innovative ideas (Katila and Ahuja,

2002) and the formation of robust networks and relationships with stakeholders (Jansen et al., 2006).

With the burgeoning growth of industries, the utilization of natural resources by manufacturing entities has witnessed exponential growth (Abbas, 2020), resulting in resource scarcity and significant environmental degradation (Ji and Zhang, 2019). In this milieu, organizations must interlace CSR practices within their operations to attain economic profitability while adhering to societal and environmental imperatives (Raimi, 2017). CSR assumes a paramount role in motivating organizations to embark upon Green Innovations (GIs), a perspective buttressed by Kesidou and Demirel (2012). Moreover, a company's commitment to environmental concerns empowers it to harmonize its practices with societal expectations, thereby ensuring the legitimacy of its business operations.

Presently, research endeavors are increasingly fixated on CSR due to heightened consumer demand for environmentally sustainable products and services (Kraus et al., 2020). Organizations find themselves increasingly subjected to social and environmental pressures from various stakeholders (Pekovic and Vogt, 2020). Consequently, sustainable companies are impelled to augment their Green Innovation Performance (GIP) as a means to enhance energy efficiency, curtail material consumption, and reduce $CO2$ emissions (Shahzad et al., 2020). In the realm of the wine industry, the impact of CSR practices on economic performance (Nirino et al., 2019), adept stakeholder management (Iaia et al., 2019), and corporate sustainability (Kariyapperuma and Collins, 2021) has been substantiated. However, scant research has probed CSR as a precursor variable of Green Innovation Performance (GIP). Therefore, the present study endeavors to address this notable void in extant literature, and in consideration of the substantial import of this relationship in the industry under investigation, we posit the following hypothesis:

H6. CSR exerts a positive influence on GIP.

Taking into account the antecedent hypotheses (H4 and H5), the subsequent hypothesis (H6) is proffered (see Figure 1), prognosticating the mediating effect of the CSR variable in catalyzing the influence of GIC on GIP.

H7. CSR serves as a mediator in the relationship between GIC and GIP.

Figure 1. Theoretical model proposed

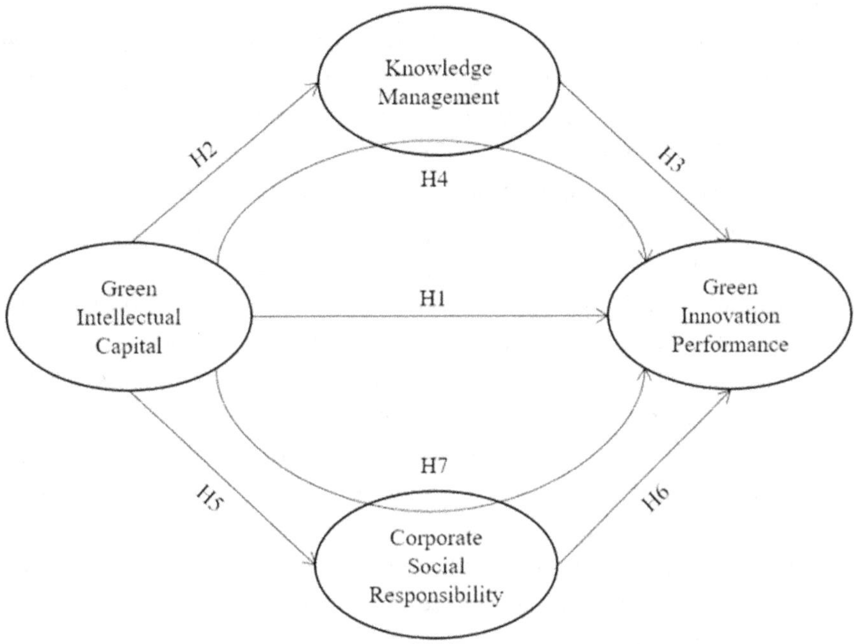

METHODOLOGY

The methodological section of this research is meticulously organized into four distinct blocks, encompassing: (1) the research context, (2) the sample and population, (3) the research questionnaire, and (4) the analysis technique. Each of these segments is expounded upon in meticulous detail below.

The rationale for situating our research within the Spanish wine industry rests on three fundamental premises. Primarily, the wine sector assumes a strategic mantle for Spain's economic and societal progress. Spain claims the title of the world's largest vineyard area and the foremost exporter in terms of volume, as corroborated by the latest data proffered by the International Organization of Vine and Wine (OIV). Secondly, knowledge emerges as the linchpin strategic determinant underpinning the sustenance of a competitive edge in the contemporary wine domain (Muller et al., 2022). Lastly, antecedent research endeavors have not hitherto scrutinized the articulated relationships posited by our theoretical model within the precincts of the wine industry. This dearth of scholarly inquiry presents a unique opportunity to advance the comprehension and elucidation of the constructs under scrutiny.

The population under consideration comprises companies operating within the Spanish wine sector, specifically those encompassed within the National Code of Economic Activities (CNAE) 1102. As per data gleaned from the Iberian Balance Sheet Analysis System (SABI), this CNAE code encompasses a comprehensive tally of 4,373 companies, thereby constituting our overarching population. To engender results of heightened representativeness, data collection was executed through a structured questionnaire, meticulously grounded in the findings of the literature review. The questionnaire, underpinned by a seven-point Likert-type scale, was administered online via the Qualtrics application during the final four months of 2021. Upon the conclusion of the data collection endeavor, an initial aggregate of 216 responses was procured. Subsequently, following a meticulous data filtering process, 202 questionnaires were adjudged as valid, ultimately forming the definitive sample, which accounts for 94.3% of the total response count. Worth underscoring is the composition of the sample, which is conspicuously reflective of the broader Spanish wine sector. The dataset spans all seventeen autonomous communities comprising Spain, with Castilla and León (14.36%), Catalonia (13.37%), and Castilla La-Mancha (10.89%) emerging as the most well-represented regions. This distribution closely mirrors the distribution within the study population, mirroring the distribution of wineries across regions, as per data sourced from the SABI database. Furthermore, in terms of organizational scale, an overwhelming majority, comprising 99.56%, of the wineries within our sample correspond to Small and Medium-sized Enterprises (SMEs), a figure congruent with the organizational size profile within the broader population, as substantiated by data pertaining to the workforce obtained from the SABI database, wherein 98.76% of Spanish wineries are designated as SMEs.

To ensure the measurement of variables is underpinned by tenets of consistency, reliability, and validity, the study relies on previously validated scales from antecedent research endeavors. For the measurement of Green Intellectual Capital (GIC), the scale propounded by Zaragoza-Sáez et al. (2020) is adopted. The scale, constituting seven items, is measured via a seven-point Likert-type scale. Green Innovation Performance (GIP), on the other hand, is gauged using the scale advanced by Chen (2008b). This variable is conceptualized as a second-order construct, comprising Green Product Innovation Performance (four items) and Green Process Innovation Performance (four items) as its primary constituents. The measurement scale for this variable, akin to GIC, employs a Likert-type scale with seven response options. Furthermore, Knowledge Management (KM) is assessed employing the 13-item scale posited by Pérez-López and Alegre (2012). This scale disaggregates the KM variable into three principal dimensions, namely knowledge acquisition (five items), knowledge transfer (four items), and knowledge utilization (four items). In the domain of Corporate Social Responsibility (CSR), the scale proposed by Salmones et al. (2005) is leveraged, encompassing 11 items. This scale discerningly measures the multidimensional construct, comprising economic responsibility (three items), ethical-legal responsibility (four items), and philanthropic responsibility (four items). In addition to these substantive variables, organizational size is integrated as a control variable, divulging the size of each organization in accordance with the criteria espoused by the Organization for Economic Cooperation and Development (OECD, 2005).

The methodological approach that governs this research entails the utilization of Partial Least Squares Structural Equation Modeling (PLS-SEM) via the SmartPLS v. 3.3.3 software. This analytical technique affords the capacity to scrutinize a network of theoretical relationships among variables, including latent constructs that are not directly observable—a characteristic that renders PLS-SEM particularly germane for social science research, given the propensity for many concepts within this discipline to be inherently unobservable. Several considerations underpin the selection of this technique. Foremost, PLS-SEM imposes relatively undemanding prerequisites regarding minimum sample size (Henseler et al., 2016), a salient advantage that aligns with our study, where the research sample (n = 202) is of moderate size.

RESULTS

Given the multidimensional nature of the CSR, KM and GIP variables, the two-stage model based on "latent variable scores" has been applied to obtain the research results (Hu and Bentler, 1998). For this purpose, the aggregate scores of the first-order constructs were calculated and then these aggregate scores were used as indicators of the second-order construct. In the following, based on the recommendations of Hair *et al.* (2019), we present the model results in three blocks: (1) the evaluation of the global model, (2) the evaluation of the measurement model, and (3) the evaluation of the structural model.

First, regarding the global model evaluation, the proposed model has a standardized root mean square residual (SRMSR) of 0.049 < 0.08 (Hu and Bentler, 1998), which means that the model has a good global fit. Moreover, it meets the strict requirement imposed by Byrne (2008), who considers that the SRMS must be less than 0.05 for an adequate overall model fit. After checking the SRMR fit criterion, it was verified whether this indicator together with the unweighted least squares discrepancy (d_ULS) and the geodesic discrepancy (d_G) were within the confidence range after applying the bootstrapping technique. As can be seen in Table 1, all values are below HI95 and HI99, which shows that the proposed model cannot be rejected (Hair *et al.,* 2019).

Table 1. Overall model fit

	Value	HI95	HI99
SRMR	0.049	0.054	0.066
d_ULS	0.298	0.402	0.456
d_G	0.233	0.279	0.302

Source: compiled by authors

Secondly, to analyze the measurement model, the following criteria set out by Hair *et al.* (2019) were followed: analyze the reliability of the individual indicators through their external loadings (λ), assess the internal consistency reliability through Cronbach's alpha and composite reliability, check the convergent validity through the average variance extracted (AVE) and analyze the discriminant validity through the heterotrait-monotrait criterion (HTMT). As can be seen in Table 2, all the indicators of the variables analyzed meet the requirement of individual item reliability, given that their loadings exceed the value 0.707 (Carmines and Zeller, 1979). For this reason, it is possible to affirm that the different indicators present sufficient levels of reliability at the individual level. As far as the analysis of internal consistency is concerned, it is possible to state that all constructs meet the criterion of internal consistency reliability, since both Cronbach's alpha and composite reliability (Pa) exceed 0.8. Furthermore, the constructs meet the requirement of convergent validity, since their AVE measures exceed the level of 0.5 (Fornell and Larcker, 1981). In other words, each construct explains more than half of the variance of its indicators. Likewise, Table 3 shows the discriminant validity test following the HTMT criterion. As can be seen, the values of the variables analyzed are clearly lower than 0.85 (Kline, 2011). This means that each construct is unique and therefore captures phenomena not represented by other constructs in the model.

Table 2. Measurement model: External loadings, construct reliability, and convergent validity

Construct/ Items	Outer Loadings	Rho (Pa)	Cronbach's Alpha	AVE
Green Intellectual Capital (GIC)		0.884	0.883	0.591
GIC 1.	0.777			
GIC 2.	0.796			
GIC 3.	0.720			
GIC 4.	0.835			
GIC 5.	0.863			
GIC 6.	0.702			
GIC 7.	0.777			
Knowledge Management (KM)		0.924	0.904	0.837
KM 1.	0.903			
KM 2.	0.927			
KM 3.	0.915			
Corporate Social Responsibility (CSR)		0.817	0.802	0.692
CSR 1.	0.770			
CSR 2.	0.862			
CSR 3.	0.860			
Green Innovation Performance (GIP)		0.925	0.924	0.929
GIP 1.	0.963			
GIP 2.	0.965			

Source: compiled by authors

Table 3. Measurement model: Discriminant validity

	GIP	GIC	CSR	KM	SIZE
GIP					
GIC	0.733				
CSR	0.641	0.532			
KM	0.581	0.527	0.545		
SIZE	0.108	0.170	0.241	0.238	

Source: compiled by authors

The evaluation of the structural model in this study encompassed an in-depth analysis of several key aspects, in line with the guidance offered by Hair et al. (2019). This comprehensive assessment included the examination of path coefficients, R-squared levels, and the predictive relevance of Q2.

The results, illustrated in Figure 2 and grounded in a bootstrap test employing 5,000 subsamples, provide a robust foundation for assessing the model's predictive capabilities and the relationships between the constructs. Through rigorous scrutiny, it is evident that the direct and indirect effects of Green Intellectual Capital (GIC) on the Green Innovation Performance (GIP) of wineries are not only positive but also statistically significant in all instances (as detailed in Table 4). This implies that both Corporate Social Responsibility (CSR) and Knowledge Management (KM) partially mediate the relationship between GIC and GIP. The direct and indirect effects, quantified at 0.448 (direct), 0.102 (indirect for KM), and 0.119 (indirect for CSR), all manifest as positive and statistically significant. Moreover, these combined effects culminate in a substantial total effect of GIC on GIP, measuring at 0.668 ($p < 0.000$). Consequently, all seven hypotheses are validated, indicating a positive and significant impact of GIC on GIP (H1, β=0.448; p<0.000), a positive and significant relationship between GIC and KM (H2, β=0.477; p<0.000), a positive and significant influence of KM on GIP (H3, β=0.213; p<0.000), a positive and significant connection between GIC and CSR (H5, β=0.467; p<0.000), a positive and significant effect of CSR on GIP (H6, β=0.255; p<0.000), the mediating role of KM in the GIC-GIP relationship (H4, β=0.102; p<0.001), and the mediating role of CSR in the GIC-GIP relationship (H7, β=0.119; p<0.002).

To assess the model's quality, the Geisser test (Q2) was conducted, revealing an average predictive relevance for the model. The Q2 values surpassing 0.25, as elucidated in Table 5, substantiate the model's predictive capabilities and relevance (Hair et al., 2016).

Regarding the control variables, the analysis discloses that the size of wineries yields a negative and non-significant impact on GIP. This implies that larger wineries exhibit lower GIP. This phenomenon may be attributed to the escalation of coordination costs, diminished organizational flexibility, and potential hindrances to achieving organizational synergies as organizational size increases. However, it's crucial to emphasize that this negative relationship between size and GIP does not attain statistical significance, and thus, the results cannot be generalized to the broader study population.

The research findings advance the proposition that the cultivation of GIC within wineries can engender heightened GIP. GIC, as a repository of environmental organizational intangibles, not only fosters environmental innovation capabilities but also cultivates vital organizational competencies such as CSR and KM. This fortifies the GIC-GIP relationship.

The documented positive and significant relationship between GIC and GIP aligns with the findings of prior research by Singh et al. (2020) and Chang (2016), which establish such a connection in the manufacturing sectors of the United Arab Emirates and Taiwan, respectively. Additionally, GIC serves as a catalytic variable for both CSR and KM. The positive and significant link between GIC and GIP is corroborated by studies such as Aslam et al. (2018) and Freeman and Velamuri (2021).

It's noteworthy that while previous research, including studies by Amores-Salvadó et al. (2014), Agyabeng-Mensah and Tang (2021), and Yu et al. (2021), has confirmed the positive relationship between environmental intangibles and enhanced organizational knowledge management, these studies have primarily focused on specific dimensions of GIC. In contrast, this study provides a holistic analysis of GIC, offering a comprehensive understanding of its relationship with KM. Furthermore, the mediation effects of KM and CSR on the GIC-GIP relationship have not been explored in the existing literature, making this research a pioneering effort in elucidating the mediating roles of these variables. The study draws from the NRBV, ICV, and KBV approaches to substantiate these mediating roles.

Figure 2. Theoretical model with R-squared, path coefficients (β), and significance
Source: compiled by authors

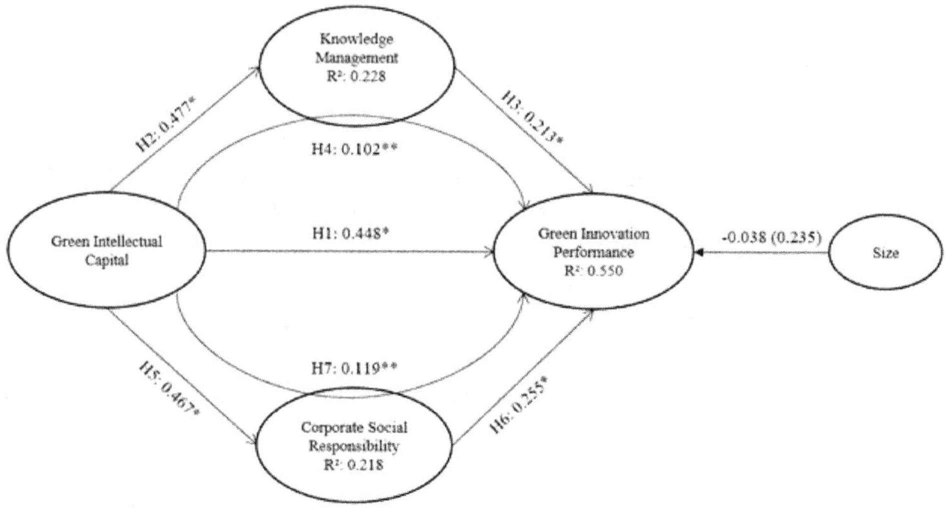

Table 4. Results of the structural model for the mediation model

Direct Effects	Path Coefficient	t-Value	p-Value	95% BCCI	Hypothesis Supported
GIC -> GIP	0.448	6.500	0.000*	[0.331; 0.551]	H1 supported
GIC -> KM	0.477	7.502	0.000*	[0.381; 0.581]	H2 supported
KM -> GIP	0.213	3.425	0.000*	[0.112; 0.307]	H3 supported
GIC -> CSR	0.467	6.945	0.000*	[0.356; 0.581]	H5 supported
CSR -> GIP	0.255	3.425	0.000*	[0.133; 0.383]	H6 supported
Indirect Effects	**Path Coefficient**	**t-Value**	**p-Value**	**95% BCCI**	**Hypothesis supported**
GIC -> KM -> GIP	0.102	3.024	0.001**	[0.047; 0.165]	H4 supported
GIC -> CSR -> GIP	0.119	2.924	0.002**	[0.060; 0.188]	H7 supported

Notes: BCCI: bias corrected confidence intervals; ** $p < 0.05$. * $p < 0.001$.
Source: compiled by authors

Table 5. Construct cross validated redundancy

	SSO	SSE	Q^2 (=1-SSE/SSO)
GIP	404	201,633	0,501
GIC	1414	1414	
CSR	606	525,604	0,133
KM	606	494,039	0,185
SIZE	202	202	

Source: compiled by authors

CONCLUSIONS AND IMPLICATIONS

In the contemporary landscape, wineries are confronting mounting pressures to enhance their environmental sustainability, given the potential adverse impacts of their operations on the environment, local communities, and the regional economy. The wine industry faces an array of exogenous challenges that pose threats to its viability, including surging energy costs, escalating water scarcity, heightened environmental consciousness among stakeholders, and the overarching specter of climate change. Within this dynamic context, the knowledge held by winegrowers, winemakers, and the wineries themselves emerges as a potent driver capable of catalyzing the adoption of sustainable practices. This, in turn, can lead to the emergence of innovative products and processes, ultimately enhancing the Green Innovation Performance (GIP) of wineries. Consequently, the analytical framework advanced in this research attains paramount relevance, particularly in light of empirical evidence illustrating the substantial influence of environmental knowledge held by organizational members, the company itself, and its network of relationships on GIP within the Spanish wine industry.

The study yields a range of both theoretical and practical implications. In terms of theoretical contributions, the findings significantly enrich the existing literature by offering empirical validation grounded in the Spanish wine industry. Notably, the research empirically substantiates the positive and statistically significant impact of Green Intellectual Capital (GIC) development on GIP. Additionally, it highlights the mediating roles played by Corporate Social Responsibility (CSR) and Knowledge Management (KM) in this intricate relationship. These results pertaining to the principal GIC-GIP nexus align with recent empirical research, such as the study by Wang and Jou (2021) conducted in the context of Taiwan's high-tech sector. Hence, the theoretical contributions address the first three research inquiries posed in this study, elucidating that: (1) a robust and positive relationship exists between GIC and GIP, (2) KM mediates the GIC-GIP association, and (3) CSR functions as a mediator in this relationship. Nevertheless, it is noteworthy that no prior research has delved into the mediating influences of CSR and KM on this relationship, underscoring the pioneering nature of this study in advancing our comprehension of how environmental intangibles can engender organizational capabilities conducive to heightened eco-innovation. Given the paucity of extant literature exploring these relationships, this study encourages scholars to embark on further exploratory research endeavors.

Turning to the practical dimension of the study, the presented findings assume a pivotal role in informing the environmental management decisions of winery managers. Within this purview, GHC can empower winery employees to undertake initiatives such as formulating codes of best environmental practices, conducting environmental education and awareness sessions, as well as participating in seminars and workshops geared towards enhancing their ecological knowledge. From the perspective of Green Structural Capital (GSC), wineries can take proactive steps to implement circular economy programs, employ computerized systems for measuring carbon and water footprints, develop eco-efficient infrastructures, cultivate sustainability-centric branding, obtain certifications affirming their environmental commitment, establish flat organizational structures conducive to the fluid dissemination of green knowledge, foster an organizational culture firmly rooted in sustainability principles, and make sustained investments in Research, Development, and Innovation (R&D&i). Lastly, with regard to GRC, nurturing and nurturing stakeholder relationships can significantly enhance wineries' environmental knowledge and, consequently, their environmental management endeavors. These strategic actions not only respond to the fourth research inquiry but also underscore the pivotal role played by GIC in amplifying GIP, in addition to generating a suite of organizational capabilities encompassing KM and CSR.

These organizational practices facilitate the accumulation of a range of green intangibles, as demonstrated, which can exert a positive influence on the GIP of wineries. Simultaneously, they contribute to the development of effective CSR policies and KM programs, facilitating the capitalization of knowledge within the organizational framework. Moreover, the integration of CSR initiatives can enhance the GIP of wineries, necessitating the incorporation of this policy at the organizational core. Similarly, proficient KM management can augment GIC, necessitating managerial efforts to advocate for a decentralized organizational structure that promotes knowledge dissemination, an open organizational culture that fosters employee creativity and tolerates mistakes, as well as a commitment to information and communication technologies to codify and transfer knowledge seamlessly among all members. These proactive measures, which winery managers can undertake concerning GIC, CSR, and KM, have the potential to elevate eco-innovation in terms of both products and processes. This, in turn, could lead to advancements such as the development of organic wines, technological enhancements in agricultural soil management, efficient waste recovery, and effective control of environmental damage and climatic risks within the winery's sphere.

Notwithstanding the substantial contributions presented in the article, it is essential to acknowledge certain limitations inherent in the research. Firstly, the significance of the subject matter warrants an extension of this analysis to encompass other wine-producing nations. Consequently, exploring the international effects of GIC on GIP assumes great significance, enabling comparisons between New World and Old World wine-producing countries. Secondly, it is noteworthy that the sample size remains relatively modest, representing a mere 4.62% of the total population. To enhance the precision and confidence level of the study, it is suggested that future research endeavors aim to investigate environmental intangible assets in the Spanish wine sector with a larger sample, approximating 10% of the total population. Additionally, it would be worthwhile to delve into the role that winery size, employed as a control variable in our study, might play in relation to GIP, given the observed negative relationship. Indeed, as a prospective avenue for research, we propose conducting a multi-group analysis to discern potential variations in the proposed model based on winery size, distinguishing between Small and Medium-sized Enterprises (SMEs) and large companies.

ACKNOWLEDGMENT

Portions of this work have been previously reported in this research: Marco-Lajara, B., Zaragoza-Sáez, P. C., Martínez-Falcó, J., & Sánchez-García, E. (2023). Does green intellectual capital affect green innovation performance? Evidence from the Spanish wine industry. *British Food Journal, 125*(4), 1469-1487.

REFERENCES

Abbas, J. (2020). Impact of total quality management on corporate green performance through the mediating role of corporate social responsibility. *Journal of Cleaner Production, 242*, 118458. doi:10.1016/j.jclepro.2019.118458

Abbas, J., & Sağsan, M. (2019). Impact of knowledge management practices on green innovation and corporate sustainable development: A structural analysis. *Journal of Cleaner Production, 229*, 611–620. doi:10.1016/j.jclepro.2019.05.024

Agyabeng-Mensah, Y., & Tang, L. (2021). The relationship among green human capital, green logistics practices, green competitiveness, social performance and financial performance. *Journal of Manufacturing Technology Management, 32*(7), 1377–1398. doi:10.1108/JMTM-11-2020-0441

Amores-Salvadó, J., Martín-de Castro, G., & Navas-López, J. (2014). Green corporate image: Moderating the connection between environmental product innovation and firm performance. *Journal of Cleaner Production, 83*, 356–365. doi:10.1016/j.jclepro.2014.07.059

Arfi, W., Hikkerova, L., & Sahut, J. (2018). External knowledge sources, green innovation and performance. *Technological Forecasting and Social Change, 129*, 210–220. doi:10.1016/j.techfore.2017.09.017

Argote, L., McEvily, B., & Reagans, R. (2003). Managing knowledge in organizations: An integrative framework and review of emerging themes. *Management Science, 49*(4), 571–582. doi:10.1287/mnsc.49.4.571.14424

Aslam, S., Ahmad, M., Amin, S., Usman, M., & Arif, S. (2018). The impact of corporate governance and intellectual capital on firm's performance and corporate social responsibility disclosure. *Pakistan Journal of Commerce and Social Sciences, 12*(1), 283–308.

Asmawanti, S., & Wijayanti, I. (2017). Intellectual capital and corporate social responsibility in banking industries in Indonesia. *Journal of Economics, Business, and Accountancy Ventura, 20*(2), 191–200.

Badir, Y., & O'Connor, G. (2015). The formation of tie strength in a strategic alliance's first new product development project: The influence of project and partners' characteristics. *Journal of Product Innovation Management, 32*(1), 154–169. doi:10.1111/jpim.12222

Barney, J. (1991). Firm resources and sustained competitive advantage. *Journal of Management, 17*(1), 99–120. doi:10.1177/014920639101700108

Byrne, B. (2008). *Structural Equation Modeling with EQS: Basic Concepts, Applications, and Programming*. Psychology Press.

Calza, F., Parmentola, A., & Tutore, I. (2021). For green or not for green? The effect of cooperation goals and type on environmental performance. *Business Strategy and the Environment, 30*(1), 267–281. doi:10.1002/bse.2620

Carmines, E., & Zeller, R. (1979). *Reliability and validity assessment* (Vol. 17). Sage. doi:10.4135/9781412985642

Cepeda-Carrion, G., Cegarra-Navarro, J., & Cillo, V. (2019). Tips to use partial least squares structural equation modelling (PLS-SEM) in knowledge management. *Journal of Knowledge Management*, *23*(1), 67–89. doi:10.1108/JKM-05-2018-0322

Chang, C. (2016). The determinants of green product innovation performance. *Corporate Social Responsibility and Environmental Management*, *23*(2), 65–76. doi:10.1002/csr.1361

Chang, C., & Chen, Y. (2012). The determinants of green intellectual capital. *Management Decision*, *50*(1), 74–94. doi:10.1108/00251741211194886

Chaudhry, N., Bilal, A., Awan, M., & Bashir, A. (2016). The role of environmental consciousness, green intellectual capital management and competitive advantage on financial performance of the firms: An evidence from manufacturing sector of Pakistan. *Journal of Quality and Technology Management*, *13*(2), 51–70.

Chen, C., Shih, H., & Yang, S. (2009). The role of intellectual capital in knowledge transfer. *IEEE Transactions on Engineering Management*, *56*(3), 402–411. doi:10.1109/TEM.2009.2023086

Chen, Y. (2008a). The positive effect of green intellectual capital on competitive advantages of firms. *Journal of Business Ethics*, *77*(3), 271–286. doi:10.100710551-006-9349-1

Chen, Y. (2008b). The driver of green innovation and green image–green core competence. *Journal of Business Ethics*, *81*(3), 531–543. doi:10.100710551-007-9522-1

Cinquini, L., Passetti, E., Tenucci, A., & Frey, M. (2012). Analyzing intellectual capital information in sustainability reports: Some empirical evidence. *Journal of Intellectual Capital*, *13*(4), 531–561. doi:10.1108/14691931211276124

Dost, M., & Badir, Y. (2018). Generation or adoption? The role of social capital. *Management Decision*, *57*(7), 1457–1471. doi:10.1108/MD-11-2017-1108

Dost, M., Badir, Y., Ali, Z., & Tariq, A. (2016). The impact of intellectual capital on innovation generation and adoption. *Journal of Intellectual Capital*, *17*(4), 675–695. doi:10.1108/JIC-04-2016-0047

European Union Monitor. (2016). *COM(2016)381 – Communication. New skills agenda for Europe: working together to strengthen Human Capital, Employability and Competitiveness*. Retrieved from https://www.eumonitor.eu/9353000/1/j9vvik7m1c3gyxp/vk4y6fuvz9um

Fornell, C., & Larcker, D. (1981). Evaluating structural equation models with unobservable variables and measurement error. *JMR, Journal of Marketing Research*, *18*(1), 39–50. doi:10.1177/002224378101800104

Freeman, R., & Velamuri, S. (2021). A New Approach to CSR. *Company Stakeholder Responsibility*, *1*, 203–213.

Frey, M., Melis, M., & Vagnoni, E. (2008). Recent developments in social and environmental reporting among Italian Universities: A critical evaluation of leading edge practices. *2nd Italian Conference on Social and Environmental Accounting*, 17-19.

Gallego-Álvarez, I., Prado-Lorenzo, J., & García-Sánchez, I. (2011). Corporate social responsibility and innovation: A resource-based theory. *Management Decision*, *49*(10), 1709–1727. doi:10.1108/00251741111183843

Ganguly, A., Talukdar, A., & Chatterjee, D. (2019). Evaluating the role of social capital, tacit knowledge sharing, knowledge quality and reciprocity in determining innovation capability of an organization. *Journal of Knowledge Management*, *23*(6), 1105–1135. doi:10.1108/JKM-03-2018-0190

Grant, R. (1996). Toward a knowledge-based theory of the firm. *Strategic Management Journal*, *17*(2), 109–122. doi:10.1002mj.4250171110

Guerrero-Villegas, J., Sierra-García, L., & Palacios-Florencio, B. (2018). The role of sustainable development and innovation on firm performance. *Corporate Social Responsibility and Environmental Management*, *25*(6), 1350–1362. doi:10.1002/csr.1644

Hair, J., Hult, G., Ringle, C., & Sarstedt, M. (2016). *A primer on partial least squares structural equation modeling (PLS-SEM)*. Sage publications.

Hair, J., Sarstedt, M., & Ringle, C. (2019). Rethinking some of the rethinking of partial least squares. *European Journal of Marketing*, *53*(4), 566–584. doi:10.1108/EJM-10-2018-0665

Hart, S., & Dowell, G. (2011). A natural-resource-based view of the firm: Fifteen years after. *Journal of Management*, *37*(5), 1464–1479. doi:10.1177/0149206310390219

Henseler, J., Hubona, G., & Ray, P. (2016). Using PLS path modeling in new technology research: Updated guidelines. *Industrial Management & Data Systems*, *116*(1), 2–20. doi:10.1108/IMDS-09-2015-0382

Hsu, Y., & Fang, W. (2009). Intellectual capital and new product development performance: The mediating role of organizational learning capability. *Technological Forecasting and Social Change*, *76*(5), 664–677. doi:10.1016/j.techfore.2008.03.012

Hu, L., & Bentler, P. (1998). Fit indices in covariance structure modeling: Sensitivity to underparameterized model misspecification. *Psychological Methods*, *3*(4), 424–453. doi:10.1037/1082-989X.3.4.424

Jansen, J., Van Den Bosch, F., & Volberda, H. (2006). Exploratory innovation, exploitative innovation, and performance: Effects of organizational antecedents and environmental moderators. *Management Science*, *52*(11), 1661–1674. doi:10.1287/mnsc.1060.0576

Jardon, C., & Dasilva, A. (2017). Intellectual capital and environmental concern in subsistence small businesses. *Management of Environmental Quality*, *28*(2), 214–230. doi:10.1108/MEQ-05-2015-0085

Ji, Q., & Zhang, D. (2019). How much does financial development contribute to renewable energy growth and upgrading of energy structure in China? *Energy Policy*, *128*, 114–124. doi:10.1016/j.enpol.2018.12.047

Katila, R., & Ahuja, G. (2002). Something old, something new: A longitudinal study of search behavior and new product introduction. *Academy of Management Journal*, *45*(6), 1183–1194. doi:10.2307/3069433

Kesidou, E., & Demirel, P. (2012). On the drivers of eco-innovations: Empirical evidence from the UK. *Research Policy*, *41*(5), 862–870. doi:10.1016/j.respol.2012.01.005

Kline, R. (2011). *Principles and practice of structural equation modelling*. Guilford Press.

Kraus, S., Rehman, S., & García, F. (2020). *Corporate social responsibility and environmental performance: The mediating role of environmental strategy and green innovation*. Academic Press.

Li, Y. (2014). Environmental innovation practices and performance: Moderating effect of resource commitment. *Journal of Cleaner Production*, *66*, 450–458.

Lim, M., Tseng, M., Tan, K., & Bui, T. (2017). Knowledge management in sustainable supply chain management: Improving performance through an interpretive structural modelling approach. *Journal of Cleaner Production*, *162*, 806–816. doi:10.1016/j.jclepro.2017.06.056

Luo, X., & Du, S. (2015). Exploring the relationship between corporate social responsibility and firm innovation. *Marketing Letters*, *26*(4), 703–714. doi:10.100711002-014-9302-5

Madhoushi, M., Sadati, A., Delavari, H., Mehdivand, M., & Mihandost, R. (2011). Entrepreneurial orientation and innovation performance: The mediating role of knowledge management. *Asian Journal of Business Management*, *3*(4), 310–316.

Marin, G., & Lotti, F. (2017). Productivity effects of eco-innovations using data on eco-patents. *Industrial and Corporate Change*, *26*(1), 125–148. doi:10.1093/icc/dtw014

Martins, V., Rampasso, I., Anholon, R., Quelhas, O., & Leal Filho, W. (2019). Knowledge management in the context of sustainability: Literature review and opportunities for future research. *Journal of Cleaner Production*, *229*, 489–500. doi:10.1016/j.jclepro.2019.04.354

Muller, C., Canale, F., & Cruz, A. (2022). Green innovation in the Latin American agri-food industry: understanding the influence of family involvement and business practices. British Food Journal. doi:10.1108/BFJ-09-2021-0994

Nahapiet, J., & Ghoshal, S. (1998). Social capital, intellectual capital, and the organizational advantage. *Academy of Management Review*, *23*(2), 242–266. doi:10.2307/259373

Nirino, N., Ferraris, A., Miglietta, N., & Invernizzi, A. (2020). Intellectual capital: The missing link in the corporate social responsibility–financial performance relationship. *Journal of Intellectual Capital*, *23*(2), 420–438. doi:10.1108/JIC-02-2020-0038

Nonaka, I. (1994). A Dynamic Theory of Organizational Knowledge Creation. *Organization Science*, *5*(1), 14-37.

Nonaka, I., & Takeuchi, H. (1995). *The knowledge-creating company: How Japanese companies create the dynamics of innovation*. Oxford University Press.

OCDE. (2005). *Manual de Oslo: Guía para la recogida e interpretación de datos sobre innovación*. Retrieved from: http://www.itq.edu.mx/convocatorias/manualdeoslo.pdf

Olivera, F., Goodman, P., & Tan, S. (2008). Contribution behaviors indistributed environments. *Management Information Systems Quarterly*, *32*(1), 23–42. doi:10.2307/25148827

Paoloni, P., Modaffari, G., Paoloni, N., & Ricci, F. (2021). The strategic role of intellectual capital components in agri-food firms. *British Food Journal*, *124*(5), 1430–1452. doi:10.1108/BFJ-01-2021-0061

Pekovic, S., & Vogt, S. (2021). The fit between corporate social responsibility and corporate governance: The impact on a firm's financial performance. *Review of Managerial Science, 15*(4), 1095–1125. doi:10.100711846-020-00389-x

Pérez-López, S., & Alegre, J. (2012). Information technology competency, knowledge processes and firm performance. *Industrial Management & Data Systems, 112*(4), 644–662. doi:10.1108/02635571211225521

Pérez-Luño, A., Alegre, J., & Valle-Cabrera, R. (2019). The role of tacit knowledge in connecting knowledge exchange and combination with innovation. *Technology Analysis and Strategic Management, 31*(2), 186–198. doi:10.1080/09537325.2018.1492712

Popescu, C. R. G., & Popescu G. N. (2019). An Exploratory Study Based on a Questionnaire Concerning Green and Sustainable Finance, Corporate Social Responsibility, and Performance: Evidence from the Romanian Business Environment. *Journal of Risk and Financial Management, 12*(4), 162. . doi:10.3390/jrfm12040162

Popescu, C. R. G. (2020). Sustainability Assessment: Does the OECD/G20 Inclusive Framework for BEPS (Base Erosion and Profit Shifting Project) Put an End to Disputes Over The Recognition and Measurement of Intellectual Capital? *Sustainability, 12*(23), 10004. . doi:10.3390/su122310004

Popescu, C. R. G. (2021). Measuring Progress Towards the Sustainable Development Goals: Creativity, Intellectual Capital, and Innovation. In C. Popescu (Ed.), *Handbook of Research on Novel Practices and Current Successes in Achieving the Sustainable Development Goals* (pp. 125–136). IGI Global. doi:10.4018/978-1-7998-8426-2.ch006

Raimi, L. (2017). Understanding theories of corporate social responsibility in the Ibero-American hospitality industry. In *Corporate Social Responsibility and Corporate Governance*. Emerald Publishing Limited. doi:10.1108/S2043-052320170000011004

Reed, K., Lubatkin, M., & Srinivasan, N. (2006). Proposing and testing an intellectual capital-based view of the firm. *Journal of Management Studies, 43*(4), 867–893. doi:10.1111/j.1467-6486.2006.00614.x

Reinartz, W., Haenlein, M., & Henseler, J. (2009). An empirical comparison of theefficacy of covariance-based and variance-based SEM. *International Journal of Research in Marketing, 26*(4), 332–344. doi:10.1016/j.ijresmar.2009.08.001

Roldan, J., & Cepeda, G. (2017), Modelos de Ecuaciones basados en la Varianza: Partial Least Squares (PLS) para Investigadores en Ciencias Sociales (4a ed.). Universidad de Sevilla.

Salmones, M., Crespo, A., & Bosque, I. (2005). Influence of corporate social responsibility on loyalty and valuation of services. *Journal of Business Ethics*, *61*(4), 369–385. doi:10.100710551-005-5841-2

Shahzad, M., Qu, Y., Javed, S., Zafar, A., & Rehman, S. (2019). Relation of environment sustainability to CSR and green innovation: A case of Pakistani manufacturing industry. *Journal of Cleaner Production*, *253*, 119938. doi:10.1016/j.jclepro.2019.119938

Shahzad, M., Qu, Y., Zafar, A., Rehman, S., & Islam, T. (2020). Exploring the influence of knowledge management process on corporate sustainable performance through green innovation. *Journal of Knowledge Management*, *24*(9), 2079–2106. doi:10.1108/JKM-11-2019-0624

Singh, S., Giudice, M. D., Chierici, R., & Graziano, D. (2020). Green innovation and environmental performance: The role of green transformational leadership and green human resource management. *Technological Forecasting and Social Change*, *150*, 119762. doi:10.1016/j.techfore.2019.119762

Sumita, T. (2005). *Intellectual assets & management reporting*. METI.

Szutowski, D., & Ratajczak, P. (2016). The relation between CSR and innovation. Model approach. *Journal of Entrepreneurship, Management and Innovation*, *12*(2), 77–94. doi:10.7341/20161224

Tan, B., Lau, T., Sarwar, A., & Khan, N. (2021). The effects of consumer consciousness, food safety concern and healthy lifestyle on attitudes toward eating "green. *British Food Journal*, *124*(4), 1187–1203. doi:10.1108/BFJ-01-2021-0005

The Lisbon Council. (2023). *The European Human Capital Index*. Retrieved from https://lisboncouncil.net/publications/the-european-human-capital-index/

United Nations Economic Commission for Europe. (2016). *Guide on Measuring Human Capital. The Task Force on Measuring Human Capital*. United Nations. Retrieved from https://unece.org/DAM/stats/publications/2016/ECECESSTAT20166_E.pdf

Wang, C., & Juo, W. (2021). An environmental policy of green intellectual capital: Green innovation strategy for performance sustainability. *Business Strategy and the Environment*, *30*(7), 3241–3254. doi:10.1002/bse.2800

Wimalachandra, D., Frank, B., & Enkawa, T. (2014). Strategic openness in quality control: Adjusting npd strategic orientation to optimize product quality. *International Journal of Industrial Engineering*, *21*(6), 3241–3254.

Wong, S. (2013). Environmental requirements, knowledge sharing and green innovation: Empirical evidence from the electronics industry in China. *Business Strategy and the Environment*, *22*(5), 321–338. doi:10.1002/bse.1746

Youndt, M., Subramaniam, M., & Snell, S. (2004). Intellectual capital profiles: An examination of investments and returns. *Journal of Management Studies*, *41*(2), 335–361. doi:10.1111/j.1467-6486.2004.00435.x

Yu, Y., Zhang, M., & Huo, B. (2021). The impact of relational capital on green supply chain management and financial performance. *Production Planning and Control*, *32*(10), 861–874. doi:10.1080/09537287.2020.1774675

Zameer, H., Wang, Y., Yasmeen, H., & Mubarak, S. (2020). Green innovation as a mediator in the impact of business analytics and environmental orientation on green competitive advantage. *Management Decision*, *60*(2), 488–507. doi:10.1108/MD-01-2020-0065

Zaragoza-Sáez, P., Claver-Cortés, E., Marco-Lajara, B., & Úbeda-García, M. (2020). Corporate social responsibility and strategic knowledge management as mediators between sustainable intangible capital and hotel performance. *Journal of Sustainable Tourism*, 1–23. doi:10.1080/09669582.2020.1811289

Chapter 8
Organizational Ambidexterity and Its Impact on Sustainability:
Insights From Spain's Wine Industry

Javier Martínez-Falcó
https://orcid.org/0000-0001-9004-5816
University of Alicante, Spain

Luis A. Millán-Tudela
https://orcid.org/0000-0003-3669-9960
University of Alicante, Spain

Bartolomé Marco-Lajara
https://orcid.org/0000-0001-8811-9118
University of Alicante, Spain

Cristina Raluca Gh. Popescu
https://orcid.org/0000-0002-5876-0550
University of Bucharest, Romania & The Bucharest University of Economic Studies, Romania

Eduardo Sánchez-García
https://orcid.org/0000-0002-8524-4906
University of Alicante, Spain

ABSTRACT

This study offers a pioneering exploration into the influence of organizational ambidexterity (OA) on sustainable performance (SP) within the Spanish wine sector. It further delves into the potential catalytic roles of corporate social responsibility (CSR) and knowledge management infrastructure (KMI) on these constructs. Drawing from an extensive literature review, a novel theoretical framework is proposed and empirically tested using structural equation modeling (PLS-SEM) on data sourced from 202 Spanish wineries between September 2021 and January 2022. Findings

DOI: 10.4018/979-8-3693-1151-6.ch008

reveal a robust positive correlation between OA and SP, with OA serving as a partial mediator in the CSR-SP and KMI-SP dynamics. This research not only fills a notable gap in the literature by being the first to probe the OA-SP nexus in the wine milieu but also illuminates the under-researched catalysts of OA, thereby offering a refreshed perspective on enhancing wineries' multifaceted performance.

INTRODUCTION

The worldwide wine sector is demonstrating a growing commitment to sustainability. This trend is evident in the rising number of green certifications available to vineyards and the heightened emphasis on viewing wineries' social and environmental initiatives as key strategic components (Flores, 2018). Such developments have captured the attention of scholars, prompting the establishment of research groups focused on the relationship between sustainability and the wine sector. Additionally, there's been an emergence of new scholarly journals and conferences dedicated to sharing insights on this topic (Kariyapperuma and Collins, 2021).

The industry confronts profound obstacles that threaten its continuity, encompassing environmental shifts, energy shortages, and diminishing water supplies (Bandinelli et al., 2020). In a parallel vein, stakeholders in vineyards express amplified socio-environmental anticipations (Miranda et al., 2022). In response to these pressing issues, vineyards are broadening their assessment criteria to include not only economic results but also their impact on society and the environment, emphasizing their Commitment to Sustainability (CS). The impetus for vineyards to amplify their CS may originate from reactive, anticipatory, or a combination of these drivers. By integrating practices that favor both the community and the natural world, they can mitigate the adverse effects of environmental alterations (external factors) while concurrently fortifying their market position via improved brand perception, credibility, and uniqueness (internal factors).

To enhance Sustainable Performance (SP), firms can introduce innovations that enable them to simultaneously discover and utilize new insights, essentially amplifying their Organizational Ambidexterity (OA). While efficiency-driven innovations can bolster economic gains, those centered on discovery can pave the way for novel practices that uplift societal and ecological welfare, thereby elevating a business's social and environmental outcomes. Yet, achieving OA requires the formal integration of social and environmental initiatives via a Corporate Social Responsibility (CSR) framework. Additionally, a conducive environment that promotes idea-sharing, a non-centralized organizational layout, and the incorporation of Information and Communication Technologies (ICT) - essentially a robust Knowledge Management Infrastructure (KMI) - is crucial. This ensures that knowledge isn't restricted, and employees are empowered to propose innovative concepts that can transform into organizational advancements and further SP. This research seeks to understand the potential of CSR and KMI as accelerators for OA and SP, and the connection between OA and SP.

The research seeks to address the subsequent seven inquiries: (RQ1) Does CSR positively influence OA? (RQ2) Does CSR have a favorable impact on SP? (RQ3) Does KMI positively impact OA? (RQ4) Does KMI have a beneficial effect on SP? (RQ5) Is there a favorable correlation between OA and SP? (RQ6) Does OA serve as a bridge between CSR and SP? (RQ7) Is OA the intermediary in the KMI-SP connection? To tackle these queries, a conceptual framework is designed, drawing from an extensive literature assessment, and is later examined using structural equation modeling. Primary data was gathered by distributing surveys to the top executives of Spanish vineyards between September 2021 and January 2022.

This investigation offers multiple contributions to scholarly literature. Firstly, as far as we're aware, no prior research has delved into the influence of OA on SP within the realm of winemaking, marking a step forward in academic understanding. Secondly, we're not aware of any prior academic work that has explored potential drivers of OA. Our study introduces two precursor variables, shedding light on the elements that catalyze innovation rooted in discovery and utilization. Thirdly, the theoretical framework we present is novel, offering a fresh perspective on enhancing the financial, societal, and ecological outcomes of vineyards. Fourthly, the concept of KMI hasn't been previously explored within the wine sector, making our research a trailblazer in applying this construct to the wine domain. Lastly, the relationship between KMI and SP hasn't been examined in the context of winemaking, so our investigation unveils new insights by analyzing this connection in Spain's wine sector.

To fulfill the research aims, the investigation is organized in the subsequent manner. Initially, following this concise prologue, section 2 introduces the conceptual framework slated for examination. Section 3 delineates the procedural steps undertaken for the research, denoting the methodological approach. Section 4 unveils the primary findings, drawing from the assessment of the comprehensive, measurement, and structural frameworks. Section 5 articulates the study's summative insights, coupled with its constraints and prospective research trajectories stemming from the inquiry.

LITERATURE REVIEW AND HYPOTHESIS DEVELOPMENT

Experts assert that the agricultural and rural development sectors hold significant importance for the member nations of the European Union (EU) (European Commission, 2023). The recent economic downturn caused by the COVID-19 pandemic had profound and lasting impacts on EU agricultural producers. In response, the European Commission implemented various strategies to assist and bolster EU wine manufacturers. Data released by the European Parliament in 2023 indicates that the EU leads the global wine industry, being the foremost producer, consumer, and exporter of wine (European Parliament, 2023). Beyond these points, there's a notable push within the wine sector towards sustainability, especially considering the pivotal role European viticulture plays for people, societies, and the environment (Popescu, 2020). The emphasis on producing and consuming eco-friendly products, including sustainable wines, significantly benefits the economies and industry bodies of nations like Spain, Italy, and France (Popescu, 2021). Additionally, the presence and utilization of intangible resources, especially intellectual capital, are deemed vital in the contemporary wine industry and are seen as primary contributors to sustainability, especially in Spanish vineyards (Popescu, 2022).

The enhancement of organizational skills and intangible resources, which contribute to the SP of businesses, such as CSR, KMI, and OA, can be interpreted through the combined lens of the Natural Resource-Based View (NRBV) and the Knowledge-Based View (KBV).

NRBV, perceived as an extension of the Resource-Based View (RBV), posits that internal resources are the primary determinants of competitive edge. Specifically, NRBV suggests that resources and capabilities associated with environmental conservation and social welfare enhancement are the principal distinguishing features of an enterprise in the marketplace. These are, thus, the primary elements upon which long-term competitive advantages are built. From this perspective, CSR is viewed as a strategic investment by firms to enhance their market differentiation, which subsequently boosts organizational profitability (Hart and Dowell, 2011). This theory also encompasses the firm's capacity to identify and leverage innovative avenues, as such innovations can augment both the firm's profitability and the well-being of the society and environment it operates within. Hence, NRBV offers insights into the connection between CSR, OA, and SP.

Conversely, KBV delves into the elements that either promote or hinder effective knowledge management within an entity and its subsequent impact on the development of organizational capabilities and the enhancement of operational outcomes (Nonaka, 1994). In this context, KMI can facilitate both exploratory and exploitative innovation processes, meaning it can bolster OA and, by extension, improve SP across multiple dimensions. Therefore, in this study, the KBV framework is utilized to elucidate the associations between KMI, OA, and SP. Subsequent sections provide a detailed exploration of these relationships.

Corporate Social Responsibility and Sustainable Performance

A plethora of scholarly works have been dedicated to establishing the positive correlation between Corporate Social Responsibility (CSR) initiatives undertaken by firms and their financial outcomes (for instance, Guan et al., 2022). This association can be attributed to several factors, including effective stakeholder engagement. CSR initiatives can mitigate disagreements among stakeholder groups, foster a sense of community between employees and their organization when they perceive the latter's commitment to their rights, and appeal to consumers who prioritize social and environmental responsibility. These factors can subsequently enhance financial outcomes (Raza et al., 2021).

Furthermore, CSR not only augments economic outcomes but also elevates social and environmental metrics, thereby enhancing the Sustainable Performance (SP) of entities (Abbas, 2020). Socially, CSR initiatives can facilitate talent acquisition, bolster employee retention, refine workplace conditions, and amplify satisfaction and allegiance among various stakeholders (Hussain et al., 2018). Environmentally, CSR strategies can encourage the integration of ecological considerations into managerial decisions, leading to more efficient energy and water utilization, and adding value to by-products produced during manufacturing (Shahzad et al., 2020).

Within the wine industry, Annunziata et al. (2018) have illustrated a positive correlation between the social initiatives of Italian vineyards and their financial outcomes. Similarly, a study by Pizzol et al. (2021) indicates that employees in Italian vineyards view CSR initiatives as economically advantageous. In contrast, findings by Muñoz et al. (2020) and Esposito (2021) suggest a negative correlation between CSR initiatives and financial outcomes in the Spanish and Italian wine sectors, respectively. Meanwhile, Marco-Lajara et al. (2022a) highlight a positive correlation between CSR initiatives and environmental outcomes. Given the varied findings in wine industry research, it remains ambiguous as to the definitive direction of the CSR-Performance relationship in this domain. Notably, most scholarly works in this sector have predominantly centered on financial outcomes, with limited exploration of the tri-dimensional impact of CSR. To the best of our understanding, comprehensive studies examining the influence of CSR on the economic, social, and environmental metrics of the wine industry are scarce. To address this research void and provide clarity in the domain, we propose the following hypothesis

H1. CSR has a positive effect on the SP of wineries.

Corporate Social Responsibility, Organizational Ambidexterity, and Sustainable Performance

In a recent study, Hadj (2020) posited that CSR initiatives can foster both radical (or exploratory innovation) and incremental (or exploitative innovation) advancements, simultaneously enhancing an organization's social performance. At the level of Small and Medium-sized Enterprises (SMEs), Bahta et al. (2022) affirmed a positive correlation between CSR endeavors and competitive edge, specifically in the realms of innovation and intangible outcomes. Broadstock et al. (2020) proposed that corporate engagement in CSR positively influences performance via the integration of innovative methodologies. They emphasized that CSR initiatives bolster a firm's capacity for both exploratory and exploitative innovations, thereby augmenting their differentiation potential and subsequent competitive positioning.

In a parallel vein, Halkos and Skouloudis (2018) confirmed the beneficial association between CSR and the evolution of organizational innovations, underscoring that both elements are rooted in a firm's capability to harness intangible assets pivotal for competitive leverage. In a similar context, Khan et al. (2021) discerned a favorable link between CSR and both exploratory and exploitative innovations. Their findings suggest that CSR can be instrumental in cultivating novel organizational competencies and in enhancing operational efficiency, cost-effectiveness, and superior customer satisfaction. Consequently, CSR adoption can stimulate OA by synergistically advancing both exploratory and exploitative innovation mechanisms (Shafique et al., 2021).

OA, reciprocally, augments not only the economic metrics of an entity but also its social and environmental dimensions (Aftab et al., 2022). Exploratory endeavors empower firms to sustain market growth, surmounting stagnation and complacency. Moreover, resource exploration and capability development through novel product introductions can enhance market agility and customer-centricity, thereby accelerating market entry (Cheah and Ho, 2019). Yet, neglecting resource allocation towards exploitative activities, which pertain to organizational sustenance and the enhancement of established capabilities, can jeopardize organizational longevity (Tarba et al., 2020). Thus, a balanced approach to both exploratory and exploitative activities can elevate economic outcomes by fostering organizational agility and efficiency, capitalizing on market prospects, and delivering apt products, culminating in enhanced profitability and sales trajectories (Bustinza et al., 2020). Recent empirical inquiries underscore that OA plays a pivotal role in augmenting the socio-environmental welfare of the regions where organizations operate (Jilani et al., 2020). Hence, a harmonized blend of both capabilities can elevate Sustainable Performance (SP), as exploratory activities yield broader market shares, long-term organizational returns, and innovative solutions to socio-environmental challenges, while exploitative endeavors refine and amplify the value proposition of existing offerings (Shafique et al., 2022).

Within the realm of viticulture, studies by Pizzol et al. (2021) and Marco-Lajara et al. (2022a) have empirically corroborated the synergistic relationship between CSR endeavors and organizational ingenuity in the wine sectors of Italy and Spain, respectively. Yet, to our discernment, holistic investigations delving into the impact of CSR on Organizational Agility (OA), which includes both pioneering and adaptive innovations, are notably limited. Additionally, inquiries exploring the connection between organizational ingenuity and vineyard outcomes primarily focus on financial indicators, frequently overlooking the socio-environmental facets, as evidenced in the researches of Annunziata et al. (2018), Broccardo et al. (2020), and Maghssudipour et al. (2020). In light of the literature surveyed, we put forth the ensuing postulations:

H2. CSR positively influences the OA within vineyards.

H3. OA positively impacts the SP of vineyards.

H4. OA acts as an intermediary in the correlation between CSR and the SP of vineyards.

Knowledge Management Infrastructure, Organizational Ambidexterity, and Sustainable Performance

From the perspective of the KBV, the assimilation of ICT augments the genesis, propagation, and application of knowledge (Al-Emran et al., 2018). Additionally, the escalating availability of information equips personnel to hone their skills and cultivate inventive cognition (Del Giudice and Della Peruta, 2016). Analogously, ICTs capacitate enterprises to relay crucial data, reconfiguring internal architectures to amplify organizational ingenuity (Trunfio and Campana, 2019). Therefore, adeptly channeling both intramural and extramural knowledge reservoirs and sculpting digital habitats through avant-garde technologies are quintessential for fostering both pioneering and adaptive innovations (Soto-Acosta and Cegarra-Navarro, 2016). This proficiency in birthing innovations anchored in both pioneering and adaptive facets can subsequently catalyze advancements in Sustainable Performance (SP) (Abbas et al., 2019).

In contrast, organizational ethos is discerned as an additional foundational pillar buttressing organizational ingenuity (Tian et al., 2018). An ethos harmonized with Organizational Flexibility (OF) characteristically radiates facets such as knowledge proliferation, psychological fortitude, leniency towards missteps, inclusiveness, reliance, empowerment, and collaborative decision-making (Suprapti et al., 2020). These characteristics can invigorate workforce engagement in creative pursuits. Reliance, as an illustration, fortifies synergy and magnifies knowledge reciprocation among colleagues, laying the groundwork for novel resolutions to institutional quandaries (Aureli et al., 2019). An ethos that accommodates missteps engenders a milieu of psychological assurance, propelling personnel towards imaginative ventures (Abdi et al., 2018). Furthermore, a milieu characterized by reliance, unambiguous dialogue, and collective decision-making motivates the workforce to articulate their perspectives and trailblaze innovative stratagems, leading to incessant innovation and operational refinements (Ghasemzadeh et al., 2019).

In a parallel context, organizations can exhibit ambidexterity, concurrently championing both exploration and exploitation, particularly when they adopt decentralized frameworks (Ali et al., 2018). Such decentralization cultivates a robust internal nexus of knowledge-centric assets, which eventually crystallize into organizational innovations (Kiefer et al., 2019). Decentralized structures amplify bespoke problem-solving, broadening the spectrum of potential solutions and fostering both exploratory and exploitative innovations, thereby enhancing OA (Darvishmotevali, 2019). As knowledge currents amplify within an entity, the prospects for organizational innovations burgeon, which can subsequently translate into augmented SP.

Within the viticulture realm, Marco-Lajara et al. (2022b) recently posited that an inclusive organizational culture serves as a primary impetus for innovation in Spanish vineyards, by streamlining knowledge dissemination internally. Concerning the nexus between technological adoption and OA, Stasi et al. (2016) and Frigon et al. (2020) empirically validated the beneficial impact of ICT proliferation and the instigation of exploratory and exploitative innovations in the Italian and Canadian viniculture contexts, respectively. Conversely, Giacomarra et al. (2021) discerned that top-down organizational structures stifle knowledge flows, thereby impeding innovation in Italian vineyards, with flatter structures emerging as more conducive to fostering an innovation-friendly ambiance.

While empirical evidence underscores the significance of plant organizational structures, open organizational cultures, and ICT in fostering innovations within the wine sector, scholarly endeavors exploring these interconnections remain limited. Furthermore, to our understanding, no prior studies within the wine domain have endeavored to holistically examine the catalysts of OA through the lens of Knowledge Management Initiatives (KMI). To bridge these gaps in the literature and drawing from the comprehensive literature review, we propose the ensuing hypotheses:

H5. KMI exerts a favorable influence on the OA of vineyards.

H6. OA serves as an intermediary conduit between KMI and the SP of vineyards.

Knowledge Management Infrastructure and Sustainable Performance

KMI holds a cardinal significance in the genesis, propagation, and application of knowledge, setting the stage for entities to achieve augmented SP (Obeidat et al., 2016). As a corollary, nurturing a collaborative institutional ethos, embracing a non-hierarchical structure, and assimilating ICT can chart a course towards progress in the economic, societal, and ecological dimensions of organizations (Di Vaio and Varriale, 2020).

The quintessence of organizational ethos is indispensable for enterprises, as it stimulates personnel to create, absorb, and spread knowledge, leading to amplified institutional financial returns (Alrowwad et al., 2017). In settings where a spirit of teamwork is fostered, and where staff members collectively support and elevate each other, it results in superior financial dividends, emanating from heightened efficiency, alongside improved societal and ecological outcomes, linked to enriched staff welfare and an elevated institutional ecological awareness (Razzaq et al., 2018). Analogously, researches by Iranmanesh et al. (2019), Isensee et al. (2020), Asadi et al. (2020), and Duke and Edet (2012) emphasize the paramountcy of organizational ethos in relation to three-dimensional performance metrics. They advocate that a resilient organizational ethos can catalyze both the financial and societal well-being of its affiliates and foster an inclination towards environmentally-conscious behaviors.

ICTs have the potential to amplify productivity and streamline operational processes, not merely by curtailing costs but also by enhancing various intangible facets, such as design prowess, inventory control systems, or knowledge stewardship (Guerola-Navarro et al., 2021). Furthermore, ICT bolsters synchronization across tasks by refining both internal and external communication frameworks, facilitating optimal information utilization between staff and leadership, and fostering robust employee interactions, thereby elevating the SP of organizations (Galati et al., 2016).

Regarding organizational architecture, it should be strategically crafted to bolster knowledge-centric endeavors, subsequently leading to performance augmentation by surmounting obstacles to knowledge inception and dissemination (Köhr et al., 2019). Modern-day entities are inclined to metamorphose their structural designs, rendering them more horizontal, thereby embedding knowledge as an integral organizational component (Guerola-Navarro et al., 2021). To realize optimal SP, the organizational blueprint must exhibit sufficient flexibility to promote collaboration and knowledge exchange among its constituents (Gold et al., 2001).

Within the viticultural domain, Marco-Lajara et al. (2022c) emphasize the significance of a collaborative ethos in augmenting the economic, social, and environmental welfare of Spanish winery personnel and pertinent stakeholders. Richter and Hanf (2021) deduce that digital transformation acts as a catalyst for the holistic sustainability of German wine cooperatives. Pertaining to organizational design, Corbo et al. (2014) ascertain that a horizontal structure promotes knowledge dissemination in Italian vineyards, leading to enhanced sustainability. Nonetheless, the academic discourse linking KMI and SP in the wine sector reveals two primary gaps. Firstly, there's a conspicuous dearth of scholarly contributions addressing the impact of KMI on winery SP. Secondly, KMIs haven't been holistically examined, with individual mechanisms aimed at refining wineries' knowledge management, and their subsequent influence on performance, being assessed in isolation. To bridge these lacunae and drawing from the comprehensive literature review, we posit the subsequent hypotheses:

H7. KMI has a positive effect on SP of wineries.

Figure 1 shows a graphical representation of the theoretical model to be tested.

Figure 1. Theoretical model

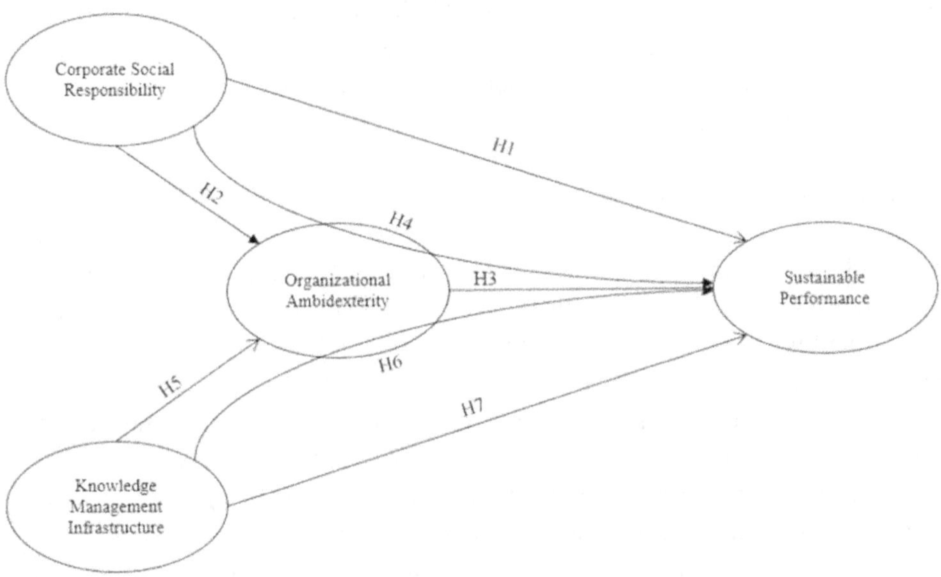

METHODOLOGY

To facilitate understanding of the methodological section, it has been divided into four blocks: (1) research context, (2) population and sample, (3) variables analyzed and (4) analysis technique.

Research Context

The focal point of this study is the viticulture sector of Spain. Several factors underpin this choice. Primarily, the Spanish viticulture sector holds a distinguished stature within the nation's economy, accounting for 2.2% of its Gross Value Added (GVA) (AFI, 2020). Beyond its economic significance, the sector is also renowned for its socio-environmental contributions. It plays a pivotal role in job creation within rural regions where vineyards are situated, safeguards the scenic beauty and historical essence of coastal viticulture zones that have witnessed urban expansion in recent times, and champions the biodiversity of the regions dedicated to wine production (Mozas-Moral et al., 2021). Additionally, knowledge has emerged as a paramount strategic resource for the Spanish viticulture sector, given its strategic evolution from mass-produced wine to premium wines endorsed by Protected Designations of Origin (PDOs) (Marco-Lajara et al., 2022d). Furthermore, the imperative for innovation within Spanish vineyards is escalating, as innovation is deemed a crucial competency for their sustained viability (Rabadán, 2021). Lastly, there exists a lacuna in empirical studies that have examined the proposed theoretical framework within the context of the Spanish viticulture sector, presenting a unique avenue to enrich academic insights.

Population and Sample

The study's target group encompasses all enterprises classified under the National Economic Activities Classification (CNAE, as denoted in Spanish) 1102, associated with viticulture. As per the records from the Iberian Financial Statement Analysis System (SABI, as termed in Spanish), there are 4,373 operational enterprises bearing the 1102 code, signifying wine production, which constitutes our study's demographic. Primary data was amassed via an online survey executed using the Qualtrics platform between September 2021 and January 2022. The survey incorporated previously authenticated scales, the specifics of which will be delineated in the ensuing subsection. It's imperative to highlight that an initial pilot test was conducted to ascertain the comprehension level of the general managers regarding the posed queries. Once their grasp of the questions was confirmed, the survey was disseminated to the general managers of Spanish viticulture enterprises, given their holistic insight, making them apt to respond accurately to the chosen scales. The initial collection yielded 216 responses, but post a meticulous scrutiny, 202 were deemed appropriate, forming the conclusive sample. At this stage, an examination for non-response bias was undertaken, comparing the initial 216 responses with the final 202. A T-test was utilized for this comparison, producing p-values exceeding 0.05 at a significance threshold of 0.05, indicating negligible variances in the analyzed responses. It's pivotal to recognize that the survey was tailored for the senior leadership of viticulture firms, predominantly the CEOs. This is attributed to the fact that top-tier executives possess a comprehensive grasp of the firm's overarching strategies and operations, rendering them more adept at addressing the survey's themes. Consequently, the findings are predicated on 202 submissions from general managers, each representing distinct wineries. These CEOs were tasked with addressing the constructs elaborated in the subsequent subsection.

Variables Analyzed

The questionnaire was meticulously designed, leveraging scales that have garnered validation in academic discourse, thus fortifying the constructs' reliability and authenticity. To measure the dimension of CSR, we embraced the metric delineated by Salmones et al. (2005). This methodology interprets CSR as an intricate variable, integrating three cardinal dimensions: economic stewardship (3 markers), ethical-juridical obligation (4 markers), and benevolent commitment (4 markers). In evaluating KMI, the 15-marker scale propounded by Lee et al. (2012) was assimilated. This metric conceptualizes KMI as an intricate variable, comprising: (1) a collaborative institutional culture, (2) ICT assimilation, and (3) a non-hierarchical institutional architecture. In congruence with antecedent studies, the OA dimension was perceived as an intricate entity, partitioned into: pioneering innovation and adaptive innovation. Notably, the 8-marker scale from Jansen et al. (2006) was harnessed, esteemed for its scholarly endorsement and its aptitude to differentiate between pioneering innovation (4 markers) and adaptive innovation (4 markers). To appraise SP, an intricate methodology was imperative, merging economic, societal, and ecological dimensions. A bespoke SP scale, inspired by Wang and Wang (2012), Paulraj (2012), and Paillé et al. (2014), was amalgamated. This gauge encompasses 15 markers, envisioning SP as a superior-tier entity, divided into: economic yield (4 markers), societal yield (6 markers), and ecological yield (5 markers). It's salient to underscore that all quartet constructs utilize a septenary Likert scale (spanning from 1-7). In summation, pertaining to control determinants, institutional magnitude, longevity, and PDO association were integrated. Institutional magnitude was ascertained per the benchmarks established by the Organization for Economic Co-operation and Development (OECD, 2005). The institution's longevity was ascertained by enumerating the years from its foundation to the investigative year (2022). PDO association was perceived as a dichotomous determinant, attributed a value of 1 if the vineyard maintained a PDO linkage and 0 in the absence of such a connection.

Analysis Technique

To evaluate the proposed theoretical framework, the study employed partial least squares structural equation modeling (PLS-SEM) via the SmartPLS software, version 4.0.0. This method facilitates the examination of interrelations between both manifest and latent variables. Given its capability to analyze unobservable phenomena, PLS-SEM is highly regarded in social sciences and notably within the domain of Management, as many of the subjects under investigation are inherently intangible (Henseler et al., 2016). Several rationales underpin the adoption of this methodology. Firstly, the sample size in this research (n=202) aligns with the recommended minimum threshold of 100, as suggested by Reinartz et al. (2009). Secondly, the study aims to assess both direct and indirect associations among variables, making PLS-SEM an apt choice for such evaluations (Roldan and Cepeda, 2017). Lastly, given the composite nature of the constructs under scrutiny (namely CSR, KMI, OA, and SP), PLS-SEM emerges as a potent instrument for dissecting such multidimensional constructs (Sarstedt et al., 2022; Sánchez-García et al., 2023; Martínez-Falcó et al., 2023).

RESULTS

Given the intricate constitution of the variables under scrutiny, a bifurcated model predicated on variable scores was utilized. In the preliminary phase, scores for the latent determinants were ascertained, which were subsequently regarded as markers for the superior-tier determinants. To elucidate the research's outcomes, we conformed to the protocols delineated by Hair et al. (2019), which recommend partitioning the results into a triad of discrete segments: (1) scrutiny of the holistic model, (2) examination of the measurement model, and (3) analysis of the structural model.

Commencing with the holistic model scrutiny, the empirical evidence indicates a commendable alignment for the model. The Standardized Root Mean Squared Residual (SRMSR) metric is registered at a value marginally below 0.08 (precisely, 0.074), signifying the model's appropriateness (Hu and Bentler, 1998). Moreover, determinants linked to the unweighted least squares discrepancy (d_ULS) and the geodesic discrepancy (d_G) reside beneath the HI95 and HI99 thresholds, corroborating their positioning within the bootstrapped confidence spectrum.

Following the comprehensive alignment assessment, the research advanced to inspect the measurement model, emphasizing indicator dependability, intrinsic consistency, convergent authenticity, and discriminant authenticity. In relation to indicator dependability, as expounded in Table 1, all markers fulfill individual dependability standards, with their loadings eclipsing the 0.707 benchmark, a demarcation pinpointed by Carmines and Zeller (1979). This validates the markers' proficiency in capturing the intended determinants. It's imperative to accentuate that these loadings are statistically consequential post bootstrapping.

Regarding intrinsic consistency, Table 1 portrays that metrics such as Cronbach's alpha, composite dependability (Pc), and the Dijkstra-Henseler criterion (Pa) consistently surpass the 0.80 demarcation, thereby satisfying the prescribed standards. This connotes a uniform linkage amidst the markers, highlighting the interconnected essence of the determinants (Dijkstra and Henseler, 2015). Additionally, the constructs fulfill the convergent authenticity standards, with Average Variance Extracted (AVE) metrics exceeding the 0.50 demarcation, suggesting that the items represent a notable segment of the variance (Hair et al., 2019). Discriminant authenticity, as depicted in Table 2, is also corroborated, with metrics registering beneath the 0.85 demarcation (Kline, 2011). This emphasizes the uniqueness of each determinant, certifying they represent distinct dimensions of the investigated phenomena.

Table 1. Measurement model analysis: external loadings, construct reliability, and convergent validity

Construct/Items	Outer Loadings	Rho_c (Pc)	Rho_a (Pa)	Cronbach's Alpha	AVE
Corporate Social Responsibility (CSR)		0.867	0.845	0.782	0.685
CSR 1	0.803				
CSR 2	0.805				
CSR 3	0.872				
Kowledge Management Infrastructure (KMI)		0.887	0.817	0.809	0.723
KMI 1	0.847				
KMI 2	0.836				
KMI 3	0.868				
Organizational Ambidexterity (OA)		0.942	0.881	0.878	0.942
OA 1	0.940				
OA 2	0.948				
Sustainable Performance (SP)		0.894	0.826	0.820	0.738
SP 1	0.799				
SP 2	0.850				
SP 3	0.922				

Note: The indicators for the second-order variables are: CSR 1= Economic Responsibility; CSR 2= Ethical-legal Responsibility; CSR 3= Philanthropic Responsibility; KMI 1= Collaborative Organizational Culture; KMI 2= ICTs; KMI 3= Decentralized Organizational Structure; OA 1= Exploratory innovation; OA 2= Exploitative innovation; SP 1= Economic Performance; SP 2= Social Performance, SP 3= Green Performance.

Source: compiled by authors

Table 2. Discriminant validity analysis based on the Heterotrait-Monotrait criterion

	OA	AGE	PDO	KMI	SP	CSR	SIZE
OA							
AGE	0.113						
PDO	0.143	0.123					
KMI	0.669	0.078	0.059				
SP	0.619	0.075	0.310	0.519			
CSR	0.494	0.079	0.058	0.669	0.424		
SIZE	0.194	0.113	0.134	0.124	0.262	0.241	

Source: compiled by authors

Subsequent to the evaluations of the holistic and measurement models, the research transitioned to the structural model, scrutinizing the path coefficients, the R-squared metric, and the predictive significance as indicated by Q2. Figure 2 showcases the information related to the path and R-squared coefficients, extracted from a bootstrap analysis comprising 5,000 subsets. Manifestly, both direct and mediated effects emerge as positive and possess statistical relevance. This accentuates that the CSR endeavors, OA, and KMI undertaken by Spanish vineyards wield a positive and pronounced impact on their SP. Additionally, the propitious character of both direct and mediated linkages implies a partial intermediation of OA in the CSR-SP linkage and the KMI-SP association, with an aggregate effect of CSR on SP recorded at 0.183 ($p<0.000$) and an aggregate effect of KMI on SP amounting to 0.340 ($p<0.000$).

The model's findings thereby validate the septet of hypotheses proposed, as there exists a positive and consequential influence of CSR on SP (H1. $\beta=0.121$; $p<0.092$), a positive and consequential influence of CSR on SP (H2. $\beta=0.189$; $p<0.017$), a positive and consequential influence of OA on SP (H3. $\beta=0.326$; $p<0.000$), a positive and consequential influence of KMI on OA (H5. $\beta=0.464$; $p<0.000$), and a positive and consequential influence of KMI on SP (H7. $\beta=0.189$; $p<0.085$). Moreover, OA operates as a partial intermediary in the CSR-SP bond (H4. $\beta=0.062$; $p<0.048$) and the KMI-SP nexus (H6. $\beta=0.151$; $p<0.002$). This insinuates that the most robust affiliations are those tethering KMI and OA to SP. In relation to the control determinants, the model's findings unveil that both magnitude ($\beta=0.106$; $p<0.028$) and PDO association ($\beta=0.244$; $p<0.000$) sustain a positive and consequential relationship, with confidence intervals of 95% and 99%, respectively. To assess the model's proficiency, the Geisser examination (Q2) was conducted, which necessitates metrics surpassing 0 ($Q2 > 0$) to validate the model's predictive relevance.

Figure 2. Results of the theoretical model formulated

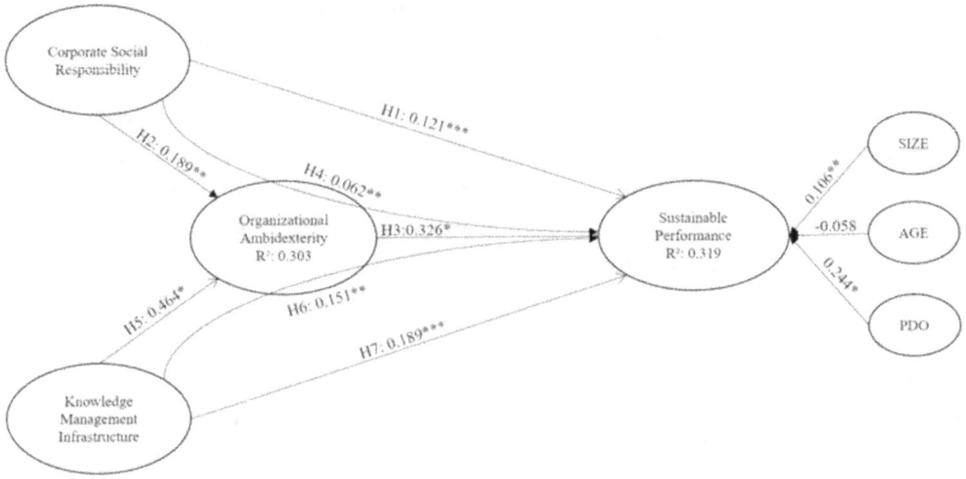

DISCUSSION AND CONCLUSION

In contemporary times, wineries face escalating demands to enhance the societal and environmental spheres they operate within. Within this backdrop, the CSR initiatives and KMI strategies adopted by wineries become pivotal, not only in countering the negative ramifications of winery operations but also in fostering both exploratory and operational innovations, culminating in an uplifted SP.

The outcomes of this investigation suggest that the embracement of CSR initiatives, cultivation of a synergistic milieu, assimilation of ICT, and advocacy for a non-hierarchical institutional architecture collectively amplify the emergence of both pioneering and adaptive innovations, leading to the augmentation of the SP within Spanish vineyards. Consequently, within the Spanish wine-producing domain, both CSR and KMI materialize as cardinal catalysts for OA and SP.

The discerned affirmative association between CSR and the SP of vineyards resonates with perspectives articulated by Annunziata et al. (2018) and Pizzol et al. (2021) within the Italian wine-producing realm. This inquiry also harmonizes with observations from Marco-Lajara et al. (2022a), emphasizing the paramountcy of CSR endeavors by Spanish vineyards in steering organizational innovative pathways. Nonetheless, this scholarly endeavor probes more profoundly, scrutinizing the aptitude to simultaneously nurture pioneering and adaptive innovations, denominated as OA. Furthermore, while antecedent inquiries predominantly fixated on financial outcomes, this exploration expands the purview to include societal and ecological outcomes, drawing from both the NRBV and KBV paradigms.

The identified affirmative linkage between KMI and SP reflects conclusions from researches such as Corbo et al. (2014), Richter and Hanf et al. (2021), and Marco-Lajara et al. (2022c) within the Italian, German, and Spanish viticultural sectors, respectively. Yet, this investigation distinctively amalgamates diverse knowledge management enablers under the consolidated KMI determinant, proffering a comprehensive viewpoint on the role of a synergistic ethos, ICT assimilation, and non-hierarchical configurations in knowledge fluxes within vineyards.

From a pragmatic standpoint, these insights can guide top-tier management in wineries aiming to bolster their economic, social, and environmental dividends. Wineries should cultivate a collaborative ethos, digitalize processes, and decentralize their organizational frameworks to enhance knowledge dynamics, thereby positively influencing their innovation trajectories and, by extension, their SP. Ethically, wineries should not only adhere to extant regulations but also champion ethical practices, embracing initiatives like circular economy programs, by-product valorization, and adherence to quality seals like organic or vegan wine certifications.

Theoretically, this research elucidates the positive influence of OA on the SP of Spanish wineries and underscores the catalytic roles of CSR and KMI. Consequently, the research questions posited are addressed, highlighting the interplay between CSR, KMI, OA, and SP, and offering a novel perspective on enhancing wineries' multifaceted performance.

Despite its contributions, the study isn't devoid of limitations. Given the study's significance and the limited literature on the topic, it's imperative to expand the analysis to other viticultural regions. Future research endeavors could explore the South African wine sector, drawing comparisons between Old and New World wine nations. Additionally, while the study incorporates age, size, and PDO membership as control variables, other influential variables remain unexplored. Future research could integrate factors like export orientation and R&D budgets to offer a more comprehensive analysis.

ACKNOWLEDGMENT

Portions of this work have been previously reported in this research: Marco-Lajara, B., Zaragoza-Saez, P., Falcó, J. M., & Millan-Tudela, L. A. (2022). Analysing the relationship between green intellectual capital and the achievement of the sustainable development goals. In *Handbook of Research on Building Inclusive Global Knowledge Societies for Sustainable Development* (pp. 111-129). IGI Global.

REFERENCES

Abbas, J. (2020). Impact of total quality management on corporate green performance through the mediating role of corporate social responsibility. *Journal of Cleaner Production, 242*, 118458. doi:10.1016/j.jclepro.2019.118458

Abbas, J., Hussain, I., Hussain, S., Akram, S., Shaheen, I., & Niu, B. (2019). The impact of knowledge sharing and innovation on sustainable performance in Islamic banks: A mediation analysis through a SEM approach. *Sustainability (Basel), 11*(15), 4049. doi:10.3390u11154049

Abdi, K., Mardani, A., Senin, A., Tupenaite, L., Naimaviciene, J., Kanapeckiene, L., & Kutut, V. (2018). The effect of knowledge management, organizational culture and organizational learning on innovation in automotive industry. *Journal of Business Economics and Management, 19*(1), 1–19. doi:10.3846/jbem.2018.1477

AFI. 2020. *Importancia económica y social del sector vitivinícola en España* [Economic and social importance of the wine sector in Spain]. Available at: https://www.interprofesionaldelvino.es/publicaciones/informes-importancia-sector/nacional/

Aftab, J., Veneziani, M., Sarwar, H., & Ishaq, M. (2022). Organizational ambidexterity, firm performance, and sustainable development: Mediating role of entrepreneurial orientation in Pakistani SMEs. *Journal of Cleaner Production, 367*, 132956. doi:10.1016/j.jclepro.2022.132956

Al-Emran, M., Mezhuyev, V., Kamaludin, A., & Shaalan, K. (2018). The impact of knowledge management processes on information systems: A systematic review. *International Journal of Information Management, 43*, 173–187. doi:10.1016/j.ijinfomgt.2018.08.001

Ali, M., Ali, I., Al-Maimani, K., & Park, K. (2018). The effect of organizational structure on absorptive capacity In single and dual learning modes. *Journal of Innovation & Knowledge, 3*(3), 108–114. doi:10.1016/j.jik.2017.03.007

Alrowwad, A., Obeidat, B., Tarhini, A., & Aqqad, N. (2017). The impact of transformational leadership on organizational performance via the mediating role of corporate social responsibility: A structural equation modeling approach. *International Business Research, 10*(1), 199–221. doi:10.5539/ibr.v10n1p199

Annunziata, E., Pucci, T., Frey, M., & Zanni, L. (2018). The role of organizational capabilities in attaining corporate sustainability practices and economic performance: Evidence from Italian wine industry. *Journal of Cleaner Production, 171*, 1300–1311. doi:10.1016/j.jclepro.2017.10.035

Asadi, S., Pourhashemi, S., Nilashi, M., Abdullah, R., Samad, S., Yadegaridehkordi, E., & Razali, N. (2020). Investigating influence of green innovation on sustainability performance: A case on Malaysian hotel industry. *Journal of Cleaner Production, 258*, 120860. doi:10.1016/j.jclepro.2020.120860

Aureli, S., Giampaoli, D., Ciambotti, M., & Bontis, N. (2019). Key factors that improve knowledge-intensive business processes which lead to competitive advantage. *Business Process Management Journal, 25*(1), 126–143. doi:10.1108/BPMJ-06-2017-0168

Bahta, D., Yun, J., Islam, M., & Ashfaq, M. (2020). Corporate social responsibility, innovation capability and firm performance: Evidence from SME. *Social Responsibility Journal, 17*(6), 840–860. doi:10.1108/SRJ-12-2019-0401

Bahta, D., Yun, J., Islam, M., & Bikanyi, K. (2021). How does CSR enhance the financial performance of SMEs? The mediating role of firm reputation. *Ekonomska Istrazivanja, 34*(1), 1428–1451. doi:10.1080/1331677X.2020.1828130

Bandinelli, R., Acuti, D., Fani, V., Bindi, B., & Aiello, G. (2020). Environmental practices in the wine industry: An overview of the Italian market. *British Food Journal, 122*(5), 1625–1646. doi:10.1108/BFJ-08-2019-0653

Broadstock, D., Matousek, R., Meyer, M., & Tzeremes, N. (2020). Does corporate social responsibility impact firms' innovation capacity? The indirect link between environmental & social governance implementation and innovation performance. *Journal of Business Research, 119*, 99–110. doi:10.1016/j.jbusres.2019.07.014

Broccardo, L., & Zicari, A. (2020). Sustainability as a driver for value creation: A business model analysis of small and medium entreprises in the Italian wine sector. *Journal of Cleaner Production, 259*, 120852. doi:10.1016/j.jclepro.2020.120852

Bustinza, O., Vendrell-Herrero, F., & Gomes, E. (2020). Unpacking the effect of strategic ambidexterity on performance: A cross-country comparison of MMNEs developing product-service innovation. *International Business Review, 29*(6), 101569. doi:10.1016/j.ibusrev.2019.01.004

Carmines, E., & Zeller, R. (1979). *Reliability and validity assessment* (Vol. 17). SAGE. doi:10.4135/9781412985642

Cheah, S., & Ho, Y. (2019). Coworking and sustainable business model innovation in young firms. *Sustainability (Basel), 11*(10), 2959. doi:10.3390u11102959

Corbo, C., Lamastra, L., & Capri, E. (2014). From environmental to sustainability programs: A review of sustainability initiatives in the Italian wine sector. *Sustainability (Basel)*, *6*(4), 2133–2159. doi:10.3390u6042133

Darvishmotevali, M. (2019). Decentralization and innovative behavior: The moderating role of supervisor support. *International Journal of Organizational Leadership*, *8*(1), 31–45. doi:10.33844/ijol.2019.60204

Del Giudice, M., & Della Peruta, M. (2016). The impact of IT-based knowledge management systems on internal venturing and innovation: A structural equation modeling approach to corporate performance. *Journal of Knowledge Management*, *20*(3), 484–498. doi:10.1108/JKM-07-2015-0257

Di Vaio, A., & Varriale, L. (2020). Blockchain technology in supply chain management for sustainable performance: Evidence from the airport industry. *International Journal of Information Management*, *52*, 102014. doi:10.1016/j.ijinfomgt.2019.09.010

Dijkstra, T., & Henseler, J. (2015). Consistent partial least squares path modeling. *Management Information Systems Quarterly*, *39*(2), 297–316. doi:10.25300/MISQ/2015/39.2.02

Esposito, B., Sessa, M., Sica, D., & Malandrino, O. (2021). Exploring Corporate Social Responsibility in the Italian wine sector through websites. *The TQM Journal*, *33*(7), 222–252. doi:10.1108/TQM-11-2020-0264

European Commission. (2023). *European Commission Adopts Market Measures to Support EU Wine Producers*. https://agriculture.ec.europa.eu/news/european-commission-adopts-market-measures-support-eu-wine-producers-2023-06-23_en

European Parliament. (2023). *Briefing: The EU Wine Sector*. https://www.europarl.europa.eu/RegData/etudes/BRIE/2023/751399/EPRS_BRI(2023)751399_EN.pdf

Flores, S. (2018). What is sustainability in the wine world? A cross-country analysis of wine sustainability frameworks. *Journal of Cleaner Production*, *172*, 2301–2312. doi:10.1016/j.jclepro.2017.11.181

Frigon, A., Doloreux, D., & Shearmur, R. (2020). Drivers of eco-innovation and conventional innovation in the Canadian wine industry. *Journal of Cleaner Production*, *275*, 124115. doi:10.1016/j.jclepro.2020.124115

Galati, A., Crescimanno, M., Tinervia, S., & Siggia, D. (2016). Website quality and internal business factors: An empirical investigation in the Italian wine industry. *International Journal of Wine Business Research*, *28*(4), 308–326. doi:10.1108/IJWBR-08-2015-0026

Ghasemzadeh, P., Nazari, J., Farzaneh, M., & Mehralian, G. (2019). Moderating role of innovation culture in the relationship between organizational learning and innovation performance. *The Learning Organization*, *26*(3), 289–303. doi:10.1108/TLO-08-2018-0139

Giacomarra, M., Shams, S., Crescimanno, M., Sakka, G., Gregori, G., & Galati, A. (2021). Internal vs. external R&D teams: Evidences from the Italian wine industry. *Journal of Business Research*, *128*, 752–761. doi:10.1016/j.jbusres.2019.05.029

Guan, X., Ahmad, N., Sial, M., Cherian, J., & Han, H. (2022). CSR and organizational performance: The role of pro-environmental behavior and personal values. *Corporate Social Responsibility and Environmental Management*, *2022*, 1–18.

Guerola-Navarro, V., Oltra-Badenes, R., Gil-Gomez, H., & Fernández, A. (2021). Customer relationship management (CRM) and Innovation: A qualitative comparative analysis (QCA) in the search for improvements on the firm performance in winery sector. *Technological Forecasting and Social Change*, *169*, 120838. doi:10.1016/j.techfore.2021.120838

Hadj, T. (2020). Effects of corporate social responsibility towards stakeholders and environmental management on responsible innovation and competitiveness. *Journal of Cleaner Production*, *250*, 119490. doi:10.1016/j.jclepro.2019.119490

Hair, Hult, Ringle, Sarstedt, Danks, & Ray. (2021). *Partial least squares structural equation modeling (PLS-SEM) using R: A workbook*. Springer.

Hair, J., Sarstedt, M., & Ringle, C. (2019). Rethinking some of the rethinking of partial least squares. *European Journal of Marketing*, *53*(4), 566–584. doi:10.1108/EJM-10-2018-0665

Halkos, G., & Skouloudis, A. (2018). Corporate social responsibility and innovative capacity: Intersection in a macro-level perspective. *Journal of Cleaner Production*, *182*, 291–300. doi:10.1016/j.jclepro.2018.02.022

Henseler, J., Hubona, G., & Ray, P. (2016). Using PLS path modeling in new technology research: Updated guidelines. *Industrial Management & Data Systems*, *116*(1), 2–20. doi:10.1108/IMDS-09-2015-0382

Hu, L., & Bentler, P. (1998). Fit indices in covariance structure modeling: Sensitivity to underparameterized model misspecification. *Psychological Methods*, *3*(4), 424–453. doi:10.1037/1082-989X.3.4.424

Hussain, N., Rigoni, U., & Cavezzali, E. (2018). Does it pay to be sustainable? Looking inside the black box of the relationship between sustainability performance and financial performance. *Corporate Social Responsibility and Environmental Management*, *25*(6), 1198–1211. doi:10.1002/csr.1631

Iranmanesh, M., Zailani, S., Hyun, S., Ali, M., & Kim, K. (2019). Impact of lean manufacturing practices on firms' sustainable performance: Lean culture as a moderator. *Sustainability (Basel)*, *11*(4), 1112. doi:10.3390u11041112

Isensee, C., Teuteberg, F., Griese, K., & Topi, C. (2020). The relationship between organizational culture, sustainability, and digitalization in SMEs: A systematic review. *Journal of Cleaner Production*, *275*, 122944. doi:10.1016/j.jclepro.2020.122944

Jansen, J., Van Den Bosch, F., & Volberda, H. (2006). Exploratory Innovation, Exploitative Innovation, and Performance: Effects of Organizational Antecedents and Environmental Moderators. *Management Science*, *52*(11), 1661–1674. doi:10.1287/mnsc.1060.0576

Jilani, M., Fan, L., Islam, M., & Uddin, A. (2020). The influence of knowledge sharing on sustainable performance: A moderated mediation study. *Sustainability (Basel)*, *12*(3), 908. doi:10.3390u12030908

Kariyapperuma, N., & Collins, E. (2021). Family logics and environmental sustainability: A study of the New Zealand wine industry. *Business Strategy and the Environment*, *30*(8), 3626–3650. doi:10.1002/bse.2823

Khan, S., Yu, Z., & Umar, M. (2021). How environmental awareness and corporate social responsibility practices benefit the enterprise? An empirical study in the context of emerging economy. *Management of Environmental Quality*, *32*(5), 863–885. doi:10.1108/MEQ-08-2020-0178

Kiefer, C., Del Rio Gonzalez, P., & Carrillo-Hermosilla, J. (2019). Drivers and barriers of eco-innovation types for sustainable transitions: A quantitative perspective. *Business Strategy and the Environment*, *28*(1), 155–172. doi:10.1002/bse.2246

Kline, R. (2011). *Principles and practice of structural equation modelling*. Guilford Press.

Köhr, C., Corsi, A., Capitello, R., & Szolnoki, G. (2019). Family culture and organisational systems as antecedents of market orientation and performance among family wineries. *International Journal of Wine Business Research*, *31*(2), 180–202. doi:10.1108/IJWBR-09-2017-0054

Lee, S., Kim, B., & Kim, H. (2012). An integrated view of knowledge management for performance. *Journal of Knowledge Management*, *16*(2), 183–203. doi:10.1108/13673271211218807

Maghssudipour, A., Lazzeretti, L., & Capone, F. (2020). The role of multiple ties in knowledge networks: Complementarity in the Montefalco wine cluster. *Industrial Marketing Management*, *90*, 667–678. doi:10.1016/j.indmarman.2020.03.021

Marco-Lajara, B., Seva-Larrosa, P., Martínez-Falcó, J., & García-Lillo, F. (2022d). Wine clusters and Protected Designations of Origin (PDOs) in Spain: An exploratory analysis. *Journal of Wine Research*, *33*(3), 146–167. doi:10.1080/09571264.2022.2110051

Marco-Lajara, B., Zaragoza-Sáez, P., Martínez-Falcó, J., & Ruiz-Fernández, L. (2022b). The Effect of Green Intellectual Capital on Green Performance in the Spanish Wine Industry: A Structural Equation Modeling Approach. *Complexity*, *2022*, 1–17. doi:10.1155/2022/6024077

Marco-Lajara, B., Zaragoza-Sáez, P., Martínez-Falcó, J., & Sánchez-García, E. (2022a). *Does green intellectual capital affect green innovation performance? Evidence from the Spanish wine industry. British Food Journal.*

Marco-Lajara, B., Zaragoza-Sáez, P., Martínez-Falcó, J., & Sánchez-García, E. 2022c. Green Intellectual Capital in the Spanish Wine Industry. In Innovative Economic, Social, and Environmental Practices for Progressing Future Sustainability (pp. 102-120). IGI Global. doi:10.4018/978-1-7998-9590-9.ch006

Martínez-Falcó, J., Marco-Lajara, B., Zaragoza-Sáez, P. D. C., & Millan-Tudela, L. A. (2023). Do circular economy practices moderate the wine tourism–green performance relationship? A structural analysis applied to the Spanish wine industry. *British Food Journal*. Advance online publication. doi:10.1108/BFJ-10-2022-0833

Miranda, B., Ross, B., Franken, J., & Gómez, M. (2022). Plural forms and differentiation strategies in the agri-food sector: Evidence from the US wine industry. *Agribusiness*, *38*(3), 486–504. doi:10.1002/agr.21741

Mozas-Moral, A., Fernández-Uclés, D., Medina-Viruel, M., & Bernal-Jurado, E. (2021). The role of the SDGs as enhancers of the performance of Spanish wine cooperatives. *Technological Forecasting and Social Change*, *173*, 121176. doi:10.1016/j.techfore.2021.121176

Muñoz, R., Fernández, M., & Salinero, Y. (2020). Sustainability, corporate social responsibility, and performance in the Spanish wine sector. *Sustainability (Basel)*, *13*(1), 7. doi:10.3390u13010007

Obeidat, B., Al-Suradi, M., Masa'deh, R., & Tarhini, A. (2016). The impact of knowledge management on innovation: An empirical study on Jordanian consultancy firms. *Management Research Review*, *39*(10), 1214–1238. doi:10.1108/MRR-09-2015-0214

OECD. (2005). *Manual de Oslo: Guía para la recogida e interpretación de datos sobre innovación* [Oslo Manual: A Guide to Collecting and Interpreting Innovation Data]. Retrieved from: http://www.itq.edu.mx/convocatorias/manualdeoslo.pdf

Paillé, P., Chen, Y., Boiral, O., & Jin, J. (2014). The impact of human resource management on environmental performance: An employee-level study. *Journal of Business Ethics*, *121*(3), 451–466. doi:10.100710551-013-1732-0

Paulraj, A. (2011). Understanding the relationships between internal resources and capabilities, sustainable supply management and organizational sustainability. *The Journal of Supply Chain Management*, *47*(1), 19–37. doi:10.1111/j.1745-493X.2010.03212.x

Pizzol, L., Luzzani, G., Criscione, P., Barro, L., Bagnoli, C., & Capri, E. (2021). The Role of Corporate Social Responsibility in the Wine Industry: The Case Study of Veneto and Friuli Venezia Giulia. *Sustainability (Basel)*, *13*(23), 13230. doi:10.3390u132313230

Podsakoff, P. M., & Organ, D. W. (1986). Self-reports in organizational research: Problems and prospects. *Journal of Management*, *12*(4), 531–544. doi:10.1177/014920638601200408

Popescu, C. R. G. (2020). Approaches to Sustainable and Responsible Entrepreneurship: Creativity, Innovation, and Intellectual Capital as Drivers for Organization Performance. In B. Hernández-Sánchez, J. Sánchez-García, & A. Moreira (Eds.), *Building an Entrepreneurial and Sustainable Society* (pp. 75–95). IGI Global. doi:10.4018/978-1-7998-2704-7.ch004

Popescu, C. R. G. (2021). Sustainable and Responsible Entrepreneurship for Value-Based Cultures, Economies, and Societies: Increasing Performance Through Intellectual Capital in Challenging Times. In C. Popescu & R. Verma (Eds.), *Sustainable and Responsible Entrepreneurship and Key Drivers of Performance* (pp. 33–58). IGI Global. doi:10.4018/978-1-7998-7951-0.ch002

Popescu, C. R. G. (2022). Mindfulness Business Principles: Producing Outstanding Value and Encouraging Community Connections. In C. Popescu (Ed.), *COVID-19 Pandemic Impact on New Economy Development and Societal Change* (pp. 196–228). IGI Global. doi:10.4018/978-1-6684-3374-4.ch010

Rabadán, A. (2021). Consumer attitudes towards technological innovation in a traditional food product: The case of wine. *Foods*, *10*(6), 1363. doi:10.3390/foods10061363 PMID:34204607

Raza, A., Farrukh, M., Iqbal, M., Farhan, M., & Wu, Y. (2021). Corporate social responsibility and employees' voluntary pro-environmental behavior: The role of organizational pride and employee engagement. *Corporate Social Responsibility and Environmental Management*, *28*(3), 1104–1116. doi:10.1002/csr.2109

Razzaq, S., Shujahat, M., Hussain, S., Nawaz, F., Wang, M., Ali, M., & Tehseen, S. (2018). Knowledge management, organizational commitment and knowledge-worker performance: The neglected role of knowledge management in the public sector. *Business Process Management Journal*, *25*(5), 923–947. doi:10.1108/BPMJ-03-2018-0079

Reinartz, W., Haenlein, M., & Henseler, J. (2009). An empirical comparison of theefficacy of covariance-based and variance-based SEM. *International Journal of Research in Marketing*, *26*(4), 332–344. doi:10.1016/j.ijresmar.2009.08.001

Richter, B., & Hanf, J. (2021). Cooperatives in the wine industry: Sustainable management practices and digitalisation. *Sustainability (Basel)*, *13*(10), 5543. doi:10.3390u13105543

Roldan, J., & Cepeda, G. (2017). Modelos de Ecuaciones basados en la Varianza: Partial Least Squares (PLS) para Investigadores en Ciencias Sociales (4a ed.). Universidad de Sevilla.

Salmones, M., Crespo, A., & Bosque, I. (2005). Influence of corporate social responsibility on loyalty and valuation of services. *Journal of Business Ethics*, *61*(4), 369–385. doi:10.100710551-005-5841-2

Sánchez-García, E., Martínez-Falcó, J., Alcon-Vila, A., & Marco-Lajara, B. (2023). Developing Green Innovations in the Wine Industry: An Applied Analysis. *Foods*, *12*(6), 1157. doi:10.3390/foods12061157 PMID:36981084

Sarstedt, M., Radomir, L., Moisescu, O. I., & Ringle, C. M. (2022). Latent class analysis in PLS-SEM: A review and recommendations for future applications. *Journal of Business Research*, *138*, 398–407. doi:10.1016/j.jbusres.2021.08.051

Shafique, I., Kalyar, M., & Mehwish, N. (2021). Organizational ambidexterity, green entrepreneurial orientation, and environmental performance in SMEs context: Examining the moderating role of perceived CSR. *Corporate Social Responsibility and Environmental Management*, *28*(1), 446–456. doi:10.1002/csr.2060

Soto-Acosta, P., & Cegarra-Navarro, J. (2016). New ICTs for knowledge management in organizations. *Journal of Knowledge Management*, *20*(3), 417–422. doi:10.1108/JKM-02-2016-0057

Stasi, A., Muscio, A., Nardone, G., & Seccia, A. (2016). New technologies and sustainability in the Italian wine industry. *Agriculture and Agricultural Science Procedia*, *8*, 290–297. doi:10.1016/j.aaspro.2016.02.023

Suprapti, S., Asbari, M., Cahyono, Y., Mufid, A., & Khasanah, N. (2020). Leadership style, organizational culture and innovative behavior on public health center performance during Pandemic Covid-19. *Journal of Industrial Engineering & Management Research*, *1*(2), 76–88.

Tarba, S., Jansen, J., Mom, T., Raisch, S., & Lawton, T. (2020). A microfoundational perspective of organizational ambidexterity: Critical review and research directions. *Long Range Planning*, *53*(6), 102048. doi:10.1016/j.lrp.2020.102048

Tian, M., Deng, P., Zhang, Y., & Salmador, M. (2018). How does culture influence innovation? A systematic literature review. *Management Decision*, *56*(5), 1088–1107. doi:10.1108/MD-05-2017-0462

Trunfio, M., & Campana, S. (2019). Drivers and emerging innovations in knowledge-based destinations: Towards a research agenda. *Journal of Destination Marketing & Management*, *14*, 100370. doi:10.1016/j.jdmm.2019.100370

Wang, Z., & Wang, N. (2012). Knowledge sharing, innovation and firm performance. *Expert Systems with Applications*, *39*(10), 8899–8908. doi:10.1016/j.eswa.2012.02.017

Chapter 9
Project Management Maturity:
OPM3 Study

Jorge Vareda Gomes
https://orcid.org/0000-0003-0656-9284
Universidade Lusófona, Lisboa, Portugal

Mário Batista Romão
https://orcid.org/0000-0003-4564-1883
ISEG, Universidade de Lisboa, Portugal

Ilércio Bento
ISEG, Universidade de Lisboa, Portugal

ABSTRACT

The objective of this chapter is to study the impact of organisational project management (OPM3) on the project performance (PP). PP performed by the organisations was assessed, based on interviews with project managers. Currently, little evidence is found in the academic literature regarding the impacts of the maturity models (MM) on the PP. The results show that the OPM3 provided a positive contribution to PP. Some of the interviewees stated that the adoption of OPM3 brought improvements at the process level, which made it possible to define in a more appropriate way, the scope, schedule, costs, and goals to perform improvements in the stakeholder's communication.

DOI: 10.4018/979-8-3693-1151-6.ch009

INTRODUCTION

In nowadays, there is a need to work with faster and more flexible organisational structures, which force companies to operate through projects which usually help them to successfully achieve their objectives. Furthermore, in an increasingly competitive business environment, it is necessary to ensure that the successful results of one project can be extended to future initiatives and investments, using standardised procedures (Gomes & Romão, 2014).

Projects are discrete but multidimensional activities that serve as vehicles of change, promoting investments made by the organisations with the goal of obtaining internal process enhancements and business benefits (Bannerman, 2008). In fact, projects are unique and designed to deliver beneficial change, so managing project goals and business benefits underpins all aspects of successful projects (Gomes & Romão, 2015). Projects are temporary endeavors undertaken to create a product, service, or result (PMI, 2016).

Project success means different things to different stakeholders. A project that seems successfully for customers could be a completely failed experience for contractors or to the end-users (Toor & Ogunlana, 2008). Stakeholders have distinct interests in different projects and therefore the perception of success vary differently across the various stakeholders (Bryde & Brown, 2005).

The definition of project success is not consensual and several authors agree that success can be achieved by the action of the project manager (Baccarini, 1999; Pinto & Slevin, 1988; Ika, 2009; McLeod et al., 2012). The *iron triangle,* the classic criterion is a measure of the immediate PP against the main design parameters - schedule (time), budget (cost) and technical requirements (quality) (Bannerman, 2008).

The *iron triangle criteria* were the very first approach of PM success (De Wit, 1988), which has later proven to be only a part of overall project success. Project manager is not responsible only for time, cost and quality management, but also to other factors, such as, integration, scope, human resource, communication, risk, procurement and stakeholder's management (PMI (2013a).

Maturity models have become an essential tool for assessing organisations' current capabilities and helping them to implement change and improvement in a structured way (Jia et al., 2011). Maturity model is a set of characteristics, attributes, indicators, or patterns that represent progression and achievement in a specific domain or discipline (Caralli et al., 2012). Maturity is often associated with step stages schema, presented in the organisational management practices that make it possible to achieve project success (Besner, & Hobbs, 2013). Not surprisingly, the concept of maturity was also diffused to the project management field. Different views exist regarding maturity in relation to project management. A significant number of competing perspectives attempt to describe mature project management practices (Cooke-Davies & Arzymanow, 2003; Hillson, 2003; Ibbs & Kwak, 2000; Jachimowicz, 2003; Mullaly, 2006; PMI, 2013a; Sawaya & Trapanese, 2004; Skulmoski, 2001). These approaches assume that increasing maturity of project management will lead to improvements in performance and results of more consistent and successful projects.

Many project maturity models emerged last decades and have been described in the PM literature (Hillson, 2001; Kerzner, 2001; Crawford, 2006; Ibbs, Reginato & Kwak, 2003). As organisations grow in terms of PM maturity, they achieve better performance at lower costs (Ibbs & Reginato, 2002). The existence of an appropriate organisational structure and economies of scale maximise the efficiency of PM efforts in obtaining projects that accomplished predefined goals.

These different stages of maturity that organisations present in terms of PM practices are defined as the level of sophistication of the PM practices development, processes and performance (Kwak & Ibbs, 2000). However, each organisation has an intrinsic operation mode that sets it apart from other organisations and, as such, implements different practices in the execution of its projects. This is a main factor that contributes to the failure of the projects (Jugdev & Thomas, 2002). To overcome this difficulty best practice frameworks emergence to help organisations to achieve their goals.

According to Grant & Pennypacker (2006), MM support the development capacity of organisations, which in turn reinforce the internal processes used to manage all the projects and relate them to the best of the organisational strategy. Despite the apparent benefits of MM for PM in the organisations, there is insufficient evidence to support the relationship between MM and improvements in the performance of organisations' projects (Grant & Pennypacker, 2006; Brookes et al., 2014; Yazici, 2009). Mullaly (2006, 2014) claimed the real contribution of MM to the success of the projects of organisations in to obtaining competitive advantage. Recognition of the maturity models' approach is also evidenced by the large investments made by businesses, governments and the third sector in developing skills and abilities in this area (Söderlund & Maylor, 2012).

In our study, were analysed the application of OPM3 in Portuguese organisations and also how managers perceived that its use improved the PP.

The present research intends to answer the following research questions:

- How do organisations manage their projects using the OPM3 maturity model?
- How does the adoption of OPM3 contributed to PP?

LITERATURE REVIEW

Project Management

Nowadays projects are regarded as an important tool for value creation in the organisations (Gomes & Romão 2016; Ingason & Jónasson, 2009; Williams & Samset, 2010; Winter et al., 2006), improve business success (Forsberg, et al., 2000; Pinto, 2002; Poli & Shenhar, 2003), and for helping the process of change and that when used timely, it can lead to the problem solving of critical issues for an organization (Clarke, 1999; Gunduz & Almuajebh, 2020; Radujkovića & Sjekavica, 2017).

There is a significant growth in the adoption of project management disciplines to accomplish work in different sectors and industries (Winter & Szczepanek, 2008). Project management coordinates a set of competencies, skills and organisational knowledge, and carries out the monitoring of pre-established activities to evaluate the project progress (Kerzner, 2013; Kronbichel, et al., 2009). These skills enable project managers to achieve the pre-defined objectives. Project management also creates value and provides relevant information to help organisations respond quickly and more effectively to customers, thus improving their own performance (PMI, 2015; Zwikael & Smyrk, 2011).

Project management has experienced a very important growth and its economic impact is considerable in different sectors, industries and countries (Turner et al, 2010; Winter et al, 2006). The projects have become a tool for organizing and structuring work in most of the organisations on which they depend (Bakker, 2010), constituting one of the most important organisational developments of the last decades (Winter et al., 2006).

One main reason for this diffusion seems to be that the project-viewed as a task-specific and time-limited form of working – is perceived as a controllable way of avoiding all the classic problems which most the organisations are struggle (e.g., bureaucracy) (Cicmil et al., 2009; Hodgson, 2004).

The origin of project management is strongly linked to the demands of planned military projects in the United States, and it emerged during the post-war period, as there was a need to coordinate a wide range of activities. In this way, traditional project management skills were developed from the requirements of construction and defence industries to plan, control and manage large and complex tangible projects (Bourne & Walker, 2004).

The PMI (2016) defined project management as the application of knowledge, skills, tools and techniques in activities project to meet project requirements. Kerzner (2013) and APM (2012) highlighted the importance of project management in planning, organizing and control the organisations resources to accomplish short-term targets to complete specific goals and wider objectives. Project management is then the process of applying the skills, knowledge and techniques and tools to assure that the project meets the required standards.

Practices and techniques of project management are recognised by many organisations in various industries as being essential skills, which benefit businesses and conducted the project to an end of success (Shenhar & Dvir, 2007). Project Management received increasing attention in the business and academic world, as projects are important tools for change and organisational development. In an environment where projects are increasingly becoming the fundamental component of the business, project management has recently been the subjected to a closer scrutiny. Over the last decades, more organisations are employing project management as a way of developing a competitive advantage, although projects do not always progress as planned (Grant & Pennypacker, 2006).

Maturity Models

As organisations are continuously looking at improving project management practices, they have increasingly adopted maturity models even though these have received numerous criticisms (Albrecht & Spang, 2014). The basic concept of maturity drives organizational processes to continuous improvement and so requires a thorough understanding of an organization's current position and where it aims to be in the future. The maturity models are based on the premise that entities (people, organisations, functional areas or processes) evolve through a process of growth or development towards a more advanced maturity, across several distinct stages (Becker et al., 2009). Maturity will affect the value which an organization can gain by implementing project management (Shi, 2011). Given the numerous best practices and capabilities involved, improving maturity requires a properly structured action plan (Crawford, 2005).

The last years have seen the publication of several articles about maturity models (Wendler, 2012). Maturity models have become an important evaluation tool for measuring the internal and external organisations capabilities, providing a framework which helps organisations to increase their ability to deliver projects on schedule and within the established budget, according to the technical requirements and the agreed levels of quality (Levin & Skulmoski, 2000). Mature organisations exhibit specific elements that reflects their maturity, namely in the levels of performance, degrees of competence and focus on the customer satisfactions (Barber, 2004; Cooke-Davies & Arzymanow, 2003; Jung & Wang, 2006). Mature organisations have ability to manage initiatives based on the standardized and defined management processes (Axelos, 2016).

Organisations with higher maturity levels are expected to be more successful in terms of project effectiveness and efficiency and also have a superior competitive advantage in the marketplace although the current research offers little to support this argument (Yazici, 2009). Measuring the maturity of organisations is a difficult and somewhat subjective task; as such an audit process focuses mainly on individuals' tasks (Andersen & Jessen, 2003). Evaluating the current performance, skills and capabilities of an organization is not easy to do; in fact, the use of maturity models simplifies our interpretation of the entire organization and makes this task possible (Kalantjakos, 2001). Maturity models focus on the organization know-what, codifying the explicit knowledge and formally documented internal processes (Jugdev & Thomas, 2002).

The value of a generic methodology like the maturity models lies on the ability to develop a model which is characterized by a high generalisability and standardization, rather than in a specific stage-model (De Bruin & Rosemann, 2005). Use of a standard methodology enables a state of model development to be reached and for incremental improvements to be made over time. The value to organisations of applying such a model lies in the ability to measure and assess domain capabilities at a certain point in time, thus achieving sustainability (De Bruin & Rosemann, 2005). Overall, maturity models reflect the characteristics of an organization as they move through different stages in a change cycle, providing conceptual guidelines on essential requirements and components at each stage, including key success drivers and indicators (Kim & Grant, 2010)

The assessment procedures helped an organization understand where they have been, where they are now, and what processes they need to implement, to continue their implementation of management methodologies. As organisations mature in business and project management processes, and their use of information technology, they implement centralized solutions to facilitate these processes (Smith, 2010). Working with different types of projects within an organization requires standard models to deliver successful future projects repeatedly, improve both the quality of future projects and gain knowledge and learn from past successes and mistakes (Hellered, 2010).

The origin of MM has its roots in the Capability Maturity Model (CMM) developed in 1991 by the Software Engineering Institute (SEI) (Grant & Pennypacker, 2006). Since then, the model has received wide acceptance as a standard for process modelling and the evaluation of organisational maturity in various process areas. CMM is intended to assess the maturity of software development organisation processes on a five-stage scale (Dooley, Subra & Anderson, 2001), and compare practices applied by an organisation with respect to a standard criterion (SEI, 2010), to develop and maintain their products (Skulmoski, 2001). The CMM has different stages to help organisations prioritise their investment intentions and each of them serves as the basis for their continuous improvement process benefiting their performance and productivity (Besner & Hobbs, 2013; Cooke-Davies & Arzymanow, 2003; Paulk et al., 1993). However, CMM is geared towards software engineering organisations and not so much for organisations from other industries and businesses.

Organisations have invested to manage their activities and failures better, and most of them have been adopting PM practices to gain competitive advantage (Jugdev & Thomas, 2002; Farrokh & Mansur, 2013), i.e., the organisations adopted practices that help them achieve their goals more efficiently and effectively. Here, the value of a formal and structured approach is recognised by practitioners of PM, as it is through this proactive management that benefits are obtained for the projects (Hillson, 2001). For an organisation to know whether its PM processes are appropriate, it must consider certain indicators that allow a comparison of their current practices. This allows for the evaluation of the PP, i.e., within the scope and the calendar, respecting the cost, and fulfilling the expectations of the clients and the satisfaction of the project team (Hillson, 2001).

Following the CMM approach, most of MM have a five-stage scale. This schema guarantees the visualisation of the maturity, from their immature PM realisation to a more structured level needed to support projects, i.e., through best practices (Kerzner, 2013). Best practices are generally defined in an appropriate way, which is currently recognised by the industry to achieve an objective set by a particular organisation. When it comes to PM at the organisation level, best practices include the ability to implement predictable, consistent, and successful organisational strategies. The use of PM also increases the likelihood of achieving the proposed goals or objectives (PMI, 2013a). In general, MM are linked to PM reference frameworks, such as, the Guide to the Project Management Body of Knowledge (PMBOK) (Skulmoski, 2001; Jugdev & Thomas, 2002; PMI, 2013a).

MM provides companies with the necessary mechanisms to identify the key areas of opportunities for improvement in project management tasks. Additionally, it serves to develop comparative indicators for the application of PM practices and techniques across organisations which operate in the same business environment or sector (Gomes & Romão, 2015). According to Crawford (2006) MM are frameworks that allow organisations to create a strategic plan that will help them to develop their PM practices. These frameworks can also be used to transform an organisation into being more standardised and documented, with potential for better results in a more consistent way (Ofori & Deffor, 2013). Organisations can clearly benefit from the adoption of a MM for PM, namely, as the chance of interconnecting all its stakeholders and, achieving success in their projects is more likely, as is the chance of the achieving repeatability success in the projects (Backlund et al., 2014; Voivedich & Jones, 2001; Eskerod & Riis, 2009).

Carefully applied, MM can gain credibility in a fast and sustainable way, both at the level of clients and to the organisational internal structures. Operations become more efficient and effective (Hillson, 2001). The study of Eskerod & Riis (2009) demonstrates that MM assist in the fulfilment and/or reduction of the schedule and cost, by increasing the efficiency of projects. MM for PM will provide an incentive and a map for the development of the formalised management of project portfolios, a library of best practices and a broad team of professional and competent project managers (Rad & Levin, 2006). This is especially the case if they are meticulously and intelligently framed with the application of the existing PM (Voivedich & Jones, 2001).

There are several reasons why organisations might choose to use a MM to assess their current performance, such as (Gomes & Romão, 2015):

- Justifying their investment portfolio, programme or project management improvements.
- Gaining recognition of service quality to support proposals.
- Gaining a better understanding of their strengths and weakness to enable improvement to happen.

Organisational Project Management Maturity Model (OPM3)

Following the CMM development, the concept of maturity has expanded in organisations reaching the project management area, which aroused the interest of PMI members to develop a standard for the maturity model on projects (Zhang et al., 2012).

PMI released the first edition of the OPM3 standard in 2003 (PMI, 2003). OPM3 is meant to enable organisations to bridge the gap between organisational strategy and successful projects (Schlichter, 2001).

OPM3 focuses on the comparison of organisational activities to best practices, defined by PMI as the optimal method of meeting a specific stated objective (Crawford, 2006). The OPM3´s intent is (Fahrenkrog et al., 2004):

- To guide the development of capabilities necessary to execute organisational strategy through successful projects, distinguished from capabilities associated only with the management of individual projects; and
- To be able to be used by organisations of all sizes and types, in virtually any industry or culture.

The OPM3 also assesses the PM maturity of the organisations through the four following stages of process improvement (Kerzner, 2013):

- Standardisation - Ensure that a process governing body is in place, develop and document the process, communicate the process to those responsible for executing the process and apply the process consistently across the organisation.

- Measurement - The measurement stage quantifies the quality of the processes.
- Control - Once a process is measured, the organisation may gather trend data to determine if it is under control.
- Improvement - Once a process has been standardized, measured, and controlled, organisations can continuously improve them.

According to Schlichter (2001), there are different motivations that lead to organisations to adopting OPM3, such as:

- The possibility for organisations to know which are the best practices in their industry and market.
- The balance between reputation and best practices, implementation of improvement plans and evaluation to be continued.
- Reducing the variability of project performance and increasing its predictability.
- Improving management and stakeholder satisfaction.
- The focus of project efforts on strategic goals.

OPM3 is a conceptual structure composed of standardized elements, evaluation, control, and improved governance, which provides visible benefits, being developed in a systematic way to achieve the objective of the project working the points of greatest relevance. The purpose of OPM3 is not to prescribe what kind of improvements users should make or how they should make them. Rather, by providing a broad-based set of organisational project management best practices, this standard allows an organization to use it as a basis for study and self-examination, and consequently to make its own informed decision regarding potential initiatives for changes (PMI, 2013b).

OPM3 provides a method to evaluate and improve systematically the organization of a single project to a portfolio of projects (Zhang et al., 2012). There are three basic elements to implement the OPM3 (PMI, 2003):

- Knowledge: The description of the contents of the management and organisational maturity model projects.
- Evaluation: The methods, processes and procedures that serve as the basis for organizing self-diagnose of the maturity of the project. This review is carried out through a questionnaire with 151 questions that allows verify the strengths and weaknesses of the project against the best practices.

- Improvement: Considering a continuous improvement process that helps managers to modify the organization of the current stage for a more mature stage.

The OPM3 program aims to support organisations to improve the capabilities that strengthen the enterprise-wide processes used in the domains of Portfolio, Programme, and Project management within the organization in alignment with the strategic objectives (Grant & Pennypacker, 2006).

The concept of organisational project management is based on the idea that there is a correlation between an organization capability in project, programme and portfolio management, and its effectiveness in implementing strategy. The degree to which an organization practices this type of project management is referred to as its organisational project management maturity (PMI, 2003).

OPM3 does not measure the maturity of the organization by assigning an achieved level, like most maturity models, but as a percentage of best practices achieved. A good understanding of OPM3 contents should be developed before carrying out an assessment. A framework cycle constitutes following steps for measuring maturity:

- Acquire knowledge – this component of OPM3 cycle requires preparation for assessment of project management maturity.
- Perform assessment – involves gathering all the data required for measurement of maturity assessment.
- Manage improvements – the results from perform assessment stage are compared against best practices standard of project, programme and portfolio management.

Because project management practices may vary from organization to organization, a set of best practices have been defined by PMI (2013a) for the comparison and improvement. According to the PMI (2003), the model brings the following benefits to the organization:

- Helps organisations who wish to increase their maturity to plan improvements, and assess its maturity compared with best practices to be used in project management.
- Enables greater consistency with the PMBOK and provides the application of the model in any kind of independent of their size, industry or segmentation.
- Provides discussions of programme management and portfolio and improved schedule and budget predictability.
- Helps organisations implement projects correctly aligned strategically in a dynamic and global economy.

- Promote de integration of separate organisational functions:
- Improved quality and customer satisfaction.
- Provide guidance for quality process and provide point of reference for appraisal (benchmarking).

The OPM3 model consists of three dimensions or ways to visualize an organization's maturity level:

- The first dimension involves the stages of improvement processes that enable organisations to visualize best practices. Standardization, measurement, control and continuous improvement.
- The second dimension is the relationship between best practices and its management domain capabilities in project, programme and portfolio.
- The third dimension involves the stages of process improvement. Initiating, planning, executing, controlling and closing.

Ghoddousi et al., 2011 presented some reasons to explain why an organization chooses the OPM3 to assess their maturity in project management, namely:

- Continuous approach with a percentage score. Most of other models used a process divided into five levels.
- Supported on PMI standards.
- Applied in all business sectors.
- Results based on the industry feedback and has been modified repeatedly.
- Great emphasis to the determination of weaknesses and continual improvement.

OPM3 is by far the most sophisticated and the most resource intensive of the maturity models in the discipline of project management (Hillson, 2003; Cooke-Davies, 2004; Backlund et al., 2014). Some inconsistencies are noted:

- Lack a well-researched and theoretical understanding of what is needed for successful project management outcomes.
- Founded on the assumption that there is an ideal path of development towards maturity that most organisations should pursue regardless of discipline area, project scope, competitive marketplace context or chosen strategy.
- The lack of reference processes for the areas of programme and portfolio, which became the Best Practices repetitive causing difficulty in their interpretation.

- The self-assessment questionnaire that is too bureaucratic and repetitive and the absence of a rating scale of measurable maturity as used in other models, which make it difficult to understand, internal communication, targets and commitments for the improvement of organisational maturity through the OPM3.

OPM3 can benefit organisations by ensuring the efficient use of project resources and by providing cost savings associated with the elimination of projects that are not tied to the organisation's strategic goals (Matassa, 2006). The present study focuses exclusively on OPM3. The reasons for this choice are the followings:

- The wide dissemination of the model in Portuguese organisations (Silva et al., 2014).
- The easy access to interviews.
- Its recognition as a universal approach to assess PM maturity.

Table 1. Highlights the main aspects related to three of the most popular MM

Maturity Model	CMMI©	P3M3©	OPM3©
Constructor	SEI	OGC/AXELOS	PMI
Version/Date	V.1.3 /2010 [33]	V.3 /2016 [51]	V.3 /2013 [37]
Theoretical background	-	Managing Successful Programmes	PMBOK
Continuity between editions	Yes	Yes	Yes
Sector	Software/engineering	All	All
Domains	Project	Project, Programme & Portfolio	Project, Programme & Portfolio
Scope	22 process areas	32 process areas	*Best practices*
Representation	Staged/ Continuous	Staged	Continuous
Levels	5	5	4
Self-Assessed	Yes	Yes	Yes
Links to strategy	Yes	Yes	Yes
Continuous improvement	Yes	Yes	Yes
Interpretation	Medium	Medium	Yes
Ease of execution	Yes	Yes	Yes

METHODOLOGY

Research Methodology

Our research follows a multiple case study strategy. According to Yin (2014), a multiple case study is the selection of two or more cases, considered as possible replications, from which one can obtain answers to research questions. However, it should be emphasised that in the case studies, whether they be single case or multiple case studies, the aim is not to obtain statistical generalisations or to measure their representativeness, but rather their particularisation (Yin, 2014).

The nature of the study was characterised as being explanatory (Saunders et al., 2009), i.e., to better understand the problem proposed, the approach adopted was inductive and the method of research qualitative.

The unit of analysis considered was the organisations' projects. It should be highlighted that the projects selected by the present study were only considered after the adoption of OPM3. Since our study focused on a phenomenon that occurred during a certain period of activity of the organisations, the time horizon was characterised as being cross-sectional (Saunders et al., 2009).

Data Collection

Six semi-structured interviews were undertaken and it was ensured that the interviewer did not influence the interviewees and thus more precise information was assured (Yin, 2014). The research was established considering the interviewees' availability, so that interviews could be conducted without time constraints. The detailed information is presented in Table 2.

Table 2. The interviewees

Interviewees	Date	Duration (mn)	Organisation	Age (years)	Gender	Years on the organisation	PM Experience (years)	Certification
E1	11/05/2016	30	O1	47	Male	5	31	PMP, OPM3
E2	13/05/2016	60	O2	51	Female	7	30	PMP
E3	16/05/2016	30	O3	37	Female	5	10	PMP
E4	19/05/2016	30	O4	37	Female	5	10	PMP
E5	13/06/2016	Email	O5	33	Male	8	5	PMP
E6	27/07/2016	30	O6	33	Male	5	9	PMP

Reliability

When conducting case studies, one of the most important sources of data collection is the interviews (Yin, 2014), which in this case focused only on project managers. The script of the interviews contained closed and open answers and was presented to the interviewees in a similar way, so that the bias effect of the data was reduced. Subsequently, the data collected were encoded and transcribed. It should be noted that research ethics have been safeguarded in terms of confidentiality, anonymity and voluntary participation. This study adopted a protocol of interviews, in order that the opinion of the interviewees was respected and it was ensured that the objective of the data collection was run in the best conditions.

Validity

Firstly, a pilot study was conducted to test the questionnaire and to understand whether the questions in fact corresponded to the predefined objective. Therefore, the scope, motivation and participation conditions were presented to the interviewees. The pilot study served to make small adjustments in the question formulation, however, the data collected from this interview were also considered, since the interviewee provided important data for the variables under analysis. This step was performed to clear any doubts that might appear regarding the focus of the research (Saunders et al., 2009). The data collection process was performed with informed consent. The interview script was elaborated considering the seven stages presented by Brinkmann & Kvale study (2015). Due to the research option, the data collected from the interviews could not be generalised to other organisations of some sector, or others.

Encoding

The encoding process was all elaborated through the content analysis. The codes were created from those expressions most often repeated by the respondents, which were important aspects of the research and somehow aroused some interest (e.g., the fact that the respondents often referred to the adaptation of practices in their projects).

Figure 1 show the codes identified and some excerpts of what was reported by each of the interviewees are presented in Table 3.

Figure 1. Encoding. Most often repeated terms/expressions.

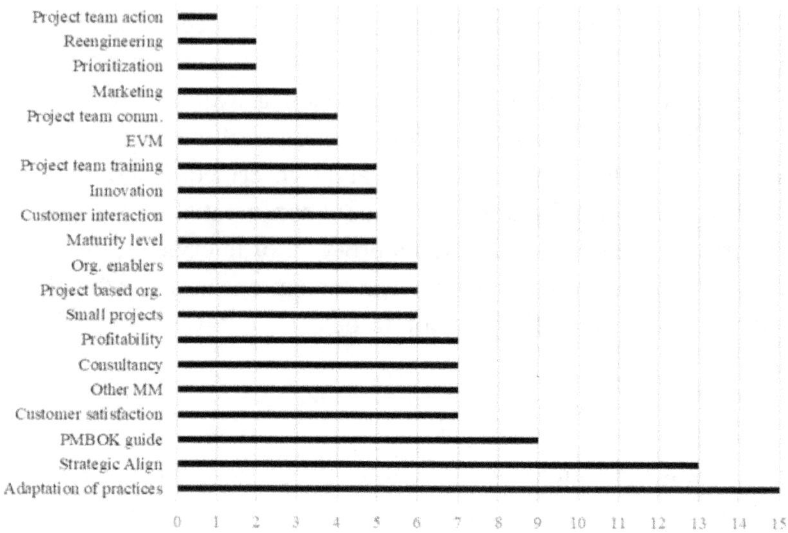

Table 3. Encoding (e.g., adaption of practices and strategic alignment)

Codes	Interviewees	Comments
Adaption of practices	1	In most cases of innovative projects, we must adapt the processes.
	2	Initially it was necessary to align the model and thereafter do some work to maintain the practices
	3	If the project starts to cost more than the planned, then we need to act quickly.
	4	Combinations were done with other approaches, such as Agile, or Scrum.
	5	In my view, it is difficult to say whether the scope of a project has been fulfilled by using the OPM3 or another framework.
Strategic alignment	1	OPM3 makes the alignment easier by improving the processes of portfolio management, aligning the projects with the objectives.
	2	The combination of the three dimensions (projects, programmes and portfolios) really promotes the alignment with the objectives and leads to implementation of the practices.
	3	By doing this, what will happen is that organisations strategies will be materialised in the field.
	4	Our objective is to have a financial margin, if we do not control costs, then the margin will also be lower. Alignment is the key.
	5	Good practices in MM help project performance improve within organisations. They help to define the best path in order that the success of the projects in the organisation is truly achieved.

RESULTS AND DISCUSSIONS

The interviewees affirmed a consensual view regarding what OPM3 represented for their organisations' PM. The question of the alignment between the organisational strategy and the project objectives was widely referenced throughout the interview sessions, confirming what was stated on the literature review about the usefulness of OPM3 in assisting organisations to develop their capacity to manage projects and to move them towards achieving their strategic objectives. In other words, for the interviewees, OPM3 enablers improve the pre-identified PM practices. The Tables 4, 5 and 6 highlighted several important research issues.

Table 4. Mapping research questions, variables, and items

Research Questions	Observed Variables	Items
How do organisations manage their projects using the OPM3 maturity model?	Questions about the OPM3	1,2,3,11
How does the adoption of the OPM3 contributed to the performance of organisations' projects?	Scope	4
	Schedule	5
	Cost	6
	Customer expectations	7, 8
	Project team satisfaction	9, 10

Table 5. The importance of OPM3 for organisations' projects

Interviewees	Answer
1	OPM3 improves our portfolio management processes and align projects with strategic objectives
2	Best practices are used to measure whether we are achieving the strategic objectives or not. The combination of the three dimensions (projects, programmes and portfolios) allows the aligning of objectives and leads the organisation to implementation of the practices.
3	OPM3 identify the gap between the *as-is* and the *to-be* and map out a roadmap of improvements. Implementing these improvements will enable happen the achievement of goals of the projects.
4	Best practices have allowed us to better control the state of the project, identify risks, and manage the stakeholders and our client.
5	The implementation of OPM3 best practices support organisations develop their PM processes in the best possible way. These processes also allow us to create a framework among the organisation's various projects.
6	OPM3 has a basic problem that makes it difficult to exactly identify the level of maturity of the organisation.

Table 6. Answers by variable

Variables Observed	Summary of the Answers
Scope Management	The implementation of OPM3 helps to improve processes by providing a better definition of the scope of a project. OPM3 allows one to confirm that the organisation makes a good planning of what will be the management of its scope and prepares and correctly identifies the requirements. Allows the documents to be structured according to PM good practices and helps to improve stakeholder communication processes.
Schedule Management	Compliance with the schedule is regularly monitored by the project manager using Earned Value Management (EVM). When the project uses agile methodologies, daily meetings are held to monitor and verify the status of the activities. OPM3 also helps build the organisational processes necessary for EVM to work
Cost Management	By applying OPM3 practices, organisations have all the necessary tools to plan, control, and for indicators and metrics. The ultimate tool for cost control is EVM.
Customer expectations	This model has a whole set of management practices to deal with customer expectations. We achieve a greater volume of commitment when deliveries meet customer expectations leading to customer satisfaction. OPM3 allows management to be very close to customer expectations.
Project team satisfaction	The main factor for the team to be satisfied is to know that the customer was satisfied and acknowledges the work done. As we often hold meetings with the customer, we make the product very close to the customer's needs. A short questionnaire was sent to collect customer feedback to analyse which points need to be improved.

In response to the research questions, it was possible to ascertain that the adoption of OPM3 did not bring immediate improvements, as these practices alone do not cause significant improvements in the projects in terms of the variables analysed. It was necessary for project managers to make good use of these practices. All respondents considered that there were situations in the projects that would not be appropriate for the use of OPM3 practices and that they had to adapt to the situation to some extent to that which they were in, and sometimes to help others industry benchmark practices.

Each project is unique and for organisations it does not make sense, in a simple and short-term project to use all range of tools and techniques prescribed by the methodology extensively. The organisational OPM3 facilitators played the role that had been proposed by PMI. Briefly the project managers claimed that the adoption of OPM3 brought significant improvements to Project Management, namely:

- Scope Management - Improvements in planning, document support structure and the construction and use of the front process.
- Schedule Management - Use of EVM, project status viewing, and improvement maps.
- Cost Management - Greater predictability, cost-effectiveness and preventive and corrective actions.
- Management of Customer Expectations - Application of the methodology, interaction with customers, commitment, and collaboration.

- Management of Project Team Satisfaction - Training and certification, and improvement of the relationship with all stakeholders and clients.

CONCLUSION

The credibility of PMI led these organisations to adopt the OPM3 maturity model and their best practices and enabled them to obtain improvements in the management of their projects. The interviewees reported by that their organisations managed their projects based on best practices However, there was a certain demand for the adaptation of other practices and, industry benchmarks, throughout the realisation of their projects, to cover certain gaps they faced, i.e., the processes that organisations should adopt in their projects. Respondents affirmed a consensual view of what OPM3 represented for their organisations' PM. The question of the alignment between the organisational strategy and the objectives of the projects was often mentioned during the interview sessions.

Among the project managers interviewed, the opinion regarding the improvements provided by the adoption of OPM3 for their projects was not consensual. Some of the interviewees had the opinion that the single use of OPM3 did not guarantee improvement in the projects, as in their opinion, the results depended much more on the capabilities of the project managers than the methodology adopted. What happened was that the model only provided recommendations for the organisations in the form of useful PM practices, and it was up to the project managers to implement them in the best possible way to obtain the necessary improvements.

OPM3 provides significant improvements for the projects and their organisations as previously described. It also seems clear that those project managers who make the best use of OPM3 practices had to adapt some practices, in order that their projects could meet the proposed objectives.

There was also agreement that OPM3 helps organisations considerably in measuring the level of achievement of their strategic objectives, to manage stakeholders, customers and contracts better, and to identify the risks associated with projects better and develop their PM processes.

REFERENCES

Albrecht, J. C., & Spang, K. (2014). Linking the benefits of project management maturity to project complexity: Insights from a multiple case study. *International Journal of Managing Projects in Business*, *7*(2), 285–301. doi:10.1108/IJMPB-08-2013-0040

Andersen, E. S., & Jessen, S. A. (2003). Project maturity in organisations. *International Journal of Project Management, 21*(6), 457–461. doi:10.1016/S0263-7863(02)00088-1

APM. (2012). *Body of Knowledge* (6th ed.). Association for Project Management.

AXELOS. (2016). *Introduction to P3M3©, version 3*. AXELOS Limited.

Baccarini, D. (1999). The logical framework method for defining project success. *Project Management Journal, 30*(4), 25–32. doi:10.1177/875697289903000405

Backlund, F., Chronéer, D., & Sundqvist, E. (2014). Project management maturity models - A critical review: A case study within Swedish engineering and construction organisations. *Procedia: Social and Behavioral Sciences, 119*, 837–846. doi:10.1016/j.sbspro.2014.03.094

Bakker, R. M. (2010). Taking stock of temporary organizational forms: A systematic review and research agenda. *International Journal of Management Reviews, 12*(4), 466–486. doi:10.1111/j.1468-2370.2010.00281.x

Bannerman, P. L. (2008). Defining project success: a multilevel framework. *Proceedings of the PMI Research Conference: Defining the Future of Project Management.*

Barber, E. (2004). Benchmarking the Management of Projects: A Review of Current Thinking. *International Journal of Project Management, 22*(4), 301–307. doi:10.1016/j.ijproman.2003.08.001

Becker, J., Knackstedt, R., & Pöppelbuß, J. (2009). Developing Maturity Models for IT Management: A Procedure Model and its Application. *Business & Information Systems Engineering, 1*(3), 213–222. doi:10.100712599-009-0044-5

Besner, C., & Hobbs, B. (2013). Contextualized Project Management Practice: A Cluster Analysis of Practices and Best Practice. *Project Management Journal, 44*(1), 17–34. doi:10.1002/pmj.21291

Bourne, L., & Walker, D. H. T. (2004). Advancing Project Management in Learning Organisations. *The Learning Organization, 11*(3), 226–243. doi:10.1108/09696470410532996

Brinkmann, S., & Kvale, S. (2015). *Interviews: Learning the Craft of Qualitative Research Interviewing* (3rd ed.). Sage.

Brookes, N., Butler, M., Dey, P., & Clark, R. (2014). The use of maturity models in improving project management performance. *International Journal of Managing Projects in Business*, *7*(2), 231–246. doi:10.1108/IJMPB-03-2013-0007

Bryde, D. J., & Brown, D. (2005). The influence of a project performance measurement system on the success of a contract for maintaining motorways and trunk roads. *Project Management Journal*, *35*(4), 57–65. doi:10.1177/875697280403500407

Caralli, R., Knight, M., & Montgomery, A. (2012). Maturity Models 101: A Primer for Applying Maturity Models to Smart Grid Security, Resilience, and Interoperability. CERT, Software Engineering Institute, Carnegie Mellon University. doi:10.21236/ADA610461

Cicmil, S., Hodgson, D., Lindgren, M., & Packendorff, J. (2009). Project management behind the facade. *Ephemera*, *9*(2), 78–92.

Clarke, A. (1999). A practical use of key success factors to improve the effectiveness of project management. *International Journal of Project Management*, *17*(3), 139–145. doi:10.1016/S0263-7863(98)00031-3

Cooke-Davies, T. J. (2004). Measurement of organizational maturity: what are the relevant questions about maturity and metrics for a project-based organization to ask, and what do these imply for project management research? In D. I. C. Slevin & J. K. Pinto (Eds.), *Innovations, project management research* (pp. 211–228). Project Management Institute.

Cooke-Davies, T. J., & Arzymanow, A. (2003). The maturity of project management in different industries - An investigation into variations between project management models. *International Journal of Project Management*, *21*(6), 471–478. doi:10.1016/S0263-7863(02)00084-4

Cooke-Davies, T. J., Schlichter, F. J., & Bredillet, C. (2001). *Beyond the PMBOK Guide.* PMI Annual Seminars and Symposium 2001, Nashville, TN.

Crawford, J. K. (2006). The Project Management Maturity Model. *Information Systems Management*, *23*(4), 50–58. doi:10.1201/1078.10580530/46352.23.4.20060901/95113.7

Crawford, L. (2005). Senior management perceptions of project management competence. *International Journal of Project Management*, *23*(1), 7–16. doi:10.1016/j.ijproman.2004.06.005

de Bruin, T., & Rosemann, M. (2005). Towards a Business Process Management Maturity Model. *Proceedings of the 13th European Conference on Information Systems (ECIS 2005)*. Available at: http://eprints.qut.edu.au/25194/

de Wit, A. (1988). Measurement of project success. *International Journal of Project Management*, *6*(3), 164–170. doi:10.1016/0263-7863(88)90043-9

Dooley, K., Subra, A., & Anderson, J. (2001). Maturity and its Impact on New Product Development Project Performance. *Research in Engineering Design*, *13*(1), 23–29. doi:10.1007001630100003

Eskerod, P., & Riis, E. (2009). Project Management Models as Value Creators. *Project Management Journal*, *40*(1), 4–18. doi:10.1002/pmj.20098

Fahrenkrog, S. L., Haeck, W., Abrams, F., & Whelbourn, D. (2003). PMI's organizational project management maturity model. *Proceedings of PMI Global Congress 2003*.

Farrokh, J., & Mansur, A. (2013). Project Management Maturity Models and Organisational Project Management Maturity Model (OPM3®): A Critical Morphological Evaluation. *International Scholarly and Scientific Research & Innovation*, *7*(5).

Forsberg, K., Mooz, H., & Cotterman, H. (2000). *Visualizing project management*. John Wiley & Sons, Inc.

Gomes, J., & Romão, M. (2014). Advantages and Limitations of Performance Measurement Tools: The Balanced Scorecard. *Proceedings of the 7th IADIS International Conference*, 19-26.

Gomes, J., & Romão, M. (2015). Achieving project success through alignment with organisational strategy: Balanced Scorecard approach. *Proceedings of the 8th IADIS International Conference - Information's Systems 2015*.

Gomes, J., & Romão, M. (2015). Enhancing Organisational Maturity with Benefits Management. *International Journal of Information Technology Project Management*, *6*(4), 34–47. doi:10.4018/IJITPM.2015100103

Gomes, J., & Romão, M. (2015). Maturity, Benefits and Project Management shaping Project Success. In *the series Advances in Intelligent Systems and Computing* (Vol. 353, pp. 435–448). New Contributions in Information Systems and Technologies. doi:10.1007/978-3-319-16486-1_43

Gomes, J., & Romão, M. (2016). Improving project success: A case study using benefits and project management. *Procedia Computer Science, 100*, 489–497. doi:10.1016/j.procs.2016.09.187

Grant, K. P., & Pennypacker, J. S. (2006). Project Management Maturity: An assessment of Project Management Capabilities among and between Selected Industries. *IEEE Transactions on Engineering Management, 53*(1), 59–68. doi:10.1109/TEM.2005.861802

Gunduz, M., & Almuajebh, M. (2020). Critical Success Factors for Sustainable Construction Project Management. *Sustainability (Basel), 12*(5), 1990. doi:10.3390u12051990

Hellered, C. (2010). *Benchmarking project management maturity in two organisations: A case study focusing on the value of having an established project management model in an organization* [Master of Science Thesis]. Chalmers University of Technology, Göteborg, Sweden.

Hillson, D. (2001). Benchmarking Organizational Project Management Capability. *Proceedings of the Project Management Institute Annual Seminars & Symposium.*

Hillson, D. (2003). Assessing Organisational Project Management Capability. *Journal of Facilities Management, 2*(3), 298–311. doi:10.1108/14725960410808276

Hodgson, D. (2004). Project work: The legacy of bureaucratic control in the post-bureaucratic organization. *Organization, 11*(1), 81–100. doi:10.1177/1350508404039659

Ibbs, C. W., & Kwak, Y. H. (2000). Assessing project management maturity. *Project Management Journal, 31*(1), 32–43. doi:10.1177/875697280003100106

Ibbs, C. W., & Reginato, J. M. (2002). Quantifying the value of Project Management. Project Management Institute, Inc.

Ibbs, C. W., Reginato, J. M., & Kwak, Y. H. (2003). Developing project management capability – Benchmarking, Maturity, Modeling, Gap Analyses, ROI studies. The Wiley Managing Projects Resources Book, John Wiley.

Ika, L. A. (2009). Project success as a topic in project management journals. *Project Management Journal, 40*(4), 6–19. doi:10.1002/pmj.20137

Ingason, H., & Jónasson, H. (2009). Contemporary Knowledge and Skill Requirements in Project Management. *Project Management Journal, 40*(2), 59–69. doi:10.1002/pmj.20122

Jachimowicz, V. A. (2003). Project management maturity model. *Project Management Journal, 34*(1), 55–56. doi:10.1177/875697280303400108

Jia, G., Chen, Y., Xue, X., Chen, J., Cao, J., & Tang, K. (2011). Program management organisation maturity integrated model for mega construction programs in China. *International Journal of Project Management, 29*(7), 834–845. doi:10.1016/j.ijproman.2011.03.003

Jugdev, K., & Thomas, J. (2002). Project management maturity models: The silver bullets of competitive advantage? *Project Management Journal, 33*(4), 4–14. doi:10.1177/875697280203300402

Jung, J. Y., & Wang, Y. J. (2006). Relationship between total quality management (TQM) and continuous improvement of international project management (CIIPM). *Technovation, 16*(5-6), 716–722. doi:10.1016/j.technovation.2006.01.003

Kalantjakos, N. J. (2001). Assessing Organizational Project Management Maturity. *Proceedings of Project Management Institute Annual Seminars & Symposium 2001.*

Kerzner, H. (2001). *Applied Project Management: Best Practices on Implementation.* John Wiley and Sons, Inc.

Kerzner, H. (2013). *Project Management: a systems approach to planning, scheduling and controlling* (11th ed.). John Wiley and Sons.

Kim, D., & Grant, G. (2010). E-government maturity model using the capability maturity model. *Journal of Systems and Information Technology, 12*(3), 230–244. doi:10.1108/13287261011070858

Kronbichel, S. A., Ostermann, H., & Staudinger, R. (2009). A review of critical success factors for ERP-projects. *The Open Information Systems Journal, 3*(1), 14–25. doi:10.2174/1874133900903010014

Kwak, Y. H., & Ibbs, C. W. (2000). The Berkley Project Management Process Maturity Model: Measuring the Value of Project Management. *Proceedings of the 2000 IEEE Engineering Management Society.*

Levin, G., & Skulmoski, G. (2000). The project management maturity. *ESI Horizons, 2*(3), 1–7.

Matassa, P. (2006). Grow up already! An OPM3® primer. *Proceedings of PMI Global Congress 2006.*

McLeod, L., Doolin, B., & MacDonell, S. G. (2012). A perspective-based understanding of project success. *Project Management Journal, 43*(5), 68–86. doi:10.1002/pmj.21290

Mullaly, M. (2006). Longitudinal Analysis of Project Management Maturity. *Project Management Journal, 36*(3), 62–73. doi:10.1177/875697280603700307

Mullaly, M. (2014). If maturity is the answer, then exactly what was the question? *International Journal of Managing Projects in Business, 7*(2), 169–185. doi:10.1108/IJMPB-09-2013-0047

Ofori, D., & Deffor, E. (2013). Assessing Project Management Maturity in Africa: A Ghanaian Perspective. *International Journal of Business Administration, 4*(6), 41–61. doi:10.5430/ijba.v4n6p41

P3M3. (2016). *Introduction to P3M3©,* version 3. AXELOS Limited.

Paulk, M. C., Curtis, B., Chrissis, M. B., & Weber, C. V. (1993). *The Capability Maturity Model for Software* (v.1.1). Technical Report CMU/SEI-93-TR-024. Carnegie Mellon University.

Pinto, J. K. (2002). Project management 2002. *Research Technology Management, 45*(2), 22–37. doi:10.1080/08956308.2002.11671489

Pinto, J. K., & Slevin, D. P. (1988). Critical success factors across the project life cycle. *Project Management Journal*, (June), 67–75.

PMI. (2003). *Organizational Project Management Maturity Model (OPM3): Knowledge Foundations*. Project Management Institute Inc.

PMI. (2013). *Project Management Body of Knowledge (PMBOK) Guide* (5th ed.). Project Management Institute Inc.

PMI. (2013a). A Guide to the Project Management Body of Knowledge: PMBOK® guide, v5.0. Project Management Institute Inc.

PMI. (2013b). *Organizational project management maturity model (OPM3): Knowledge Foundation* (3rd ed.). Project Management Institute.

PMI. (2014). *Implementing Organizational Project Management: A Practice Guide*. Project Management Institute.

PMI. (2015). *PMI's Pulse of the Profession: Capturing the Value of Project Management*. Project Management Institute.

PMI. (2016). PMI Lexicon of Project Management Terms (version 3.1). Project Management Institute Inc.

Poli, M., & Shenhar, A. J. (2003). Project strategy: The key to project success. *Proceedings of the Portland International Conference on Management of Engeneering and Technology*, 231–235. 10.1109/PICMET.2003.1222799

Rad, P., & Levin, G. (2006). Project Management Maturity Assessment. *AACE International Transactions,* PM61-PM64.

Radujkovića, M., & Sjekavica, M. (2017). Project Management Success Factors. *Procedia Engineering*, *196*, 607–615. doi:10.1016/j.proeng.2017.08.048

Saunders, M., Lewis, P., & Thornhill, A. (2009). *Research Methods for Business Students* (5th ed.). Pearson Education Limited.

Sawaya, N., & Trapanese, P. (2004). Measuring project management maturity. *Security Distributing and Marketing*, *34*(1), 44–66.

Schlichter, J. (2001). PMI's organizational project management maturity model: emerging standards. *Proceedings of PMI Annual Seminars & Symposium.*

SEI. (2010). *CMMI for Services (v.1.3): Improving processes for providing better services.* Technical report CMU/SEI-2010-TR-034, November 2010. Carnegie Mellon University.

Shenhar, A. J., & Dvir, D. (2007). *Reinventing Project Management: The Diamond Approach to Successful Growth and Innovation.* Harvard Business School Press.

Shi, Q. (2011). Rethinking the implementation of project management: A value adding path map approach. *International Journal of Project Management*, *29*(3), 295–302. doi:10.1016/j.ijproman.2010.03.007

Silva, D., Tereso, A., Fernandes, G., & Pinto, J. A. (2014). OPM3® Portugal Project: Analysis of Preliminary Results. *Procedia Technology*, *16*, 1027–1036. doi:10.1016/j.protcy.2014.10.057

Skulmoski, G. (2001). Project maturity and competence interface. *Cost Engineering (Morgantown, W. Va.)*, *43*(6), 11–18.

Smith, D. A. (2010). *Knowledge Management as an indicator of Organizational Maturity in Project Management: An enhancement of OPM3 Model* [PhD thesis]. Capella University.

Söderlund, J., & Maylor, H. (2012). Project management scholarship: Relevance, impact and five integrative challenges for business and management schools. *International Journal of Project Management, 30*(6), 686–696. doi:10.1016/j.ijproman.2012.03.007

Toor, S. R., & Ogunlana, S. O. (2008). Critical COMs of success in large-scale construction projects: Evidence from Thailand construction industry. *International Journal of Project Management, 26*(4), 420–430. doi:10.1016/j.ijproman.2007.08.003

Turner, J. R., Huemann, M., Anbari, F., & Bredillet, C. (2010). *Perspectives on projects*. Routledge. doi:10.4324/9780203891636

Voivedich, B., & Jones, M. (2001). Developing and Applying a Project Management Capability Maturity Model. *Proceedings of the PMI Annual Seminars & Symposium*.

Wendler, R. (2012). The Maturity of Maturity Model Research: A systematic mapping study. *Information and Software Technology, 54*(12), 1317–1339. doi:10.1016/j.infsof.2012.07.007

Williams, T., & Samset, K. (2010). Issues in Front-End Decision Making on Projects. *Project Management Journal, 41*(2), 38–49. doi:10.1002/pmj.20160

Winter, M., Smith, C., Morris, P., & Cicmil, S. (2006). Directions for future research in project management: The main findings of a UK government-funded research network. *International Journal of Project Management, 24*(8), 638–649. doi:10.1016/j.ijproman.2006.08.009

Winter, M., & Szczepanek, T. (2008). Projects and programmes as value creation processes: A new perspective and some practical implications. *International Journal of Project Management, 26*(1), 95–103. doi:10.1016/j.ijproman.2007.08.015

Yazici, H. J. (2009). The Role of Project Management Maturity and Organizational Culture in Perceived Performance. *Project Management Journal, 40*(3), 14–33. doi:10.1002/pmj.20121

Yin, R. (2014). *Case Study Research: Design and Methods* (5th ed.). Sage.

Zhang, L. Y., He, J., & Zhang, X. X. (2012). The Project Management Maturity Model and Application Based on PRINCE2. *Proceedings of International Workshop on Information and Electronics Engineering, 29*, 3691-3697.

Zwikael, O., & Smyrk, J. (2011). *Project Management for the Creation of Organisational Value*. Springer-Verlag. doi:10.1007/978-1-84996-516-3

Chapter 10
Advancing Sustainability:
ESG Evolution and the AI Edge

Nitish Kumar Minz
https://orcid.org/0009-0000-4770-0336
K.R. Mangalam University, India

Yash Khattar
Guru Gobind Singh Indraprastha University, India

ABSTRACT

This research explores how artificial intelligence (AI) can enhance corporate sustainability by leveraging environmental, social, and governance (ESG) practices. It investigates the effective integration of AI into ESG initiatives, addressing challenges and ethical considerations. The study employs a literature review and case studies to demonstrate AI's impact on ESG efforts, focusing on data analysis, predictive modeling, and risk assessment. The research highlights AI's potential to revolutionize ESG, enabling data-driven decision-making and fostering sustainability-driven innovation. This chapter contributes to understanding the expanding role of ESG and AI's integration for sustainability, emphasizing its importance in today's business landscape.

1. INTRODUCTION

The global business landscape is experiencing a profound transformation characterized by a shift towards emphasizing environmental, social, and governance (ESG) practices as fundamental elements of corporate sustainability. Simultaneously, the emergence of artificial intelligence (AI) technologies presents promising avenues

DOI: 10.4018/979-8-3693-1151-6.ch010

for enhancing sustainability efforts. This paper delves into the intersection of ESG and AI, aiming to address a pressing research problem: How can organizations effectively harness AI to advance their ESG initiatives while navigating potential implications and challenges?

1.1 Relevance and Novelty

ESG practices have evolved from peripheral considerations to integral components of corporate strategies. This transformation is driven by stakeholder demands, regulatory changes, and a heightened awareness of global sustainability challenges (Burnaev, 2023). AI, with its proficiency in data analysis, predictive modelling, and risk assessment (Huang, 2021), offers unprecedented opportunities to bolster ESG efforts. Understanding the ethical implications and practical implementation of AI-driven sustainability strategies is vital as organizations strive to thrive in this evolving landscape.

1.2 Importance of Policy Implications

As ESG becomes increasingly intertwined with business operations, the policy implications of AI integration cannot be understated. Ethical considerations, data privacy, transparency, and inclusivity must be at the forefront of AI implementations (Saxena, 2022). This paper sheds light on the ethical challenges and offers insights for responsible AI-driven ESG practices.

1.3 Methodology and Data

The study employs a comprehensive literature review, drawing insights from recent research papers and case studies that demonstrate AI's impact on ESG initiatives. These insights are critical in identifying best practices (Chauhan, 2022) and understanding AI's role in driving sustainability-driven innovation (Pan, 2023).

1.4 Contribution to Literature

This research contributes to the literature by providing a holistic exploration of the expanding significance of ESG in business and the potential integration of AI to achieve sustainability goals. It addresses a knowledge gap by offering practical insights into AI implementation and ethical considerations in sustainability strategies.

1.5 Limitations

While this paper offers valuable insights, it acknowledges that the landscape of AI and ESG is continually evolving. Future research may delve deeper into specific industry applications and evolving regulatory frameworks.

This research unfolds the historical development of ESG practices and their increasing prominence, coupled with AI's potential to amplify sustainability endeavours. It underscores the importance of responsible AI integration to navigate ESG complexities, ultimately fostering responsible and resilient corporate practices in an era where sustainability is not merely an option but a necessity.

2. LITERATURE REVIEW

Burnaev (2023) explored practical applications of artificial intelligence (AI) to address environmental, social, and governance (ESG) challenges. It presented various case studies demonstrating how AI technologies can be leveraged to enhance ESG initiatives in businesses. The study provided valuable insights into the implementation of AI-driven solutions to achieve sustainability goals, making it a valuable resource for organizations seeking innovative ways to improve their ESG performance.

Chauhan (2022) focused on the digitalization of supply chain management using Industry 4.0 technologies from a sustainability perspective. It examined how digitalization can contribute to sustainable practices in supply chains. The study highlighted the importance of adopting modern technologies, including AI, to enhance the efficiency and sustainability of supply chain operations. It offered valuable insights for organizations aiming to integrate sustainability into their supply chain management strategies.

Elouidani et al. (2022) conducted a bibliometric analysis of the use of artificial intelligence (AI) in sustainable finance. It provided an overview of the research landscape and trends in this domain. The study highlighted the increasing importance of AI in the context of sustainable finance and offered a comprehensive perspective on the current state of research in this field. It is a valuable resource for scholars and practitioners interested in the intersection of AI and finance for sustainability.

Huang (2021) explored the use of AI-driven digital twins in the context of Industry 4.0, focusing on smart manufacturing and advanced robotics. It provided an overview of the current state of AI-driven digital twin technologies and their applications in enhancing manufacturing processes. The study offered valuable insights into how AI can optimize operations in Industry 4.0, contributing to sustainability through improved efficiency and resource utilization.

Liu (2023) investigated public perceptions of environmental, social, and governance (ESG) issues based on social media data in China. It utilized AI-driven sentiment analysis to understand how ESG topics are discussed and perceived on social media platforms. The research provided valuable insights into the public's attitudes towards sustainability and ESG, offering a unique perspective on the role of AI in gauging public sentiment regarding ESG issues.

Mourtzis (2022) explored the challenges and opportunities associated with the transition from Industry 4.0 to Society 5.0, emphasizing the role of AI and technology in shaping sustainable societies. It provides a comprehensive overview of the key concepts and discusses how AI can contribute to societal sustainability. The review offered valuable insights into the broader context of technological transitions and their implications for sustainability.

Pan (2023) provided an insightful examination of the role of artificial intelligence (AI) in achieving digital sustainability. It offered a domain-specific analysis of AI's applications in sustainability, highlighting current research trends and future directions. The study served as a valuable resource for understanding how AI can contribute to sustainability efforts across various domains, including energy, environment, and social impact.

Saxena (2022) explored the intersection of technologies, particularly Industry 4.0, and environmental, social, and governance (ESG) considerations. It examined how technologies empowered by Industry 4.0 can enhance ESG practices in organizations. The study provided insights into the potential of technological advancements, including AI, to drive sustainability within the framework of ESG, offering guidance for businesses seeking to leverage technology for sustainable development.

Smokova (2022) investigated how technology giants, Microsoft, Google, and Apple (GAFAM), utilize artificial intelligence (AI) systems to advance their environmental, social, and governance (ESG) and corporate social responsibility (CSR) initiatives. It provided case studies and insights into how these influential companies harness AI to address sustainability challenges, offering a glimpse into best practices for integrating AI into ESG and CSR strategies.

3. METHODOLOGY

This research employs a methodology centred on an extensive literature review and case study analysis. The study commences with a comprehensive review of academic literature, reports, and case studies related to ESG practices, corporate sustainability, and the role of AI in enhancing sustainability efforts. Real-world case studies across diverse industries will be examined to illustrate practical applications of AI within ESG strategies. This combined approach of literature analysis and case study examination aims to provide a holistic understanding of AI's integration in ESG initiatives, considering ethical dimensions. Figure 1 mentions the Research Methodology Flowchart: Integrating AI into ESG Practices in an easier way to comprehend.

Figure 1. Research methodology flowchart: Integrating AI into ESG practices
Source: Author's compilation

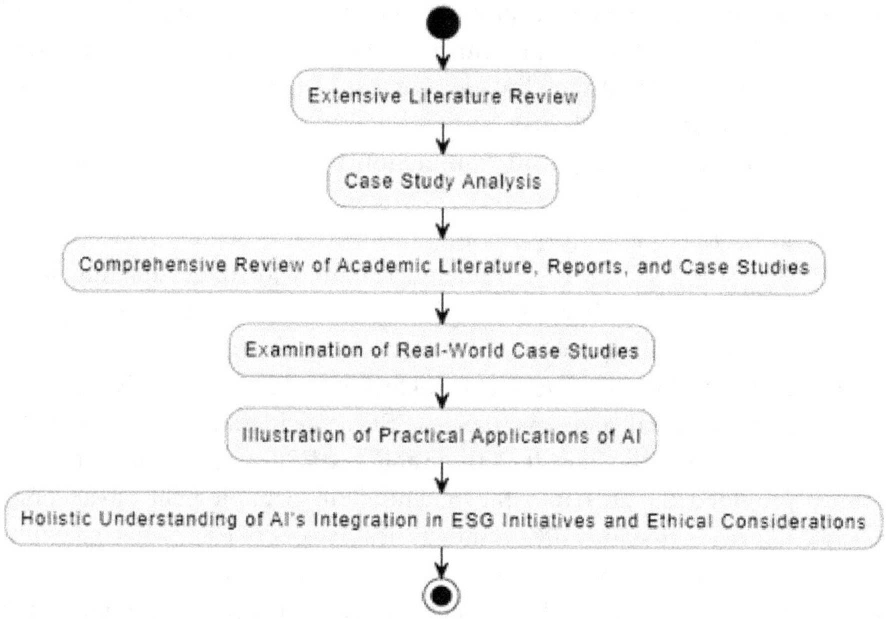

4. ESG EVOLUTION: A HISTORICAL PERSPECTIVE

4.1 Early ESG Initiatives

The origins of ESG practices in corporate governance date back to the early 20th century, as noted in historical research (Burnaev, 2023). During this period, corporate leaders recognized the need for ethical and responsible business conduct beyond mere profit generation. These early efforts laid the foundation for considering environmental, social, and governance factors as integral components of corporate strategies.

As elucidated by Chauhan (2022), the mid-20th century marked a significant milestone with the emergence of concepts like sustainability and ethical supply chain management. Corporations began to integrate environmental and social considerations into their operations, reflecting a growing awareness of global sustainability challenges. This transformative phase set the stage for the comprehensive ESG framework we see today.

4.2 Regulatory Frameworks

Government regulations have played a pivotal role in shaping the trajectory of ESG practices (Elouidani et al., 2022). Over the years, governments worldwide have recognized the importance of sustainability and ethical governance. Regulatory changes, such as environmental protection laws and corporate governance reforms, have compelled organizations to adopt ESG principles (Huang, 2021).

Global ESG standards and reporting requirements, as highlighted by Pan (2023), have further standardized ESG practices. Organizations adhere to frameworks like the Global Reporting Initiative (GRI) and the Task Force on Climate-related Financial Disclosures (TCFD), ensuring transparency and comparability in their ESG disclosures. This standardization not only bolsters ESG's significance but also fosters a more accountable and sustainable corporate landscape, aligning with global sustainability goals.

The historical evolution of ESG practices, influenced by regulatory frameworks and global standards, underscores the dynamic journey from early corporate governance principles to the comprehensive ESG framework embraced by organizations today (Saxena, 2022). This journey reflects a growing recognition of the interconnectedness between environmental responsibility, social equity, and effective governance in the pursuit of corporate sustainability (Selim, 2020).

5. THE EXPANDING SIGNIFICANCE OF ESG

5.1 Stakeholder Expectations

Stakeholders, comprising investors, consumers, and employees, have become instrumental in driving the adoption of ESG practices (Burnaev, 2023). Investors, in particular, are increasingly factoring in a company's ESG performance when making investment decisions, recognizing the inherent risks and opportunities associated with sustainable practices.

Consumer preferences and ethical considerations have also played a pivotal role in influencing companies to embrace ESG initiatives. Research by Liu (2023) demonstrates the impact of public perceptions, often shaped by social media discourse, on a company's reputation and market position. Companies responsive to these dynamics understand that their ESG performance directly correlates with their brand image and, consequently, their bottom line.

5.2 Integration Into Business Strategy

The integration of ESG considerations into corporate strategy is a strategic imperative (Saxena, 2022). Organizations are increasingly aligning ESG goals with long-term business objectives to reap a multitude of benefits. These include improved risk management, enhanced brand reputation, and access to capital that is attuned to sustainable practices.

Mourtzis (2022) highlights the importance of this alignment within the context of Industry 4.0 and Society 5.0 transitions. The adoption of advanced technologies, including artificial intelligence, facilitates this integration by providing data-driven insights into ESG-related opportunities and challenges.

In conclusion, the expanding significance of ESG is driven by stakeholder expectations and its integration into corporate strategy, reflecting the realization that sustainable practices are not only ethically responsible but also pivotal for long-term business success.

6. LEVERAGING AI FOR ENHANCED ESG PRACTICES

6.1 Data Analysis and ESG Metrics

Artificial Intelligence (AI) is at the forefront of transforming the way organizations manage their environmental, social, and governance (ESG) data. One of its key roles is in data analysis, where AI systems excel at collecting, processing, and interpreting vast and complex datasets (Burnaev, 2023). This capability allows companies to enhance their ESG reporting and benchmarking efforts significantly.

AI-driven ESG reporting ensures that data is collected accurately and consistently, reducing the risk of errors or omissions. For instance, AI can automate the collection of data from various sources, ranging from supply chain information to energy consumption data. By doing so, it streamlines the reporting process, saving time and resources. This not only leads to more comprehensive ESG reporting but also allows for real-time monitoring and adjustments, promoting transparency and accountability (Chauhan, 2022).

Furthermore, AI's data analysis capabilities enable companies to derive meaningful insights from their ESG metrics. Through machine learning algorithms, AI can identify trends, patterns, and correlations within the data that might not be apparent through traditional analysis methods. This can help organizations pinpoint areas for improvement, set ambitious sustainability goals, and make data-driven decisions to drive ESG initiatives forward (Liu, 2023).

6.2 Predictive Modeling for Risk Assessment

Predictive modelling is another critical aspect of AI's contribution to ESG practices. AI algorithms can assess historical ESG data to identify potential risks and opportunities (Huang, 2021). For example, they can predict the environmental impact of specific business practices or anticipate social and governance-related issues that might arise in the future. This foresight enables organizations to proactively address ESG challenges, minimize risks, and seize opportunities for sustainable growth.

Moreover, predictive analytics can assist in anticipating market trends and regulatory changes that may impact ESG performance (Mourtzis, 2022). By staying ahead of these shifts, companies can adapt their strategies and policies accordingly, ensuring compliance with evolving ESG standards. This adaptability not only mitigates risks but also positions organizations to take advantage of emerging opportunities in sustainable markets (Pan, 2023).

In conclusion, the integration of AI into ESG practices represents a transformative shift in how companies approach sustainability. AI streamlines data management and analysis enhances ESG reporting accuracy and empowers organizations with predictive capabilities to navigate the dynamic landscape of sustainability. However, it is crucial to consider the ethical aspects of AI in ESG, ensuring that responsible and transparent AI practices are adhered to (Selim, 2020).

7. CASE STUDIES

7.1 Companies Leading in ESG Integration

In the realm of environmental, social, and governance (ESG) integration, several companies have emerged as leaders, setting the benchmark for sustainable practices. These exemplary companies showcase not only their commitment to ESG but also the tangible benefits of such integration.

One such leader is Microsoft, a technology giant that has taken a comprehensive approach to ESG integration. Microsoft's ESG initiatives span from reducing carbon emissions through sustainable data centres to fostering diversity and inclusion in its workforce. This multifaceted approach aligns with its long-term business objectives and has earned Microsoft recognition as a leader in ESG integration (Smokova, 2022).

Another notable example is Unilever, a consumer goods company that has made sustainability a core part of its business strategy. Unilever's Sustainable Living Plan commits the company to reducing its environmental footprint while simultaneously increasing social impact. Through initiatives like sustainable sourcing, reducing plastic waste, and promoting hygiene and sanitation, Unilever exemplifies how ESG can be deeply integrated into the core of a business's operations (Selim, 2020).

7.2 AI-Driven ESG Initiatives

Organizations across various industries are harnessing the power of artificial intelligence (AI) to augment their ESG efforts, showcasing the versatility and impact of AI in sustainability.

Siemens, a global leader in industrial automation and sustainable technologies, exemplifies the use of AI in ESG. Siemens employs AI-driven digital twins to optimize its manufacturing processes, reducing energy consumption and emissions. These digital twins simulate real-world production scenarios, allowing for precise adjustments and minimizing environmental impact. This AI-driven approach not only enhances sustainability but also contributes to cost savings (Huang, 2021).

In the financial sector, BlackRock, one of the world's largest asset management firms, utilizes AI to strengthen its ESG investment strategies. AI algorithms analyze vast amounts of ESG data to identify sustainable investment opportunities and potential risks. This data-driven approach allows BlackRock to align its investments with ESG principles, promoting responsible investing and sustainable financial growth (Elouidani et al., 2022).

Additionally, Google, a technology conglomerate, employs AI to optimize its data centre operations. Through predictive analytics and machine learning, Google maximizes energy efficiency, reducing its environmental footprint. This AI-driven initiative not only demonstrates Google's commitment to ESG but also showcases the potential for technology companies to lead in sustainable practices (Smokova, 2022).

These case studies highlight that AI-driven ESG initiatives are not limited to specific industries but are adaptable and applicable across sectors. They underscore the transformative potential of AI in enhancing sustainability efforts, whether through optimizing manufacturing processes, enabling responsible investing, or improving energy efficiency. As more organizations embrace AI for ESG, these examples serve as inspirations for others to follow suit and drive positive change in the pursuit of sustainable business practices.

8. CHALLENGES AND ETHICAL CONSIDERATIONS

8.1 Data Privacy and Transparency

While the integration of artificial intelligence (AI) in environmental, social, and governance (ESG) initiatives offers promising benefits, it also presents significant challenges related to data privacy and transparency.

One of the primary concerns is data privacy. AI systems rely on vast amounts of data, including sensitive information, to make informed decisions. Collecting and analyzing this data raises ethical questions about how it is sourced, stored, and protected. Ensuring the privacy of individuals and organizations whose data is utilized in AI-driven ESG initiatives is paramount. Transparent data handling practices, secure storage, and adherence to data protection regulations are essential to address these concerns (Liu, 2023).

Transparency is another critical consideration. The opacity of AI algorithms and decision-making processes can create scepticism and erode trust in AI-driven ESG efforts. Companies must be transparent about how AI is being used in their sustainability initiatives, including the algorithms and data sources employed. Providing stakeholders with insights into the AI-driven decision-making process can help build trust and ensure accountability (Selim, 2020).

8.2 Ethical AI in Sustainability

Deploying AI in sustainability efforts necessitates a commitment to ethical practices to avoid exacerbating ESG issues. Ethical AI in sustainability encompasses various facets, including avoiding bias, ensuring fairness, and promoting inclusivity.

One challenge is addressing algorithmic bias. AI systems can inadvertently perpetuate biases present in the data they are trained on, leading to discriminatory outcomes. To mitigate this, organizations must carefully curate training datasets and implement bias-detection mechanisms. Regular audits of AI systems to identify and rectify bias are crucial to ensuring that AI does not exacerbate existing social inequalities (Liu, 2023).

Fairness is another ethical consideration. AI algorithms should not favour or discriminate against particular groups or communities when making decisions related to ESG. Fairness-aware AI development involves defining fairness metrics, actively monitoring for disparities, and adjusting algorithms as needed to ensure equitable outcomes (Chauhan, 2022).

Inclusivity is essential to ethical AI in sustainability. It involves ensuring that AI-driven ESG initiatives consider the diverse perspectives and needs of all stakeholders. This includes involving marginalized communities and stakeholders in decision-making processes and actively seeking their input to avoid unintended negative consequences (Elouidani et al., 2022).

In conclusion, while AI offers tremendous potential to enhance ESG practices, addressing the associated challenges and ethical considerations is paramount. Data privacy and transparency must be upheld to protect sensitive information and build trust with stakeholders. Ethical AI practices, including combating bias, ensuring fairness, and promoting inclusivity, are essential to prevent AI from exacerbating ESG issues and to create genuinely sustainable and responsible solutions. As organizations continue to embrace AI in their sustainability efforts, ethical considerations will play a pivotal role in achieving meaningful and positive impacts on environmental, social, and governance fronts.

9. FUTURE DIRECTIONS AND RECOMMENDATIONS

9.1 The Potential of AI-ESG Integration

The integration of artificial intelligence (AI) and environmental, social, and governance (ESG) practices holds vast potential for shaping the future of sustainable business. Several promising developments are on the horizon. Figure 2 provides an overview of the Potential of AI-ESG Integration.

i. **Enhanced Predictive Analytics:** AI will continue to advance predictive modelling capabilities, enabling organizations to anticipate ESG risks and opportunities with greater precision. This will empower businesses to make proactive decisions that align with sustainability goals and adapt to rapidly changing ESG landscapes (Pan, 2023).
ii. **AI for Impact Measurement:** Future AI systems will play a pivotal role in accurately measuring the impact of ESG initiatives. Enhanced data analytics and AI-driven impact assessments will provide organizations with a comprehensive understanding of their ESG performance and help them communicate their achievements more effectively (Saxena, 2022).
iii. **Responsible AI:** The future of AI-ESG integration will prioritize responsible AI practices. Ethical considerations, fairness, and transparency will be embedded into AI systems, ensuring that AI-driven sustainability efforts align with ethical standards and do not inadvertently exacerbate ESG issues (Selim, 2020).

Figure 2. The potential of AI-ESG integration
Source: Author's compilation

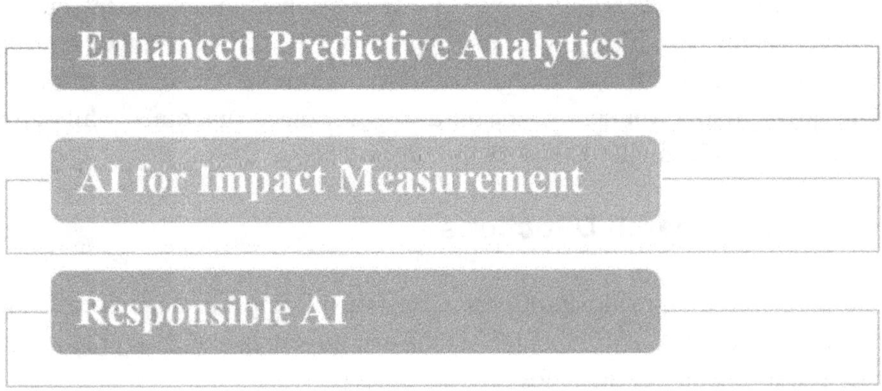

9.2 Recommendations for Organizations

As organizations seek to harness the potential of AI to enhance their ESG initiatives, several practical recommendations can guide their efforts:

i. **Data Governance:** Establish robust data governance frameworks to ensure the ethical and responsible use of data in AI-driven ESG initiatives. Data privacy, security, and transparency should be central considerations.
ii. **Skill Development:** Invest in building AI-related skills and capabilities within the organization. Training employees to work effectively with AI systems is crucial for successful integration.
iii. **Collaborative Partnerships:** Collaborate with AI experts, sustainability organizations, and industry peers to leverage collective knowledge and resources in advancing ESG goals.
iv. **Impact Measurement:** Develop clear and measurable ESG goals and regularly assess the impact of AI-driven initiatives. Transparency in reporting progress is key to building trust with stakeholders.
v. **Ethical AI Guidelines:** Establish guidelines and policies for the ethical use of AI in ESG. This includes addressing bias, ensuring fairness, and promoting inclusivity in AI systems.
vi. **Stakeholder Engagement:** Engage with stakeholders, including investors, consumers, employees, and communities, to gather input and feedback on AI-driven ESG initiatives. This fosters transparency and aligns efforts with stakeholder expectations (Mourtzis, 2022).

In summary, the future of AI-ESG integration offers exciting opportunities for organizations committed to sustainability. By embracing responsible AI practices, enhancing predictive capabilities, and prioritizing impact measurement, businesses can navigate the complex ESG landscape more effectively. Implementing the recommended steps will enable organizations to leverage AI as a powerful tool for driving positive environmental, social, and governance outcomes while aligning with evolving ESG standards and expectations.

9.3 Future Research Directions

While this research has made significant strides in exploring the integration of artificial intelligence (AI) into environmental, social, and governance (ESG) practices, there are several promising avenues for future research:

i. **Ethical AI in ESG:** Investigate the development of ethical frameworks and guidelines specifically tailored to the use of AI in ESG. Explore how organizations can ensure that their AI-driven ESG initiatives are aligned with ethical principles and societal values.
ii. **AI and Sustainable Finance:** Examine the role of AI in sustainable finance in greater detail. Explore how AI can optimize investment decisions, risk assessment, and portfolio management to promote ESG objectives while maximizing financial returns.
iii. **AI and Climate Change Mitigation:** Investigate how AI can be harnessed to address climate change challenges. Research the potential of AI-driven solutions in areas such as renewable energy, carbon footprint reduction, and climate risk modelling.
iv. **AI and Social Impact:** Explore the applications of AI in addressing social inequalities and promoting social responsibility. Investigate how AI can be utilized to enhance access to education, healthcare, and basic amenities, contributing to a more equitable society.
v. **AI Governance and Regulation:** Study the regulatory landscape surrounding AI applications in ESG. Analyze how governments and international bodies are shaping policies and regulations to ensure responsible AI use in sustainability efforts.

9.4 Limitations of the Study

It is important to acknowledge the limitations of this research:

i. **Scope:** This study provides a broad overview of AI's role in ESG, but it does not delve deeply into specific industry sectors or geographic regions. Future research can offer more granular insights into sector-specific challenges and opportunities.
ii. **Temporal Scope:** The study primarily focuses on recent developments in ESG and AI. Long-term trends and their impact on sustainability efforts could benefit from further exploration.
iii. **Ethical Considerations:** While ethical considerations associated with AI in ESG are discussed, a comprehensive ethical framework is beyond the scope of this paper. Future research can provide in-depth ethical guidelines and assessments.
iv. **Data Privacy:** The study briefly mentions data privacy concerns in AI but does not extensively explore this critical issue. Future research should delve into the intricacies of data privacy in AI-driven sustainability initiatives.
v. **Quantitative Analysis:** This research adopts a qualitative approach. Future studies can complement this with quantitative analyses, surveys, and empirical data to validate findings and identify quantitative relationships between AI adoption and ESG performance.

Addressing these limitations and pursuing future research in these areas can contribute to a more nuanced understanding of the complex interplay between AI and ESG, further advancing sustainable practices across industries and regions.

10. CONCLUSION

The journey documented in this research paper has offered profound insights into the transformation of environmental, social, and governance (ESG) practices from mere peripheral concerns to becoming fundamental pillars of corporate sustainability strategies. ESG, over the years, has metamorphosed into a driving force that fundamentally reshapes how organizations operate, transcending the realm of profitability alone (Burnaev, 2023).

Moreover, our exploration has illuminated the immense potential of artificial intelligence (AI) in elevating sustainability endeavours to unprecedented heights. AI's exceptional capabilities in data analysis, predictive modelling, and risk assessment equip organizations with the essential tools required to navigate the intricate landscape of ESG challenges and opportunities (Huang, 2021). Through the lens of case studies and insights derived from AI applications (Pan, 2023), we have witnessed the transformative power of AI, enabling data-driven decision-making and fostering innovation in sustainability practices (Chauhan, 2022).

The integration of AI into ESG practices transcends the fulfilment of stakeholder expectations; it has become a strategic imperative for ensuring long-term business resilience and success. It empowers organizations to not only meet regulatory requirements but also instigate significant and impactful change in environmental conservation, social responsibility, and ethical governance (Saxena, 2022).

As organizations embark on this transformative journey, it is imperative to acknowledge the ethical considerations and challenges intertwined with AI-driven ESG initiatives (Selim, 2020). Upholding principles of data privacy, transparency, fairness, and inclusivity should be at the forefront of AI implementations. Only by doing so can technology truly enhance, rather than hinder, the pursuit of sustainability (Smokova, 2022).

This research paper has not only shed light on the historical evolution of ESG practices and their mounting prominence in the corporate landscape but has also underscored the pivotal role of AI as a catalyst for advancing sustainability. By wholeheartedly embracing AI-driven solutions, businesses can not only navigate the intricacies of ESG but also thrive in an era where sustainability is not merely an option but an imperative. This journey toward sustainable and responsible business practices not only aligns with the expectations of an increasingly conscientious world but also paves the way for a more resilient and sustainable future, where businesses play a vital role in shaping a better world for all.

REFERENCES

Burnaev, E. M., Mironov, E., Shpilman, A., Mironenko, M., & Katalevsky, D. (2023). Practical AI Cases for Solving ESG Challenges. *Sustainability (Basel)*, *12731*(17), 12731. Advance online publication. doi:10.3390u151712731

Chauhan, S. S., Singh, R., Gehlot, A., Akram, S. V., Twala, B., & Priyadarshi, N. (2022). Digitalization of Supply Chain Management with Industry 4.0 Enabling Technologies: A Sustainable Perspective. *Processes (Basel, Switzerland)*, *96*(1), 96. Advance online publication. doi:10.3390/pr11010096

Elouidani, R. (2022). Artificial Intelligence for a Sustainable Finance: A Bibliometric Analysis. *International Conference on Advanced Intelligent Systems for Sustainable Development*, 536-551. Retrieved from https://link.springer.com/chapter/10.1007/978-3-031-26384-2_46

Huang, Z. S., Shen, Y., Li, J., Fey, M., & Brecher, C. (2021). A survey on AI-driven digital twins in industry 4.0: Smart manufacturing and advanced robotics. *Sensors (Basel)*, *6340*(19), 6340. Advance online publication. doi:10.339021196340 PMID:34640660

Liu, M. L., Luo, X., & Lu, W.-Z. (2023). Public perceptions of environmental, social, and governance (ESG) based on social media data: Evidence from China. *Journal of Cleaner Production*, 135840. Advance online publication. doi:10.1016/j.jclepro.2022.135840

Mourtzis, D. A., Angelopoulos, J., & Panopoulos, N. (2022). A Literature Review of the Challenges and Opportunities of the Transition from Industry 4.0 to Society 5.0. *Energies*, *6276*(17), 6276. Advance online publication. doi:10.3390/en15176276

Pan, S. L., & Nishant, R. (2023). Artificial intelligence for digital sustainability: An insight into domain-specific research and future directions. *International Journal of Information Management*, 102668. Advance online publication. doi:10.1016/j.ijinfomgt.2023.102668

Saxena, A. S., Singh, R., Gehlot, A., Akram, S. V., Twala, B., Singh, A., Montero, E. C., & Priyadarshi, N. (2022). Technologies Empowered Environmental, Social, and Governance (ESG): An Industry 4.0 Landscape. *Sustainability (Basel)*, *309*(1), 309. Advance online publication. doi:10.3390u15010309

Selim, O. (2020). *ESG and AI: the beauty and the beast of sustainable investing.* Academic Press.

Smokova, D. (2022). *How are GAFAM companies-Microsoft, Google, and Apple-utilizing AI systems' capabilities to drive their ESG/CSR initiatives?* [Bachelor's thesis]. University of Twente. Retrieved from https://purl.utwente.nl/essays/91325

Chapter 11
Benefits Management and Balanced Scorecard in Dynamic Environments

Jorge Vareda Gomes
https://orcid.org/0000-0003-0656-9284
Universidade Lusófona, Lisboa, Portugal

Mário Batista Romão
https://orcid.org/0000-0003-4564-1883
ISEG, Universidade de Lisboa, Portugal

ABSTRACT

In the rapidly-changing environments characterizing most industries today, organizations face intense competitive pressure to do things better, faster, and cheaper. Most markets are becoming increasingly dynamic. Organizations can no longer rely on a traditional analytical approach to understand their industry or market, since that market is changing in rapid and unexpected ways. In spite of its worldwide dissemination, balanced scorecard (BSC) has demonstrated inadequacy in certain circumstances. Some of the original advantages of the BSC can nowadays be interpreted as weaknesses. The authors suggest that in business dynamic environments, the benefits management approach, by using the benefits dependency network, can help BSCs to guide and support the benefits achievement related with investments, in a complementary way. By using a case study, they try to show how a BSC exhibits limitations to deal with business disruptive environments and how a benefits management approach brings a strengthened business implementation vision, from strategy down to operations.

DOI: 10.4018/979-8-3693-1151-6.ch011

INTRODUCTION

With the increasing pressure to achieve performance improvement, the need to implement highly effective efficient and integrated management systems is continuously increasing. There has been an emphasis on understanding how performance is created within the firm. To understand what drives performance, managers must have in place performance measurement systems designed to capture information on all aspects of the business (Pravdić & Kučinar, 2015). Strategies often fail in organizations, not because of poor design but because they are poorly implemented. Since strategy implementation is critical to the continued success of any organization, the study of specific management tools that can help in this regard is of great interest (Bisbe & Barrubés, 2012). Most markets are becoming increasingly dynamic; organizations cannot rely on an analytical approach to understanding their industry or market, since that market is changing in rapid and unexpected ways. Equally, they cannot rely on the collection of resources that have provided them with competitive advantage in the past. Rather, they must learn to develop capabilities that allow them to integrate, reconfigure, gain and release resources (Eisenhardt and Martin, 2000).

With a shift from the industrial economy towards a *new economy* that is now predominantly characterized by intangible assets, such as knowledge and innovative capability, organizations must manage increasing levels of complexity, mobility and uncertainty (Voelpel *et al.* 2005). The ability to manage knowledge-based intellect is of critical important in this new environment (Quinn, 1992). Competition in this *new economy* is now increasingly characterized by the rapid emergence of brand-owning companies that devote their energies to organizational fitness (Beer, 2002).

The development of a dynamic business environment affects every company (Friesenbichler & Reinstaller, 2022). Technological changes and product variations are two factors that significantly affect business development (Liu et al., 2020). In today's intensely competitive business environments, it is vital for enterprises to adopt swift actions that guarantee their financial security and market position (Lee et al., 2022). For many companies' competitive advantage is a continuous process of performance improvements and search for better practices and development of new capabilities. This includes a search for more efficient process technologies, new or improved products and procedures in the manufacturing process but also development of dynamic capabilities (Teece, Pisano and Shuen 1997) to respond and adapt to change and new trends in the sector. Prahalad and Hamel (1990) argue that sustainable competitive advantage is dependent upon building and exploiting *core competences*.

Porter's recent work emphasizes the need for firms and countries to broaden and upgrade their internal advantages to sustain and extend competitive advantages (Porter 1991, 1992).

Firms obtain sustained competitive advantage by implementing strategies that exploit their internal strengths through responding to environmental opportunities, improving internal weaknesses and eliminated the external threats (Barney, 1991).

For managers the challenge is to identify, develop, protect, and deploy resources and capabilities in a way that provides the firm with a sustainable competitive advantage and, thereby, a superior return on capital (Amit & Schoemaker, 1993).

Teece *et al.*, (1997) originally defined the dynamic capabilities approach as ways of exploiting existing internal and external firm specific competences to address changing investments.

Some authors have long recognized the importance of firm differences and distinctive competencies (Selznick, 1957; Ansoff, 1965; Andrews, 1971; Hofer and Schendel, 1978).

The resource-based view (RBV) of the firm is an influential theoretical framework for understanding how competitive advantage within firms is achieved and how that advantage might be sustained over time (Barney, 1991; Nelson, 1991; Penrose, 1959; Peteraf, 1993; Prahalad & Hamel, 1990; Teece, Pisano & Shuen, 1997; Wernerfelt, 1984). This perspective focuses on the internal organization of firms, and so is a complement to the traditional emphasis of strategy on industry structure and strategic positioning within that structure as the determinants of competitive advantage (Henderson & Cockburn, 1994; Porter, 1979).

RBV approach assumes that organizations can be conceptualized as sets of resources that are heterogeneously distributed across the organizations and their differences persist over the time (Amit and Schoemaker, 1993; Mahoney & Pandian, 1992; Penrose, 1959; Wernerfelt, 1984) and emphasizes firm-specific capabilities and assets and the existence of isolating mechanisms as the fundamental determinants of firm performance (Penrose, 1959; Rumelt, 1984; Teece, 1984; Wernerfelt 1984).

Authors writings such as Irvin and Michaels (1989), Wernerfelt (1989), Prahalad and Hamel (1990), Grant (1991), or Stalk, Evans, and Shulman (1992) further evidence a continuing interest in core skills and capabilities as a source of competitive advantage.

According to Barney (1991) a firm resource to have the potential of generating competitive advantage, it must have the following the four empirical indicators:

(1) Valuable, in the sense that it exploits opportunities.
(2) Rare, among a firm's current and potential competition.
(3) Imperfectly imitable
(4) Without strategically equivalent substitutes.

The research has theorized when firms have resources that are valuable, rare, inimitable and non replaceable, so called VRIN attributes, they can achieve sustainable competitive advantage by implementing fresh value-creating strategies that cannot be easily duplicated by competing firms (Barney, 1991; Conner and Prahalad, 1996; Nelson, 1991; Peteraf, 1993; Wernerfelt, 1984, 1995).

According to Amit & Schoemaker (1993), managerial decisions concerning such resources and capabilities are ordinarily made in a setting that is characterized by:

(1) Uncertainty about the economic, industry, regulatory, social, and technological environments, competitors' behavior, and customers preferences.
(2) Complexity concerning the interrelated causes that shape the firm's environments, the competitive interactions ensuing from differing perceptions about these environments.
(3) Intra organizational conflicts among those who make managerial decisions and those affected by them.

These conditions of uncertainty, complexity and conflict are usually difficult to articulate or model. To answer to the new business constrains, better, faster and cheaper, the successful organizations have developed three broad strategies:

(1) Companies have hired, trained and empowered employees to use information and skills so that the organization will be more knowledgeable and responsive to pressures for change,
(2) many companies have chosen to collaborate more fully with key stakeholders, particularly customers, suppliers and employees to design more effective, efficient process,
(3) companies have begun to better understand what creates success; however, they define it and to effectively manage process to achieve success.

Recently, scholars have extended RBV to dynamic markets (Teece *et al.,*1997), in these markets, where the competitive environment is continuously changing the dynamic capabilities by which the firms' managers integrate, build, and reconfigure internal and external competencies to address rapidly changing environments (Teece *et al.,*1997) become the source of sustained competitive advantage.

While extreme forms of dynamic competition (termed "hypercompetition" by D'Aveni 1994) are characteristic of product markets, dynamically competitive conditions also are present in the markets for resources. Indeed, competitive conditions in product markets are driven, in part, by the conditions of competition in the markets for resources (Barney 1986).

The problems that companies address today require enterprise-wide solutions that call for an integrated approach and effective management of organizational resources to achieve business objectives. Benefits Management (BM) approach proposes a continuous mapping of benefits of IS/IT investments, implementing and monitoring intermediate results. Balanced Scorecard (BSC) is an innovative approach that considers the financial and non-financial perspectives in determining the performance level of organization. Not only represents a measurement tool, but it is also a multi-dimensional system of performance management focuses on the alignment of all business initiatives with the strategy. In this paper the authors propose a link between these two approaches to improve the management of business benefits and to ensure that actions taken along the investment life-cycle lead to foreseen benefits realization.

BACKGROUND

The Performance Measurement

In recent years, traditional performance management techniques measure the organizational financial performance such as revenue, sales volume and profit are blamed for that they are one-dimensional and they are backward-looking in the record (David, 2011). Financial measures describe only a small part of the firm performance. Traditional financial measures, like ROI and EPS, can give misleading signals (Sambharya, 2011). As a result, managers want a balanced presentation of both financial and new operational measures. The company's success for tomorrow depends on its ability today of intangible assets such as customer relation, internal business process and employee learning (Kaplan & Norton, 2004). Measuring organizational success and implementing effective strategies for future success represent continuous challenges for managers, researchers and consultants. According to Kaplan & Norton (2000) strategy is the movement of an organization towards a desired but uncertain future position. "Management control systems provide information that is intended to be useful to managers in performing their jobs and to assist organizations in developing and maintaining viable patterns of behavior." (Otley, 1999: 364).

Ittner and Larcker (2003) highlighted some mistakes companies make when trying to measure nonfinancial performance:

(1) Not linking measures to strategy - Using an approach such as the Balanced Scorecard by itself does not identify which performance areas make the greatest contributions to the company's financial outcomes.

(2) Not validating the links - Not validating the model leads to measuring too many things, and areas of performance that don't have much effect on what really matters.
(3) Not setting the right performance targets - Outstanding nonfinancial performance does not always translate into outstanding financial performance.
(4) Measuring incorrectly - Companies used metrics that lacked statistical validity and reliability

With the help of performance measurement tools, companies can monitor the implementation of their business plans and strategies, thereby contributing to their organizational success. With performance measurement an organization can monitor the implementation of its plans and determine when plans are unsuccessful and how to improve them. According to Atkinson *el al.*, (1997) the performance measurement system must do four things: (1) Help the company evaluate whether it is receiving the expected contribution from employees and suppliers, the elements of its internal group and the expected returns from customer group. (2) Help the company evaluate whether it is giving each stakeholder group what it needs to continue to contribute so the company can meet its primary objectives. (3) Guide the design and implementation of process that contribute to the companies' secondary objectives. (4) Help the company evaluate its planning and he contracts, both implicit and explicit that it has negotiated with its stakeholders by helping it evaluate the effect of secondary objectives on its primary objectives.

Reilly & Reilly (2000) identifies a role of characteristics that managers would like to see in a measurement system:

(1) The system should ensure that value is created for the stakeholders and help managers in their decision making by giving insight into future outcomes.
(2) Measurements should be systematic.
(3) Measurements should help the company accomplishment a strategy by tracking its activities.
(4) A measure should be logical and express what stakeholders want delivered.
(5) The number of measurements within the organization should be limited by including only those that are most important.
(6) Measurement standards should take into consideration what is going on in the rest of the industry.
(7) A measurement system should inspire users to understand the system and create a culture that understands the power of the information that measurements provide. Results should be openly communicated, and the system should be easy for everyone to use.

Ittner & Larcker (2003) highlights the mistakes that companies make when trying to measure nonfinancial performance:

(1) Not linking measures to strategy – A major challenges for companies is determining which nonfinancial measures to track.
(2) Not validating the links - Not validating the model leads to measuring too many things, and areas of performance that don't have much effect on what really matters.
(3) Setting the right performance targets - Outstanding nonfinancial performance does not always translate into outstanding financial performance.
(4) Measuring incorrectly - Research also indicated that 70% of the company's used metrics that lacked statistical validity.

Once a performance measurement system has been developed it has to be implemented. This system will have to interact with two fundamental environments:

(1) Internal – The organization.
(2) External – The market where the organization competes that includes two distinct elements, customers, and competitors (Neely *et al.,* 2003).

According to Atkinson *et al.,* (1997) most companies use formal performance measurements systems that are extensions of their financial reporting systems, and they justify this practice because the financial reporting system provides measures that are generally regarded as reliable and consistent and connected with the primary objective of creating profits for the shareholders. The traditional financial accounting measures can give misleading signals for continuous improvement and innovation and are out of step with the skills and competencies needed by today´s organizations (Maltz *et al.*, 2003). Measurement has been recognized as a crucial element to improve business performance (Sharma *et al.,* 2005).

Balanced Scorecard and Strategy Maps

In an article published in the Harvard Business Review, Kaplan and Norton (1992) introduced BSC in response to growing dissatisfaction of the inadequacy of traditional performance measurement systems and its dependence of exclusively financial. Proponents of the balanced scorecard have long suggested the use of non-financial performance measures via customer, internal business process, and learning and innovation to supplement traditional financial measures. (Kaplan & Norton 1992). The authors proposed an integrated framework for the implementation of financial and nonfinancial performance measures to help organizations align their initiatives with the organization's strategy. The BSC is recognized as a comprehensive system of strategically aligned performance measures (Decoene & Bruggeman, 2006) and is used extensively in business and industry, government, and non-profit organizations worldwide. BSC suggests that as well as financial measures of performance, attention should be paid to the requirements of customers, business processes, learning and growth and longer-term sustainability.

The BSC translates the vision and strategy of a business unit into objectives and measures in four different areas:

- Customer perspective: how the company wishes to be viewed by its customers. The indicators are such as customer satisfaction, customer retention, new customer acquisition, customer response time, market share and customer profitability.
- Internal business process perspective: in which processes the company must do to satisfy shareholders and customers. The key measures include product design, product development, post-sale service, manufacturing efficiency and quality. We must excel at maximizing on-time delivery and minimizing defect rates.
- Learning and growth perspective: which improvements the company must achieve to implement its vision. The key measures include the ability of employees, information systems, and organizational procedures to manage the business and adapt to change.
- Financial perspective: how the company wishes to be viewed by its shareholders. The indicators include profitability measures such as operating income, earnings per share, return-on-capital-employed and sales growth.

A major strength of the BSC approach is the emphasis it places linking performance measures with business unit strategy (Otley, 1999). According to Ahn (2001) the BSC bridges the gap between the development of a strategy and its realization by supporting and linking four critical management processes:

1. Clarifying and translate vision and strategy.
2. Communicate and linking strategic objectives and measures.
3. Planning, set targets, and aligning strategic initiatives.
4. Enhancing strategic feedback and learning.

A well designed BSC should be able to describe the strategies through the objectives and measures previously chosen (Niven, 2002). In modern business models, intangible assets such as employees' skills and knowledge levels, customers and suppliers' relationships, and an innovative culture are critical in providing the much-needed cutting-edge to the organization (Margarita, 2008). The BSC has evolved and morphed from measurement tool to strategic change framework, and most recently to a tool to measure the readiness of intangible value drivers (Marr & Adams, 2004).

Reshaping the BSC it can also be applied to IS/IT in four specific domains (Van Grembergen & DE Haes, 2005; Van Grembergen et al, 2003):

1. The business contribution perspective capturing the business value created from IS/IT investments.
2. The user perspective representing the user evaluation of IS/IT.
3. The operational excellence perspective evaluating the IS/IT processes employed to develop and deliver applications.
4. The future perspective representing the human and technology resources needed by IS/IT to deliver its services over time.

The first step in creating the management processes for implementation of strategy relying on the construction of a reliable and consistent framework for describing strategy, known as Strategy Map (SM). The SM outlines all the cause-and-effect linkages between what an organization's strategy is and what everyone does on a day-to-day basis (Kaplan & Norton, 2000). The SM identify how to get the destinations, the strategic objectives, how tangible and intangible assets are involved, outlines how assets of all types are combined to create customer value propositions, specifies how the desired financial outcomes will be realized and detail the relationships between shareholders, customers, business processes and competencies (Kaplan & Norton, 2000).

Benefits Management and Benefits Dependency Networks

Ward et al, (1996) developed an approach for identifying, structuring, planning, monitoring and delivery benefits. The model introduced the idea of a distinct process targeted towards managing the benefits realization of IS/IT projects to improve the results. The process of BM based on the management model of strategic change developed by Pettigrew and Whipp (1991), recognizes that the process by which a major change is managed needs to be relevant to the content of the change involved both internal and external. The process model of BM includes the following set of steps:

1. Identifying and structuring benefits - The proposed benefits are identified and, for each proposed benefit, business measures are developed, both financial and

non-financial. The benefits are structured to understand the linkages between technology effects, business changes and business objectives.

2. Planning benefits realization - For each benefit, specific responsibility for realizing the benefits are allocated within the stakeholders. The required business benefits and changes are also assessed and planned for, and a Benefits Realization Plan (BRP) is produced.
3. Executing the benefits realization plan - Alongside the implementation of the proposed IS/IT investments, the necessary business changes as detailed in the benefits realization plan are carried out.
4. Evaluating and reviewing results - Following the full implementation of IS/IT and business changes, the previously developed business measures are used to evaluate the effects of the project.
5. Potential for further benefits - As a result of the post-project review, it may become apparent that further benefits are now achievable.

Several authors recognized the importance of the BM initial phases. Bennington & Baccarini (2004) suggest that the benefits identification should be a combined approach of interviews and workshops involving key stakeholders. Best practice is to involve key stakeholders to identify and agree desired benefits maximizing the likelihood of commitment to realize those benefits across a range of levels in the business or the organization (Glynne, 2007). The key tool of this approach is the Benefits Dependency Network (BDN) that was introduced for the first time by Ward & Elvin (1999), and was designed to enable the investment objectives and their resulting benefits to be linked in a structured way to the business, organization and IS/IT changes required to realize those benefits.

LIMITATIONS OF THE TRADITIONAL FRAMEWORKS

Increasing turbulence of the external business environment has focused attention upon resources and organizational capabilities as the principal source of sustainable competitive advantage and the foundation for strategy formulation (Grant, 1996). A business manager should be able to analyze the environment to profit the opportunities or face the threats. Organizations need to build strength and fight their weakness available in the business environment.

The Balanced Scorecard (BSC) is one of the most popular frameworks with a wide usage and as known as a multi-dimensional approach to performance measurement and management that is linked specifically to organizational strategy. BSC suggests that as well as financial measures of performance, attention should be paid to the requirements of customers, business processes and longer-term sustainability. Thus, four areas of performance are defined now labelled as financial, customer, internal business and innovation and learning and it is suggested that up to four measures of performance should be developed in each area.

The BSC is a hierarchical model in which financial performance forms the primary goal to which the other dimensions contribute rather than a truly "balanced" model affording equal status to non-financial objectives (Valmohammadi & Servati, 2011). The "balance" of the scorecard is reflected by the balance between lagging (outcome measures) and leading (performance drivers) indicators, and between financial and nonfinancial measures (De Haas, 2000). A major strength of the Balanced Scorecard approach is the emphasis it places on linking performance measures with business unit strategy (Otley, 1999). According to Neely (1998), one of the hidden strengths of a balanced measurement framework is that it forces management teams to explore the beliefs and assumptions, which underpin their strategy. Banker, Chang, Pizzini (2004) highlighted the linkage between performance measures and strategy objectives, once linkage is understood, strategic objectives can be further translated into actionable measures to help organizations improve performance. The BSC represent not a way of measuring the success of an organization but go future in that they offer managers a "road-map" by which they can manage (Rafiq et al., 2020).

Despite its worldwide dissemination BSC has demonstrated inadequacy in certain circumstances. Interestingly, some of the advantages of the BSC can also be interpreted as disadvantages. Atkinson *el al.,* (1997) note BSC model incomplete because fails to: (1) Adequately highlight the contributions that the employees and suppliers make to help the company achieve its objectives, (2) identify the role of the community in defining the environment within which the company works, (3) identify performance measures to assess stakeholders' contributions. Smith (1998) note that the BSC fails to account for the role of employee's motivation and finally while BSC provides constructs for multiple measures and overcoming the limitations of single measures, there is no clear provision for very long-term measures; the distinctions between means and ends is not well define, and the model probably needs additional empirical validation (Maltz *et al.*, 2003).

The BSC does not define appropriate balance, particularly in terms of stakeholder value. In addition, a BSC designed around a company's strategy is not necessarily complete, and the linkages among measurements and between perspectives are not explicit (Reilly & Reilly, 2000). The BSC contains a serious flaw because if a manager were to introduce a set of measures based solely on it, he would not be able to answer one of the most fundamental questions of all – what are our competitors doing (the competitor perspective)? (Neely and Kennerley, 2003).

According to Voelpel (2005), the BSC when applied in the *new economy* display significant limitations in dealing with new rapidly changing and networked corporate environment. BSC have been very much engaged in improving measurable performance to optimize operational efficiency (Roos *et al.,* 1997; Bontis *et al.,* 1999; Russ, 2001). The BSC follows this logic of seeking efficiency and enables organizations to react to changes by aligning business processes to a defined strategy what causes severe damage to the firm in the innovation economy. Voelpel (2005) identifies on BSC five major problems categories that could endanger the organizations survival:

(1) The BSC is a measurement tool that is relatively rigid; tend to force indicators into one of the four perspectives.
(2) The BSC creates a statics organization that tends to struggle with the challenges of a highly competitive and changing business world.
(3) The external innovative connectivity of an organization is difficult by BSC, which shows to be mostly an internal document thereby depicting a critical limitation in its ability to account for the external environment and systematic linkages.
(4) BSC inability to deal with knowledge creation, learning and growth, BSC follows the traditional logic of innovation, working internally, keeping secret from the external environment.
(5) The BSC have a linear thinking with no room available for understanding more complex business processes.

BALANCED SCORECARD LIMITATIONS

Using the five major problems categories identified by Voelpel (2005) we suggested that a Benefits Management (BM) approach could help BSC to achieve the benefits related with investments in a logical complementary.

The purpose of the benefits management process is to improve the identification of achievable benefits and to ensure that decisions and actions taken over the life of the investment lead to realizing all the feasible benefits (Ward & Daniel, 2006). But, perhaps more importantly, the approach and the associated tools and techniques change the nature of the involvement of business managers and other stakeholders in the management of the investment throughout its lifecycle.

(a) **Rigidity** – The BSC tends to force indicators into one of the four perspectives it limits the view on the company, since it leaves little room for cross-perspectives that might have a simultaneous impact on the company. Those that do not fit or cannot be categorized within the given framework of the four dimensions are in danger of being neglected. BSC might not only enhance a confirmation bias, enabling managers only to see what they want to see (or measure), but it ignores the changing nature of today's business environment.

The BSC concept provides no mechanism for maintaining the relevance of defined measures (Hudson *et al.,* 2001). Neely *et al.,* (1995) also found that the problem for managers is usually not identifying what could be measured but reducing the list of possible measures to a manageable (and relevant) set. Platts and Kim (2002) agree that simply looking at different measures simultaneously is not enough. The linkages between them must also be understood. Mooraj *et al.,* (1999) state that the BSC fails to identify performance measurement as a two-way process. It focuses primarily on top-down performance measurement. Hudson *et al.*, (2001) also acknowledge this and write that BSCs have a lack of integration between the top-level, strategic scorecard, and operational-level measures.

(b) **Immobility** - The BSC creates statics organizations that tend to struggle with the challenges of a highly competitive and changing business world (Voelpel, 2005). Within the BSC approach, a centrally defined strategy is translated into certain measures that align all company activities to achieving these BSC goals. This increases and possibly maximizes the focus on the given goal but limits any further activities and initiatives that might go beyond the originally set targets (Voelpel, 2005). In such an aligned organization, employees, for instance, might have a clear perception of their job, the achievements of BSC metrics, but they will only do little more than achieving just these (Falk and Kosfeld, 2004).

(c) **Inadequacy to external innovative connectivity -** The BSC is a management and measurement tool that is primarily focus is in driving performance and translating strategy into action promoting the organizational efficiency. The BSC ignores the needs of linking the organization to innovative enhanced economy where the companies evolve, establish partnerships, and compete, developing the products and services to answer to the market needs. Mooraj *et al.*, (1999) note that the BSC does not consider the extended value chain in which employee and supplier contributions are highlighted. The BSC may be too narrowly defined. Business is more and more based on networks of firms or so-called business ecosystems in which successful firms collaborate within their network and thereby improve their own performance significantly (Iansiti & Levien, 2004). Since today's business operations are not carried out anymore in isolation until the final product is delivered, but accompanied closely by stakeholder interaction, so the BSC approaches should consider these networks both competitive and collaborative. The BSC is based on the view of the firm in relative isolation and adversarial in relationships with suppliers. Such limitations about a systemic systems orientation become more pronounced, the more a company has to deal with rapid and disruptive change as well as a networked environment such as in today's business world (Voelpel, 2005).

(d) **Dealing with knowledge creation, learning and growth** -The BSC follows the traditional logic of innovation through internal developments, which work on an innovation from its beginning to its end, keeping it secret from the external environment and especially from competitors. The nature of innovation is similarly changing from incremental towards more and more dynamic, from closed to open, meanwhile becoming increasingly networked. In contrast to the BSC internally focused learning and growth perspective the organizations should acknowledges the potential of the entire system. It needs to become a cross-section through all business areas that transcends the traditional internal innovations focus. Innovation, a key factor to intellectual capital (IC) is viewed by the BSC as an internal business process and categorized under this perspective, appearing to be a routine process rather than a creative endeavour by skilled employees all over the company. Knowledge, learning and growth have become essential and good measurement systems need to acknowledge that innovation has to be practiced in all business areas.

The difficulty, which is not limited to the BSC only, is to measure such distributed innovation (Voelpel, 2005).

(e) **Linear thinking** - As business processes become more complex, the understanding of most of the key success factors within a firm, especially today, needs to take a cross-perspective into account. Simple cause-and-effect relationships are not sufficient anymore to understand complex relationships that the BSC tries to reduce to a linear one-way relationship. Customer satisfaction for instance might be linked to various factors such as employee satisfaction, quality, delivery time, and so on. The problem of how to link the indicators of the BSC is still unsolved (Andréasson and Svartling, 1999).

The predominant mindset connected to the application of the BSC is that of a mechanistic and linear thinking, making it difficult to deal with an interconnected and networked world (Voelpel, 2005).

Benefits Management

Tracking the markets and the competitors often, make the changes and redefined the performance measures should be the role of any organization operating dynamic environments. Analysing and choosing the correct drivers that will be the input to the business case for investments that lead to changes on the ways of the work is done. Most of the value from investments comes from the business changes that it enables the organization to make:

(1) Adoption of new or redefined processes
(2) New roles and responsibilities.
(3) Operation of new teams, groups, divisions.
(4) New governance arrangements.
(5) Use of new measures and metrics
(6) Use of new appraisal and reward schemes.
(7) New practices for managing and sharing information.

The investment is in enabled change, not just technology, to achieve improvements in business and organizational performance through better processes, relationships, and ways of working. The achievement of benefits obviously depends on effective implementation of the technology, but evidence from project success and failure suggests that it is organizations inability to accommodate and exploit the capabilities of the technology that causes the poor return from many investments. While business changes may be considered as the way the organization wishes to work 'for ever more', it is recognized that the organization will be undertaking other investments and changes (Ward & Daniel, 2006).

The benefits management helps the BSC on the [(a)] rigidity and [(b)] immobility problems because BM answers continuously to the market requests through the business drivers and agreeing with all the stakeholders on the goals and benefits of the investments building a cause-and-effect network that highlights all the changes needed on the business. This network show how the goals and benefits were reached putting on the stakeholders the responsibility of tracking and achieving the goals and benefits. Since the objectives are phrased in terms of targets for achievement wanted from the investment, the benefits can be identified by considering the performance improvements that will be realised if each of these objectives or targets is achieved. The performance indicators follow all benefits and business changes and give a full perspective how the investments were tracking and accomplish. Further benefits identified were analysed and prosecuted.

The benefits management approach encourages a range of staff to work together because no single individual or group has all the knowledge necessary to identify all the benefits, changes, and IT enablers.

[(c)] The linking BSC to the external innovation environment could improve keeping a open mindset to the markets, competitors, and rapidly reacting to all the situations that generates disadvantage to the organization introducing new ways of doing the work powered by the IS/IT investments, "upgrading" constantly the resources. The BM approaches through the benefits dependency network, draw on a map all the objectives, benefits and changes needed from the business drivers and the path to reach them, setting responsibilities, targets, and performance measures.

(d) (e) In dynamic environments is crucial a close market survey to observe the way how consumers, competitors and suppliers are touched by the different factors that shape the business. The benefits management enhance the discussion and the agreement around the business objectives and related benefits answering to external and internal drivers.

The BSC is grounded in a mechanistic mindset. Business processes become more complex, the understanding of most of the key success factors within a firm, especially today. In a knowledge driven company, simple cause effect relationships are not sufficient anymore to understand complex relationships that the BSC tries to reduce to a linear one-way relationship.

The BSC discipline through the performance measures applied to all organization tasks causes a total focus on the measures accomplishment that leads to successful achievement of the priority objectives, therefore, no room left for other initiatives besides the pre-defined ones. The benefits management consider five stages:

(1) Identifying and structuring benefits – For each proposed benefit suitable business measures are developed, and they are structured to understand the linkages between technology effects, business changes and business objectives.
(2) Planning benefits realisation – For each benefit, specific responsibility for realising the benefit is allocated within the business.
(3) Executing the benefits realisation plan – Carrying out the necessary business changes detailed in the benefits realisation plan.
(4) Evaluating and reviewing results – Review provides an explicit tool for evaluating whether the proposed business benefits have been delivered.
(5) Potential for further benefits - As a result of the post-project review, it may become apparent that further benefits are now achievable.

The benefits management process includes a post-implementation benefits review as an important component of the project. This review should not concentrate on the use of technology or on the project management, rather technology and project audits should be carried out separately. Instead, the benefits review should explore which of the planned benefits have been realized, whether there were any unexpected benefits arising and which planned benefits are still expected but may need additional attention to ensure they are realized. Actions should then be put in place to ensure that these benefits are realized.

CASE STUDY

The VIAPAV investment was a result of a disruptive solution on the products line of the company's portfolio. The organizations BSC shows the inability to deal with these disruptive solutions once the system is extremely focused on implementing the organization strategy in a top-down way, rejecting all new activities or initiatives. The system reviled incapacity to deal and to build a logical cross-perspective in a cause-and-effect process that improved the flexibility and create a set of system indicators that track the development of the investment.

Building the BDN of VIAPAV case study investment (Gomes, 2011) shown on Figure 1 and 4, highlights that the objectives and the related benefits were achieved by the combination of the business changes (T1 to T4) powered by the enabling changes (F1 to F6) and IS/IT enablers (I1 to I4).

Figure 1. Benefits dependency network (Gomes, 2011)

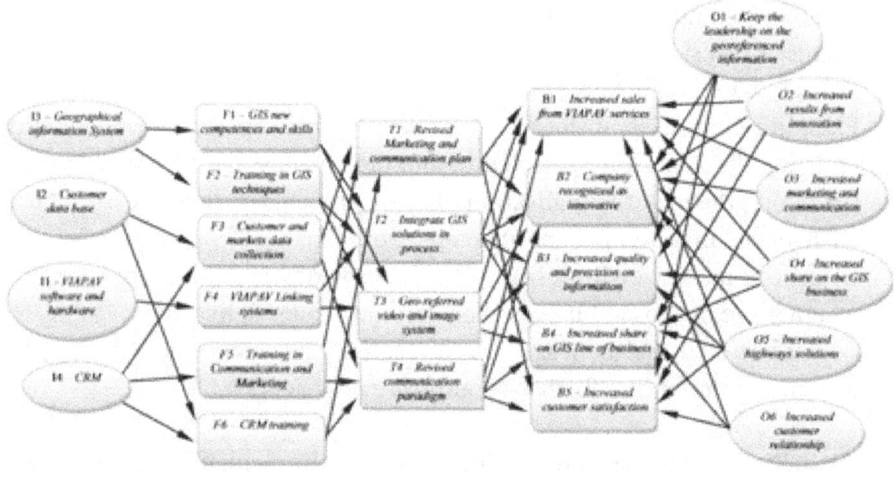

This framework shows in a simple way the cause-and-effect actions to fulfil the end goals.

Table 1. Owners and targets on the benefits dependency network

F1 – Human Resources Manager 6 months	**T1 – Marketing Manager 6 months**	**B1 – Sales Manager 3% Annual Revenue**
F2 – **Human Resources Manager and** I&D Manager *6 months*	T2 – *I&D Manager 16 months*	B2 – *Marketing Manager Annual Inquiry. Better than 70% (Scale 1 – 100%)*
F3 – *Marketing Manager 6 months*	T3 – *Project Manager 12 months*	B3 – *Project Manager Time reduction 30%*
F4 - *Project manager 12 months*	T4 – *Marketing Manager 6 months*	B4 – *Sales Manager 3% Annual revenue*
F5 – ***Human Resources** Manager 6 months*		B5 – *Marketing Manager Annual Inquiry. Better than 70% (Scale 1 – 100%)*
F6 – ***Human Resources** Manager 6 months*		

Following the O2 objective we can build a *specific stream* that shows how the *increased results from innovation* were reach following the network showed in the Figure 2.

Figure 2. O2 specific stream

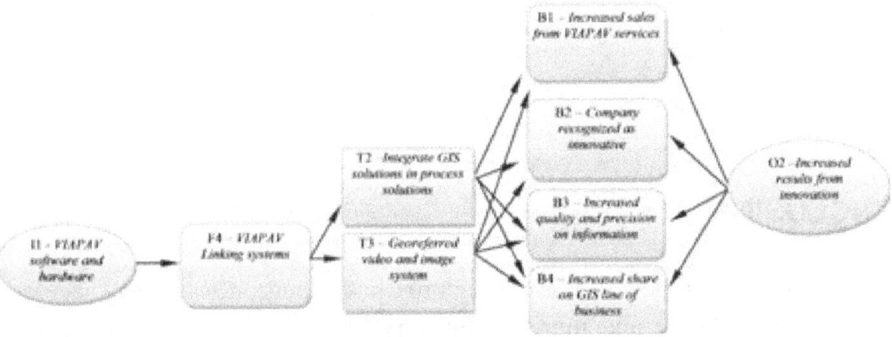

Integration of the Benefits Dependency Network on the BSC Strategic Map is shown on the Figure 3.

Figure 3. Integrated benefits on the strategy map

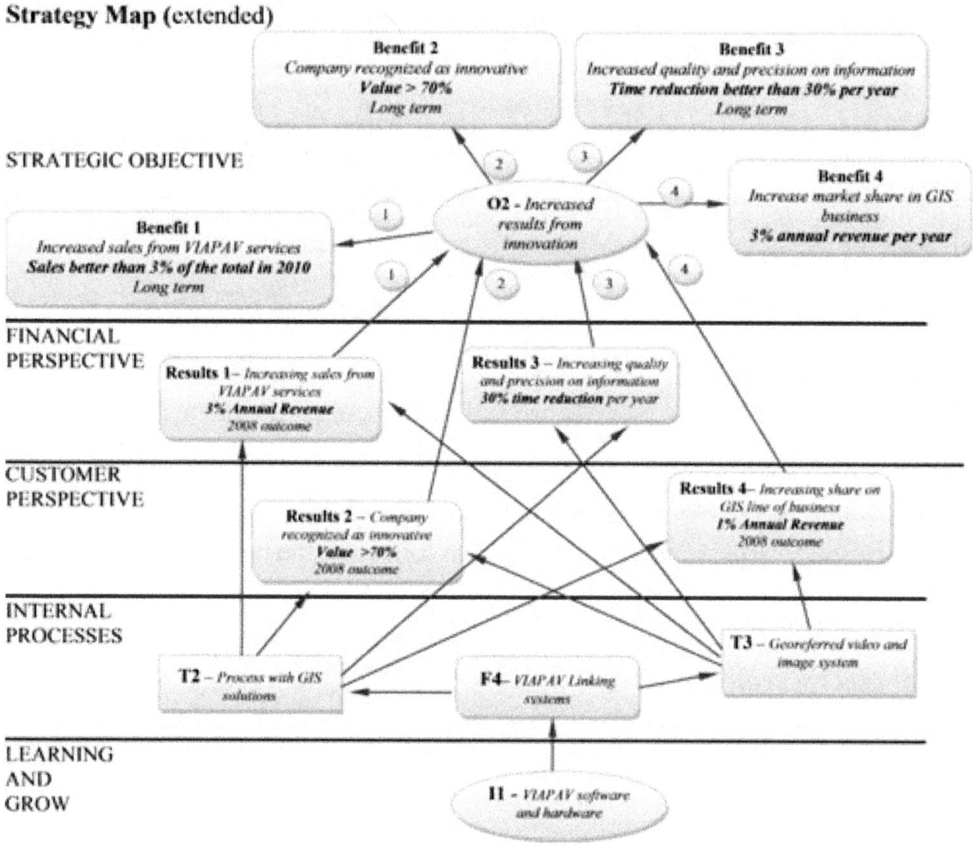

CONCLUSION

The business environment of this new century has undergone rapid and accelerating change, creating more and more uncertainty and complexity. Most markets are becoming increasingly dynamic. Companies compete in this fierce environment to achieve a sustainable competitive advantage, positioning itself strategically in their industries or developing durable and distinctive firm capabilities and resources or through knowledge and innovation.

Organizations are becoming interested in finding ways in which they can ensure their long-term sustainability, whether they are private firms, looking to maximize their shareholder value, or public sector and non-profit organizations, seeking to maximize their quality of service to citizens and/or effectiveness.

Given the dynamic and rapidly changing environment in which the organizations compete, it is important that organisations effectively manage their outcomes form investments. To achieve that they must continuously improve their measurement systems so that it remains appropriate and aligned with their strategies.

Although an increasing number of companies have been using nonfinancial performance measurements in areas such as customer loyalty and employee satisfaction, few have realized the potential benefits of these relatively new measurement systems. These days, performance measurement systems are attracting more and more attention, both among academics and practitioners. Many organizations have shown a complete disconnection between their strategy and how they measure it.

The BSC has become a popular concept for performance measurement, and it focuses attention of management on only a few performance measures and bridges different functional areas as it includes both financial and non-financial measure.

BSC through strategy maps became a powerful tool, allowing organizations to convert its initiatives and resources – including intangible assets such as corporate cultures and employee knowledge, into tangible outcomes. We claim that by the integration between the Balanced Scorecard and the Benefits Management approach can increase the effectiveness of the strategic projects portfolio and improve the confidence of business sponsors that their investments in projects will return benefits that they perceived to be of value.

The BSC represents the natural evolution of management practices, which began to take shape in the post-industrial era. It arises with the necessity to complete the traditional approach of measuring the financial success of organizations in the way that organizational vision and strategy are converted into goals, strategic indicators, targets and initiatives and that its unfolding occurs through other perspectives beyond the financial, with the focus of maintaining long-term sustainability. In addition to the BSC advantages, some criticism has also been presented. The aim is to highlight some rigidity and immobility of the BSC, which advises its use in combination with other approaches, joining the best of their potential. The BSC needs to be complemented with other less vertically integrated tools that enable greater stakeholder participation in setting strategic objectives, so that everyone feels involved and committed with the organizations destiny. The ability to react to the dynamic business environment, interconnected with the necessary internal changes, is challenges that call for a particular attention, deserving higher usefulness in a performance management tool.

Our case study provides an example on how Benefits Management can help Balanced Scorecard with a continuous market follow up and a client intimacy management strategy. Using a benefits Management approach, we've shown how to collect the business drivers, discuss with all the relevant stakeholders, agree on the objectives and the benefits, as well as on on the organizational changes and on the right set of IS/IT enablers.

Benefits Management adds value providing relevant information to the strategic framework of the BSC, by identifying the goals and the benefits and by mapping the way to get them, supported on the right combination of organizational changes, enabling factors and IS/IT enablers.

Benefits Management consider both short- and long-term business benefits. Short term benefits are more likely to be realised and give the stakeholders an idea on if and how the program is going to achieve its goals. Long term benefits may not appear until long after the program has closed and may generate less commitment and enthusiasm.

The authors claimed that Benefits Management provide a richer and more useful decision support and monitoring tool, making the strategy implementation visible, testable, and measurable.

Developing a Benefits Dependency Network results in a clear statement of the benefits from an investment, the activities and the IT capabilities required to achieve those benefits. A complete Benefits Dependency Network also shows how different groups need to work together to achieve the desired benefits.

Benefits Management not only increase the value of investment but also avoid spending money on projects that would not have delivered benefits, increasing greatly the likelihood of the benefits expected from the investment being realized.

REFERENCES

Ahn, H. (2001). Applying the Balanced Scorecard Concept: An Experience Report. *Long Range Planning*, *34*(4), 441–461. doi:10.1016/S0024-6301(01)00057-7

Amit, R., & Schoemaker, P. J. H. (1993). Strategic assets and organizational rent. *Strategic Management Journal*, *14*(1), 33–46. doi:10.1002mj.4250140105

Andréasson, M., & Svartling, A. (1999). *Knowledge Management Methods: Practical approaches to managing knowledge in The Balanced Scorecard - A tool for managing knowledge?* https://www.handels.gu.se/epc/archive/00001973/01/Andreasson_1999_7.pdf

Andrews, K. R. (1971). *The Concept of Corporate Strategy*. Irwin.

Ansoff, H. I. (1965). *Corporate Strategy*. McGraw Hill.

Atkinson, A., Waterhouse, J., & Wells, R., (1997). A Stakeholder Approach to Strategic Performance Measurement. *Sloan Management Review, 38*(3), 5.

Banker, R., Chang, H., & Pizzini, M. (2004). The Balanced Scorecard judgemental effects of performance measures linked to strategy. *The Accounting Review*, *79*(1), 1–23. doi:10.2308/accr.2004.79.1.1

Barney, J. (1986). Strategic Factor Markets: Expectations, Luck and Business Strategy. *Management Science*, *32*(10), 1231–1241. doi:10.1287/mnsc.32.10.1231

Barney, J. (1991). Firm resources and sustained competitive advantage. *Journal of Management*, *17*(1), 99–120. doi:10.1177/014920639101700108

Beer, M. (2002). Building Organizational Fitness. In *Organizations 21C* (pp. 311-330). Financial Times Prentice Hall.

Bennington, P., & Baccarini, D. (2004, June). Project benefits management in IT projects – An Australian perspective. *Project Management Journal*.

Bisbe, J., & Barrubés, J. (2012). The Balanced Scorecard as a Management Tool for Assessing and Monitoring Strategy Implementation in Health Care Organizations. *Revista Española de Cardiología*, *65*(10), 919–927. doi:10.1016/j.recesp.2012.05.014 PMID:22917775

Bontis, N., Dragonetti, N. C., Jacobsen, K., & Roos, G. (1999). The knowledge toolbox: A review of the tools available to measure and manage intangible resources. *European Management Journal*, *17*(4), 391–403. doi:10.1016/S0263-2373(99)00019-5

Conner, K. R., & Prahalad, C. K. (1996). A resource-based theory of the firm: Knowledge versus opportunism. *Organization Science*, *7*(5), 477–501. doi:10.1287/orsc.7.5.477

D'Aveni, R. (1994). *Hypercompetition: Managing the dynamics of strategic manoeuvring*. The Free Press.

David, F. R. (2011). Strategic management: concepts and cases (13th ed.). Prentice Hall.

De Haas, M. (2000). *Strategic dialogue: in search of goal coherence* [PhD thesis]. Eindhoven University of Technology.

Decoene, V., & Bruggeman, W. (2006). Strategic alignment and middle-level managers' motivation in a Balanced Scorecard setting. *International Journal of Operations & Production Management*, *26*(4), 3–4, 429–448. doi:10.1108/01443570610650576

Eisenhart, K. M., & Martin, J. A. (2000). Dynamic capabilities: What they are? *Strategic Management Journal*, *21*(10-11), 1105–1211. doi:10.1002/1097-0266(200010/11)21:10/11<1105::AID-SMJ133>3.0.CO;2-E

FalkA.KosfeldM. (2004). *Distrust - The Hidden Cost of Control.* CEPR Discussion Paper No.4512. https://ssrn.com/abstract=590102

Friesenbichler, K., & Reinstaller, A. (2022). Do firms facing competitors from emerging markets behave differently? Evidence from Austrian manufacturing firms. *European Business Review, 34*(2), 153–170. doi:10.1108/EBR-09-2020-0216

Glynne, P. (2007). *Benefits Management-changing the focus of delivery*. Association for Progress Management.

Gomes, J. (2011). *Gestão de benefícios numa empresa de Geoengenharia* [Master thesis]. ISCTE.

Grant, R. M. (1991). A resource-based theory of competitive advantage: Implications for strategy formulation. *California Management Review, 33*(3), 114–135. doi:10.2307/41166664

Grant, R. M. (1996). Toward a knowledge-based theory of the firm. *Strategic Management Journal, 17*, 109–122.

Henderson, R., & Cockburn, I. (1994). Measuring competence? Exploring firm effects in pharmaceutical research. *Strategic Management Journal, 15*, 63–84.

Hofer, C. W., & Schendel, D. (1978). *Strategy Formulation: Analytical Concepts*. West Publishing Company.

Hudson, M., Smart, A., & Bourne, M. (2001). Theory and Practice in SME Performance Measurement Systems. *International Journal of Operations & Production Management, 21*(8), 1096–1115. doi:10.1108/EUM0000000005587

Iansiti, M., & Levien, R. (2004). *The keystone advantage: what the new dynamics of business ecosystems mean for strategy, innovation, and sustainability*. Harvard Business School Press.

Irvin, R. A., & Michaels, E. G. (1989). Core skills: Doing the right things right. *The McKinsey Quarterly*, (Summer), 4–19.

Ittner, C. D., & Larcker, D. F. (2003). Coming up short on nonfinancial performance measurement. *Harvard Business Review, 81*(11), 88–95. PMID:14619154

Kaplan, R. S., & Norton, D. P. (1992). The Balanced Scorecard: Measures that drive performance. *Harvard Business Review, 70*(1), 71–79. PMID:10119714

Kaplan, R. S., & Norton, D. P. (2000). *The Strategy-Focused Organization: How Balanced Scorecard companies thrive in the new business environment*. Harvard Business School Press.

Kaplan, R. S., & Norton, D. P. (2004, February). Measuring the Strategic Readiness of Intangible Assets. *Harvard Business Review*. PMID:14971269

Lee, C., Wu, C., & Jong, D. (2022). Understanding the Impact of Competitive Advantage and Core Competency on Regional Tourism Revitalization: Empirical Evidence in Taiwan. *Frontiers in Psychology*, *20*(13), 922211. doi:10.3389/fpsyg.2022.922211 PMID:35668969

Liu, J., Li, X., & Wang, S. (2020). What have we learnt from 10 years of fintech research? a scientometric analysis. *Technological Forecasting and Social Change*, *155*, 120022. doi:10.1016/j.techfore.2020.120022

Mahoney, J. T., & Pandian, J. R. (1992). The resource-based view within the conversation of strategic management. *Strategic Management Journal*, *13*(5), 363–380. doi:10.1002mj.4250130505

Maltz, A. C., Shenhar, A. J., & Reilly, R. R. (2003). Beyond the Balanced Scorecard: Refining the Search for Organizational Success Measures. *Long Range Planning*, *36*(April), 187–204. doi:10.1016/S0024-6301(02)00165-6

Margarita, I. (2008). The Balanced Scorecard Method, From Theory to Practice. *Intellectual Economics.*, *1*(3), 18–28.

Marr, B., & Adams, C. (2004). The balanced scorecard and intangible assets: Similar idea, unaligned concepts. *Measuring Business Excellence*, *8*(3), 18–27. doi:10.1108/13683040410555582

Mooraj, S., Oyon, D., & Hostettler, D. (1999). The Balanced Scorecard: A Necessary Good or an Unnecessary Evil? *European Management Journal*, *17*(5), 481–491. doi:10.1016/S0263-2373(99)00034-1

Neely, A. (1998). *Measuring Business Performance: Why, What and How*. Economist Books.

Neely, A., Gregory, M., & Platts, K. (1995). Performance measurement system design: A literature review and research agenda. *International Journal of Operations & Production Management*, *15*(4), 80–116. doi:10.1108/01443579510083622

Neely, A., & Kennerley, M. (2003). Measuring Performance in a Changing Environment. *International Journal of Operations & Production Management*, *23*(2), 213–229. doi:10.1108/01443570310458465

Nelson, R. R. (1991). Why do firms differ, and how does it matter? *Strategic Management Journal*, *12*, 61-74.

Niven, P. R. (2002). *Balanced scorecard step-by-step: Maximizing performance and maintaining results*. Wiley & Sons.

Otley, D. (1999). Performance management: A framework for management control systems research. *Management Accounting Research, 10*(4), 363–382. doi:10.1006/mare.1999.0115

Penrose, E. T. (1959). *The Theory of the Growth of the Firm*. Wiley.

Peteraf, M. A. (1993). The cornerstones of competitive advantage. *Strategic Management Journal, 14*(3), 179–191. doi:10.1002mj.4250140303

Pettigrew, A., & Whipp, R. (1991). *Managing change for competitive success.* Blackwell Publishers.

Platts, K. W., & Tan, K. H. (2002). Designing linked performance measures – A connectance based approach. *Pre-prints 12th Intern. Seminar on Production Economics, 2*, 367-373.

Porter, M. E. (1979). How competitive forces shape strategy. *Harvard Business Review, 57*(2), 137–145. PMID:18271320

Porter, M. E. (1991). *The Competitive Advantage of Nations*. Free Press.

Porter, M. E. (1992). Towards a Dynamic Theory of Strategy. *Strategic Management Journal, 12*, 95-118.

Prahalad, C. K., & Hamel, G. (1990). The core competence of the corporation. *Harvard Business Review, 68*(3), 79–91.

Pravdić, P., & Kučinar, R. (2015). A balanced scorecard analysis of performance metrics in profit organization. *Anali poslovne ekonomije, 13*, 14- 31.

Quinn, J. B. (1992). *Intelligent Enterprise: A Knowledge and Service Based Paradigm for Industry*. Free Press.

Rafiq, M., Zhang, X., Yuan, J., Naz, S., & Maqbool, S. (2020). Impact of a Balanced Scorecard as a Strategic Management System Tool to Improve Sustainable Development: Measuring the Mediation of Organizational Performance through PLS-Smart. *Sustainability (Basel), 12*(4), 1365. doi:10.3390u12041365

Reilley, G., & Reilley, R. (2000). Using a measure network to understand and delivery value. *Journal of Cost Management.*

Roos, J., Roos, G., Dragonetti, N.C., & Edvinsson, L. (1997). *Intellectual Capital: Navigating in the New Business Landscape.* Macmillan.

Rumelt, R. P. (1984). Towards a strategic theory of the firm. In R. B. Lamb (Ed.), *Competitive Strategic Management* (pp. 556–570). Prentice-Hall.

Russ, R. (2001). Economic value added: Theory, evidence, a missing link. *Review of Business*, *22*(1), 66–71.

Sambharya, R. B. (2011). Security analysts' earnings forecasts as a measure of firm performance: An empirical exploration of its domain. *Management Decision*, *49*(7), 1160–1181. doi:10.1108/00251741111151190

Selznick, P. (1957). *Leadership in Administration: A Sociological Interpretation*. Harper and Row.

Sharma, M. K., Bhagwat, R., & Dangayach, G. S. (2005). Practice of performance measurement: Experience from Indian SMEs. *International Journal of Globalisation and Small Business*, *1*(2), 183–213. doi:10.1504/IJGSB.2005.008014

Smith, M. (1998). Measuring Organizational Effectiveness. *Management Accounting*, 34-36.

Stalk, G., Evans, P., & Shulman, E. (1992). Competing on capabilities: The new rules of corporate strategy. *Harvard Business Review*, (March-April), 57–69. PMID:10117369

Teece, D. J. (1984). Economic analysis and strategic management. *California Management Review*, *26*(3), 87–110. doi:10.2307/41165082

Teece, D. J., Pisano, G., & Shuen, A. (1997). Dynamic capabilities and strategic fit. *Strategic Management Journal*, *18*(7), 510–533. doi:10.1002/(SICI)1097-0266(199708)18:7<509::AID-SMJ882>3.0.CO;2-Z

Valmohammadi, C., & Servati, A. (2011). Performance measurement system implementation using Balanced Scorecard and statistical methods. *International Journal of Productivity and Performance Management*, *60*(5), 493–511. doi:10.1108/17410401111140400

Van Grembergen, W., & De Haes, S. (2005). Measuring and improving information technology governance through the balanced scorecard. *Information Systems Control Journal*, 2.

Van Grembergen, W. Saull, R., & De Haes, S. (2003). Linking the IT balanced scorecard to the business objectives at a major Canadian financial group. *Journal of Information Technology Cases and Applications*.

Voelpel, S., Leibold, M., Eckhoff, R., & Davenport, T. (2005). The Tyranny of the Balanced Scorecard in the Innovation Economy. In *4th International Critical Management Studies Conference - Intellectual Capital Stream*. Cambridge University.

Ward, J., & Daniel, E. (2006). *Benefits Management, Delivering Value from IS and IT Investments*. John Wiley & Sons.

Ward, J., & Elvin, R. (1999). A new framework for managing IT-enabled business change. *Information Systems Journal*, *9*(3), 197–221. doi:10.1046/j.1365-2575.1999.00059.x

Wernerfelt, B. (1984). A resource-based view of the firm. *Strategic Management Journal*, *5*(2), 171–180. doi:10.1002mj.4250050207

Wernerfelt, B. (1989). From critical resources to corporate strategy. *Journal of General Management*, *5*, 171–180.

Wernerfelt, B. (1995). The resource-based view of the firm: Ten years after. *Strategic Management Journal*, *16*(3), 171–174. doi:10.1002mj.4250160303

Chapter 12
Digital Transformation in Public Administration

Jorge Vareda Gomes
https://orcid.org/0000-0003-0656-9284
Universidade Lusófona, Lisboa, Portugal

Mário Batista Romão
https://orcid.org/0000-0003-4564-1883
ISEG, Universidade de Lisboa, Portugal

ABSTRACT

At a global level, governments are implementing transformation projects and initiatives to respond to a changing society and as part of a drive for efficiency and cost savings. Considering the profile of digital transformation (DT) projects within the context of the Portuguese public administration (PA), the proposal for a framework was developed which contains a set of attributes and criteria to identify the feasibility and adequacy of the projects submitted for evaluation. The study identifies the set of characteristics, critical success factors, challenges, and difficulties of DT projects in this public administration context. A qualitative methodological approach was used, and a single case study strategy was applied. The proposed framework enables a better alignment of strategies, as well as an improved allocation of resources and the consequent improvement of the performance objectives defined by the PA.

DOI: 10.4018/979-8-3693-1151-6.ch012

INTRODUCTION

Business and government have long recognized the potential of technology and both are strongly committed to ongoing digital transformation (DT) programmes. The ongoing digital revolution has changed the frame of contemporary economies, modern businesses, and public administration by promoting and implementing new technological solutions for digitalization (Rymarczyk, 2021). Datta et al. (2020) state that DT can bring about various benefits, such as the reduction of corruption and inefficiencies in the Public Administration (PA), as well as increased transparency and increased public confidence in the government resulting from accountability, which leads to an increase in security with regards data privacy and sustainability. In countries where these changes occurred, they have been proven to be an effective way to reduce corruption (Mouna, Nedra & Khaireddine, 2020).

Portugal's initiatives also reinforce this topic, examples being the launch of the second phase of the national strategy of Industry 4.0 for the digitization of the economy in 2019, with associated financing of approximately 600 million euros for the two years duration (European Commission, 2020a). According to Schwab (2016), the impact of Industry 4.0 implies flexible cooperation between the virtual and the physical and also between industries at a global level, which consequently enables product customization and the creation of new operational models.

This paper relates the analysis of a case study of the Agency for Administrative Modernization (AMA) – a public institute that is responsible for the promotion and development of administrative modernization in Portugal. AMA operates under the auspices of the Secretary of State for Innovation and Administrative Modernization in the areas of administrative modernization, including simplification and electronic administration. The relevance of this study is related to the primordial role played by DT in the Portuguese Administration, as manifested by the development and management of new service models which enable citizens and companies to interact with the State in an innovative and efficient manner. Another relevant reason for this study is the fact that the public sector is part of the Innovation System (Freeman, 2008). The Innovation System are constructed in developing countries by building capacities of learning, which are structured more or less formally between actors and communities. Innovation only makes sense through the formalization of these national capacities, conveyers of new knowledge (Casadella & Uzunidis, 2017). The Innovation System has now expanded its concept and is starting to be recognized as an innovation process (Godinho, 2013) as it is characterized by collaboration between different actors and the respective interactions among themselves, namely: companies, customers, financiers, and the State. AMA has a department called the Project Management Office (PMO), which is dedicated to project portfolio management, with more than 80 currently active projects. According to Too &

Weaver (2014), when a lot of projects are being carried out simultaneously, the effect is that the associated project management becomes more complex, due to its interdependencies and multiple implementations. The main driver for our proposal is the current absence of an adequate DT model, which is necessary to enable the evaluation as to whether a project meets the conditions to be approved. Accordingly, the objective of the study was to elaborate a proposal for a framework to be used to evaluate whether DT projects meet the necessary conditions to be initiated, based on the characteristics of projects of this nature and the context of the Portuguese Administration. This framework needs to be simple to use, with the possibility be tested in the near future. The study is conditional on the following three research questions:

QInv1 - What are the main factors that influence the success of a DT project?

QInv2 - What are the main challenges and difficulties of carrying out a DT project?

QInv3 - How can a framework be built to evaluate the needs of the PA's DT projects?

Another objective of this proposal for a framework is to enable the organization and coherent integration of the diverse range of elements which are considered for the assessment and evaluation of DT projects.

LITERATURE REVIEW

Digital Transformation

Digital transformation is a top priority for organizations of all sizes and sectors. By leveraging technology, companies can streamline operations, improve efficiency and provide better customer experiences. However, digital transformation requires more than just implementing new technologies. It requires a fundamental change in the way organizations operate, communicate and interact with their customers and partners. Interoperability is increasingly important, as e-government continues to add and improve services (Sharma & Panigrahi, 2015) Achieving organizational interoperability in public administration is a crucial factor for successful digital transformation, although there are still many challenges and limitations regarding organizational factors (Margariti et al., 2022). Interoperability is the path that enables the integration of various entities. Enhanced interoperability among public bodies and public and private organizations respectively is of critical importance for building e-Government added value models (Pardo & Tayi, 2007). AMA uses a platform which encourages the development of interoperability which is called iAP. This tool is extendable to the private sector through the means of legal support. Multichannel electronic services are made available on the iAP platform, which are aimed at meeting the needs of citizens and companies alike. Mergel et al. (2019) refers to DT as being a holistic effort to review key government processes and services, in addition to the traditional digitization efforts. Among others, the result of these DT efforts are focused on meeting users' needs, as well as new ways of providing services and expanding the user base. DT is a continuous process, which requires constant adjustments to the entire chain, products, and services offered to the population and most likely leads to better relations between entities and stakeholders, as well as an increase in satisfaction among the population, with the most relevant impact being the promotion of change in a bureaucratic and organizational culture (Mergel et al., 2019). For those responsible for the implementation of DT, the ability to make essential, yet sometimes disruptive changes is a necessity (Iannacci et al., 2019; Pittaway & Montazemi, 2020).

E-Government

E-Government interoperability represents a set of multidimensional, complementary, and dynamic capabilities needed among these networks of organizations in order to achieve successful information sharing (Pardo, Nam & Burke, 2012). Interoperability in e-Government aims to link multiple systems, information, and work models among different government agencies in a state or around the world (Ordiyasa et al., 2016). Currently, studies on the interoperability of e-government applications have become the focus of research, by previous researchers, to develop information and communication technology systems, to realize the smooth exchange of information across all elements of government (El Benany & El Beqqali, 2017). According to Barcevičius et al. (2019), the PA took the first steps towards e-government during the late 90s. Based on a broad literature review, these authors conceived a framework which describes the path to date (Figure 1).

Figure 1. eGovernment evolution

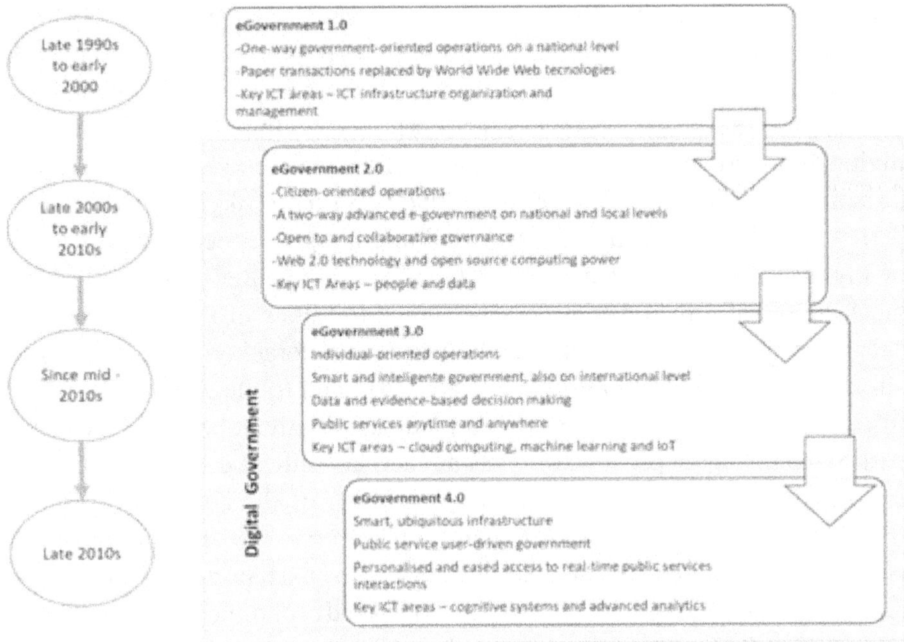

Importantly, e-government acquired a new and larger dimension in the early 2000s, called Digital Government. Digital Government refers to the concept of a digital ecosystem which is composed of various actors besides the government, such as non-governmental organizations, companies, and citizens' associations that support the production and access to data, services, and content through interaction with the government (OECD, 2014). Digital government represents the transformation of the public sector into the next phase of public management and delivery of Information and Communication Technology (ICT)-based services (OECD, 2014). According to the report of the Digital Economy and Society Index (DESI) (European Commission, 2020b), Portugal is in 13th place among the 28 Member States with regards the provision of digital public services. Another report that assesses the European digital situation is the eGovernment Benchmark issued by the European Commission (2020a), which is an annual monitoring instrument (Table 1).

Table 1. Performance of PT compared to EC and United Kingdom (UK)

	Penetration	Digitization
EC27 + UK	60%	72%
PT	53%	82%

Source: European Commission (2020b)

The European Commission report reveals that the innovation process in Portugal was carried out efficiently, although there is an underlying desire to expand the number of users online and to realize all the potential benefits. The country had significant growth from 2017 to 2018 and its performance remained constant in 2019. The same report also concludes that Portugal is within the European average for digitization and when combining relative and absolute indicators, has a better performance than expected. To understand the meaning of 'digitization', Mergel et al. (2019) state that digitization goes beyond migrating a service from the physical to the digital sphere, as it also includes focusing on potential changes which can promote the transformation of processes. The difficulties of PA with regards the digital dimension on a global scale are known, and Weerakkody et al. (2016) state that in most cases the frustrating results are attributed to the technology itself. A significant number of DT projects are implemented without being integrated into the institutional change process, often as a reactive political decision based on the private sector mentality, without due consideration of the complex institutional environment of the PA (Currie & Guah, 2007; Currie, 2012; Janowski, 2015). Situations of competition between public entities are also reported, in the search for power and institutional legitimacy, as well as social and economic adequacy (Cordella & Tempini, 2015). The challenge is not only to introduce digital technologies in the PA, but rather to integrate its use in the modernization of the PA (OECD, 2014).

Successful Strategies, Critical Success Factors (FCS), Challenges, and Difficulties of Digital Transformation

Based on an extensive literature review, García & Pablo (2005) identified a set of strategies which resulted in e-government initiatives being successful, and yet at the same time met the challenges involved. A summary of the main findings of these authors is outline below:

1. Information and data strategies: adopt comprehensive planning, quality assurance and compliance; the involvement of the right partners, common structure, and standards to facilitate iteration, continuous feedback from users.
2. Information technology strategies: useful and easy-to-use information systems; raise awareness of the topic, and focus initial efforts on developing prototypes of system and process; project leader with strong technical skills and specialization, as well as at least some team members to create ways to deal with the insufficiency of a qualified technical workforce.
3. Organizational and managerial strategies: clear, realistic and measurable goals; identify the most important stakeholders and insert them in the project's development, especially users; good communication channels and process

improvements are extremely important to map out the current capacities and training needs of developers and users; political skills and experience among its members; and financial resources where managers often need to develop innovative financial schemes and partnerships to implement the initiatives.

4. Legal and regulatory strategies: invest in changes in the regulatory environment which permit or enable the adoption of emerging technologies, policies, and appropriate IT standards to provide a common framework.

Critical success factors (CSF) can be described as the set of situations, factors, or actions which contribute to meeting the success criteria of a project (Gomes & Romão, 2016). Carrasqueiro et al. (2018) concluded that there are three main critical success factors for DT projects:

1. Articulation between the sponsors of the initiative.
2. Federated architecture which implements interoperability through pre-existing components.
3. Existence of governance and management of multilevel structures.

Other CSF can also be cited and can be generalized as the following: the existence of a clear vision and strategy; leadership with a high level of commitment; identifying and engaging stakeholders; clear communication for stakeholders to promote trust; the existence of legal and regulatory framework; adequate project management; the profile of the project; the skills of the technical teams involved; and the existence of adequate infrastructure. Chandler & Thomas (2015) highlight the role played by the sponsor as an influencing factor in the project. For the sponsor can exercise their influence in the following two ways (Crawford et al., 2006, Crawford et al., 2008):

1. Through their governance in coordinating activities, such as taking responsibility for the project plan and obtaining the forecast benefits, guiding and making decisions, critically evaluating the outcome of the project's progress, and being senior enough to be able to represent the project.
2. In the form of their support, through their availability to support, and through their credibility to be able to influence the relationship and leadership network.

Interoperability is a key requirement for the digitalisation of processes that involve different systems and sectors (Franzl, Wanzenböck & Berger, 2023). According to Bousdekis and Kardaras (2020), interoperability is also considered to be an FCS, and these authors argue that when capacity is limited between the various information systems, then the result is a repetitive and time-consuming processes. They also reinforce the role of Corporate Architecture (CA) as a tool which provides a coherent set of principles, methods, and models used in the design and execution of business processes, information systems, and infrastructure, which contribute to a better alignment between the business domains and TI (Jensen et al., 2011). Through an analysis of 528 articles on DT, Pihir et al. (2019) concluded that the main factors which determine and influence the views of success and challenge are the following:

- Orientation to the strategy and support of senior leadership.
- The customer is the starting point for development through the monitoring of their needs.
- ICT and process infrastructure, where the level of digital maturity of an organization is directly related to the introduction of technology in the execution of processes.
- Strengthening talent and employee capacity through the investment in training human resources.
- Innovation culture and organizational commitment, where employees need to be committed to innovation and the organization, and steps must be taken to ensure that the work environment is conducive to innovation and change.

Still focused on the challenges and difficulties, Datta et al. (2020) describe the experience of DT in Italy:

- The level of adoption of digital services by the population.
- The risk of non-continuity of the projects due to the inconsistency of the objectives of the PA, due to political changes.
- Low level of digital skills, not only for users, but also for public servants, which reveals digital exclusion, even at the labor level.
- The bureaucracy that undermines efficiency increases complexity and costs and also undermines confidence in the government.

Public entities aim to achieve high levels of cooperation between stakeholders to improve the efficiency and quality of public service delivery (Chourabi et al., 2012; Van Veenstra et al., 2011; Kohli & Johnson, 2011; Matt et al., 2015).

Frameworks and Models

Next the construction of the proposal, some frameworks, business models, methods of evaluation and decision making were identified, whose objectives have a greater affinity with the objective of the study (Table 2).

Table 2. Frameworks, business models, methods of evaluation, and decision

Montagna (2005)	A framework to evaluate e-government initiatives regarding the feasibility, benefits and advantages generated by each initiative. Five dimensions were defined: product, time, distance, iteration, and procedures. Each dimension can be assessed by using four criteria: efficiency, effectiveness, strategic benefits, and also transparency and institutional value. According to the author, the dimension-criterion relationship must be viewed from the point of view of the government, the citizen, and the company.
Chesbrough (2011)	Open Service Innovation – this concept is recognized when the organization uses internal and external knowledge to accelerate internal and market innovation. The framework uses the participation of customers for co-creation, due to the difficulty of describing tacit knowledge and service innovation. This framework encourages consumer appreciation and rewards and uses open innovation to accelerate and strengthen innovation, leading to a less costly, less risky, and faster innovation.
Datta et al. (2020)	Carried out a study on DT projects in the Italian PA, and recommend best practices for managing the projects, including the affirmation of their broad degree of generalization. The key measure identified in the Italian study was the division of large projects into smaller modules to make them more understandable and manageable. According to the authors, modularity allows dealing quickly with any problems from the beginning to control costs and complete projects on time and within budget.
Osterwalder & Pigneur, 2010	Consider an organization's business model to be a tool which creates, delivers, and captures value. It consists of nine blocks which are developed according to the customer's needs. A resource used by Canvas is to establish a Minimum Viable Product that works as a prototype before starting the project and will later be increased. Al-Debei & Avison (2010) recognize that the business model can play an essential role in the face of the complex and turbulent scenario of the current world, because it is versatile, multipurpose, and has high levels of flexibility.
Hanelt et al. (2020)	The multidimensionality of DT projects – where these authors concluded about the existence of three fundamental dimensions for the success of DT projects: (1) Contextual Conditions – which initially act in the definition of DT (Henfridsson and Yoo, 2013) and which result from the material, environmental, and managerial antecedents and the respective interaction; (2) Mechanisms – strategic and operational innovation mechanisms which involve the application of resources, processes, and capabilities that are new to the organization. Integration mechanisms which include their alignment with existing resources, processes, and capabilities (Daniel & Wilson, 2003; Henfridsson & Yoo, 2013; Ranganathan et al., 2003); (3) Results – organizational results resulting from the change caused by DT. Economic results, better performance, and new forms of value which are caused by better service quality or cost reductions. Spillovers – the effect on the organizational environment caused by DT, which has an effect on systems, industry, information security, and individual effects.
Ross et al. (2019)	Accountability framework – which is based on large private sector companies and does not follow a technical approach, but rather adds value. This framework has eight principles: (1) Owner with responsibility for the entire product life cycle instead of project manager; (2) Continuous launches, rather than a scheduled agenda; (3) A mission that guides the team through objectives and limits, rather than a formal organizational structure; (4) Metrics, rather than directives designed to allow teams to define how they intend to achieve their mission; (5) Experiments to perceive the user's response in phases, rather than major launches; (6) Teams which have complete and even multifunctional autonomy and resources, rather than a traditional matrix structure; (7) Collaboration with inter-coordination between teams, rather than a hierarchy; (8) The trust of leaders in teams which results in the team assuming full responsibility, rather than of controlling the team's routine.

RESEARCH METHODOLOGY

Methodological Approach

The research carried out for this paper used a qualitative approach and its underlying philosophy underlying is the interpretivist approach – which states that reality originates by means of a social construction, where the meanings that social actors attribute to their experiences predominate (Saunders et al., 2019). A survey was carried out for which the respondents were selected from a group of targeted professionals who had experience of acting on and/or deciding about DT projects, who were therefore potentially capable of clearly identifying their points of view according to their own experiences. To analyses the data collected in the research, an inductive approach was used (Saunders et al., 2019) which enables the identification of themes and patterns in the results of the collected data which can somehow be related to the existing literature to improve or build new theories, that is to say, to migrate from the specific to a more general view of the phenomena. Three research questions were defined. The first two research questions and a questionnaire with semi-structured questions were used as a source to answer the third research question. The collection of all the research questions was used to achieve the objective of the work (Figure 2).

Figure 2. Relationship between investigation and inquiry questions

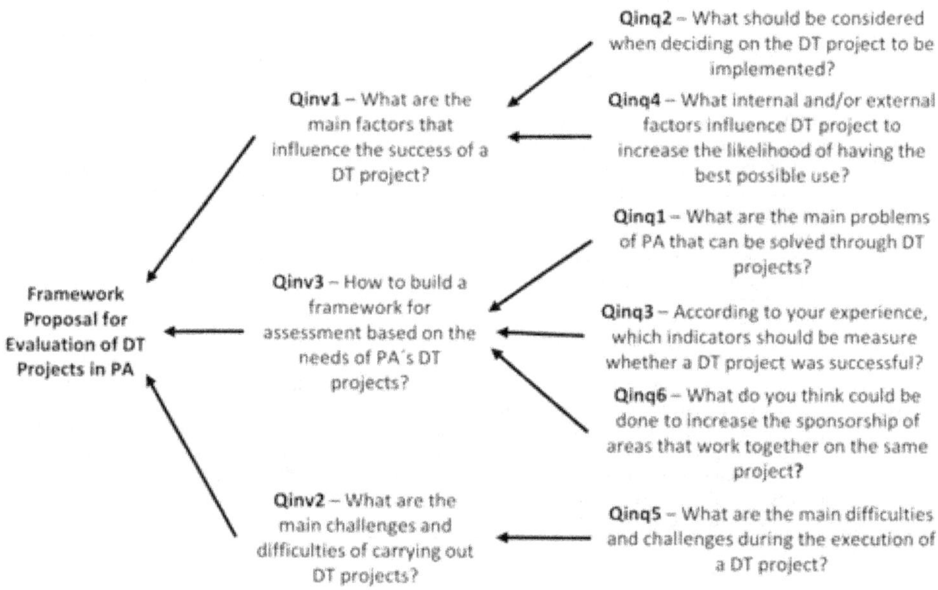

The survey was then prepared and subjected to a pre-test. The interviewees were sent an e-mail in which they were informed about the reason for the contact and the estimated duration of the interview. The identifications of the most cited themes in each response to questions were used as a source to define the categories (Yin, 2018) and to answer the research questions. These categories were then used to identify the factors that influence the success of DT projects, which were then used as the basis for constructing the framework (Montagna, 2005; Hanelt et al., 2020). The sampling was shaped by four attributes:

1. Convenience: due to the easy access to the interviewees, as they work in the same organization and have common projects with the researcher.
2. Intentional: the interviewees were chosen on purpose, in order to make it possible to collect more appropriate data to answer the research questions.
3. Type: is characterized as being homogeneous, as the interviewees occupy managerial and/or leadership positions in the same entity. Additionally, their functions have a direct relationship or influence on DT projects, thus making it possible to explore particular issues more profoundly and, consequently, the small differences that arose would be more easily exposed.
4. Size: the minimum acceptable for a non-probabilistic sample from a homogeneous group – which is 4 to 12 people, according to Saunders et al. (2019).

In the sample, from among the directors and team leaders of AMA who were either directly connected with or had influence on the DT projects, 13 were invited to participate in the survey, although only 11 actually accepted and were interviewed. As mentioned above, the most-cited themes of each question were used as a source to define the categories for the CSFs (Yin, 2018) and to answer the four research questions. These categories were the critical success factors for the success of TD and were used as the basis for the construction of the framework (Montagna, 2005; Hanelt et al., 2020). An analysis was first made of the consolidation of the responses of all the interviewees, identifying which themes were the most cited and the least cited, after which a second analysis was made of the answers to the other questions if anything was identified as being complementary. The themes which were cited at least three times were transformed into categories. All interviews were conducted individually and remotely, using video and audio communication software. The respondents spontaneously filled out the responses, which were often similar to other interviewees' responses. All the issues were then analyzed and all the complementary contributions were identified as well. At the end, the respondents were also given the opportunity to add any further information or comment that they considered relevant to the study.

ANALYSIS AND DISCUSSION

The answers to the research questions are presented below, which are based on the analysis of the interviews, the establishment of categories and the literature, as well as the respective transversality between the data (Table 3). The compilation of the survey responses is reproduced in Appendix I.

Table 3. Identified categories and related survey questions (Qinq)

	Category	Qinq1	Qinq2	Qinq3	Qinq4	Qinq5	Qinq6
01	Citizen at the center	+	+		+		
02	Human resources	+	+		+	+	
03	Clear definition of projects		+		+		+
04	Entities, areas and partners		+		+		+
05	Sponsor		+		+		+
06	Political, strategic, operational and technological alignment		+		+	+	
07	Communication		+		+		+
08	Suppliers		+		+		
09	Product management	+	+			+	
10	Technological Infrastructure and process integration	+	+		+		
11	Stakeholders			+		+	+
12	Monitoring						
13	Legal and regulatory environment					+	

QInv1: What Are the Main Factors That Influence the Success of a DT Project?

The answers to questions from the Qinq 2 and Qinq 4 questionnaire were used mainly to answer QInv1. Correspondences were found in the literature regarding the responses of Qinq 2 and Qinq 4, for different degrees of intensity. The most common topics were classified into 10 categories (Table 4).

Table 4. The most common topics related to the QInv1

	Category	Explanation
01	Citizen at the center	Projects must be designed by taking into consideration the needs of the citizen and/or the company, where they can exercise the role of co-creators of the services and their experiences are monitored, their opinions collected, and prototypes are created before the products are implemented (Ross et al., 2019) and systems should focus on usability.
02	Human resources	Technical qualification and adequate profile to lead, according to the profile of the project (Carrasqueiro et al., 2018). This category was also supported in the literature by Pihir et al. (2019), when they emphasized the importance of investing in the training and management of human resources, and also by Datta et al. (2020) with regards the difficulties derived from the low digital skills of civil servants.
03	Clear definition of projects	Includes the objective, the viability of the final product, the target audience, how performance will be measured, budget control, team responsibilities, priorities, and the justification for carrying out the project. The adoption of Agile methodology. This category was supported by García & Pablo (2005) and Datta et al, (2020) through the recommendation of the roadmap of project deliveries and reverse engineering to meet the planned deadline. Another correspondence is the dimension of the success of projects by Shenhar et al. (2001), as the expected impact for dimension depends on the level of technology required by the project.
04	Entities, areas, and partners	Mentioned the need to map the reality and the business of the partners involved to get to know their capabilities and limitations. Manage the relationship and deal with dependency and competition between entities (Weerakkody et al., 2016; Cordella & Tempini, 2015).
05	Sponsor	The need for the commitment of a representative sponsor throughout the project, as well as in the other entities involved, together with decision-making power and influence (Chandler & Thomas (2015).
06	Political, strategic, operational, and technological alignment	The need to meet the political agenda and whether there is congruence with the master plan of PA, AMA, and the partner entities and the design of projects. Projects fail because they are not integrated into the process of institutional change (Weerakkody et al., 2016)
07	Communication	A communication strategy and plan and the sharing of information in the rendering of accounts during the project up until the results are released. Transparency in the sense of promoting trust through the flow of communication (Datta et al., 2020)
08	Suppliers	Quality is an important point as there is a shortage of specialized ICT labor. The element of the successful strategy (García & Pablo, 2005).
09	Product management	Who will be responsible and how will the final product be managed after the project is completed?
10	Technological infrastructure and process integration	Align expectations concerning availability, technological maturity, integration, network, and data security (Hanelt et al., 2020)

QInv2: What Are the Main Challenges and Difficulties in Carrying Out a DT Project?

As mentioned in QInv1, the factors and elements that influence success can also be seen from the point of view of challenges and difficulties when faced with the reality of the DT project environment. This was confirmed by the responses to the Qinq5 interview. Almost the same categories as QInv1 were found, with the exception of a new category entitled (11) Stakeholders. With regards the other categories already mentioned in QInv1, what occurred was the expansion of the responses of the categories under the view of the challenge and difficulty (Table 5).

Table 5. The most common topics related to the QInv2

	Category	Explanation
02	Human resources	The difficulty of maintaining the best human resources, whether owned or outsourced, is added due to the intense need in the market for professionals with digital skills, high remuneration, and the number of people needed to execute the projects.
04	Entities, areas, and partners	Reinforcing the importance of relationship management
06	Political, strategic, operational, and technological alignment	Decision dependencies and obligation to adjust to political urgencies (Datta et al., 2020)
10	Technological infrastructure and process integration	Measure the performance of projects in general due to data access restrictions, whether for legal or operational reasons, the integration of processes, and also about the interconnection of infrastructures (Pihir et al., 2019; Datta et al., 2020; Rogers, 2016)
11	Stakeholders	The importance of keeping the various stakeholders aligned throughout the project

QInv3: How to Build an Assessment Framework Based on the Needs of DT Projects in PA

The answer to this question is the result of the analysis of the first two research questions and the survey questions that are presented below. In this stage, two final and new categories were identified, in addition to those already mentioned above. From this point onwards the framework proposal was developed. Reducing bureaucracy for citizens/companies and internal PA was one of the most cited points of Qinq1, however it is not considered to be a category, as it is more of an objective, rather than an attribute (Table 6).

Table 6. The most common topics related to QInv3

	Category	Explanation
03	Clear definition of projects	There is a strict pre-start plan for projects and a clear definition of support requirements in project management, through the use of tools such as a Balanced Scorecard or gamification
07	Communication	Is primarily to maintain a high level of collaboration and make it explicit where it does not exist. Visibility with stakeholders to attract and maintain support (Pihir et al., 2019; Hanelt et al., 2020). Sufficient and easily-accessible documentation.
12	Monitoring	Measure the success of a DT project. The following subcategories were also considered in monitoring: the impact produced for society (Panagiotopoulos et al., 2012); adherence to the budget; level of adoption of public services by citizens/companies (Datta et al., 2020 and Panagiotopoulos et al., 2012); time of the execution of the service for both the user and the public servant; saving human and financial resources when migrating the service from physical to digital; level of user satisfaction and level of achievement of objectives; the importance of metrics rather than directives (Ross et al., 2019).
13	The legal and regulatory environment	Legal and regulatory environment in which the project is to be developed (Carrasqueiro et al., 2018; García & Pablo, 2005; Hanelt et al., 2020), which can be considered to be both a success factor and also a difficulty.

Framework Proposal for DT Project Evaluation

A matrix structure was designed using the principle that there is an order of categories which are independent of the others, in the sense of being used as a construction base for the others and also as a filter. The framework presents seven layers of filters that should be used in the evaluation of a project. Each layer is an evaluation phase to ascertain whether the project starts, or not. If the sequence of layers does not meet the requirements of the project, the proponent must be advised that their proposal needs to be revised to validate those layers that did not present consistency, and the evaluation should only be resumed again afterwards (Table 7).

Table 7. Framework proposal for DT project evaluation

Layer	Description
First	The project addresses the following categories: *(01) Citizen at the Centre*, including the aspect of participation in the creation of the project (Barcevičius et al., 2019; Chesbrough, 2011; Datta et al., 2020; Garcia & Pablo, 2005; Greve, 2015; Hanelt et al., 2020; Montagna, 2005; Osterwalder et., 2010; Pihir et al., 2019; Ross et ., 2019) and *(03) Clear definition of projects* (Carrasqueiro et al., 2018; Chesbrough, 2011; Garcia & Pablo, 2005; Hanelt et al., 2020; Montagna, 2005; Too& Weaver, 2014; Weerakkody et al., 2016).
Second	Includes *(06) Political, strategic, operational, and technological alignment* during the initial phase (Bousdekis & Kardaras, 2020; Carrasqueiro et al., 2018; Datta et al., 2020; Hanelt et al., 2020) and also whether the conditions of the *(13) The Legal and regulatory environment* have been validated (Carrasqueiro et al., 2018; Datta et al., 2020; Hanelt et al., 2020). Although these categories were not those most frequently present in the study, they can be restrictive factors for categories *(04)*, *(05)*, *(08)*, and *(10)*.
Third	Human Resources are sufficient and have the appropriate skills for the type of project (Carrasqueiro et al., 2018; Datta et al., 2020; Garcia & Pablo, 2005; Hanelt et al., 2020; Pihir et al., 2019), in *(04) Entities, areas, and partners* (Carrasqueiro et al., 2018; Pittaway & Montazemi, 2020; Weerakkody et al., 2016) and *(08) Suppliers* (Carrasqueiro et al., 2018; Datta et al., 2020; Garcia & Pablo, 2005).
Fourth	The mapping plan for *(10) Technological and Process Infrastructure* at AMA, entities and suppliers is planned. Including corporate architecture (Bousdekis & Kardaras, 2020; Carrasqueiro et al., 2018; Chesbrough, 2011; Garcia & Pablo, 2005; Greve, 2015; Hanelt et al., 2020; Pihir et al., 2019; Rogers, 2016; Weerakkody et al., 2016), also *(04) Entities* and *(08) Suppliers*.
Fifth	Who is the *(5) Sponsor* and has leadership power and influence in the relationship network according to the characteristics identified in the previous layers (Carrasqueiro et al., 2018; Chandler & Thomas, 2015; Datta et al., 2020; Pihir et al., 2019)
Sixth	How *(07) Communication* (Carrasqueiro et al., 2018; Datta et al., 2020; Greve, 2015; Montagna, 2005) and *(12) Monitoring* (Garcia & Pablo, 2005; Panagiotopoulos et al., 2012; Ross et al., 2019) will be conducted throughout the project, as the second will be one of the sources of the first, favouring transparency, as well as the relationship with *(11) Stakeholders* (Carrasqueiro et al., 2018; Datta et al., 2020; Hanelt et al., 2020; Pihir et al., 2019) which include the categories *(01)*, *(02)*, *(04)*, *(05)* and *(08)*.
Seventh	What will be the minimum viable product at the end of the project and who will be responsible for managing the product (Montagna, 2005; Osterwalder et al., 2010).

As mentioned in the introduction, the framework needs to be tested to verify how it behaves in practice. The ideal would be to also define a specific area for the pilot to be carried out – such as health, education, or social security – as this would facilitate the analysis of the tool's performance by evaluating projects which satisfy similar conditions.

CONCLUSION

The end objective of this research is to create a proposed framework for project evaluation which is customized for DT, taking into consideration the characteristics and complexity of the Portuguese PA in order to confirm whether the project already satisfies the necessary conditions to be started. This objective was partially achieved, in that the framework is capable of identifying those factors that are most relevant to DT for the reality of PA and it presents a matrix structure. In total, thirteen factors were identified. Furthermore, the complexity of the projects was also confirmed, based on the dynamics of the relationship between them and the number of actors involved. The co-creation and co-participation between the State and the citizen were identified as being the most relevant factors for the success of DT in both the interviews and the literature, and accordingly this principle is also applied in the development of the framework proposal. This tool will be presented to the AMA, with the aim that it can be jointly developed by this organization's leaders and teams and will consequently be subject to internal and external criticism and adaptations and later be tested in practice by project decision-makers and managers. After experimentation, this tool can be improved, and if its application is found to promote a positive impact, then it can be adopted by the AMA as a means of support for decision making.

CONTRIBUTIONS, LIMITATIONS, AND FUTURE RESEARCH

The first contribution of this research was to identify those factors that influence the success of a DT project in the specific environment of the PA in Portugal, in alignment with the vision of the AMA's leadership. This identification was corroborated by the correlation with the literature, which added more credibility to the result. A significant part of the objective of the research was achieved, namely the proposal of a personalized tool, which is more likely to succeed in terms of its application, as it was constructed by those who work with and know the reality of the projects in question. A second contribution is the framework structure, which represents a structured and straightforward starting point for leaders and teams who can use and develop it – even if they possess differing levels of knowledge and experience of the project. The simplicity of the tool was another objective of the study, and an additional contribution is the fact that by being a simple and visual tool, it will enable better choices to be made, and assist in achieving better results. Certain limitations exist, such as the lack of information regarding the reasons that lead to the failure of DT projects in the PA and also the fact that there are very few references concerning frameworks for the evaluation or approval of specific projects for the management of DT in the PA. Further research is required to identify how human resources can be trained and developed to manage the complexity of DT better. It would also be relevant to investigate ways of increasing the involvement of the Digital Government ecosystem actors in the creation of public policies, as it is they who are often responsible for the initial creation of programmes and plans. The consequent increased level of involvement would promote both support for the political system and also commitment to the success of the public policy. In turn, this sharing of a certain part of the responsibility for implementing DT would result in the government becoming more experienced in carrying out the process of stakeholder consultation.

REFERENCES

Al-Debei, M., & Avison, D. (2010). Developing a unified framework of the business model concept. *European Journal of Information Systems, 19*(3), 359–376. doi:10.1057/ejis.2010.21

Barcevičius, M., Cibaitė, E., Codagnone, G., Gineikytė, C., Klimavičiūtė, V., Liva, L., Matulevič, G., & Vanini, G. (2019). *Exploring Digital Government transformation in the EU - Analysis of the State of the art and review of literature*. Publications Office of the European Union. doi:10.2760/17207

Bousdekis, A., & Dimitris, K. (2020). Digital transformation of local government: A case study from Greece. *Proceedings IEEE 22nd Conference on Business Informatics, 2*, 131-140. 10.1109/CBI49978.2020.10070

Carrasqueiro, S., Monteiro, M., Pereira, R., Pereira, C., & Martins, H. (2018). Dematerialization of the medical certificate for driving license in Portugal: a case study of success factors of whole-of-Government e-Government initiatives. *Proceedings of the 11th International Conference on Theory and Practice of Electronic Governance*. 10.1145/3209415.3209510

Casadella, V., & Uzunidis, D. (2017). National Innovation Systems of the South, Innovation and Economic Development Policies: A multidimensional approach. *Journal of Innovation Economics & Management*, *2*(23), 137–157. doi:10.3917/jie.pr1.0007

Chandler, D., & Thomas, J. (2015). Does executive sponsorship matter for realizing project management value. *Project Management Journal*, *46*(5), 46–61. doi:10.1002/pmj.21521

Chesbrough, H. (2011). *Open Services Innovation: Rethinking Your Business to Grow and Compete in a New Era* (1st ed.). Jossey-Bass.

Chourabi, H., Nam, T., Walker, S., Gil-Garcia, J., Mellouli, S., Nahon, K., Pardo, T., & Scholl, H. (2012). Understanding Smart Cities: An Integrative Framework. *Proceedings of the 45th Hawaii International Conference on System Sciences.*

Cordella, A., & Tempini, N. (2015). E-government and organizational change: Reappraising the role of ICT and bureaucracy in public service delivery. *Government Information Quarterly*, *32*(3), 279–286. doi:10.1016/j.giq.2015.03.005

Crawford, L., Cooke-Davies, T., Hobbs, B., Labuschagne, L., Remington, K., & Chen, P. (2008). Governance and Support in the Sponsoring of Projects and Programs. *Project Management Journal, 39*, S43–S55. doi:10.1002/pmj.20059

Crawford, L., Pollack, J., & England, D. (2006). Uncovering the trends in project management: Journal emphases over the last 10 years. *International Journal of Project Management*, *24*(2), 175–184. doi:10.1016/j.ijproman.2005.10.005

Currie, W. (2012). Institutional Isomorphism and Change: The National Programme for IT – 10 Years On. *Journal of Information Technology*, *27*(3), 236–248. doi:10.1057/jit.2012.18

Currie, W., & Guah, M. (2007). Conflicting institutional logics: A national programme for IT in the organizational field of healthcare. *Journal of Information Technology*, *22*(3), 235–247. doi:10.1057/palgrave.jit.2000102

Daniel, E., & Wilson, H. (2003). The role of dynamic capabilities in e-business transformation. *European Journal of Information Systems*, *12*(4), 282–296. doi:10.1057/palgrave.ejis.3000478

Datta, P., Walker, L., & Amarilli, F. (2020). Digital transformation: Learning from Italy's public administration. *Journal of Information Technology Teaching Cases,* 1-18. doi:10.1177/2043886920910437

El Benany, M. M., & El Beqqali, O. (2017). Cross-organizational orchestrator for e-government interoperability. *Proceedings of the 13th IEEE/ACS International Conference of Computer Systems and Applications, AICCSA 2016*. 10.1109/AICCSA.2016.7945750

European Commission. (2020a). eGovernment Benchmark 2020: eGovernment that works for the people. Luxembourg: Publications Office of the European Union.

European Commission. (2020b). *Digital Economy and Society Index: Digital public services*. https://ec.europa.eu/digital-single-market/en/news/digital-economy-and-society-index-desi-2020

Franzl, G., Wanzenböck, C., & Berger, A. (2023). Interoperability as a key factor for digitalisation — A success story for cross-sector knowledge transfer. *E&I Elektrotechnik und Informationstechnik*, *140*(5), 471–477. doi:10.100700502-023-01143-3

Freeman, C. (2008). *Systems of Innovation Selected Essays in Evolutionary Economics*. Edward Elgar Publishing. doi:10.4337/9781035306176

García, J., & Pardo, T. (2005). E-government success factors: Mapping practical tools to theoretical foundations. Government, IT implementation, Information Technology, Relevance, Success factors. *Government Information Quarterly*, *22*(2), 187–216. doi:10.1016/j.giq.2005.02.001

Godinho, M. (2013). Inovação em Portugal. Lisboa: Fundação Francisco Manuel dos Santos.

Gomes, J., & Romão, M. (2016). Improving Project Success: A Case Study Using Benefits and Project Management. *Procedia Computer Science*, *100*, 489–497. doi:10.1016/j.procs.2016.09.187

Hanelt, A., Bohnsack, R., Marz, D., & Marante, C. (2020). A Systematic Review of the Literature on Digital Transformation: Insights and Implications for Strategy and Organizational Change. *Journal of Management Studies*. Advance online publication. doi:10.1111/joms.12639

Henfridsson, O., & Yoo, Y. (2013). The Liminality of Trajectory Shifts in Institutional Entrepreneurship. *Organization Science*. Advance online publication. doi:10.1287/orsc.2013.0883

Iannacci, F., Seepma, A., Blok, C., & Resca, A. (2019). Reappraising maturity models in e-Government research: The trajectory-turning point theory. *The Journal of Strategic Information Systems*, *28*(3), 310–329. Advance online publication. doi:10.1016/j.jsis.2019.02.001

Janowski, T. (2015). Digital government evolution: From transformation to contextualization. *Government Information Quarterly*, *32*(3), 221–236. doi:10.1016/j.giq.2015.07.001

Jensen, C., Cline, O., & Owen, M. (2011). *Combining Business Process Management and Enterprise Architecture for Better Business Outcomes* (1st ed.). IBM Redbooks.

Jones, B., & Baumgartner, F. (2012). From There to Here: Punctuated Equilibrium to the General Punctuation Thesis to a Theory of Government Information Processing. *The Policy Studies Journal*, *40*(1).

Kohli, R., & Johnson, S. (2011). Digital Transformation in Latecomer Industries: CIO and CEO Leadership Lessons from Encana Oil & Gas (USA) Inc. *MIS Quarterly Executive*, *10*(4), 141–156.

Margariti, V., Stamati, T., Anagnostopoulos, D., Nikolaidou, M., & Papastilianou, A. (2022). A holistic model for assessing organizational interoperability in public administration. *Government Information Quarterly*, *39*(3), 101712. Advance online publication. doi:10.1016/j.giq.2022.101712

Matt, C., Hess, T., & Benlian, A. (2015). Digital Transformation Strategies. *Business & Information Systems Engineering*, *57*(5), 339–343. doi:10.100712599-015-0401-5

Mergel, I., Edelmann, N., & Haug, N. (2019). Defining digital transformation: Results from expert interviews. *Government Information Quarterly*, *36*(4), 101385. doi:10.1016/j.giq.2019.06.002

Montagna, J. (2005). A framework for the assessment and analysis of electronic government proposals. *Electronic Commerce Research and Applications*, *4*(3), 204–219. doi:10.1016/j.elerap.2005.01.003

Mouna, A., Nedra, B., & Khaireddine, M. (2020). International Comparative Evidence of E-Government Success and Economic Growth: Technology Adoption as an Anti-Corruption Tool. *Transforming Government: People. Process and Policy*, *14*(5), 713–736.

OECD. (2014). *Recommendation of the Council on Digital Government Strategies*. Public Governance Committee. https://www.oecd.org/gov/digital-government/Recommendation-digital-government-strategies.pdf

Ordiyasa, I. W., Nugroho, L. E., Santosa, P. I., Ferdiana, R., & Kumorotomo, W. (2016). Review: Interoperability model of e-Government services. In *2nd International Conference on Information Technology, Computer, and Electrical Engineering, ICITACEE 2015* (pp. 177–182). Institute of Electrical and Electronics Engineers Inc. 10.1109/ICITACEE.2015.7437794

Osterwalder, A., & Pigneur, Y. (2010). *Business Model Generation: Handbook for Visionaries, Game Changers, and Challengers*. John Wiley & Sons, Inc.

Panagiotopoulos, P., Al-Debei, M., Fitzgerald, G., & Elliman, T. (2012). A business model perspective for ICTs in public engagement. *Government Information Quarterly*, *29*(2), 192–202. doi:10.1016/j.giq.2011.09.011

Pardo, T. A., Nam, T., & Burke, G. B. (2012). E-Government Interoperability: Interaction of Policy, Management, and Technology Dimensions. *Social Science Computer Review*, *30*(1), 7–23. doi:10.1177/0894439310392184

Pardo, T. A., & Tayi, G. K. (2007). Interorganizational information integration: A key enabler for digital government. *Government Information Quarterly*, *24*(4), 691–715. doi:10.1016/j.giq.2007.08.004

Pihir, I., Tomičić-Pupek, K., & Tomičić, M. (2019). Digital transformation playground - literature review and framework of concepts. *Journal of Information and Organizational Sciences*, *43*(1), 33–48. doi:10.31341/jios.43.1.3

Pittaway, J., & Montazemi, A. (2020). Know-how to lead digital transformation: The case of local governments. *Government Information Quarterly*, *37*(4), 101474. doi:10.1016/j.giq.2020.101474

Ranganathan, C., Goode, V., & Ramaprasad, A. (2003). Managing the transition to bricks and clicks. *Communications of the ACM*, *46*(12), 308–316. doi:10.1145/953460.953515

Rogers, D. (2016). *The digital transformation playbook: rethink your business for the digital age*. Columbia University Press. doi:10.7312/roge17544

Ross, J., Beath, C., & Mocker, M. (2019). *Designed for Digital How to Architect Your Business for Sustained Success*. MIT Press. doi:10.7551/mitpress/12188.001.0001

Rymarczyk, J. (2012). The Impact of Industrial Revolution 4.0 on International Trade. *Entrepreneurial Business and Economics Review*, *9*(1), 105–117. doi:10.15678/EBER.2021.090107

Saunders, M., Thornhill, A., & Lewis, P. (2019). *Research methods for business students* (8th ed.). Pearson Education Limited. ISBN.

Schwab, K. (2016). *The Fourth Industrial Revolution*. World Economic Forum.

Sharma, R., & Panigrahi, P. K. (2015). Developing a roadmap for planning and implementation of interoperability capability in e-government. *Transforming Government*, *9*(4), 426–447. doi:10.1108/TG-06-2014-0023

Shenhar, A., Dvir, D., Levy, O., & Maltz, A. C. (2001). Project success: A multidimensional strategic concept. *Long Range Planning*, *34*(6), 699–725. doi:10.1016/S0024-6301(01)00097-8

Too, E., & Weaver, P. (2014). The management of project management: A conceptual framework for project governance. *International Journal of Project Management*, *32*(8), 1382–1394. doi:10.1016/j.ijproman.2013.07.006

Van Veenstra, A. F., Klievink, B., & Janssen, M. (2011). Barriers and impediments to transformational government: Insights from literature and practice. *Electronic Government. International Journal (Toronto, Ont.)*, *8*(2/3), 226–241. doi:10.1504/EG.2011.039838

Weerakkody, V., Omar, A., El-Haddadeh, R., & Al-Busaidy, M. (2016). Digitally-enabled service transformation in the public sector: The lure of institutional pressure and strategic response towards change. *Government Information Quarterly*, *33*(4), 658–668. doi:10.1016/j.giq.2016.06.006

Yin, R. (2018). *Case Study Research and Applications: Design and Methods* (6th ed.). Sage Publications, Inc.

APPENDIX 1: COMPILATION OF THE RESULTS OF THE SURVEY RESPONSES

Qinq1: What Are the Main Problems of Public Administration (PA) That Can Be Solved Through Digital Transformation (DT) Projects?

Most cited problems:

· Bureaucracy for citizens and companies.
· PA internal bureaucracy.
· Digital services which are not centered on the citizen and fail to consider the usability and the full range of the facilities of the technology.
· Citizens' access barriers, such as distance and difficulty in moving.
· Interoperability.
· High costs for the citizen.
· Insufficient level of digital skills among the human resources to meet demand and at the requested speed.

Other problems:

· Reduced level of accessibility for citizens with physical or cognitive limitations.
· Failure to meet the State's duty of transparency regarding the results of the government's activity.
· High public costs and difficulty in integrating service procedures that involve more than one entity.
· There is a lack of a consolidated database of government data on project results.
· Difficulty in managing emerging technologies.
· Low level of knowledge of citizens and companies with regards the digital products and services available.

Qinq2: What Should Be Considered When Deciding on the Digital Transformation (DT) Project to Be Implemented?

Most cited issues:

· Know the service or product as well as the business of the entity that will experience a DT process.
· Clear definition of the problem to be solved.

· Clear definition of which stakeholder will benefit from the service.
· The project must have a strong and motivated Sponsor.
· Sufficient human resources who are trained in accordance with the needs of the project.
· Which political impact for citizens and companies is to be promoted and whether this is sufficient to justify implementing the project.
· How will both impact and performance be measured during the project?
· Map in detail the platforms involved (interoperability).
· Political, strategic, operational, and technological alignment.
· Who will be responsible and how the final product will be managed after the conclusion of the project?

Other issues:

· Context costs.
· Political will.
· Lack of necessary information and the need for more planning.
· Public departments must be provided with visibility to projects.
· Less ambitious and consequently more feasible objectives.
· The need for a communication plan.
· Usability of the services.
· If the ecological sustainability of resources is considered, then what is the applicable governing legislation?
· The need for an organizational risk analysis and information security risk analysis at the level of personal data.

Qinq3: According to Your Experience, Which Indicators Should Be Used to Measure Whether a DT Project Was Successful?

Most cited indicators:

· Compliance with the deadline.
· The impact produced for society.
· Adherence to the budget.
· Percentage of user adoption.
· Service execution time for both users and civil servants.
· The number of human resources made redundant by the implementation of the digital service.
· The cost reduction resulting from the implementation of the digital service
· The level of user satisfaction and the level of achievement of the objectives

Other indicators:

· Maintenance of the structure to perform the service after implementation, in accordance with the impact caused.
· Fulfilments of the function.
· Measurement of the level of difficulty in performing the service.
· Level of stakeholder involvement.
· Reduction of the number of iterations between the citizen and the PA.
· The achievement of the objective resulting from implementation of the policy measures.
· Quality, productivity, and return on investment.

Qinq4: Which Internal and/or External Factors Influence the Likelihood of a DT Project Having the Best Possible Use?

Most cited internal factors:

· Communication during all phases of the project.
· Sufficient human resources according to the requirements of the projects.
· Active involvement of the top leadership.
· The projects are focused on citizens' needs.

Other internal factors:

· Clear definition of the problem by the entity or business.
· Clear definition of the target stakeholders.
· Involvement of direct and indirect stakeholders.
· The political relationship between the departments.
· The approach to managing the projects.
· Insufficient and/or inaccessible documentation.
· Feedback on the progress of the project delivery.
· Definition of responsibilities and deadlines.
· Limitations and bureaucracy regarding the public procurement of goods, services, and people,
· Ability to establish alternative scenarios.
· Consumption of resources within the budget cycle,
· Level of services between different areas.
· Clear definition of requirements, the setting of priorities, and carrying out a detailed risk analysis.

Most cited external factors:

· The Sponsor being more senior that the management of the AMA.
· Reconciliation of political interests.
· Dependence on teams from other entities.
· The quality of suppliers due to the limited resources available and the scarcity of technology specialists.
· The relationship between entities during the implementation of the project.

Other external factors:

· Adequate information, especially regarding projects that involve a high degree of integration.
· People with the right skills. in the right places.
· Measuring the impact of the project to ensure that the Sponsor and the steering committee are aware.
· Competition between entities.
· Influences of business, political. and external interests.
· Budget and time available.
· Interoperability, risk analysis. and governance of the PA.

Qinq5: What Are the Main Difficulties and Challenges During the Execution of a DT Project?

Most cited difficulties and challenges:

· External dependence on other entities to carry out the project.
· Dependent on decision and political urgencies.
· Human resources management of the entities.
· Insufficient number of human resources.
· Capture and maintain the best human resources.
· Digital training and planning failures.
· Keeping stakeholders on board and alignment between areas and entities.
· Managing the final product.

Other difficulties and challenges:

· Level and number of technology providers available.
· Alignment between support areas.
· Delay in responding to expert validation.

· Lack of access to available data from other entities' services to measure performance or user satisfaction.
· Lack of a clear definition of requirements and clarity of the project scope.
· Lack of direction for the usability of the services.
· How financial resources are distributed over time.
· Difficulty and delay in hiring consultants.
· Lack of a systematic and integrated process.
· Validation of deliveries and acceptance criteria.
· Impaired performance of long projects and failure to test the solutions.
· Lack of a defined process for suspending or canceling a project.
· Permission to use data from interoperability.
· Sponsorship, communication, and bureaucracy,

Qinq6: What Do You Think Could Be Done to Increase the Sponsorship of Areas That Work Together on the Same Project?

Most cited suggestions:

· Strict planning during the pre-start phase of projects.
· A greater level of knowledge sharing, which is well documented and easily accessible.
· Continuous communication of progress and results.
· A strong Sponsor and alignment between stakeholders.

Other suggestions:

· Integrated product view and clarity in setting priorities.
· Implement a Balanced Scorecard and Gamification.
· A change in the organizational culture.
· Build trust between teams and permanently involve the teams.
· Reduce dependence on people and areas.
· Bi-weekly meetings with all areas.
· All areas should sign the work plan.
· A plan which involves all stakeholders who are linked to a service level.
· A plan to mitigate damages due to a delay in the schedule.
· Accountability and the elimination of redundancies.
· Leaders who can increase collaborative logic.
· Tender documents which are written with the strategy in mind.
· Exchange of information between all those involved.
· Lack of collaboration, being a political priority, and project control.

Compilation of References

Abbas, J. (2020). Impact of total quality management on corporate green performance through the mediating role of corporate social responsibility. *Journal of Cleaner Production*, *242*, 118458. doi:10.1016/j.jclepro.2019.118458

Abbas, J., Hussain, I., Hussain, S., Akram, S., Shaheen, I., & Niu, B. (2019). The impact of knowledge sharing and innovation on sustainable performance in Islamic banks: A mediation analysis through a SEM approach. *Sustainability (Basel)*, *11*(15), 4049. doi:10.3390u11154049

Abbas, J., & Sağsan, M. (2019). Impact of knowledge management practices on green innovation and corporate sustainable development: A structural analysis. *Journal of Cleaner Production*, *229*, 611–620. doi:10.1016/j.jclepro.2019.05.024

Abdi, K., Mardani, A., Senin, A., Tupenaite, L., Naimaviciene, J., Kanapeckiene, L., & Kutut, V. (2018). The effect of knowledge management, organizational culture and organizational learning on innovation in automotive industry. *Journal of Business Economics and Management*, *19*(1), 1–19. doi:10.3846/jbem.2018.1477

Acemoglu, D., Hazell, J., & Restrepo, P. (2022). Artificial Intelligence and Jobs: Evidence from Online Vacancies. *Journal of Labor Economics*, *40*(S1), S293–S340. doi:10.1086/718327

Acemoglu, D., Lelarge, C., & Restrepo, P. (2020). Competing With Robots: Firm-Level Evidence from France. *AEA Papers and Proceedings. American Economic Association*, *110*, 383–388. doi:10.1257/pandp.20201003

Acemoglu, D., & Restrepo, P. (2022). Tasks, automation, and the rise in U.S. wage inequality. *Econometrica*, *90*(5), 1973–2016. doi:10.3982/ECTA19815

AFI. 2020. *Importancia económica y social del sector vitivinícola en España* [Economic and social importance of the wine sector in Spain]. Available at: https://www.interprofesionaldelvino.es/publicaciones/informes-importancia-sector/nacional/

African Development Bank. (2022). *Ethiopia Economic Outlook*. Available online: https://www.afdb.org/en/countries/east-africa/ethiopia/ethiopia-economic-outlook

Aftab, J., Veneziani, M., Sarwar, H., & Ishaq, M. (2022). Organizational ambidexterity, firm performance, and sustainable development: Mediating role of entrepreneurial orientation in Pakistani SMEs. *Journal of Cleaner Production*, *367*, 132956. doi:10.1016/j.jclepro.2022.132956

Agyabeng-Mensah, Y., & Tang, L. (2021). The relationship among green human capital, green logistics practices, green competitiveness, social performance and financial performance. *Journal of Manufacturing Technology Management*, *32*(7), 1377–1398. doi:10.1108/JMTM-11-2020-0441

Ahmad, H., Yaqub, M., & Lee, S. H. (2023). Environmental-, social-, and governance-related factors for business investment and sustainability: A scientometric review of global trends. *Environment, Development and Sustainability*. Advance online publication. doi:10.100710668-023-02921-x PMID:36714213

Ahn, H. (2001). Applying the Balanced Scorecard Concept: An Experience Report. *Long Range Planning*, *34*(4), 441–461. doi:10.1016/S0024-6301(01)00057-7

Al Amosh, H., Khatib, S. F. A., Alkurdi, A., & Bazhair, A. H. (2022). Capital structure decisions and environmental, social and governance performance: Insights from Jordan. *Journal of Financial Reporting and Accounting*. doi:10.1108/JFRA-12-2021-0453

Alareeni, B. A., & Hamdan, A. (n.d.). *ESG impact on performance of US S&P 500-listed firms*. Academic Press.

Albrecht, J. C., & Spang, K. (2014). Linking the benefits of project management maturity to project complexity: Insights from a multiple case study. *International Journal of Managing Projects in Business*, *7*(2), 285–301. doi:10.1108/IJMPB-08-2013-0040

Al-Debei, M., & Avison, D. (2010). Developing a unified framework of the business model concept. *European Journal of Information Systems*, *19*(3), 359–376. doi:10.1057/ejis.2010.21

Al-Emran, M., Mezhuyev, V., Kamaludin, A., & Shaalan, K. (2018). The impact of knowledge management processes on information systems: A systematic review. *International Journal of Information Management*, *43*, 173–187. doi:10.1016/j.ijinfomgt.2018.08.001

Ali, M., Ali, I., Al-Maimani, K., & Park, K. (2018). The effect of organizational structure on absorptive capacity In single and dual learning modes. *Journal of Innovation & Knowledge*, *3*(3), 108–114. doi:10.1016/j.jik.2017.03.007

Alrowwad, A., Obeidat, B., Tarhini, A., & Aqqad, N. (2017). The impact of transformational leadership on organizational performance via the mediating role of corporate social responsibility: A structural equation modeling approach. *International Business Research*, *10*(1), 199–221. doi:10.5539/ibr.v10n1p199

Al-Sartawi, A. M. M., Hussainey, K., & Razzaque, A. (2022). The role of artificial intelligence in sustainable finance. *Journal of Sustainable Finance & Investment*, 1–6. doi:10.1080/20430795.2022.2057405

Amit, R., & Schoemaker, P. J. H. (1993). Strategic assets and organizational rent. *Strategic Management Journal*, *14*(1), 33–46. doi:10.1002mj.4250140105

Amores-Salvadó, J., Martín-de Castro, G., & Navas-López, J. (2014). Green corporate image: Moderating the connection between environmental product innovation and firm performance. *Journal of Cleaner Production*, *83*, 356–365. doi:10.1016/j.jclepro.2014.07.059

Andersen, E. S., & Jessen, S. A. (2003). Project maturity in organisations. *International Journal of Project Management*, *21*(6), 457–461. doi:10.1016/S0263-7863(02)00088-1

Andréasson, M., & Svartling, A. (1999). *Knowledge Management Methods: Practical approaches to managing knowledge in The Balanced Scorecard - A tool for managing knowledge?* https://www.handels.gu.se/epc/archive/00001973/01/Andreasson_1999_7.pdf

Andrews, K. R. (1971). *The Concept of Corporate Strategy*. Irwin.

Annunziata, E., Pucci, T., Frey, M., & Zanni, L. (2018). The role of organizational capabilities in attaining corporate sustainability practices and economic performance: Evidence from Italian wine industry. *Journal of Cleaner Production*, *171*, 1300–1311. doi:10.1016/j.jclepro.2017.10.035

Ansoff, H. I. (1965). *Corporate Strategy*. McGraw Hill.

Apergis, N., Poufinas, T., & Antonopoulos, A. (2022). ESG scores and cost of debt. *Energy Economics*, *112*, 106186. doi:10.1016/j.eneco.2022.106186

APM. (2012). *Body of Knowledge* (6th ed.). Association for Project Management.

Arfi, W., Hikkerova, L., & Sahut, J. (2018). External knowledge sources, green innovation and performance. *Technological Forecasting and Social Change*, *129*, 210–220. doi:10.1016/j.techfore.2017.09.017

Argote, L., McEvily, B., & Reagans, R. (2003). Managing knowledge in organizations: An integrative framework and review of emerging themes. *Management Science*, *49*(4), 571–582. doi:10.1287/mnsc.49.4.571.14424

Asadi, S., Pourhashemi, S., Nilashi, M., Abdullah, R., Samad, S., Yadegaridehkordi, E., & Razali, N. (2020). Investigating influence of green innovation on sustainability performance: A case on Malaysian hotel industry. *Journal of Cleaner Production*, *258*, 120860. doi:10.1016/j.jclepro.2020.120860

Ashok, M., Madan, R., Joha, A., & Sivarajah, U. (2022). Ethical framework for Artificial Intelligence and Digital technologies. *International Journal of Information Management*, *62*, 102433. doi:10.1016/j.ijinfomgt.2021.102433

Aslam, S., Ahmad, M., Amin, S., Usman, M., & Arif, S. (2018). The impact of corporate governance and intellectual capital on firm's performance and corporate social responsibility disclosure. *Pakistan Journal of Commerce and Social Sciences*, *12*(1), 283–308.

Asmawanti, S., & Wijayanti, I. (2017). Intellectual capital and corporate social responsibility in banking industries in Indonesia. *Journal of Economics, Business, and Accountancy Ventura*, *20*(2), 191–200.

Atkinson, A., Waterhouse, J., & Wells, R., (1997). A Stakeholder Approach to Strategic Performance Measurement. *Sloan Management Review, 38*(3), 5.

Aureli, S., Giampaoli, D., Ciambotti, M., & Bontis, N. (2019). Key factors that improve knowledge-intensive business processes which lead to competitive advantage. *Business Process Management Journal, 25*(1), 126–143. doi:10.1108/BPMJ-06-2017-0168

AXELOS. (2016). *Introduction to P3M3©, version 3*. AXELOS Limited.

Baccarini, D. (1999). The logical framework method for defining project success. *Project Management Journal, 30*(4), 25–32. doi:10.1177/875697289903000405

Backlund, F., Chronéer, D., & Sundqvist, E. (2014). Project management maturity models - A critical review: A case study within Swedish engineering and construction organisations. *Procedia: Social and Behavioral Sciences, 119*, 837–846. doi:10.1016/j.sbspro.2014.03.094

Badir, Y., & O'Connor, G. (2015). The formation of tie strength in a strategic alliance's first new product development project: The influence of project and partners' characteristics. *Journal of Product Innovation Management, 32*(1), 154–169. doi:10.1111/jpim.12222

Bahta, D., Yun, J., Islam, M., & Ashfaq, M. (2020). Corporate social responsibility, innovation capability and firm performance: Evidence from SME. *Social Responsibility Journal, 17*(6), 840–860. doi:10.1108/SRJ-12-2019-0401

Bahta, D., Yun, J., Islam, M., & Bikanyi, K. (2021). How does CSR enhance the financial performance of SMEs? The mediating role of firm reputation. *Ekonomska Istrazivanja, 34*(1), 1428–1451. doi:10.1080/1331677X.2020.1828130

Bakker, R. M. (2010). Taking stock of temporary organizational forms: A systematic review and research agenda. *International Journal of Management Reviews, 12*(4), 466–486. doi:10.1111/j.1468-2370.2010.00281.x

Bandinelli, R., Acuti, D., Fani, V., Bindi, B., & Aiello, G. (2020). Environmental practices in the wine industry: An overview of the Italian market. *British Food Journal, 122*(5), 1625–1646. doi:10.1108/BFJ-08-2019-0653

Banker, R., Chang, H., & Pizzini, M. (2004). The Balanced Scorecard judgemental effects of performance measures linked to strategy. *The Accounting Review, 79*(1), 1–23. doi:10.2308/accr.2004.79.1.1

Bannerman, P. L. (2008). Defining project success: a multilevel framework. *Proceedings of the PMI Research Conference: Defining the Future of Project Management.*

Barabanov, S. S., Basnet, A., Walker, T. J., Yuan, W., & Wendt, S. (2021). Firm-and country-level determinants of green investments: An empirical analysis. *Managerial Finance, 47*(11), 1672–1692. doi:10.1108/MF-06-2020-0311

Barber, E. (2004). Benchmarking the Management of Projects: A Review of Current Thinking. *International Journal of Project Management, 22*(4), 301–307. doi:10.1016/j.ijproman.2003.08.001

Barcevičius, M., Cibaitė, E., Codagnone, G., Gineikytė, C., Klimavičiūtė, V., Liva, L., Matulevič, G., & Vanini, G. (2019). *Exploring Digital Government transformation in the EU - Analysis of the State of the art and review of literature*. Publications Office of the European Union. doi:10.2760/17207

Barney, J. (1986). Strategic Factor Markets: Expectations, Luck and Business Strategy. *Management Science*, *32*(10), 1231–1241. doi:10.1287/mnsc.32.10.1231

Barney, J. B. (1991). Firm resources and sustained competitive advantage. *Journal of Management*, *17*(1), 99–120. doi:10.1177/014920639101700108

Becker, J., Knackstedt, R., & Pöppelbuß, J. (2009). Developing Maturity Models for IT Management: A Procedure Model and its Application. *Business & Information Systems Engineering*, *1*(3), 213–222. doi:10.100712599-009-0044-5

Beer, M. (2002). Building Organizational Fitness. In *Organizations 21C* (pp. 311-330). Financial Times Prentice Hall.

Bennington, P., & Baccarini, D. (2004, June). Project benefits management in IT projects – An Australian perspective. *Project Management Journal*.

Besner, C., & Hobbs, B. (2013). Contextualized Project Management Practice: A Cluster Analysis of Practices and Best Practice. *Project Management Journal*, *44*(1), 17–34. doi:10.1002/pmj.21291

Bhatt, P. R., & Bhatt, R. R. (2017). Corporate governance and firm performance in Malaysia. *Corporate Governance (Bradford)*, *17*(5), 896–912. doi:10.1108/CG-03-2016-0054

Bisbe, J., & Barrubés, J. (2012). The Balanced Scorecard as a Management Tool for Assessing and Monitoring Strategy Implementation in Health Care Organizations. *Revista Española de Cardiología*, *65*(10), 919–927. doi:10.1016/j.recesp.2012.05.014 PMID:22917775

Blackman, R. (2020, October 15). *A Practical Guide to Building Ethical AI*. Retrieved from https://hbr.org/2020/10/a-practical-guide-to-building-ethical-ai

Boarini, R., Murtini, F., Schreyeri, P., & Fleurbaey, M. (2016). *Multi-dimensional Living Standards: A Welfare Measure Based on Preferences*. OECD Statistics Working Papers 5. OECD Publishing. doi:10.1787/18152031

Bohm, S., Carrington, M., Cornelius, N., de Bruin, B., Greenwood, M., Hassan, L., & Shaw, D. (2022). Ethics at the centre of global and local challenges: Thoughts on the future of business ethics. *Journal of Business Ethics*, *180*(3), 835–861.

Bolton, M., Raven, R., & Mintrom, M. (2021). Can AI transform public decision-making for sustainable development? An exploration of critical earth system governance questions. *Earth System Governance*, *9*, 100116. doi:10.1016/j.esg.2021.100116

Bontis, N., Dragonetti, N. C., Jacobsen, K., & Roos, G. (1999). The knowledge toolbox: A review of the tools available to measure and manage intangible resources. *European Management Journal*, *17*(4), 391–403. doi:10.1016/S0263-2373(99)00019-5

Booth, A. (2019). Living Standards in Southeast Asia. Changes over the Long Twentieth Century, 1900-2015. Amsterdam University Press.

Bourne, L., & Walker, D. H. T. (2004). Advancing Project Management in Learning Organisations. *The Learning Organization*, *11*(3), 226–243. doi:10.1108/09696470410532996

Bousdekis, A., & Dimitris, K. (2020). Digital transformation of local government: A case study from Greece. *Proceedings IEEE 22nd Conference on Business Informatics*, *2*, 131-140. 10.1109/CBI49978.2020.10070

BožićV. (2023). Environmental, social, and governance approach (ESG) & artificial intelligence (AI). *ResearchGate*. doi:10.13140/RG.2.2.34753.12641

Brinkmann, S., & Kvale, S. (2015). *Interviews: Learning the Craft of Qualitative Research Interviewing* (3rd ed.). Sage.

Brito, D., & Curl, R. F. (2020). *Automation Does Not Kill Jobs. It Increases Inequality*. Baker Institute Report no. 11.06.20. Rice University's Baker Institute for Public Policy.

Broadstock, D., Matousek, R., Meyer, M., & Tzeremes, N. (2020). Does corporate social responsibility impact firms' innovation capacity? The indirect link between environmental & social governance implementation and innovation performance. *Journal of Business Research*, *119*, 99–110. doi:10.1016/j.jbusres.2019.07.014

Broccardo, L., & Zicari, A. (2020). Sustainability as a driver for value creation: A business model analysis of small and medium entreprises in the Italian wine sector. *Journal of Cleaner Production*, *259*, 120852. doi:10.1016/j.jclepro.2020.120852

Brookes, N., Butler, M., Dey, P., & Clark, R. (2014). The use of maturity models in improving project management performance. *International Journal of Managing Projects in Business*, *7*(2), 231–246. doi:10.1108/IJMPB-03-2013-0007

Bryde, D. J., & Brown, D. (2005). The influence of a project performance measurement system on the success of a contract for maintaining motorways and trunk roads. *Project Management Journal*, *35*(4), 57–65. doi:10.1177/875697280403500407

Buallay, A., Hamdan, A., & Zureigat, Q. (2017). Corporate governance and firm performance: Evidence from Saudi Arabia. Australasian Accounting. *Business and Finance Journal*, *11*(1), 78–98.

Bukowski, P., & Novokmet, F. (2021). Between communism and capitalism: Long-term inequality in Poland, 1892-2015. *Journal of Economic Growth*, *26*(2), 187–239. doi:10.100710887-021-09190-1 PMID:34776755

Burnaev, E. M., Mironov, E., Shpilman, A., Mironenko, M., & Katalevsky, D. (2023). Practical AI Cases for Solving ESG Challenges. *Sustainability (Basel)*, *12731*(17), 12731. Advance online publication. doi:10.3390u151712731

Burns, E. (2023). Machine Learning. *TechTarget network*. https://www.techtarget.com/searchenterpriseai/definition/machine-learning-ML

Busco, C., Consolandi, C., Eccles, R. G., & Sofra, E. (2020). A preliminary analysis of SASB reporting: Disclosure topics, financial relevance, and the financial intensity of ESG materiality. *The Bank of America Journal of Applied Corporate Finance*, *32*(2), 117–125. doi:10.1111/jacf.12411

Bustinza, O., Vendrell-Herrero, F., & Gomes, E. (2020). Unpacking the effect of strategic ambidexterity on performance: A cross-country comparison of MMNEs developing product-service innovation. *International Business Review*, *29*(6), 101569. doi:10.1016/j.ibusrev.2019.01.004

Byrne, B. (2008). *Structural Equation Modeling with EQS: Basic Concepts, Applications, and Programming*. Psychology Press.

Calza, F., Parmentola, A., & Tutore, I. (2021). For green or not for green? The effect of cooperation goals and type on environmental performance. *Business Strategy and the Environment*, *30*(1), 267–281. doi:10.1002/bse.2620

Cantino, V., Devalle, A., & Fiandrino, S. (2017). *ESG Sustainability and Financial Capital Structure: Where they Stand Nowadays*. Academic Press.

Caralli, R., Knight, M., & Montgomery, A. (2012). Maturity Models 101: A Primer for Applying Maturity Models to Smart Grid Security, Resilience, and Interoperability. CERT, Software Engineering Institute, Carnegie Mellon University. doi:10.21236/ADA610461

Carmines, E., & Zeller, R. (1979). *Reliability and validity assessment* (Vol. 17). Sage. doi:10.4135/9781412985642

Carrasqueiro, S., Monteiro, M., Pereira, R., Pereira, C., & Martins, H. (2018). Dematerialization of the medical certificate for driving license in Portugal: a case study of success factors of whole-of-Government e-Government initiatives. *Proceedings of the 11th International Conference on Theory and Practice of Electronic Governance*. 10.1145/3209415.3209510

Carufel, R. (2019). *Companies embrace AI, but execs cite challenges on alignment, ethics*. Agility, PR Solutions. Retrieved from: https://www.agilitypr.com/pr-news/public-relations/companies-embrace-ai-but-execs-

Casadella, V., & Uzunidis, D. (2017). National Innovation Systems of the South, Innovation and Economic Development Policies: A multidimensional approach. *Journal of Innovation Economics & Management*, *2*(23), 137–157. doi:10.3917/jie.pr1.0007

Caselli, F., & Michaels, G. (2013). Do Oil Windfalls Improve Living Standards? Evidence from Brazil. *American Economic Journal. Applied Economics*, *5*(1), 208–238. doi:10.1257/app.5.1.208

Central Statistics Agency (CSA) of Ethiopia. (2010a). *Household Income, Consumption and Expenditure Survey 1995-1996. Study Documentation*. http://www.csa.gov.et/survey-report/category/72-hice-1995

Central Statistics Agency (CSA) of Ethiopia. (2010b). *Revised Report on the 1995-1996 Household Income, Consumption and Expenditure Survey. Study Documentation. Statistical Bulletin No. 204*. http://www.csa.gov.et/survey-report/category/72-hice-1995

Central Statistics Agency (CSA) of Ethiopia. (2010c). *Household Income, Consumption and Expenditure Survey 1999-2000. Study Documentation. February 2001. Statistical Bulletin No. 258.* http://www.csa.gov.et/survey-report/category/73-hice-2000

Central Statistics Agency (CSA) of Ethiopia. (2010d). *Report on the 1999-2000 Household Income, Consumption and Expenditure Survey. Study Documentation.* http://www.csa.gov.et/survey-report/category/73-hice-2000

Central Statistics Agency (CSA) of Ethiopia. (2011a). *Household Consumption and Expenditure (HCE) Survey 2010/11. Analytical Report. Statistical Bulletin No. 563.* http://www.csa.gov.et/survey-report/category/75-hice-2011

Central Statistics Agency (CSA) of Ethiopia. (2011b). *The 2010/11 Ethiopian Households Consumption – Expenditure (HCE). Survey Results For: Country Level. Statistical Report.* http://www.csa.gov.et/survey-report/category/75-hice-2011

Central Statistics Agency (CSA) of Ethiopia. (2011c). *Ethiopian Data Quality Assessment Framework (EDQAF).* Addis Ababa. http://www.csa.gov.et/component/phocadownload/category/310?Itemid=310

Central Statistics Agency (CSA) of Ethiopia. (2018a). *The 2015/16 Ethiopian Household Consumption – Expenditure (HCE) Survey Results For: Country Level. Statistical Report. Statistical Bulletin No. 585.* http://www.csa.gov.et/survey-report/category/350-hice-2016

Central Statistics Agency (CSA) of Ethiopia. (2018b). *Statistical Data report on 3rd mission to Ethiopia- June 2018.* http://www.csa.gov.et/survey-report/category/350-hice-2016

Cepeda-Carrion, G., Cegarra-Navarro, J., & Cillo, V. (2019). Tips to use partial least squares structural equation modelling (PLS-SEM) in knowledge management. *Journal of Knowledge Management, 23*(1), 67–89. doi:10.1108/JKM-05-2018-0322

Chadha, S., & Sharma, A. K. (2015). Capital Structure and Firm Performance: Empirical Evidence from India. *Vision, 19*(4), 295-302. doi:10.1177/0972262915610852

Chandler, D., & Thomas, J. (2015). Does executive sponsorship matter for realizing project management value. *Project Management Journal, 46*(5), 46–61. doi:10.1002/pmj.21521

Chang, C. (2016). The determinants of green product innovation performance. *Corporate Social Responsibility and Environmental Management, 23*(2), 65–76. doi:10.1002/csr.1361

Chang, C., & Chen, Y. (2012). The determinants of green intellectual capital. *Management Decision, 50*(1), 74–94. doi:10.1108/00251741211194886

Charl, D. V. (2022). *The Global Reporting Initiative's (GRI) Past, Present and Future: Critical reflections and a research agenda on sustainability reporting (standard-setting).* https://papers.ssrn.com/sol3/papers.cfm?abstract_id=4099915

Chaudhry, N., Bilal, A., Awan, M., & Bashir, A. (2016). The role of environmental consciousness, green intellectual capital management and competitive advantage on financial performance of the firms: An evidence from manufacturing sector of Pakistan. *Journal of Quality and Technology Management*, *13*(2), 51–70.

Chauhan, S. S., Singh, R., Gehlot, A., Akram, S. V., Twala, B., & Priyadarshi, N. (2022). Digitalization of Supply Chain Management with Industry 4.0 Enabling Technologies: A Sustainable Perspective. *Processes (Basel, Switzerland)*, *96*(1), 96. Advance online publication. doi:10.3390/pr11010096

Che Haat, M. H., Abdul Rahman, R., & Mahenthiran, S. (2008). Corporate Governance, transparency and performance of Malaysian companies. *Managerial Auditing Journal*, *23*(8), 744–778. doi:10.1108/02686900810899518

Cheah, S., & Ho, Y. (2019). Coworking and sustainable business model innovation in young firms. *Sustainability (Basel)*, *11*(10), 2959. doi:10.3390u11102959

Chen, C., Shih, H., & Yang, S. (2009). The role of intellectual capital in knowledge transfer. *IEEE Transactions on Engineering Management*, *56*(3), 402–411. doi:10.1109/TEM.2009.2023086

Chen, W., & Wellman, B. (2004). The global digital divide–within and between countries. *ITandSociety*, *1*(7), 39–45.

Chen, Y. (2008a). The positive effect of green intellectual capital on competitive advantages of firms. *Journal of Business Ethics*, *77*(3), 271–286. doi:10.100710551-006-9349-1

Chen, Y. (2008b). The driver of green innovation and green image–green core competence. *Journal of Business Ethics*, *81*(3), 531–543. doi:10.100710551-007-9522-1

Chesbrough, H. (2011). *Open Services Innovation: Rethinking Your Business to Grow and Compete in a New Era* (1st ed.). Jossey-Bass.

Chouaibi, Y., Rossi, M., & Zouari, G. (2021). The Effect of Corporate Social Responsibility and the Executive Compensation on Implicit Cost of Equity: Evidence from French ESG Data. *Sustainability (Basel)*, *13*(20), 11510. doi:10.3390u132011510

Chourabi, H., Nam, T., Walker, S., Gil-Garcia, J., Mellouli, S., Nahon, K., Pardo, T., & Scholl, H. (2012). Understanding Smart Cities: An Integrative Framework. *Proceedings of the 45th Hawaii International Conference on System Sciences.*

Chu, C. I., Chatterjee, B., & Brown, A. (2013). The current status of greenhouse gas reporting by Chinese companies: A test of legitimacy theory. *Managerial Auditing Journal*, *28*(2), 114–139.

Cicmil, S., Hodgson, D., Lindgren, M., & Packendorff, J. (2009). Project management behind the facade. *Ephemera*, *9*(2), 78–92.

Cinquini, L., Passetti, E., Tenucci, A., & Frey, M. (2012). Analyzing intellectual capital information in sustainability reports: Some empirical evidence. *Journal of Intellectual Capital*, *13*(4), 531–561. doi:10.1108/14691931211276124

Clarke, A. (1999). A practical use of key success factors to improve the effectiveness of project management. *International Journal of Project Management, 17*(3), 139–145. doi:10.1016/S0263-7863(98)00031-3

Conner, K. R., & Prahalad, C. K. (1996). A resource-based theory of the firm: Knowledge versus opportunism. *Organization Science, 7*(5), 477–501. doi:10.1287/orsc.7.5.477

Cooke-Davies, T. J., Schlichter, F. J., & Bredillet, C. (2001). *Beyond the PMBOK Guide.* PMI Annual Seminars and Symposium 2001, Nashville, TN.

Cooke-Davies, T. J. (2004). Measurement of organizational maturity: what are the relevant questions about maturity and metrics for a project-based organization to ask, and what do these imply for project management research? In D. I. C. Slevin & J. K. Pinto (Eds.), *Innovations, project management research* (pp. 211–228). Project Management Institute.

Cooke-Davies, T. J., & Arzymanow, A. (2003). The maturity of project management in different industries - An investigation into variations between project management models. *International Journal of Project Management, 21*(6), 471–478. doi:10.1016/S0263-7863(02)00084-4

Copenhagen Business School (CBS). (2023). *Center for Corporate Governance.* https://www.cbs.dk/en/research/departments-and-centres/department-of-accounting/center-corporate-governance

Corbo, C., Lamastra, L., & Capri, E. (2014). From environmental to sustainability programs: A review of sustainability initiatives in the Italian wine sector. *Sustainability (Basel), 6*(4), 2133–2159. doi:10.3390u6042133

Cordella, A., & Tempini, N. (2015). E-government and organizational change: Reappraising the role of ICT and bureaucracy in public service delivery. *Government Information Quarterly, 32*(3), 279–286. doi:10.1016/j.giq.2015.03.005

Costantiello, A., & and Leogrande, A. (2023). *The Determinants of CO2 Emissions in the Context of ESG.* Academic Press.

CostantielloA.LeograndeA. (2023). The Impact of Research and Development Expenditures on ESG Model in the Global Economy. SSRN(4414232). doi:10.2139/ssrn.4414232

CostantielloA.LeograndeA. (2023). The Role of Political Stability in the Context of ESG Models at World Level. SSRN (4406997). doi:10.2139/ssrn.4406997

Council of Europe. (2023). *Good Governance. 12 Principles of Good Governance.* https://www.coe.int/en/web/good-governance/12-principles

Crawford, L., Cooke-Davies, T., Hobbs, B., Labuschagne, L., Remington, K., & Chen, P. (2008). Governance and Support in the Sponsoring of Projects and Programs. *Project Management Journal, 39*, S43–S55. doi:10.1002/pmj.20059

Crawford, J. K. (2006). The Project Management Maturity Model. *Information Systems Management, 23*(4), 50–58. doi:10.1201/1078.10580530/46352.23.4.20060901/95113.7

Crawford, L. (2005). Senior management perceptions of project management competence. *International Journal of Project Management*, *23*(1), 7–16. doi:10.1016/j.ijproman.2004.06.005

Crawford, L., Pollack, J., & England, D. (2006). Uncovering the trends in project management: Journal emphases over the last 10 years. *International Journal of Project Management*, *24*(2), 175–184. doi:10.1016/j.ijproman.2005.10.005

Currie, W. (2012). Institutional Isomorphism and Change: The National Programme for IT – 10 Years On. *Journal of Information Technology*, *27*(3), 236–248. doi:10.1057/jit.2012.18

Currie, W., & Guah, M. (2007). Conflicting institutional logics: A national programme for IT in the organizational field of healthcare. *Journal of Information Technology*, *22*(3), 235–247. doi:10.1057/palgrave.jit.2000102

D'Aveni, R. (1994). *Hypercompetition: Managing the dynamics of strategic manoeuvring*. The Free Press.

Dahiya, M., & Singh, S. (2020). The linkage between CSR and cost of equity: An Indian perspective. Sustainability Accounting. *Management and Policy Journal*, *12*(3), 499–52.

Dahiya, M., & Singh, S. (2021). The linkage between CSR and cost of equity: An Indian perspective. *Sustainability Accounting, Management and Policy Journal*, *12*(3), 499–521. doi:10.1108/SAMPJ-10-2019-0379

Daniel, E., & Wilson, H. (2003). The role of dynamic capabilities in e-business transformation. *European Journal of Information Systems*, *12*(4), 282–296. doi:10.1057/palgrave.ejis.3000478

Darvishmotevali, M. (2019). Decentralization and innovative behavior: The moderating role of supervisor support. *International Journal of Organizational Leadership*, *8*(1), 31–45. doi:10.33844/ijol.2019.60204

Datta, P., Walker, L., & Amarilli, F. (2020). Digital transformation: Learning from Italy's public administration. *Journal of Information Technology Teaching Cases,* 1-18. doi:10.1177/2043886920910437

David, F. R. (2011). Strategic management: concepts and cases (13th ed.). Prentice Hall.

Davis, G. F., & Adam-Cobb, J. (2010). Resource dependence theory: Past and future. *Research in the Sociology of Organizations*, *28*, 21–42. doi:10.1108/S0733-558X(2010)0000028006

de Bruin, T., & Rosemann, M. (2005). Towards a Business Process Management Maturity Model. *Proceedings of the 13th European Conference on Information Systems (ECIS 2005).* Available at: http://eprints.qut.edu.au/25194/

De Haas, M. (2000). *Strategic dialogue: in search of goal coherence* [PhD thesis]. Eindhoven University of Technology.

de Jong, H. (2015). Living Standards in a Modernizing World: A Long-Run Perspective on Material Wellbeing and Human Development. In W Glatzer (ed.), *Global Handbook of Quality of Life: exploration of well-being of nations and continent*. Springer. Available online: https://research.rug.nl/en/publications/living-standards-in-a-modernizing-world-a-long-run-perspective-on

De Villiers, C., Dimes, R., & Molinari, M. (2023). *How will AI text generation and processing impact sustainability reporting? Critical analysis, a conceptual framework and avenues for future research*. Sustainability Accounting, Management and Policy Journal. doi:10.1108/SAMPJ-02-2023-0097

de Wit, A. (1988). Measurement of project success. *International Journal of Project Management*, *6*(3), 164–170. doi:10.1016/0263-7863(88)90043-9

Decoene, V., & Bruggeman, W. (2006). Strategic alignment and middle-level managers' motivation in a Balanced Scorecard setting. *International Journal of Operations & Production Management*, *26*(4), 3–4, 429–448. doi:10.1108/01443570610650576

Dedunu, H. H., & Sedara, D. (2023). Impact of environmental, social, and governance practices on the consumer buying decision. In Advances in business strategy and competitive advantage book series (pp. 129–147). doi:10.4018/978-1-6684-6815-9.ch008

Deegan, C. (2002). Introduction. *Accounting, Auditing & Accountability Journal*, *15*(3), 282–311. doi:10.1108/09513570210435852

Del Giudice, M., & Della Peruta, M. (2016). The impact of IT-based knowledge management systems on internal venturing and innovation: A structural equation modeling approach to corporate performance. *Journal of Knowledge Management*, *20*(3), 484–498. doi:10.1108/JKM-07-2015-0257

Del Vitto, A., Marazzina, D., & Stocco, D. (2023). ESG ratings explainability through machine learning techniques. *Annals of Operations Research*. Advance online publication. doi:10.100710479-023-05514-z

DesJardins, J. (1998). Corporate environmental responsibility. *Journal of Business Ethics*, *17*(8), 825–838. doi:10.1023/A:1005719707880

Deutsche Welle (DW). (2022). *Global Issues. Living Standards Declining in 90% of Countries — UN*. Available online: https://www.dw.com/en/un-index-shows-living-standards-declining-in-90-of-countries/a-63052023

Devalle, A., Fiandrino, S., & Cantino, V. (2017). ESG Sustainability and Financial Capital Structure: Where they Stand Nowadays. *International Journal of Business and Social Science*, *8*(5).

Dhankar, R. S., & Boora, A. S. (1996). Cost of capital, optimal capital structure, and value of firm: An empirical study of Indian companies. *Vikalpa*, *21*(3), 29–36. doi:10.1177/0256090919960303

Di Vaio, A., & Varriale, L. (2020). Blockchain technology in supply chain management for sustainable performance: Evidence from the airport industry. *International Journal of Information Management*, *52*, 102014. doi:10.1016/j.ijinfomgt.2019.09.010

Dijkstra, T., & Henseler, J. (2015). Consistent partial least squares path modeling. *Management Information Systems Quarterly*, *39*(2), 297–316. doi:10.25300/MISQ/2015/39.2.02

Dimri, V. (2020). A study on the weak form efficiency of chemicals sector in BSE. *International Research Journal of Management Sociology & Humanity*, *11*(1), 64–73.

Donaldson, T., & Preston, L. E. (1995). The stakeholder theory of the corporation: Concepts, evidence, and implications. *Academy of Management Review*, *20*(1), 65–91. doi:10.2307/258887

Dooley, K., Subra, A., & Anderson, J. (2001). Maturity and its Impact on New Product Development Project Performance. *Research in Engineering Design*, *13*(1), 23–29. doi:10.1007001630100003

Dost, M., & Badir, Y. (2018). Generation or adoption? The role of social capital. *Management Decision*, *57*(7), 1457–1471. doi:10.1108/MD-11-2017-1108

Dost, M., Badir, Y., Ali, Z., & Tariq, A. (2016). The impact of intellectual capital on innovation generation and adoption. *Journal of Intellectual Capital*, *17*(4), 675–695. doi:10.1108/JIC-04-2016-0047

Dowling, J., & Pfeffer, J. (1975). Organizational legitimacy: Social values and organizational behavior. *Pacific Sociological Review*, *18*(1), 122–136. doi:10.2307/1388226

Durnev, A., & Kim, E. (2005). To steal or not to steal: Firm attributes, legal environment, and valuation. *The Journal of Finance*, *60*(3), 1461–1493. doi:10.1111/j.1540-6261.2005.00767.x

Egger, D., Miguel, E., Warren, S. S., Shenoy, A., Collins, E., Karlan, D., Parkerson, D., Mobarak, A. M., Fink, G., Udry, C., Walker, M., Haushofer, J., Larreboure, M., Athey, S., Lopez-Pena, P., Benhachmi, S., Humphreys, M., Lowe, L., Meriggi, N. F., ... Vernot, C. (2021). Falling living standards during the COVID-19 crisis: Quantitative evidence from nine developing countries. *Science Advances*, *7*(6), eabe0997. Advance online publication. doi:10.1126ciadv.abe0997 PMID:33547077

Eisenhart, K. M., & Martin, J. A. (2000). Dynamic capabilities: What they are? *Strategic Management Journal*, *21*(10-11), 1105–1211. doi:10.1002/1097-0266(200010/11)21:10/11<1105::AID-SMJ133>3.0.CO;2-E

El Benany, M. M., & El Beqqali, O. (2017). Cross-organizational orchestrator for e-government interoperability. *Proceedings of the 13th IEEE/ACS International Conference of Computer Systems and Applications, AICCSA 2016*. 10.1109/AICCSA.2016.7945750

El Ghoul, S., Guedhami, O., Kwok, C., & Mishra, D. (2011). Does corporate social responsibility affect the cost of capital? *Journal of Banking & Finance*, *35*(9), 2388–2406. doi:10.1016/j.jbankfin.2011.02.007

Eliwa, Y., Aboud, A., & Saleh, A. (2021). ESG practices and the cost of debt: Evidence from EU countries. *Critical Perspectives on Accounting*, *79*, 102097. doi:10.1016/j.cpa.2019.102097

Elouidani, R. (2022). Artificial Intelligence for a Sustainable Finance: A Bibliometric Analysis. *International Conference on Advanced Intelligent Systems for Sustainable Development*, 536-551. Retrieved from https://link.springer.com/chapter/10.1007/978-3-031-26384-2_46

Eskerod, P., & Riis, E. (2009). Project Management Models as Value Creators. *Project Management Journal*, *40*(1), 4–18. doi:10.1002/pmj.20098

Esposito, B., Sessa, M., Sica, D., & Malandrino, O. (2021). Exploring Corporate Social Responsibility in the Italian wine sector through websites. *The TQM Journal*, *33*(7), 222–252. doi:10.1108/TQM-11-2020-0264

European Commission. (2020a). eGovernment Benchmark 2020: eGovernment that works for the people. Luxembourg: Publications Office of the European Union.

European Commission. (2020b). *Digital Economy and Society Index: Digital public services.* https://ec.europa.eu/digital-single-market/en/news/digital-economy-and-society-index-desi-2020

European Commission. (2023). *European Commission Adopts Market Measures to Support EU Wine Producers.* https://agriculture.ec.europa.eu/news/european-commission-adopts-market-measures-support-eu-wine-producers-2023-06-23_en

European Parliament. (2023). *Briefing: The EU Wine Sector.* https://www.europarl.europa.eu/RegData/etudes/BRIE/2023/751399/EPRS_BRI(2023)751399_EN.pdf

European Union Monitor. (2016). *COM(2016)381 – Communication. New skills agenda for Europe: working together to strengthen Human Capital, Employability and Competitiveness.* Retrieved from https://www.eumonitor.eu/9353000/1/j9vvik7m1c3gyxp/vk4y6fuvz9um

Fahrenkrog, S. L., Haeck, W., Abrams, F., & Whelbourn, D. (2003). PMI's organizational project management maturity model. *Proceedings of PMI Global Congress 2003.*

FalkA.KosfeldM. (2004). *Distrust - The Hidden Cost of Control.* CEPR Discussion Paper No.4512. https://ssrn.com/abstract=590102

Fama, E. F. (1980). Agency problems and the theory of the firm. *Journal of Political Economy*, *88*(2), 288–307. doi:10.1086/260866

Farrokh, J., & Mansur, A. (2013). Project Management Maturity Models and Organisational Project Management Maturity Model (OPM3®): A Critical Morphological Evaluation. *International Scholarly and Scientific Research & Innovation, 7*(5).

Federal Reserve Bank of Saint Louis. (2015). *What Causes a Country's Standard of Living to Rise?* Available online: https://www.stlouisfed.org/on-the-economy/2015/december/what-causes-countrys-standard-living-rise

Federal Statistical Office. (2022). *Quality of Life Indicators.* Available online: https://www.bfs.admin.ch/bfs/en/home/statistics/cross-sectional-topics/city-statistics/indicators-quality-life.html

Fiorillo, P., Meles, A., Mustilli, M., & Salerno, D. (2022). How does the financial market influence firms' Green innovation? The role of equity analysts. *Journal of International Financial Management & Accounting*, *33*(3), 428–458. doi:10.1111/jifm.12152

Fleurbaey, M., & Gaulier, G. (2009). International Comparisons of Living Standards by Equivalent Incomes. *The Scandinavian Journal of Economics*, *111*(3), 597–624. doi:10.1111/j.1467-9442.2009.01578.x

Flores, S. (2018). What is sustainability in the wine world? A cross-country analysis of wine sustainability frameworks. *Journal of Cleaner Production*, *172*, 2301–2312. doi:10.1016/j.jclepro.2017.11.181

Foote, D. (2022). ESG reporting: Seven steps to get started. *Our Insights | Plante Moran*. https://www.plantemoran.com/explore-our-thinking/insight/2021/10/esg-reporting-seven-steps-to-get-started

Fornell, C., & Larcker, D. (1981). Evaluating structural equation models with unobservable variables and measurement error. *JMR, Journal of Marketing Research*, *18*(1), 39–50. doi:10.1177/002224378101800104

Forsberg, K., Mooz, H., & Cotterman, H. (2000). *Visualizing project management*. John Wiley & Sons, Inc.

Forsyth, T. (1997). Environmental responsibility and business regulation: The case of sustainable tourism. *The Geographical Journal*, *163*(3), 270–280. doi:10.2307/3059723

Francová, O., Korhonen, K., & Kovačević, D. (2022). *How programme evaluations can benefit from quality of life considerations*. European Stability Mechanism.

Franzl, G., Wanzenböck, C., & Berger, A. (2023). Interoperability as a key factor for digitalisation — A success story for cross-sector knowledge transfer. *E&I Elektrotechnik und Informationstechnik*, *140*(5), 471–477. doi:10.100700502-023-01143-3

Freeman, C. (2008). *Systems of Innovation Selected Essays in Evolutionary Economics*. Edward Elgar Publishing. doi:10.4337/9781035306176

Freeman, R. E. (1999). Divergent stakeholder theory. *Academy of Management Review*, *24*(2), 233–236.

Freeman, R. E., & Phillips, R. A. (2002). Stakeholder theory: A libertarian defense. *Business Ethics Quarterly*, *12*(3), 331–349. doi:10.2307/3858020

Freeman, R., & Velamuri, S. (2021). A New Approach to CSR. *Company Stakeholder Responsibility*, *1*, 203–213.

Frey, M., Melis, M., & Vagnoni, E. (2008). Recent developments in social and environmental reporting among Italian Universities: A critical evaluation of leading edge practices. *2nd Italian Conference on Social and Environmental Accounting*, 17-19.

Friesenbichler, K., & Reinstaller, A. (2022). Do firms facing competitors from emerging markets behave differently? Evidence from Austrian manufacturing firms. *European Business Review*, *34*(2), 153–170. doi:10.1108/EBR-09-2020-0216

Frigon, A., Doloreux, D., & Shearmur, R. (2020). Drivers of eco-innovation and conventional innovation in the Canadian wine industry. *Journal of Cleaner Production*, *275*, 124115. doi:10.1016/j.jclepro.2020.124115

Galati, A., Crescimanno, M., Tinervia, S., & Siggia, D. (2016). Website quality and internal business factors: An empirical investigation in the Italian wine industry. *International Journal of Wine Business Research*, *28*(4), 308–326. doi:10.1108/IJWBR-08-2015-0026

Gallego-Álvarez, I., Prado-Lorenzo, J., & García-Sánchez, I. (2011). Corporate social responsibility and innovation: A resource-based theory. *Management Decision*, *49*(10), 1709–1727. doi:10.1108/00251741111183843

Gallego-Álvarez, I., & Villardón, J. L. V. (2012c). Analysis of environmental indicators in international companies by applying the logistic biplot. *Ecological Indicators*, *23*, 250–261. doi:10.1016/j.ecolind.2012.03.024

Ganguly, A., Talukdar, A., & Chatterjee, D. (2019). Evaluating the role of social capital, tacit knowledge sharing, knowledge quality and reciprocity in determining innovation capability of an organization. *Journal of Knowledge Management*, *23*(6), 1105–1135. doi:10.1108/JKM-03-2018-0190

García, J., & Pardo, T. (2005). E-government success factors: Mapping practical tools to theoretical foundations. Government, IT implementation, Information Technology, Relevance, Success factors. *Government Information Quarterly*, *22*(2), 187–216. doi:10.1016/j.giq.2005.02.001

Ghasemzadeh, P., Nazari, J., Farzaneh, M., & Mehralian, G. (2019). Moderating role of innovation culture in the relationship between organizational learning and innovation performance. *The Learning Organization*, *26*(3), 289–303. doi:10.1108/TLO-08-2018-0139

Gholami, A., Sands, J., & Shams, S. (2022). *Corporates' sustainability disclosures impact on cost of capital and idiosyncratic risk.* Meditari Accountancy Research., doi:10.1108/MEDAR-06-2020-0926

Giacomarra, M., Shams, S., Crescimanno, M., Sakka, G., Gregori, G., & Galati, A. (2021). Internal vs. external R&D teams: Evidences from the Italian wine industry. *Journal of Business Research*, *128*, 752–761. doi:10.1016/j.jbusres.2019.05.029

Giannetti, M., Jasova, M., Loumioti, M., & Mendicino, C. (2023). *"Glossy Green" Banks: The Disconnect Between Environmental Disclosures and Lending Activities*. Academic Press.

Glynne, P. (2007). *Benefits Management-changing the focus of delivery*. Association for Progress Management.

Godinho, M. (2013). Inovação em Portugal. Lisboa: Fundação Francisco Manuel dos Santos.

Gomes, J. (2011). *Gestão de benefícios numa empresa de Geoengenharia* [Master thesis]. ISCTE.

Gomes, J., & Romão, M. (2015). Achieving project success through alignment with organisational strategy: Balanced Scorecard approach. *Proceedings of the 8th IADIS International Conference - Information's Systems 2015.*

Gomes, J., & Romão, M. (2014). Advantages and Limitations of Performance Measurement Tools: The Balanced Scorecard. *Proceedings of the 7th IADIS International Conference*, 19-26.

Gomes, J., & Romão, M. (2015). Enhancing Organisational Maturity with Benefits Management. *International Journal of Information Technology Project Management*, *6*(4), 34–47. doi:10.4018/IJITPM.2015100103

Gomes, J., & Romão, M. (2015). Maturity, Benefits and Project Management shaping Project Success. In *the series Advances in Intelligent Systems and Computing* (Vol. 353, pp. 435–448). New Contributions in Information Systems and Technologies. doi:10.1007/978-3-319-16486-1_43

Gomes, J., & Romão, M. (2016). Improving project success: A case study using benefits and project management. *Procedia Computer Science*, *100*, 489–497. doi:10.1016/j.procs.2016.09.187

Góngora-Salazar, P., Casabianca, M. S., & Rodríguez-Lesmes, P. (2022). Income inequality and self-rated health status in Colombia. *International Journal for Equity in Health*, *21*(1), 69. doi:10.118612939-022-01659-8 PMID:35578287

Gopinath, G. (2023). *The Power and Perils of the "Artificial Hand": Considering AI Through the Ideas of Adam Smith Speech to commemorate 300th anniversary of Adam Smith's birth University of Glasgow.* International Monetary Fund. Retrieved from https://www.imf.org/en/News/Articles/2023/06/05/sp060523-fdmd-ai-adamsmith?cid=em-COM-123-46688

Government Finance Officers Association (GFOA) of the United States and Canada. (2023). *Best Practices. "ESG" Best Practice - "G" Governance.* https://www.gfoa.org/materials/esg-best-practice-g-governance

Government, A. C. T. (2022). *ACT Wellbeing Framework. Having the Financial Resources to Live Life Well.* Available online: https://www.act.gov.au/wellbeing/explore-overall-wellbeing/living-standards

Grant, R. M. (1996). Toward a knowledge-based theory of the firm. *Strategic Management Journal*, *17*, 109–122.

Grant, K. P., & Pennypacker, J. S. (2006). Project Management Maturity: An assessment of Project Management Capabilities among and between Selected Industries. *IEEE Transactions on Engineering Management*, *53*(1), 59–68. doi:10.1109/TEM.2005.861802

Grant, R. (1996). Toward a knowledge-based theory of the firm. *Strategic Management Journal*, *17*(2), 109–122. doi:10.1002mj.4250171110

Grant, R. M. (1991). A resource-based theory of competitive advantage: Implications for strategy formulation. *California Management Review*, *33*(3), 114–135. doi:10.2307/41166664

GRI - GRI and SASB reporting 'complement each other .' (n.d.). https://www.globalreporting.org/news/news-center/gri-and-sasb-reporting-complement-each-other/

Guan, X., Ahmad, N., Sial, M., Cherian, J., & Han, H. (2022). CSR and organizational performance: The role of pro-environmental behavior and personal values. *Corporate Social Responsibility and Environmental Management*, *2022*, 1–18.

Guerola-Navarro, V., Oltra-Badenes, R., Gil-Gomez, H., & Fernández, A. (2021). Customer relationship management (CRM) and Innovation: A qualitative comparative analysis (QCA) in the search for improvements on the firm performance in winery sector. *Technological Forecasting and Social Change*, *169*, 120838. doi:10.1016/j.techfore.2021.120838

Guerrero-Villegas, J., Sierra-García, L., & Palacios-Florencio, B. (2018). The role of sustainable development and innovation on firm performance. *Corporate Social Responsibility and Environmental Management*, *25*(6), 1350–1362. doi:10.1002/csr.1644

Gunduz, M., & Almuajebh, M. (2020). Critical Success Factors for Sustainable Construction Project Management. *Sustainability (Basel)*, *12*(5), 1990. doi:10.3390u12051990

Gu, Y., Ho, K. C., Yan, C., & Gozgor, G. (2021). Public environmental concern, CEO turnover, and green investment: Evidence from a quasi-natural experiment in China. *Energy Economics*, *100*(105379), 100. doi:10.1016/j.eneco.2021.105379

Hadj, T. (2020). Effects of corporate social responsibility towards stakeholders and environmental management on responsible innovation and competitiveness. *Journal of Cleaner Production*, *250*, 119490. doi:10.1016/j.jclepro.2019.119490

Hair, Hult, Ringle, Sarstedt, Danks, & Ray. (2021). *Partial least squares structural equation modeling (PLS-SEM) using R: A workbook.* Springer.

Hair, J., Hult, G., Ringle, C., & Sarstedt, M. (2016). *A primer on partial least squares structural equation modeling (PLS-SEM).* Sage publications.

Hair, J., Sarstedt, M., & Ringle, C. (2019). Rethinking some of the rethinking of partial least squares. *European Journal of Marketing*, *53*(4), 566–584. doi:10.1108/EJM-10-2018-0665

Halkos, G., & Skouloudis, A. (2018). Corporate social responsibility and innovative capacity: Intersection in a macro-level perspective. *Journal of Cleaner Production*, *182*, 291–300. doi:10.1016/j.jclepro.2018.02.022

Hanelt, A., Bohnsack, R., Marz, D., & Marante, C. (2020). A Systematic Review of the Literature on Digital Transformation: Insights and Implications for Strategy and Organizational Change. *Journal of Management Studies*. Advance online publication. doi:10.1111/joms.12639

Hart, S., & Dowell, G. (2011). A natural-resource-based view of the firm: Fifteen years after. *Journal of Management*, *37*(5), 1464–1479. doi:10.1177/0149206310390219

Hellered, C. (2010). *Benchmarking project management maturity in two organisations: A case study focusing on the value of having an established project management model in an organization* [Master of Science Thesis]. Chalmers University of Technology, Göteborg, Sweden.

Henderson, R., & Cockburn, I. (1994). Measuring competence? Exploring firm effects in pharmaceutical research. *Strategic Management Journal*, *15*, 63–84.

Henfridsson, O., & Yoo, Y. (2013). The Liminality of Trajectory Shifts in Institutional Entrepreneurship. *Organization Science*. Advance online publication. doi:10.1287/orsc.2013.0883

Henseler, J., Hubona, G., & Ray, P. (2016). Using PLS path modeling in new technology research: Updated guidelines. *Industrial Management & Data Systems*, *116*(1), 2–20. doi:10.1108/IMDS-09-2015-0382

HeX.XuZ.ShiJ. (2023). The Impact of Air Pollution Levels on Chinese Green Bond Market during COVID-19: A Green Preference Perspective. SSRN (4329551). doi:10.2139/ssrn.4329551

Hill, C. W., & Jones, T. M. (1992). Stakeholder-agency theory. *Journal of Management Studies*, *29*(2), 131–154. doi:10.1111/j.1467-6486.1992.tb00657.x

Hillson, D. (2001). Benchmarking Organizational Project Management Capability. *Proceedings of the Project Management Institute Annual Seminars & Symposium.*

Hillson, D. (2003). Assessing Organisational Project Management Capability. *Journal of Facilities Management*, *2*(3), 298–311. doi:10.1108/14725960410808276

Hodgson, D. (2004). Project work: The legacy of bureaucratic control in the post-bureaucratic organization. *Organization*, *11*(1), 81–100. doi:10.1177/1350508404039659

Hofer, C. W., & Schendel, D. (1978). *Strategy Formulation: Analytical Concepts*. West Publishing Company.

Hospido, L., Sanz, C., & Villanueva, E. (2023). Air pollution: a review of its economic effects and policies to mitigate them. *Banco de Espana Occasionally Paper*(2301).

Hsu, Y., & Fang, W. (2009). Intellectual capital and new product development performance: The mediating role of organizational learning capability. *Technological Forecasting and Social Change*, *76*(5), 664–677. doi:10.1016/j.techfore.2008.03.012

Huang, Z. S., Shen, Y., Li, J., Fey, M., & Brecher, C. (2021). A survey on AI-driven digital twins in industry 4.0: Smart manufacturing and advanced robotics. *Sensors (Basel)*, *6340*(19), 6340. Advance online publication. doi:10.339021196340 PMID:34640660

Hudson, M., Smart, A., & Bourne, M. (2001). Theory and Practice in SME Performance Measurement Systems. *International Journal of Operations & Production Management*, *21*(8), 1096–1115. doi:10.1108/EUM0000000005587

Hu, L., & Bentler, P. (1998). Fit indices in covariance structure modeling: Sensitivity to underparameterized model misspecification. *Psychological Methods*, *3*(4), 424–453. doi:10.1037/1082-989X.3.4.424

Humlum, A. (2020). *Robot Adoption and Labor Market Dynamics*. Working paper, University of Chicago.

Hussain, N., Rigoni, U., & Cavezzali, E. (2018). Does it pay to be sustainable? Looking inside the black box of the relationship between sustainability performance and financial performance. *Corporate Social Responsibility and Environmental Management*, *25*(6), 1198–1211. doi:10.1002/csr.1631

Iannacci, F., Seepma, A., Blok, C., & Resca, A. (2019). Reappraising maturity models in e-Government research: The trajectory-turning point theory. *The Journal of Strategic Information Systems*, *28*(3), 310–329. Advance online publication. doi:10.1016/j.jsis.2019.02.001

Iansiti, M., & Levien, R. (2004). *The keystone advantage: what the new dynamics of business ecosystems mean for strategy, innovation, and sustainability*. Harvard Business School Press.

Ibbs, C. W., & Reginato, J. M. (2002). Quantifying the value of Project Management. Project Management Institute, Inc.

Ibbs, C. W., Reginato, J. M., & Kwak, Y. H. (2003). Developing project management capability – Benchmarking, Maturity, Modeling, Gap Analyses, ROI studies. The Wiley Managing Projects Resources Book, John Wiley.

Ibbs, C. W., & Kwak, Y. H. (2000). Assessing project management maturity. *Project Management Journal*, *31*(1), 32–43. doi:10.1177/875697280003100106

IFRS - International Sustainability Standards Board. (n.d.). https://www.ifrs.org/groups/international-sustainability-standards-board/

Ika, L. A. (2009). Project success as a topic in project management journals. *Project Management Journal*, *40*(4), 6–19. doi:10.1002/pmj.20137

Inampudi, K., & Macpherson, M. (2020). The Impact of AI on Environmental, Social and Governance (ESG) Investing. *The Impact of AI on Environmental, Social and Governance (ESG) Investing*, *129–131*. Advance online publication. doi:10.1002/9781119551966.ch35

Ingason, H., & Jónasson, H. (2009). Contemporary Knowledge and Skill Requirements in Project Management. *Project Management Journal*, *40*(2), 59–69. doi:10.1002/pmj.20122

International Development Association (IDA). (2023a). *Governance and Institutions*. https://ida.worldbank.org/en/topics/cross-cutting/governance-and-institutions

International Development Association (IDA). (2023b). *IDA19 Results Measurement System*. https://ida.worldbank.org/en/rms

International Monetary Fund (IMF). (2023). *IMF and Good Governance. Why is good governance important?* https://www.imf.org/en/About/Factsheets/Sheets/2023/The-IMF-and-Good-Governance

Iranmanesh, M., Zailani, S., Hyun, S., Ali, M., & Kim, K. (2019). Impact of lean manufacturing practices on firms' sustainable performance: Lean culture as a moderator. *Sustainability (Basel)*, *11*(4), 1112. doi:10.3390u11041112

Irvin, R. A., & Michaels, E. G. (1989). Core skills: Doing the right things right. *The McKinsey Quarterly*, (Summer), 4–19.

Isensee, C., Teuteberg, F., Griese, K., & Topi, C. (2020). The relationship between organizational culture, sustainability, and digitalization in SMEs: A systematic review. *Journal of Cleaner Production*, *275*, 122944. doi:10.1016/j.jclepro.2020.122944

Ittner, C. D., & Larcker, D. F. (2003). Coming up short on nonfinancial performance measurement. *Harvard Business Review*, *81*(11), 88–95. PMID:14619154

Jachimowicz, V. A. (2003). Project management maturity model. *Project Management Journal*, *34*(1), 55–56. doi:10.1177/875697280303400108

Jain, P., Vyas, V., & Chalasani, D. P. S. (2016). Corporate Social Responsibility and Financial Performance in SMEs: A Structural Equation Modelling Approach. *Global Business Review*, *17*(3), 630–653. doi:10.1177/0972150916630827

JainY.GuptaS.YalcinerS.JoglekarY. N.KhetanP.ZhangT. (2023). Overcoming complexity in ESG Investing: The role of Generative AI integration in identifying contextual ESG factors. *Social Science Research Network*. doi:10.2139/ssrn.4495647

Janowski, T. (2015). Digital government evolution: From transformation to contextualization. *Government Information Quarterly*, *32*(3), 221–236. doi:10.1016/j.giq.2015.07.001

Jansen, J., Van Den Bosch, F., & Volberda, H. (2006). Exploratory innovation, exploitative innovation, and performance: Effects of organizational antecedents and environmental moderators. *Management Science*, *52*(11), 1661–1674. doi:10.1287/mnsc.1060.0576

Jardon, C., & Dasilva, A. (2017). Intellectual capital and environmental concern in subsistence small businesses. *Management of Environmental Quality*, *28*(2), 214–230. doi:10.1108/MEQ-05-2015-0085

Jensen, C., Cline, O., & Owen, M. (2011). *Combining Business Process Management and Enterprise Architecture for Better Business Outcomes* (1st ed.). IBM Redbooks.

Jia, G., Chen, Y., Xue, X., Chen, J., Cao, J., & Tang, K. (2011). Program management organisation maturity integrated model for mega construction programs in China. *International Journal of Project Management*, *29*(7), 834–845. doi:10.1016/j.ijproman.2011.03.003

Jilani, M., Fan, L., Islam, M., & Uddin, A. (2020). The influence of knowledge sharing on sustainable performance: A moderated mediation study. *Sustainability (Basel), 12*(3), 908. doi:10.3390u12030908

Ji, Q., & Zhang, D. (2019). How much does financial development contribute to renewable energy growth and upgrading of energy structure in China? *Energy Policy, 128*, 114–124. doi:10.1016/j.enpol.2018.12.047

Jones, B., & Baumgartner, F. (2012). From There to Here: Punctuated Equilibrium to the General Punctuation Thesis to a Theory of Government Information Processing. *The Policy Studies Journal, 40*(1).

Joseph Rowntree Foundation. (2019). *What's the best way to improve living standards?* Available online: https://www.jrf.org.uk/blog/whats-best-way-improve-living-standards

Jugdev, K., & Thomas, J. (2002). Project management maturity models: The silver bullets of competitive advantage? *Project Management Journal, 33*(4), 4–14. doi:10.1177/875697280203300402

Jung, J. Y., & Wang, Y. J. (2006). Relationship between total quality management (TQM) and continuous improvement of international project management (CIIPM). *Technovation, 16*(5-6), 716–722. doi:10.1016/j.technovation.2006.01.003

K, A., & Shanthi, V. (2020). Artificial Intelligence – A Driving way for Sustainable Organizational Growth. *ResearchGate*. https://www.researchgate.net/publication/344522304_Artificial_Intelligence_-_A_Driving_way_for_Sustainable_Organizational_Growth

Kakwani, N. (1993). Performance in living standards: An international comparison. *Journal of Development Economics, 41*(2), 307–336. doi:10.1016/0304-3878(93)90061-Q

Kalantjakos, N. J. (2001). Assessing Organizational Project Management Maturity. *Proceedings of Project Management Institute Annual Seminars & Symposium 2001*.

Kaplan, R. S., & Norton, D. P. (1992). The Balanced Scorecard: Measures that drive performance. *Harvard Business Review, 70*(1), 71–79. PMID:10119714

Kaplan, R. S., & Norton, D. P. (2000). *The Strategy-Focused Organization: How Balanced Scorecard companies thrive in the new business environment*. Harvard Business School Press.

Kaplan, R. S., & Norton, D. P. (2004, February). Measuring the Strategic Readiness of Intangible Assets. *Harvard Business Review*. PMID:14971269

Kariyapperuma, N., & Collins, E. (2021). Family logics and environmental sustainability: A study of the New Zealand wine industry. *Business Strategy and the Environment, 30*(8), 3626–3650. doi:10.1002/bse.2823

Katila, R., & Ahuja, G. (2002). Something old, something new: A longitudinal study of search behavior and new product introduction. *Academy of Management Journal, 45*(6), 1183–1194. doi:10.2307/3069433

Kerzner, H. (2001). *Applied Project Management: Best Practices on Implementation*. John Wiley and Sons, Inc.

Kerzner, H. (2013). *Project Management: a systems approach to planning, scheduling and controlling* (11th ed.). John Wiley and Sons.

Kesidou, E., & Demirel, P. (2012). On the drivers of eco-innovations: Empirical evidence from the UK. *Research Policy*, *41*(5), 862–870. doi:10.1016/j.respol.2012.01.005

Khan, S., Yu, Z., & Umar, M. (2021). How environmental awareness and corporate social responsibility practices benefit the enterprise? An empirical study in the context of emerging economy. *Management of Environmental Quality*, *32*(5), 863–885. doi:10.1108/MEQ-08-2020-0178

Kiefer, C., Del Rio Gonzalez, P., & Carrillo-Hermosilla, J. (2019). Drivers and barriers of eco-innovation types for sustainable transitions: A quantitative perspective. *Business Strategy and the Environment*, *28*(1), 155–172. doi:10.1002/bse.2246

Kiel, G. C., Nicholson, G. J., & Kiel, G. C. (2007). Can directors impact performance? A case based test of three theories of corporate governance. *Corporate Governance*, *15*(4), 585–609. doi:10.1111/j.1467-8683.2007.00590.x

Kim, D., & Grant, G. (2010). E-government maturity model using the capability maturity model. *Journal of Systems and Information Technology*, *12*(3), 230–244. doi:10.1108/13287261011070858

Kitsios, F., & Kamariotou, M. (2021). Artificial Intelligence and Business Strategy towards Digital Transformation: A Research Agenda. *Sustainability (Basel)*, *13*(4), 2025. doi:10.3390u13042025

Kline, R. (2011). *Principles and practice of structural equation modelling*. Guilford Press.

Kocmanová, A., Hřebíček, J., & Dočekalová, M. (2011). Corporate governance and sustainability. *Economics & Management, 16*.

Kohli, R., & Johnson, S. (2011). Digital Transformation in Latecomer Industries: CIO and CEO Leadership Lessons from Encana Oil & Gas (USA) Inc. *MIS Quarterly Executive*, *10*(4), 141–156.

Köhr, C., Corsi, A., Capitello, R., & Szolnoki, G. (2019). Family culture and organisational systems as antecedents of market orientation and performance among family wineries. *International Journal of Wine Business Research*, *31*(2), 180–202. doi:10.1108/IJWBR-09-2017-0054

Kotsantonis, S., & Serafeim, G. (2019). Four Things No One Will Tell You About ESG Data. *The Bank of America Journal of Applied Corporate Finance*, *31*(2), 50–58. doi:10.1111/jacf.12346

Kraus, S., Rehman, S., & García, F. (2020). *Corporate social responsibility and environmental performance: The mediating role of environmental strategy and green innovation*. Academic Press.

Kronbichel, S. A., Ostermann, H., & Staudinger, R. (2009). A review of critical success factors for ERP-projects. *The Open Information Systems Journal*, *3*(1), 14–25. doi:10.2174/1874133900903010014

Kuhn, T. (1962). *The structure of scientific revolutions*. University of Chicago Press.

Kushwaha, A. K., & Kar, A. K. (2021). *MarkBot – A Language Model-Driven Chatbot for Interactive Marketing in Post-Modern World*. Information Systems Frontiers. . doi:10.1007/s10796-021-10184-y

Kwak, Y. H., & Ibbs, C. W. (2000). The Berkley Project Management Process Maturity Model: Measuring the Value of Project Management. *Proceedings of the 2000 IEEE Engineering Management Society*.

Laureti, L., Costantiello, A., & Leogrande, A. (2022). *The Role of Renewable Energy Consumption in Promoting Sustainability and Circular Economy. A Data-Driven Analys*. Academic Press.

Lee, C., Wu, C., & Jong, D. (2022). Understanding the Impact of Competitive Advantage and Core Competency on Regional Tourism Revitalization: Empirical Evidence in Taiwan. *Frontiers in Psychology*, *20*(13), 922211. doi:10.3389/fpsyg.2022.922211 PMID:35668969

Lee, O., Joo, H., Choi, H., & Cheon, M. (2022). Proposing an integrated approach to analyzing ESG data via machine learning and deep learning algorithms. *Sustainability (Basel)*, *14*(14), 8745. doi:10.3390u14148745

Lee, S., Kim, B., & Kim, H. (2012). An integrated view of knowledge management for performance. *Journal of Knowledge Management*, *16*(2), 183–203. doi:10.1108/13673271211218807

LeograndeA.CostantielloA. (2023). The Labor Force Participation Rate in the Context of ESG Models at World Level. SSRN (4466452). doi:10.2139/ssrn.4466452

Levin, G., & Skulmoski, G. (2000). The project management maturity. *ESI Horizons*, *2*(3), 1–7.

Levy, D. H. F., & Murnane, R. J. (2003). The Skill Content of Recent Technological Change: An Empirical Exploration. *The Quarterly Journal of Economics*, *118*(4), 1279–1333. doi:10.1162/003355303322552801

Li, Y. (2014). Environmental innovation practices and performance: Moderating effect of resource commitment. *Journal of Cleaner Production*, *66*, 450–458.

Lim, M., Tseng, M., Tan, K., & Bui, T. (2017). Knowledge management in sustainable supply chain management: Improving performance through an interpretive structural modelling approach. *Journal of Cleaner Production*, *162*, 806–816. doi:10.1016/j.jclepro.2017.06.056

Lindkvist, L., & Saric, O. (2020). *Sustainability Performance and Capital Structure: An analysis of the relationship between ESG rating and debt ratio*. Academic Press.

Liu, J., Li, X., & Wang, S. (2020). What have we learnt from 10 years of fintech research? a scientometric analysis. *Technological Forecasting and Social Change*, *155*, 120022. doi:10.1016/j.techfore.2020.120022

Liu, M. L., Luo, X., & Lu, W.-Z. (2023). Public perceptions of environmental, social, and governance (ESG) based on social media data: Evidence from China. *Journal of Cleaner Production*, 135840. Advance online publication. doi:10.1016/j.jclepro.2022.135840

Living Standard. (2022). *A New Living Standard.* Available online: https://livingstandard.org/about/

Lokman, A. S., & Ameedeen, M. A. (2018). Modern chatbot systems: A technical review. In *Proceedings of the Future Technologies Conference* (pp. 1012–1023). Springer. 10.1007/978-3-030-02683-7_75

Luo, X., & Du, S. (2015). Exploring the relationship between corporate social responsibility and firm innovation. *Marketing Letters*, *26*(4), 703–714. doi:10.100711002-014-9302-5

Lu, P., Hamori, S., & Tian, S. (2023). Can ESG investments and new environmental law improve social happiness in China? *Frontiers in Environmental Science*, *11*(1089486), 1089486. doi:10.3389/fenvs.2023.1089486

Luque González, A., Guamán, L. K., & Popescu, C. R. G. (2022a). Market Economy and Good Living: Obstacles to Its Achievement in Orellana, Ecuador. In C. Popescu (Ed.), *Frameworks for Sustainable Development Goals to Manage Economic, Social, and Environmental Shocks and Disasters* (pp. 35–56). IGI Global. doi:10.4018/978-1-6684-6750-3.ch003

Luque González, A., Soledispa Ibarra, R. E., & Popescu, C. R. G. (2022b). Analysis of Labor Reform During COVID-19: The Case of Ecuador. In C. Popescu (Ed.), *Handbook of Research on SDGs for Economic Development, Social Development, and Environmental Protection* (pp. 1–25). IGI Global. doi:10.4018/978-1-6684-5113-7.ch001

Madhoushi, M., Sadati, A., Delavari, H., Mehdivand, M., & Mihandost, R. (2011). Entrepreneurial orientation and innovation performance: The mediating role of knowledge management. *Asian Journal of Business Management*, *3*(4), 310–316.

Maghssudipour, A., Lazzeretti, L., & Capone, F. (2020). The role of multiple ties in knowledge networks: Complementarity in the Montefalco wine cluster. *Industrial Marketing Management*, *90*, 667–678. doi:10.1016/j.indmarman.2020.03.021

Mahoney, J. T., & Pandian, J. R. (1992). The resource-based view within the conversation of strategic management. *Strategic Management Journal*, *13*(5), 363–380. doi:10.1002mj.4250130505

Majumder, A., & Chakravarty, S. R. (1996). Achievement and improvement in living standards—An empirical analysis. *Social Indicators Research*, *37*(3), 269–280. doi:10.1007/BF00286234

Malik, M. S., & Makhdoom, D. D. (2016). Does corporate governance beget firm performance in fortune global 500 companies? *Corporate Governance (Bradford)*, *16*(4), 747–764. doi:10.1108/CG-12-2015-0156

Maltz, A. C., Shenhar, A. J., & Reilly, R. R. (2003). Beyond the Balanced Scorecard: Refining the Search for Organizational Success Measures. *Long Range Planning*, *36*(April), 187–204. doi:10.1016/S0024-6301(02)00165-6

Ma, N., Cheong, T. S., & Li, J. (2022). Evaluating Global Inequality Using Decomposition Approach. *Front Psychol.* 12:809670. *Frontiers in Psychology*, *2022*(Jan), 26. doi:10.3389/fpsyg.2021.809670 PMID:35153930

Mansour, M., Al Amosh, H., Alodat, A. Y., Khatib, S. F. A., & Saleh, M. W. A. (2022). The Relationship between Corporate Governance Quality and Firm Performance: The Moderating Role of Capital Structure. *Sustainability, 14*(17), 10525. doi:10.3390/su141710525

Marco-Lajara, B., Zaragoza-Sáez, P., Martínez-Falcó, J., & Sánchez-García, E. 2022c. Green Intellectual Capital in the Spanish Wine Industry. In Innovative Economic, Social, and Environmental Practices for Progressing Future Sustainability (pp. 102-120). IGI Global. doi:10.4018/978-1-7998-9590-9.ch006

Marco-Lajara, B., Seva-Larrosa, P., Martínez-Falcó, J., & García-Lillo, F. (2022d). Wine clusters and Protected Designations of Origin (PDOs) in Spain: An exploratory analysis. *Journal of Wine Research*, *33*(3), 146–167. doi:10.1080/09571264.2022.2110051

Marco-Lajara, B., Zaragoza-Sáez, P., Martínez-Falcó, J., & Ruiz-Fernández, L. (2022b). The Effect of Green Intellectual Capital on Green Performance in the Spanish Wine Industry: A Structural Equation Modeling Approach. *Complexity*, *2022*, 1–17. doi:10.1155/2022/6024077

Marco-Lajara, B., Zaragoza-Sáez, P., Martínez-Falcó, J., & Sánchez-García, E. (2022a). *Does green intellectual capital affect green innovation performance? Evidence from the Spanish wine industry. British Food Journal.*

Margarita, I. (2008). The Balanced Scorecard Method, From Theory to Practice. *Intellectual Economics.*, *1*(3), 18–28.

Margariti, V., Stamati, T., Anagnostopoulos, D., Nikolaidou, M., & Papastilianou, A. (2022). A holistic model for assessing organizational interoperability in public administration. *Government Information Quarterly*, *39*(3), 101712. Advance online publication. doi:10.1016/j.giq.2022.101712

Marín, F. M. (2023). *De las humanidades digitales a la Inteligencia Artificial General.* University of Texas at San Antonio.

Marin, G., & Lotti, F. (2017). Productivity effects of eco-innovations using data on eco-patents. *Industrial and Corporate Change*, *26*(1), 125–148. doi:10.1093/icc/dtw014

Marr, B., & Adams, C. (2004). The balanced scorecard and intangible assets: Similar idea, unaligned concepts. *Measuring Business Excellence*, *8*(3), 18–27. doi:10.1108/13683040410555582

Martínez-Falcó, J., Marco-Lajara, B., Zaragoza-Sáez, P. D. C., & Millan-Tudela, L. A. (2023). Do circular economy practices moderate the wine tourism–green performance relationship? A structural analysis applied to the Spanish wine industry. *British Food Journal.* Advance online publication. doi:10.1108/BFJ-10-2022-0833

Martins, V., Rampasso, I., Anholon, R., Quelhas, O., & Leal Filho, W. (2019). Knowledge management in the context of sustainability: Literature review and opportunities for future research. *Journal of Cleaner Production*, *229*, 489–500. doi:10.1016/j.jclepro.2019.04.354

Matassa, P. (2006). Grow up already! An OPM3® primer. *Proceedings of PMI Global Congress 2006*.

Matt, C., Hess, T., & Benlian, A. (2015). Digital Transformation Strategies. *Business & Information Systems Engineering*, *57*(5), 339–343. doi:10.100712599-015-0401-5

McBride, R., Dastan, A., & Mehrabinia, P. (2022). How AI affects the future relationship between corporate governance and financial markets: A note on impact capitalism. *Managerial Finance*, *48*(8), 1240–1249. doi:10.1108/MF-12-2021-0586

McLeod, L., Doolin, B., & MacDonell, S. G. (2012). A perspective-based understanding of project success. *Project Management Journal*, *43*(5), 68–86. doi:10.1002/pmj.21290

Melinda, A., & Wardhani, R. (2020). The Effect of Environmental, Social, Governance, and Controversies on Firms' Value: Evidence from Asia. In W. A. Barnett & B. S. Sergi (Eds.), *International Symposia in Economic Theory and Econometrics* (pp. 147–173). Emerald Publishing Limited. doi:10.1108/S1571-038620200000027011

Mergel, I., Edelmann, N., & Haug, N. (2019). Defining digital transformation: Results from expert interviews. *Government Information Quarterly*, *36*(4), 101385. doi:10.1016/j.giq.2019.06.002

Ministry of Social Development. (2022a). *Direct Measurement of Living Standards: The New Zealand ELSI Scale*. Available online: https://www.msd.govt.nz/about-msd-and-our-work/publications-resources/monitoring/living-standards/living-standards-elsi.html

Ministry of Social Development. (2022b). *Living Standards Research*. Available online: https://www.msd.govt.nz/about-msd-and-our-work/publications-resources/monitoring/living-standards/index.html

Ministry of Social Development. (2022c). *Household Incomes in New Zealand: trends in indicators of inequality and hardship 1982 to 2020*. Available online: https://www.msd.govt.nz/about-msd-and-our-work/publications-resources/monitoring/household-incomes/index.html

Minkkinen, M., Niukkanen, A., & Mäntymäki, M. (2022). What about investors? ESG analyses as tools for ethics-based AI auditing. *AI & Society*. Advance online publication. doi:10.100700146-022-01415-0

Miranda, B., Ross, B., Franken, J., & Gómez, M. (2022). Plural forms and differentiation strategies in the agri-food sector: Evidence from the US wine industry. *Agribusiness*, *38*(3), 486–504. doi:10.1002/agr.21741

Mishel, L., & Bivens, J. (2021). The Productivity-Median Compensation Gap in the United States: The Contribution of Increased Wage Inequality and the Role of Policy Choices. *International Productivity Monitor*, (41), 61. https://link.gale.com/apps/doc/A689169156/AONE?u=anon~10ba8f08&sid=googleScholar&xid=5119dfa8

Mitchell, A. (2023). ChatGPT could make these jobs obsolete: 'The wolf is at the door.' *New York Post*. Retrieved from https://nypost.com/2023/01/25/chat-gpt-could-make-these-jobs-obsolete/

Montagna, J. (2005). A framework for the assessment and analysis of electronic government proposals. *Electronic Commerce Research and Applications*, *4*(3), 204–219. doi:10.1016/j.elerap.2005.01.003

Moodaley, W., & Telukdarie, A. (2023). Greenwashing, Sustainability Reporting, and Artificial Intelligence: A Systematic Literature review. *Sustainability (Basel)*, *15*(2), 1481. doi:10.3390u15021481

Mooraj, S., Oyon, D., & Hostettler, D. (1999). The Balanced Scorecard: A Necessary Good or an Unnecessary Evil? *European Management Journal*, *17*(5), 481–491. doi:10.1016/S0263-2373(99)00034-1

Mouna, A., Nedra, B., & Khaireddine, M. (2020). International Comparative Evidence of E-Government Success and Economic Growth: Technology Adoption as an Anti-Corruption Tool. *Transforming Government: People. Process and Policy*, *14*(5), 713–736.

Mourtzis, D. A., Angelopoulos, J., & Panopoulos, N. (2022). A Literature Review of the Challenges and Opportunities of the Transition from Industry 4.0 to Society 5.0. *Energies*, *6276*(17), 6276. Advance online publication. doi:10.3390/en15176276

Mozas-Moral, A., Fernández-Uclés, D., Medina-Viruel, M., & Bernal-Jurado, E. (2021). The role of the SDGs as enhancers of the performance of Spanish wine cooperatives. *Technological Forecasting and Social Change*, *173*, 121176. doi:10.1016/j.techfore.2021.121176

Muhammad, M., Yet, C. E., Tahir, M., & Nasir, A. M. (2020). Capital structure of family firms: The effect of debt and equity market timing. *Journal of Family Business Management*, *11*(1), 1–18. doi:10.1108/JFBM-09-2019-0059

Mullaly, M. (2006). Longitudinal Analysis of Project Management Maturity. *Project Management Journal*, *36*(3), 62–73. doi:10.1177/875697280603700307

Mullaly, M. (2014). If maturity is the answer, then exactly what was the question? *International Journal of Managing Projects in Business*, *7*(2), 169–185. doi:10.1108/IJMPB-09-2013-0047

Muller, C., Canale, F., & Cruz, A. (2022). Green innovation in the Latin American agri-food industry: understanding the influence of family involvement and business practices. British Food Journal. doi:10.1108/BFJ-09-2021-0994

Muminov, N., Kim, T., Egamberdiyev, F., & Ambartsumyan, A. (2020). The Ways Of Improvement Of Living Standards. *International Journal of Psychosocial Rehabilitation*, *24*(4), 1965–1980. doi:10.37200/IJPR/V24I4/PR201305

Muñoz, R., Fernández, M., & Salinero, Y. (2020). Sustainability, corporate social responsibility, and performance in the Spanish wine sector. *Sustainability (Basel)*, *13*(1), 7. doi:10.3390u13010007

Nahapiet, J., & Ghoshal, S. (1998). Social capital, intellectual capital, and the organizational advantage. *Academy of Management Review*, *23*(2), 242–266. doi:10.2307/259373

Neaher, G., Bray, D., Mueller-Kaler, J. & Schatz, B. (2021). *Standardizing the future: How can the United States navigate the geopolitics of international technology standards?* Atlantic Council Report.

Neely, A. (1998). *Measuring Business Performance: Why, What and How*. Economist Books.

Neely, A., Gregory, M., & Platts, K. (1995). Performance measurement system design: A literature review and research agenda. *International Journal of Operations & Production Management, 15*(4), 80–116. doi:10.1108/01443579510083622

Neely, A., & Kennerley, M. (2003). Measuring Performance in a Changing Environment. *International Journal of Operations & Production Management, 23*(2), 213–229. doi:10.1108/01443570310458465

Nelson, R. R. (1991). Why do firms differ, and how does it matter? *Strategic Management Journal, 12*, 61-74.

Nirino, N., Ferraris, A., Miglietta, N., & Invernizzi, A. (2020). Intellectual capital: The missing link in the corporate social responsibility–financial performance relationship. *Journal of Intellectual Capital, 23*(2), 420–438. doi:10.1108/JIC-02-2020-0038

Niven, P. R. (2002). *Balanced scorecard step-by-step: Maximizing performance and maintaining results*. Wiley & Sons.

Nonaka, I. (1994). A Dynamic Theory of Organizational Knowledge Creation. *Organization Science, 5*(1), 14-37.

Nonaka, I., & Takeuchi, H. (1995). *The knowledge-creating company: How Japanese companies create the dynamics of innovation*. Oxford University Press.

Obeidat, B., Al-Suradi, M., Masa'deh, R., & Tarhini, A. (2016). The impact of knowledge management on innovation: An empirical study on Jordanian consultancy firms. *Management Research Review, 39*(10), 1214–1238. doi:10.1108/MRR-09-2015-0214

OCDE. (2005). *Manual de Oslo: Guía para la recogida e interpretación de datos sobre innovación*. Retrieved from: http://www.itq.edu.mx/convocatorias/manualdeoslo.pdf

OECD. (2005). *Manual de Oslo: Guía para la recogida e interpretación de datos sobre innovación* [Oslo Manual: A Guide to Collecting and Interpreting Innovation Data]. Retrieved from: http://www.itq.edu.mx/convocatorias/manualdeoslo.pdf

OECD. (2014). *Recommendation of the Council on Digital Government Strategies*. Public Governance Committee. https://www.oecd.org/gov/digital-government/Recommendation-digital-government-strategies.pdf

OECD. (2021). *Artificial Intelligence, Machine Learning and Big Data in Finance: Opportunities, Challenges, and Implications for Policy Makers,* https://www.oecd.org/finance/artificial-intelligence-machine-learning-big-data-in-finance.htm

Ofori, D., & Deffor, E. (2013). Assessing Project Management Maturity in Africa: A Ghanaian Perspective. *International Journal of Business Administration*, *4*(6), 41–61. doi:10.5430/ijba.v4n6p41

Olivera, F., Goodman, P., & Tan, S. (2008). Contribution behaviors indistributed environments. *Management Information Systems Quarterly*, *32*(1), 23–42. doi:10.2307/25148827

Oliver, C. (1992). The antecedents of deinstitutionalization. *Organization Studies*, *13*(4), 563–588. doi:10.1177/017084069201300403

Oprean-Stan, C., Oncioiu, I., Iuga, I. C., & Stan, S. (2020). Impact of sustainability reporting and inadequate management of ESG factors on corporate performance and sustainable growth. *Sustainability (Basel)*, *12*(20), 8536. doi:10.3390u12208536

Ordiyasa, I. W., Nugroho, L. E., Santosa, P. I., Ferdiana, R., & Kumorotomo, W. (2016). Review: Interoperability model of e-Government services. In *2nd International Conference on Information Technology, Computer, and Electrical Engineering, ICITACEE 2015* (pp. 177–182). Institute of Electrical and Electronics Engineers Inc. 10.1109/ICITACEE.2015.7437794

Organization for Economic Co-operation and Development (OECD). (2022a). *Better Life Index.* Available online: https://www.oecdbetterlifeindex.org/

Organization for Economic Co-operation and Development (OECD). (2022b). *Better Life Index. Definitions and Metadata.* Available online: https://www.oecd.org/wise/OECD-Better-Life-Index-definitions-2021.pdf

Organization for Economic Co-operation and Development (OECD). (2023). *Corporate Governance*. https://www.oecd.org/corporate/

Organization for Security and Co-operation in Europe (OSCE). (2003). *OSCE Strategy Document For The Economic And Environmental Dimension. 2nd day of the Eleventh Meeting MC(11) Journal No. 2, Agenda item 8.* https://www.osce.org/files/f/documents/a/3/20705.pdf

Organization for Security and Co-operation in Europe (OSCE). (2023). *Good Governance*. https://www.osce.org/oceea/446335

Osterwalder, A., & Pigneur, Y. (2010). *Business Model Generation: Handbook for Visionaries, Game Changers, and Challengers*. John Wiley & Sons, Inc.

Otley, D. (1999). Performance management: A framework for management control systems research. *Management Accounting Research*, *10*(4), 363–382. doi:10.1006/mare.1999.0115

Ould Daoud Ellili, N. (2020). Environmental, social, and governance disclosure, ownership structure and cost of capital: Evidence from the UAE. *Sustainability (Basel)*, *12*(18), 7706. doi:10.3390u12187706

Our World in Data (WEC). (2020). *The short history of global living conditions and why it matters that we know it*. Available online: https://ourworldindata.org/a-history-of-global-living-conditions-in-5-charts

P3M3. (2016). *Introduction to P3M3©*, version 3. AXELOS Limited.

Paillé, P., Chen, Y., Boiral, O., & Jin, J. (2014). The impact of human resource management on environmental performance: An employee-level study. *Journal of Business Ethics*, *121*(3), 451–466. doi:10.100710551-013-1732-0

Pakistan Bureau of Statistics. (2022). *Pakistan Social and Living Standards Measurement. Brief on PSLM Survey*. Available online: https://www.pbs.gov.pk/content/pakistan-social-and-living-standards-measurement

Panagiotopoulos, P., Al-Debei, M., Fitzgerald, G., & Elliman, T. (2012). A business model perspective for ICTs in public engagement. *Government Information Quarterly*, *29*(2), 192–202. doi:10.1016/j.giq.2011.09.011

Pan, S. L., & Nishant, R. (2023). Artificial intelligence for digital sustainability: An insight into domain-specific research and future directions. *International Journal of Information Management*, *72*, 102668. doi:10.1016/j.ijinfomgt.2023.102668

Paoloni, P., Modaffari, G., Paoloni, N., & Ricci, F. (2021). The strategic role of intellectual capital components in agri-food firms. *British Food Journal*, *124*(5), 1430–1452. doi:10.1108/BFJ-01-2021-0061

Pardo, T. A., Nam, T., & Burke, G. B. (2012). E-Government Interoperability: Interaction of Policy, Management, and Technology Dimensions. *Social Science Computer Review*, *30*(1), 7–23. doi:10.1177/0894439310392184

Pardo, T. A., & Tayi, G. K. (2007). Interorganizational information integration: A key enabler for digital government. *Government Information Quarterly*, *24*(4), 691–715. doi:10.1016/j.giq.2007.08.004

Park, J., Park, Y., Yoo, J. L., Yue, G., & Yu, J. (2022). Can the perceived risk of particulate matter change people's desires and behavior intentions? *Frontiers in Public Health*, *10*(1035174), 1035174. doi:10.3389/fpubh.2022.1035174 PMID:36466525

Paulk, M. C., Curtis, B., Chrissis, M. B., & Weber, C. V. (1993). *The Capability Maturity Model for Software* (v.1.1). Technical Report CMU/SEI-93-TR-024. Carnegie Mellon University.

Paulraj, A. (2011). Understanding the relationships between internal resources and capabilities, sustainable supply management and organizational sustainability. *The Journal of Supply Chain Management*, *47*(1), 19–37. doi:10.1111/j.1745-493X.2010.03212.x

Pekovic, S., & Vogt, S. (2021). The fit between corporate social responsibility and corporate governance: The impact on a firm's financial performance. *Review of Managerial Science*, *15*(4), 1095–1125. doi:10.100711846-020-00389-x

Pellegrini, C. B., Caruso, R., & Mehmeti, N. (2019). The impact of ESG scores on cost of equity and firm's profitability. New Challenges in Corporate Governance. *Theory into Practice*, 38–40.

Penrose, E. T. (1959). *The Theory of the Growth of the Firm*. Wiley.

Pérez-López, S., & Alegre, J. (2012). Information technology competency, knowledge processes and firm performance. *Industrial Management & Data Systems*, *112*(4), 644–662. doi:10.1108/02635571211225521

Pérez-Luño, A., Alegre, J., & Valle-Cabrera, R. (2019). The role of tacit knowledge in connecting knowledge exchange and combination with innovation. *Technology Analysis and Strategic Management*, *31*(2), 186–198. doi:10.1080/09537325.2018.1492712

Peteraf, M. A. (1993). The cornerstones of competitive advantage. *Strategic Management Journal*, *14*(3), 179–191. doi:10.1002mj.4250140303

Pettigrew, A., & Whipp, R. (1991). *Managing change for competitive success*. Blackwell Publishers.

Pihir, I., Tomičić-Pupek, K., & Tomičić, M. (2019). Digital transformation playground - literature review and framework of concepts. *Journal of Information and Organizational Sciences*, *43*(1), 33–48. doi:10.31341/jios.43.1.3

Pinto, J. K. (2002). Project management 2002. *Research Technology Management*, *45*(2), 22–37. doi:10.1080/08956308.2002.11671489

Pinto, J. K., & Slevin, D. P. (1988). Critical success factors across the project life cycle. *Project Management Journal*, (June), 67–75.

Pittaway, J., & Montazemi, A. (2020). Know-how to lead digital transformation: The case of local governments. *Government Information Quarterly*, *37*(4), 101474. doi:10.1016/j.giq.2020.101474

Pizzol, L., Luzzani, G., Criscione, P., Barro, L., Bagnoli, C., & Capri, E. (2021). The Role of Corporate Social Responsibility in the Wine Industry: The Case Study of Veneto and Friuli Venezia Giulia. *Sustainability (Basel)*, *13*(23), 13230. doi:10.3390u132313230

Platts, K. W., & Tan, K. H. (2002). Designing linked performance measures – A connectance based approach. *Pre-prints 12th Intern. Seminar on Production Economics, 2*, 367-373.

PMI. (2003). *Organizational Project Management Maturity Model (OPM3): Knowledge Foundations*. Project Management Institute Inc.

PMI. (2013). *Project Management Body of Knowledge (PMBOK) Guide* (5th ed.). Project Management Institute Inc.

PMI. (2013a). A Guide to the Project Management Body of Knowledge: PMBOK® guide, v5.0. Project Management Institute Inc.

PMI. (2013b). *Organizational project management maturity model (OPM3): Knowledge Foundation* (3rd ed.). Project Management Institute.

PMI. (2014). *Implementing Organizational Project Management: A Practice Guide*. Project Management Institute.

PMI. (2015). *PMI's Pulse of the Profession: Capturing the Value of Project Management*. Project Management Institute.

PMI. (2016). PMI Lexicon of Project Management Terms (version 3.1). Project Management Institute Inc.

Podsakoff, P. M., & Organ, D. W. (1986). Self-reports in organizational research: Problems and prospects. *Journal of Management, 12*(4), 531–544. doi:10.1177/014920638601200408

Poli, M., & Shenhar, A. J. (2003). Project strategy: The key to project success. *Proceedings of the Portland International Conference on Management of Engeneering and Technology*, 231–235. 10.1109/PICMET.2003.1222799

Ponnu, C. H. (2008). Corporate governance structures and the performance of Malaysian public listed companies. *International Review of Business Research Papers, 4*(2), 217–230.

Popescu, C. R. G. (2020). Sustainability Assessment: Does the OECD/G20 Inclusive Framework for BEPS (Base Erosion and Profit Shifting Project) Put an End to Disputes Over The Recognition and Measurement of Intellectual Capital? *Sustainability, 12*(23), 10004.. doi:10.3390/su122310004

Popescu, C. R. G., & Popescu G. N. (2019). An Exploratory Study Based on a Questionnaire Concerning Green and Sustainable Finance, Corporate Social Responsibility, and Performance: Evidence from the Romanian Business Environment. *Journal of Risk and Financial Management, 12*(4), 162. . doi:10.3390/jrfm12040162

Popescu, C. R. G. (2020). Approaches to Sustainable and Responsible Entrepreneurship: Creativity, Innovation, and Intellectual Capital as Drivers for Organization Performance. In B. Hernández-Sánchez, J. Sánchez-García, & A. Moreira (Eds.), *Building an Entrepreneurial and Sustainable Society* (pp. 75–95). IGI Global. doi:10.4018/978-1-7998-2704-7.ch004

Popescu, C. R. G. (2021). Measuring Progress Towards the Sustainable Development Goals: Creativity, Intellectual Capital, and Innovation. In C. Popescu (Ed.), *Handbook of Research on Novel Practices and Current Successes in Achieving the Sustainable Development Goals* (pp. 125–136). IGI Global. doi:10.4018/978-1-7998-8426-2.ch006

Popescu, C. R. G. (2021). Sustainable and Responsible Entrepreneurship for Value-Based Cultures, Economies, and Societies: Increasing Performance Through Intellectual Capital in Challenging Times. In C. Popescu & R. Verma (Eds.), *Sustainable and Responsible Entrepreneurship and Key Drivers of Performance* (pp. 33–58). IGI Global. doi:10.4018/978-1-7998-7951-0.ch002

Popescu, C. R. G. (2022). Mindfulness Business Principles: Producing Outstanding Value and Encouraging Community Connections. In C. Popescu (Ed.), *COVID-19 Pandemic Impact on New Economy Development and Societal Change* (pp. 196–228). IGI Global. doi:10.4018/978-1-6684-3374-4.ch010

Popescu, C. R. G., & González, A. L. (2022b). Legendary, Life-Changing, and Memorable Benefits of Digitalization to Restart the Economy: Impact of COVID-19 on Global Economic Environment for Sustainable Development. In C. Popescu (Ed.), *Handbook of Research on Building Inclusive Global Knowledge Societies for Sustainable Development* (pp. 166–184). IGI Global. doi:10.4018/978-1-6684-5109-0.ch008

Popescu, C. R. G., & González, A. L. (2022c). Current High-Powered Challenges and High-Reaching Reforms: Moving to a New Economic Model Based on Green Energy, Digitalization, and Shock Resistance. In C. Popescu (Ed.), *Frameworks for Sustainable Development Goals to Manage Economic, Social, and Environmental Shocks and Disasters* (pp. 133–154). IGI Global. doi:10.4018/978-1-6684-6750-3.ch008

Popescu, C. R. G., & González, A. L. (2023). Digital Transformation Impact on Organizations' Culture and Employees' Motivation: Shaping the "New Normal" and Addressing Sustainable Development Goals. In C. Popescu (Ed.), *Positive and Constructive Contributions for Sustainable Development Goals* (pp. 114–130). IGI Global. doi:10.4018/978-1-6684-7499-0.ch008

Popescu, C. R. G., & Luque González, A. (2022a). Importance and Implications of Influential, Powerful, and Remarkable Economic Policy Mix: Pre-Pandemic and Post-Pandemic Challenges in Building Inclusive Global Knowledge Societies. In C. Popescu (Ed.), *Handbook of Research on SDGs for Economic Development, Social Development, and Environmental Protection* (pp. 46–65). IGI Global. doi:10.4018/978-1-6684-5113-7.ch003

Porter, M. E. (1992). Towards a Dynamic Theory of Strategy. *Strategic Management Journal, 12*, 95-118.

Porter, M. E. (1979). How competitive forces shape strategy. *Harvard Business Review, 57*(2), 137–145. PMID:18271320

Porter, M. E. (1991). *The Competitive Advantage of Nations*. Free Press.

Potter, W. (2023). *'This is not crying wolf... the wolf is at the door': Fears AI could make white collar jobs obsolete as Microsoft pumps multibillion-dollar investment into ChatGPT after laying off 10,000 workers.* Dailymail.com. Retrieved from https://www.dailymail.co.uk/news/article-11683901/ChatGPT-make-white-collar-jobs-obsolete-Microsoft-pumps-billions-AI.html

Prahalad, C. K., & Hamel, G. (1990). The core competence of the corporation. *Harvard Business Review, 68*(3), 79–91.

Pravdić, P., & Kučinar, R. (2015). A balanced scorecard analysis of performance metrics in profit organization. *Analі poslovne ekonomije, 13*, 14- 31.

Quinn, J. B. (1992). *Intelligent Enterprise: A Knowledge and Service Based Paradigm for Industry*. Free Press.

Rabadán, A. (2021). Consumer attitudes towards technological innovation in a traditional food product: The case of wine. *Foods, 10*(6), 1363. doi:10.3390/foods10061363 PMID:34204607

Rad, P., & Levin, G. (2006). Project Management Maturity Assessment. *AACE International Transactions,* PM61-PM64.

Radford, A., Narasimhan, K., Salimans, T., & Sutskever, I. (2018). *Improving Language Understanding with Unsupervised Learning*. Technical Report, OpenAI.

Radujkovića, M., & Sjekavica, M. (2017). Project Management Success Factors. *Procedia Engineering*, *196*, 607–615. doi:10.1016/j.proeng.2017.08.048

Rafiq, M., Zhang, X., Yuan, J., Naz, S., & Maqbool, S. (2020). Impact of a Balanced Scorecard as a Strategic Management System Tool to Improve Sustainable Development: Measuring the Mediation of Organizational Performance through PLS-Smart. *Sustainability (Basel)*, *12*(4), 1365. doi:10.3390u12041365

Raimi, L. (2017). Understanding theories of corporate social responsibility in the Ibero-American hospitality industry. In *Corporate Social Responsibility and Corporate Governance*. Emerald Publishing Limited. doi:10.1108/S2043-052320170000011004

Raimo, N., Caragnano, A., Zito, M., Vitolla, F., & Mariani, M. (2021). Extending the benefits of ESG disclosure: The effect on the cost of debt financing. *Corporate Social Responsibility and Environmental Management*, *28*(4), 1412–1421. doi:10.1002/csr.2134

Ramanathan, S., & Isaksson, R. (2022). Sustainability reporting as a 21st century problem statement: Using a quality lens to understand and analyse the challenges. *The TQM Journal*, *35*(5), 1310–1328. doi:10.1108/TQM-01-2022-0035

Ranganathan, C., Goode, V., & Ramaprasad, A. (2003). Managing the transition to bricks and clicks. *Communications of the ACM*, *46*(12), 308–316. doi:10.1145/953460.953515

Rao, N. D., & Min, J. (2018). Decent Living Standards: Material Prerequisites for Human Wellbeing. *Social Indicators Research*, *138*(1), 225–244. doi:10.100711205-017-1650-0 PMID:29950752

Ray, K. K., & Mitra, S. K. (2018). Firm's Financial Performance and Sustainability Efforts: Application of Classifier Models. *Global Business Review*, *19*(3), 722–736. doi:10.1177/0972150917713859

Raza, A., Farrukh, M., Iqbal, M., Farhan, M., & Wu, Y. (2021). Corporate social responsibility and employees' voluntary pro-environmental behavior: The role of organizational pride and employee engagement. *Corporate Social Responsibility and Environmental Management*, *28*(3), 1104–1116. doi:10.1002/csr.2109

Razzaq, S., Shujahat, M., Hussain, S., Nawaz, F., Wang, M., Ali, M., & Tehseen, S. (2018). Knowledge management, organizational commitment and knowledge-worker performance: The neglected role of knowledge management in the public sector. *Business Process Management Journal*, *25*(5), 923–947. doi:10.1108/BPMJ-03-2018-0079

Reed, K., Lubatkin, M., & Srinivasan, N. (2006). Proposing and testing an intellectual capital-based view of the firm. *Journal of Management Studies*, *43*(4), 867–893. doi:10.1111/j.1467-6486.2006.00614.x

Reilley, G., & Reilley, R. (2000). Using a measure network to understand and delivery value. *Journal of Cost Management*.

Reinartz, W., Haenlein, M., & Henseler, J. (2009). An empirical comparison of theefficacy of covariance-based and variance-based SEM. *International Journal of Research in Marketing*, *26*(4), 332–344. doi:10.1016/j.ijresmar.2009.08.001

Richter, B., & Hanf, J. (2021). Cooperatives in the wine industry: Sustainable management practices and digitalisation. *Sustainability (Basel)*, *13*(10), 5543. doi:10.3390u13105543

Rogers, D. (2016). *The digital transformation playbook: rethink your business for the digital age*. Columbia University Press. doi:10.7312/roge17544

Roldan, J., & Cepeda, G. (2017), Modelos de Ecuaciones basados en la Varianza: Partial Least Squares (PLS) para Investigadores en Ciencias Sociales (4a ed.). Universidad de Sevilla.

Roldan, J., & Cepeda, G. (2017). Modelos de Ecuaciones basados en la Varianza: Partial Least Squares (PLS) para Investigadores en Ciencias Sociales (4a ed.). Universidad de Sevilla.

Roos, J., Roos, G., Dragonetti, N.C., & Edvinsson, L. (1997). *Intellectual Capital: Navigating in the New Business Landscape*. Macmillan.

Ross, J., Beath, C., & Mocker, M. (2019). *Designed for Digital How to Architect Your Business for Sustained Success*. MIT Press. doi:10.7551/mitpress/12188.001.0001

Roy, A. (2016). Corporate governance and firm performance: A study of Indian listed firms. *Metamorphosis*, *15*(1), 31–46. doi:10.1177/0972622516629032

Ruiz-Guerra, I., Molina-Moreno, V., Cortés-García, F. J., & Núñez-Cacho, P. (2019). Prediction of the impact on air quality of the cities receiving cruise tourism: The case of the Port of Barcelona. *Heliyon*, *5*(2), e01280. doi:10.1016/j.heliyon.2019.e01280 PMID:30923758

Rumelt, R. P. (1984). Towards a strategic theory of the firm. In R. B. Lamb (Ed.), *Competitive Strategic Management* (pp. 556–570). Prentice-Hall.

Russ, R. (2001). Economic value added: Theory, evidence, a missing link. *Review of Business*, *22*(1), 66–71.

Rymarczyk, J. (2012). The Impact of Industrial Revolution 4.0 on International Trade. *Entrepreneurial Business and Economics Review*, *9*(1), 105–117. doi:10.15678/EBER.2021.090107

Sacks, G. (2023). *Generative AI could raise global GDP by 7% Artificial Intelligence*. Retrieved from https://www.goldmansachs.com/intelligence/pages/generative-ai-could-raise-global-gdp-by-7-percent.html

Sætra, H. S. (2021). A Framework for Evaluating and Disclosing the ESG Related Impacts of AI with the SDGs. *Sustainability (Basel)*, *13*(15), 8503. doi:10.3390u13158503

Sætra, H. S. (2022). The AI ESG protocol: Evaluating and disclosing the environment, social, and governance implications of artificial intelligence capabilities, assets, and activities. *Sustainable Development*. Advance online publication. doi:10.1002d.2438

Sagarikabiswas. (2023). *ChatGPT: 7 IT Jobs That AI Can't Replace*. Retrieved from https://www.geeksforgeeks.org/chatgpt-7-it-jobs-that-ai-cant-replace/

Saidane, D., & Ben Abdallah, S. (2021). Sustainable Finance: Concepts, Analyses and Perspectives. In D. Bourghelle, R. Pérez, & P. Rozin (Eds.), *Critical Studies on Corporate Responsibility, Governance and Sustainability* (pp. 181–192). Emerald Publishing Limited. doi:10.1108/S2043-905920210000015028

Salmones, M., Crespo, A., & Bosque, I. (2005). Influence of corporate social responsibility on loyalty and valuation of services. *Journal of Business Ethics*, *61*(4), 369–385. doi:10.100710551-005-5841-2

Sambharya, R. B. (2011). Security analysts' earnings forecasts as a measure of firm performance: An empirical exploration of its domain. *Management Decision*, *49*(7), 1160–1181. doi:10.1108/00251741111151190

Sánchez-García, E., Martínez-Falcó, J., Alcon-Vila, A., & Marco-Lajara, B. (2023). Developing Green Innovations in the Wine Industry: An Applied Analysis. *Foods*, *12*(6), 1157. doi:10.3390/foods12061157 PMID:36981084

Sarstedt, M., Radomir, L., Moisescu, O. I., & Ringle, C. M. (2022). Latent class analysis in PLS-SEM: A review and recommendations for future applications. *Journal of Business Research*, *138*, 398–407. doi:10.1016/j.jbusres.2021.08.051

Saunders, M., Lewis, P., & Thornhill, A. (2009). *Research Methods for Business Students* (5th ed.). Pearson Education Limited.

Saunders, M., Thornhill, A., & Lewis, P. (2019). *Research methods for business students* (8th ed.). Pearson Education Limited. ISBN.

Sawaya, N., & Trapanese, P. (2004). Measuring project management maturity. *Security Distributing and Marketing*, *34*(1), 44–66.

Saxena, A. S., Singh, R., Gehlot, A., Akram, S. V., Twala, B., Singh, A., Montero, E. C., & Priyadarshi, N. (2022). Technologies Empowered Environmental, Social, and Governance (ESG): An Industry 4.0 Landscape. *Sustainability (Basel)*, *309*(1), 309. Advance online publication. doi:10.3390u15010309

Schlichter, J. (2001). PMI's organizational project management maturity model: emerging standards. *Proceedings of PMI Annual Seminars & Symposium*.

Schumpeter, J. (1949). *The Theory of Economic Development, An Inquiry into Profits, Capital, Credit, Interest and the Business Cycle*. Harvard University Press.

Schumpeter, J. (1994). *Capitalism, Socialism and democracy*. Routledge.

Schwab, K. (2016). *The Fourth Industrial Revolution*. World Economic Forum.

Scott, W. R. (2005). Institutional theory: Contributing to a theoretical research program institutional theory. *Great Minds in Management: The Process of Theory Development*, *37*, 460–484.

Šebestová, J. D., & Popescu, C. R. G. (2022). Factors Influencing Investments into Human Resources to Support Company Performance. *J. Risk Financial Manag.*, *15*(1), 19. doi:10.3390/jrfm15010019

SEI. (2010). *CMMI for Services (v.1.3): Improving processes for providing better services.* Technical report CMU/SEI-2010-TR-034, November 2010. Carnegie Mellon University.

Selim, O. (2020). *ESG and AI: the beauty and the beast of sustainable investing.* Academic Press.

Selznick, P. (1957). *Leadership in Administration: A Sociological Interpretation.* Harper and Row.

Shafique, I., Kalyar, M., & Mehwish, N. (2021). Organizational ambidexterity, green entrepreneurial orientation, and environmental performance in SMEs context: Examining the moderating role of perceived CSR. *Corporate Social Responsibility and Environmental Management*, *28*(1), 446–456. doi:10.1002/csr.2060

Shahzad, M., Qu, Y., Javed, S., Zafar, A., & Rehman, S. (2019). Relation of environment sustainability to CSR and green innovation: A case of Pakistani manufacturing industry. *Journal of Cleaner Production*, *253*, 119938. doi:10.1016/j.jclepro.2019.119938

Shahzad, M., Qu, Y., Zafar, A., Rehman, S., & Islam, T. (2020). Exploring the influence of knowledge management process on corporate sustainable performance through green innovation. *Journal of Knowledge Management*, *24*(9), 2079–2106. doi:10.1108/JKM-11-2019-0624

Sharifi, A., Khavarian-Garmsir, A. R., & Kummitha, R. K. R. (2021). Contributions of smart city solutions and technologies to resilience against the COVID-19 pandemic: A literature review. *Sustainability (Basel)*, *13*(14), 1–28. doi:10.3390u13148018

Sharma, M. K., Bhagwat, R., & Dangayach, G. S. (2005). Practice of performance measurement: Experience from Indian SMEs. *International Journal of Globalisation and Small Business*, *1*(2), 183–213. doi:10.1504/IJGSB.2005.008014

Sharma, R., & Panigrahi, P. K. (2015). Developing a roadmap for planning and implementation of interoperability capability in e-government. *Transforming Government*, *9*(4), 426–447. doi:10.1108/TG-06-2014-0023

Shenhar, A. J., & Dvir, D. (2007). *Reinventing Project Management: The Diamond Approach to Successful Growth and Innovation.* Harvard Business School Press.

Shenhar, A., Dvir, D., Levy, O., & Maltz, A. C. (2001). Project success: A multidimensional strategic concept. *Long Range Planning*, *34*(6), 699–725. doi:10.1016/S0024-6301(01)00097-8

Shen, Y., Lyu, M., & Zhu, J. (2022). Air pollution and corporate green financial constraints: Evidence from China's listed companies. *International Journal of Environmental Research and Public Health*, *22*(15034), 19. doi:10.3390/ijerph192215034 PMID:36429753

Shi, Q. (2011). Rethinking the implementation of project management: A value adding path map approach. *International Journal of Project Management, 29*(3), 295–302. doi:10.1016/j.ijproman.2010.03.007

Silva, D., Tereso, A., Fernandes, G., & Pinto, J. A. (2014). OPM3® Portugal Project: Analysis of Preliminary Results. *Procedia Technology, 16*, 1027–1036. doi:10.1016/j.protcy.2014.10.057

Singh, S., Giudice, M. D., Chierici, R., & Graziano, D. (2020). Green innovation and environmental performance: The role of green transformational leadership and green human resource management. *Technological Forecasting and Social Change, 150*, 119762. doi:10.1016/j.techfore.2019.119762

Skulmoski, G. (2001). Project maturity and competence interface. *Cost Engineering (Morgantown, W. Va.), 43*(6), 11–18.

Smith, D. A. (2010). *Knowledge Management as an indicator of Organizational Maturity in Project Management: An enhancement of OPM3 Model* [PhD thesis]. Capella University.

Smith, M. (1998). Measuring Organizational Effectiveness. *Management Accounting*, 34-36.

Smokova, D. (2022). *How are GAFAM companies-Microsoft, Google, and Apple-utilizing AI systems' capabilities to drive their ESG/CSR initiatives?* [Bachelor's thesis]. University of Twente. Retrieved from https://purl.utwente.nl/essays/91325

Söderlund, J., & Maylor, H. (2012). Project management scholarship: Relevance, impact and five integrative challenges for business and management schools. *International Journal of Project Management, 30*(6), 686–696. doi:10.1016/j.ijproman.2012.03.007

Song, J. M. (2023). *Air pollution, regulations on emission and firms' social responsibility*. Singapore Management University.

Sood, K., Pathak, P., Jain, J., & Gupta, S. (2022). How does an investor prioritize ESG factors in India? An assessment based on fuzzy AHP. *Managerial Finance*. Advance online publication. doi:10.1108/MF-04-2022-0162

Soto-Acosta, P., & Cegarra-Navarro, J. (2016). New ICTs for knowledge management in organizations. *Journal of Knowledge Management, 20*(3), 417–422. doi:10.1108/JKM-02-2016-0057

Sridhar, K. (2023, August 15). The impact of AI on sustainability and ESG: Seizing opportunities and overcoming challenges. *WION*. https://www.wionews.com/opinions-blogs/the-impact-of-ai-on-sustainability-and-esg-seizing-opportunities-and-overcoming-challenges-625607

Stalk, G., Evans, P., & Shulman, E. (1992). Competing on capabilities: The new rules of corporate strategy. *Harvard Business Review*, (March-April), 57–69. PMID:10117369

Stasi, A., Muscio, A., Nardone, G., & Seccia, A. (2016). New technologies and sustainability in the Italian wine industry. *Agriculture and Agricultural Science Procedia, 8*, 290–297. doi:10.1016/j.aaspro.2016.02.023

Strand, R., & Freeman, R. E. (2015). Scandinavian cooperative advantage: The theory and practice of stakeholder engagement in Scandinavia. *Journal of Business Ethics, 127*(1), 65–85. doi:10.100710551-013-1792-1

Strauss, D. (2023). Generative AI's 'productivity revolution' will take time to pay off. *Financial Times*. Retrieved from https://www.ft.com/content/21384711-3506-4901-830c-7ecc3ae6b32a

Sumita, T. (2005). *Intellectual assets & management reporting*. METI.

Suprapti, S., Asbari, M., Cahyono, Y., Mufid, A., & Khasanah, N. (2020). Leadership style, organizational culture and innovative behavior on public health center performance during Pandemic Covid-19. *Journal of Industrial Engineering & Management Research, 1*(2), 76–88.

Syed, A. M. (2017). Environment, social, and governance (ESG) criteria and preference of managers. *Cogent Business & Management, 4*(1), 1340820. doi:10.1080/23311975.2017.1340820

Sze, A., Tang, I., Li, W., & Yu, I. W. (2021). *Is the Cost of Corporate Debt Influenced by ESG Factors?* Evidence from the EMEAP Region.

Szutowski, D., & Ratajczak, P. (2016). The relation between CSR and innovation. Model approach. *Journal of Entrepreneurship, Management and Innovation, 12*(2), 77–94. doi:10.7341/20161224

Tan, B., Lau, T., Sarwar, A., & Khan, N. (2021). The effects of consumer consciousness, food safety concern and healthy lifestyle on attitudes toward eating "green. *British Food Journal, 124*(4), 1187–1203. doi:10.1108/BFJ-01-2021-0005

Tarba, S., Jansen, J., Mom, T., Raisch, S., & Lawton, T. (2020). A microfoundational perspective of organizational ambidexterity: Critical review and research directions. *Long Range Planning, 53*(6), 102048. doi:10.1016/j.lrp.2020.102048

Teece, D. J. (1984). Economic analysis and strategic management. *California Management Review, 26*(3), 87–110. doi:10.2307/41165082

Teece, D. J., Pisano, G., & Shuen, A. (1997). Dynamic capabilities and strategic fit. *Strategic Management Journal, 18*(7), 510–533. doi:10.1002/(SICI)1097-0266(199708)18:7<509::AID-SMJ882>3.0.CO;2-Z

The Economist. (2022). *Global living standards are moving in the wrong direction. Climate change and conflict could make things even worse.* Available online: https://www.economist.com/graphic-detail/2022/09/08/global-living-standards-are-moving-in-the-wrong-direction

The Institute for Fiscal Studies (IFS). (2022a). *Living standards, poverty and inequality in the UK.* Available online: https://ifs.org.uk/living-standards-poverty-and-inequality-uk

The Institute for Fiscal Studies (IFS). (2022b). *Report. Living standards, poverty and inequality in the UK: 2022.* Available online: https://ifs.org.uk/publications/living-standards-poverty-and-inequality-uk-2022

The Institute of Chartered Accountants in England and Wales (ICAEW). (2023). *What is corporate governance?* https://www.icaew.com/technical/corporate-governance/principles/principles-articles/does-corporate-governance-matter

The Lisbon Council. (2023). *The European Human Capital Index.* Retrieved from https://lisboncouncil.net/publications/the-european-human-capital-index/

The Treasury of New Zealand. (2018). *Improving Living Standards: We Need to Talk About Productivity.* Available online: https://www.treasury.govt.nz/publications/speech/improving-living-standards-we-need-talk-about-productivity

Tian, M., Deng, P., Zhang, Y., & Salmador, M. (2018). How does culture influence innovation? A systematic literature review. *Management Decision, 56*(5), 1088–1107. doi:10.1108/MD-05-2017-0462

Tiwari, A. K. (2022). Guest editorial: Green and sustainable corporate finance: past, present and future. *International Journal of Managerial Finance, 18*(4), 613–616. doi:10.1108/IJMF-08-2022-636

Too, E., & Weaver, P. (2014). The management of project management: A conceptual framework for project governance. *International Journal of Project Management, 32*(8), 1382–1394. doi:10.1016/j.ijproman.2013.07.006

Toor, S. R., & Ogunlana, S. O. (2008). Critical COMs of success in large-scale construction projects: Evidence from Thailand construction industry. *International Journal of Project Management, 26*(4), 420–430. doi:10.1016/j.ijproman.2007.08.003

Topuz, S. G. (2022). The Relationship Between Income Inequality and Economic Growth: Are Transmission Channels Effective? *Social Indicators Research, 162*(3), 1177–1231. doi:10.100711205-022-02882-0 PMID:35103032

Trunfio, M., & Campana, S. (2019). Drivers and emerging innovations in knowledge-based destinations: Towards a research agenda. *Journal of Destination Marketing & Management, 14*, 100370. doi:10.1016/j.jdmm.2019.100370

Tsagas, G., & Villiers, C. (2020). Why "less is more" in non-financial reporting initiatives: Concrete steps towards supporting sustainability. Accounting, Economics, and Law. *Convivium, 10*(2).

Turner, J. R., Huemann, M., Anbari, F., & Bredillet, C. (2010). *Perspectives on projects.* Routledge. doi:10.4324/9780203891636

United Cities and Local Governments Asia-Pacific (UCLG ASPAC). (2021). *Good Governance: Definition and Characteristics.* https://uclg-aspac.org/good-governance-definition-and-characteristics/

United Nations (UN). (2012). *UN System Task Team on the Post-2015 UN Development Agenda. Governance and Development.* Thematic Think Piece UNDESA, UNDP, UNESCO. https://www.un.org/millenniumgoals/pdf/Think%20Pieces/7_governance.pdf

United Nations (UN). (2015). *Sustainable Development Goals (SDGs). Do You Know All 17 SDGs?* Available online: https://sdgs.un.org/goals

United Nations (UN). (2017). *Improving Living Standards through Mainstreaming of Sustainable Development Goals into the National Development Policy in Tajikistan.* Available online: https://sustainabledevelopment.un.org/content/documents/16021Tajikistan.pdf

United Nations (UN). (2018). *The 2030 Agenda and the Sustainable Development Goals: An Opportunity for Latin America and the Caribbean* (LC/G.2681-P/Rev.3). United Nations. Available online: https://repositorio.cepal.org/bitstream/handle/11362/40156/25/S1801140_en.pdf

United Nations (UN). (2019). *Raising Living Standards Boosts Overall Well-Being of Societies, Speakers Say, as Commission for Social Development Continues Session.* Available online: https://press.un.org/en/2019/soc4875.doc.htm

United Nations Development Programme (UNDP). (2022). *Human Development Report 2021-22: Uncertain Times, Unsettled Lives: Shaping our Future in a Transforming World.* Available online: https://hdr.undp.org/content/human-development-report-2021-22

United Nations Economic and Social Commission for Asia and the Pacific (UNESCAP). (2023). *What is Good Governance?* https://www.unescap.org/sites/default/files/good-governance.pdf

United Nations Economic Commission for Europe. (2016). *Guide on Measuring Human Capital. The Task Force on Measuring Human Capital.* United Nations. Retrieved from https://unece.org/DAM/stats/publications/2016/ECECESSTAT20166_E.pdf

United Nations Geneva. (2022). *Sustainable Development Goals (SDGs).* Available online: https://www.ungeneva.org/en/topics/sustainable-development-goals

United States Green Building Council (USGBC). (2022). *Healthy people in healthy places equals a healthy economy.* Available online: https://www.usgbc.org/resources/healthy-people-healthy-places-equals-healthy-economy

Valmohammadi, C., & Servati, A. (2011). Performance measurement system implementation using Balanced Scorecard and statistical methods. *International Journal of Productivity and Performance Management, 60*(5), 493–511. doi:10.1108/17410401111140400

Van Grembergen, W. Saull, R., & De Haes, S. (2003). Linking the IT balanced scorecard to the business objectives at a major Canadian financial group. *Journal of Information Technology Cases and Applications.*

Van Grembergen, W., & De Haes, S. (2005). Measuring and improving information technology governance through the balanced scorecard. *Information Systems Control Journal,* 2.

Van Veenstra, A. F., Klievink, B., & Janssen, M. (2011). Barriers and impediments to transformational government: Insights from literature and practice. *Electronic Government. International Journal (Toronto, Ont.), 8*(2/3), 226–241. doi:10.1504/EG.2011.039838

Vaswani, A., Shazeer, N., Parmar, N., Uszkoreit, J., Jones, L., Gomez, A. N., & Polosukhin, I. (2017). *Attention is all you need. Advances in neural information processing systems.* 31st Conference on Neural Information Processing Systems. https://proceedings.neurips.cc/paper/2017/file/ 3f5ee243547dee91fbd053c1c4a845aa-Paper.pdf

Vodenska, I., Trajanov, R., Chitkushev, L., & Trajanov, D. (2022). *Challenges and Opportunities in ESG Investments.* doi:10.1007/978-3-031-17292-2_14

Voelpel, S., Leibold, M., Eckhoff, R., & Davenport, T. (2005). The Tyranny of the Balanced Scorecard in the Innovation Economy. In *4th International Critical Management Studies Conference - Intellectual Capital Stream.* Cambridge University.

Voivedich, B., & Jones, M. (2001). Developing and Applying a Project Management Capability Maturity Model. *Proceedings of the PMI Annual Seminars & Symposium.*

Wan, G., Dawod, A. Y., Chanaim, S., & Ramasamy, S. S. (2023). Hotspots and trends of environmental, social and governance (ESG) research: A bibliometric analysis. *Data Science and Management, 6*(2), 65–75. doi:10.1016/j.dsm.2023.03.001

Wang, C., & Juo, W. (2021). An environmental policy of green intellectual capital: Green innovation strategy for performance sustainability. *Business Strategy and the Environment, 30*(7), 3241–3254. doi:10.1002/bse.2800

Wang, W., & Siau, K. (2019). Artificial intelligence, machine learning, automation, robotics, future of work and future of humanity. *Journal of Database Management, 30*(1), 61–79. doi:10.4018/JDM.2019010104

Wang, Z., & Wang, N. (2012). Knowledge sharing, innovation and firm performance. *Expert Systems with Applications, 39*(10), 8899–8908. doi:10.1016/j.eswa.2012.02.017

Ward, J., & Daniel, E. (2006). *Benefits Management, Delivering Value from IS and IT Investments.* John Wiley & Sons.

Ward, J., & Elvin, R. (1999). A new framework for managing IT-enabled business change. *Information Systems Journal, 9*(3), 197–221. doi:10.1046/j.1365-2575.1999.00059.x

WB. (2023)f. *Children in employment, total (% of children ages 7-14).* 27, 2023 da https://data.worldbank.org/indicator/SL.TLF.0714.ZS

WB. (2023l). *People using safely managed sanitation services (% of population).* https://data.worldbank.org/indicator/SH.STA.SMSS.ZS

WB. (2023a). *Access to electricity (% of population).* https://data.worldbank.org/indicator/EG.ELC.ACCS.ZS

WB. (2023b). *Agricultural land (% of land area).* https://data.worldbank.org/indicator/AG.LND.AGRI.ZS

WB. (2023c). *Agriculture, forestry, and fishing, value added (% of G).* https://data.worldbank.org/indicator/NV.AGR.TOTL.ZS

WB. (2023d). *Annual freshwater withdrawals, total (% of internal resources).* https://data.worldbank.org/indicator/ER.H2O.FWTL.ZS

WB. (2023e). *Cause of death, by communicable diseases and maternal, prenatal and nutrition conditions (% of total).* https://data.worldbank.org/indicator/SH.DTH.COMM.ZS

WB. (2023g). *CO2 emissions (metric tons per capita).* https://data.worldbank.org/indicator/EN.ATM.CO2E.PC

WB. (2023h). *Energy imports, net (% of energy use).* https://data.worldbank.org/indicator/EG.IMP.CONS.ZS

WB. (2023i). *Energy use (kg of oil equivalent per capita).* https://data.worldbank.org/indicator/EG.USE.PCAP.KG.OE

WB. (2023j). *Food production index (2014-2016 = 100).* https://data.worldbank.org/indicator/AG.PRD.FOOD.XD

WB. (2023k). *Fossil fuel energy consumption (% of total).* https://data.worldbank.org/indicator/EG.USE.COMM.FO.ZS

WB. (2023l). *Individuals using the Internet (% of population).* https://data.worldbank.org/indicator/IT.NET.USER.ZS

WB. (2023m). *Labor force participation rate, total (% of total population ages 15-64) (modeled ILO estimate).* World Bank.

WB. (2023n). *Life expectancy at birth, total (years).* https://data.worldbank.org/indicator/SP.DYN.LE00.IN

WB. (2023o). *Mammal species, threatened.* https://data.worldbank.org/indicator/EN.MAM.THRD.NO

WB. (2023p). *Net Migration.* https://data.worldbank.org/indicator/SM.POP.NETM

WB. (2023r). *Prevalence of overweight (% of adults).* https://genderdata.worldbank.org/indicators/sh-sta-owad-zs/

WB. (2023s). *Prevalence of undernourishment (% of population).* https://data.worldbank.org/indicator/SN.ITK.DEFC.ZS

WB. (2023t). *Proportion of seats held by women in national parliaments (%).*https://data.worldbank.org/indicator/SG.GEN.PARL.ZS

WB. (2023u). *Ratio of female to male labor force participation rate (%) (modeled ILO estimate).* https://data.worldbank.org/indicator/SL.TLF.CACT.FM.ZS

WB. (2023v). *Renewable energy consumption (% of total final energy consumption)*. https://data.worldbank.org/indicator/EG.FEC.RNEW.ZS

WB. (2023w). *Scientific and technical journal articles*. https://data.worldbank.org/indicator/IP.JRN.ARTC.SC

WB. (2023x). *Terrestrial and marine protected areas (% of total territorial area)*. https://data.worldbank.org/indicator/ER.PTD.TOTL.ZS

Weerakkody, V., Omar, A., El-Haddadeh, R., & Al-Busaidy, M. (2016). Digitally-enabled service transformation in the public sector: The lure of institutional pressure and strategic response towards change. *Government Information Quarterly*, *33*(4), 658–668. doi:10.1016/j.giq.2016.06.006

Weissglass, D. E. (2022). Contextual bias, the democratization of healthcare, and medical artificial intelligence in low- and middle-income countries. *Bioethics*, *36*(2), 201–209. doi:10.1111/bioe.12927 PMID:34460977

Wendler, R. (2012). The Maturity of Maturity Model Research: A systematic mapping study. *Information and Software Technology*, *54*(12), 1317–1339. doi:10.1016/j.infsof.2012.07.007

Wernerfelt, B. (1984). A resource-based view of the firm. *Strategic Management Journal*, *5*(2), 171–180. doi:10.1002mj.4250050207

Wernerfelt, B. (1989). From critical resources to corporate strategy. *Journal of General Management*, *5*, 171–180.

Wernerfelt, B. (1995). The resource-based view of the firm: Ten years after. *Strategic Management Journal*, *16*(3), 171–174. doi:10.1002mj.4250160303

Williams, J. (2023). How AI Will Enhance Human Capabilities. *Forbes*. Retrieved from https://www.forbes.com/sites/forbescommunicationscouncil/2018/03/19/how-ai-will-enhance-human-capabilities/?sh=1d37cd1e366f

Williams, L. (1999). *Hard Core: Power, Pleasure, and the" Frenzy of the Visible*. Univ of CA Press.

Williams, T., & Samset, K. (2010). Issues in Front-End Decision Making on Projects. *Project Management Journal*, *41*(2), 38–49. doi:10.1002/pmj.20160

Wilson, K. O. (2023, June 22). *SASB - ESG Reporting - Diversity and Inclusion - SASB Standards*. SASB. https://sasb.org/blog/exploring-diversity-inclusion-in-the-sasb-standards/

Wilson, C. (2010). Why should sustainable finance be given priority?: Lessons from pollution and biodiversity degradation. *Accounting Research Journal*, *23*(3), 267–280. doi:10.1108/10309611011092592

Wimalachandra, D., Frank, B., & Enkawa, T. (2014). Strategic openness in quality control: Adjusting npd strategic orientation to optimize product quality. *International Journal of Industrial Engineering*, *21*(6), 3241–3254.

Winter, M., Smith, C., Morris, P., & Cicmil, S. (2006). Directions for future research in project management: The main findings of a UK government-funded research network. *International Journal of Project Management, 24*(8), 638–649. doi:10.1016/j.ijproman.2006.08.009

Winter, M., & Szczepanek, T. (2008). Projects and programmes as value creation processes: A new perspective and some practical implications. *International Journal of Project Management, 26*(1), 95–103. doi:10.1016/j.ijproman.2007.08.015

Wong, S. (2013). Environmental requirements, knowledge sharing and green innovation: Empirical evidence from the electronics industry in China. *Business Strategy and the Environment, 22*(5), 321–338. doi:10.1002/bse.1746

Word Bank (WB). (1992). *Governance and Development.* https://elibrary.worldbank.org/doi/epdf/10.1596/0-8213-2094-7 doi:10.1596/0-8213-2094-7

World Bank (WB). (2017). *World Bank Group Country Partnership Framework for the Democratic Republic of Ethiopia 2018-2022.* Available online: https://documents1.worldbank.org/curated/en/202771504883944180/pdf/119576-revised-Ethiopia-Country-Partnership-Web.pdf

World Bank (WB). (2020). *How can countries support economic growth and improve living standards across all regions?* Available online: https://blogs.worldbank.org/latinamerica/how-can-countries-support-economic-growth-and-improve-living-standards-across-all

World Bank (WB). (2022a). *The World Bank in Ethiopia.* Available online: https://www.worldbank.org/en/country/ethiopia/overview

World Bank (WB). (2022b). *World Bank Group Statement on Current Situation in Ethiopia.* Available online: https://www.worldbank.org/en/news/statement/2021/03/05/world-bank-group-statement-on-current-situation-in-ethiopia

World Bank (WB). (2022c). *World Bank Boosts Pastoral Economies and Climate Action in the Horn of Africa.* Available online: https://www.worldbank.org/en/news/statement/2021/03/05/world-bank-group-statement-on-current-situation-in-ethiopia

World Bank (WB). (2022d). *World Bank Approves $180 Million to Step-Up Support for Refugees and Host Communities in Ethiopia.* Available online: https://www.worldbank.org/en/news/press-release/2022/06/28/world-bank-approves-180-million-to-step-up-support-for-refugees-and-host-communities-in-ethiopia

World Bank (WB). (2022e). *Ethiopia - Country partnership framework for the period FY18 - FY22 (English).* Available online: https://documents.worldbank.org/en/publication/documents-reports/documentdetail/202771504883944180/ethiopia-country-partnership-framework-for-the-period-fy18-fy22

World Bank (WB). (2023). *Governance.* Available online: https://www.worldbank.org/en/topic/governance/overview

World Economic Forum (WEC). (2021). *Climate Change. 5 surprising ways to increase living standards sustainably.* Available online: https://www.weforum.org/agenda/2021/10/5-surprising-ways-to-increase-living-standards-sustainably/

World Trade Organization. (2022a). *The WTO can ... cut living costs and raise living standards.* Available online: https://www.wto.org/english/thewto_e/whatis_e/10thi_e/10thi01_e.htm

World Trade Organization. (2022b). *The WTO can ... settle disputes and reduce trade tensions.* Available online: https://www.wto.org/english/thewto_e/whatis_e/10thi_e/10thi02_e.htm

World Trade Organization. (2022c). *The WTO can ... stimulate economic growth and employment.* Available online: https://www.wto.org/english/thewto_e/whatis_e/10thi_e/10thi03_e.htm

World Trade Organization. (2022d). *The WTO can ... cut the cost of doing business internationally.* Available online: https://www.wto.org/english/thewto_e/whatis_e/10thi_e/10thi04_e.htm

World Trade Organization. (2022e). *The WTO can ... support the environment and health.* Available online: https://www.wto.org/english/thewto_e/whatis_e/10thi_e/10thi08_e.htm

World Trade Organization. (2022f). *The WTO can ... contribute to peace and stability.* Available online: https://www.wto.org/english/thewto_e/whatis_e/10thi_e/10thi09_e.htm

Wu, J., & Pu, Y. (2020). Air pollution, general government public-health expenditures and income inequality: Empirical analysis based on the spatial Durbin model. *PLoS One, 15*(10). doi:10.1371/journal.pone.0240053 PMID:33002068

Xiang, G., Liu, J., Zhong, S., & Deng, M. (2022). Comprehensive metrological and content analysis of the income inequality research in health field: A bibliometric analysis. *Frontiers in Public Health, 10*, 901112. doi:10.3389/fpubh.2022.901112 PMID:36187638

Xue, S., Zhang, B., & Zhao, X. (2021). Brain drain: The impact of air pollution on firm performance. *Journal of Environmental Economics and Management, 110*(102546), 102546. doi:10.1016/j.jeem.2021.102546

Yang, Z., & Broby, D. (2020). *Sustainable Finance: AI Applications in Satellite Imagery and Data.* Financail Technology Paper.

Yazici, H. J. (2009). The Role of Project Management Maturity and Organizational Culture in Perceived Performance. *Project Management Journal, 40*(3), 14–33. doi:10.1002/pmj.20121

Yin, R. (2014). *Case Study Research: Design and Methods* (5th ed.). Sage.

Yin, R. (2018). *Case Study Research and Applications: Design and Methods* (6th ed.). Sage Publications, Inc.

Yogesh, K. (2023). "So, what if ChatGPT wrote it?" Multidisciplinary perspectives on opportunities, challenges, and implications of generative conversational AI for research, practice, and policy. *International Journal of Information Management, 71*, 102642. doi:10.1016/j.ijinfomgt.2023.102642

Youndt, M., Subramaniam, M., & Snell, S. (2004). Intellectual capital profiles: An examination of investments and returns. *Journal of Management Studies*, *41*(2), 335–361. doi:10.1111/j.1467-6486.2004.00435.x

Yu, Y., Zhang, M., & Huo, B. (2021). The impact of relational capital on green supply chain management and financial performance. *Production Planning and Control*, *32*(10), 861–874. doi:10.1080/09537287.2020.1774675

Zameer, H., Wang, Y., Yasmeen, H., & Mubarak, S. (2020). Green innovation as a mediator in the impact of business analytics and environmental orientation on green competitive advantage. *Management Decision*, *60*(2), 488–507. doi:10.1108/MD-01-2020-0065

Zaragoza-Sáez, P., Claver-Cortés, E., Marco-Lajara, B., & Úbeda-García, M. (2020). Corporate social responsibility and strategic knowledge management as mediators between sustainable intangible capital and hotel performance. *Journal of Sustainable Tourism*, 1–23. doi:10.1080/09669582.2020.1811289

Zhang, L. Y., He, J., & Zhang, X. X. (2012). The Project Management Maturity Model and Application Based on PRINCE2. *Proceedings of International Workshop on Information and Electronics Engineering, 29*, 3691-3697.

Zhang, R. L. (2021). *ESG and Cost of Debt.* Stanford University.

Zwikael, O., & Smyrk, J. (2011). *Project Management for the Creation of Organisational Value.* Springer-Verlag. doi:10.1007/978-1-84996-516-3

About the Contributors

Cristina Raluca Gh. Popescu is Full-Professor Habil. at University of Bucharest, PhD. Supervisor and Doctoral School Member at The Bucharest University of Economic Studies, Romania. She collaborates with University of Craiova and is scientific researcher at The National Institute of Research and Development for Environmental Protection and the National Institute for Research and Development Comoti Turbomotors. She is Public Policy Expert at Ministry of Research, Innovation and Digitization. She is Member of Chamber of Financial Auditors of Romania (CAFR), as Financial Auditor, and Member of Authority for the Public Oversight of the Statutory Audit Activity (ASPAAS), as Financial auditor. She is review board member: IBIMA Conferences and Journal of E-Government Studies and Best Practices, IBIMA Publishing, USA; IGI Global – Publishing House; International Journal of Health Economics (IJHE), University of Bucharest; Multidisciplinary Digital Publishing Institute (MDPI) (Basel, Switzerland) for Journal of Risk and Financial Management, Mathematics, Sustainability, Journal of Open Innovation: Technology, Market, and Complexity, Symmetry, Administrative Sciences, World, Informatics.

Poshan (Sam) Yu is a Lecturer in Accounting and Finance in the International Cooperative Education Program of Soochow University (China). He is also an External Professor of FinTech and Finance at SKEMA Business School (China), a Visiting Professor at Krirk University (Thailand), an EU-Asia Research Coordinator at the European Business University of Luxembourg and a Visiting Researcher at the Australian Studies Centre of Shanghai University (China). Sam leads FasterCapital (Dubai, UAE) as a Regional Partner (China) and serves as a Startup Mentor for AIC RAISE (Coimbatore, India) and University College London. His research interests include financial technology, regulatory technology, public-private partnerships, mergers and acquisitions, private equity, venture capital, start-ups, intellectual property, art finance, and China's "One Belt One Road" policy.

* * *

Maria Sneha A. is currently pursuing Masters of Commerce in Christ University. She received Bachelors degree from Christ University in Finance and Accountancy specialization. She is also been awarded as the best paper titled Customer-Centric Fintech in the Age of AI: Opportunities, Challenges, and Strategic Recommendations".

Jorge Gomes is Professor of Strategy and Management at Universidade Lusófona and researcher at ADVANCE/CSG/ISEG - University of Lisbon. He holds a PhD in Management from ISEG and a Master's in Management Sciences from ISCTE-IUL, a postgraduate degree in Project Management from INDEG / ISCTE and a degree in Geographic Engineering from the Faculty of Sciences of the University of Lisbon. For the last 35 years he has worked as an engineer, project manager, quality auditor and consultant. His research interests include Strategy and Operations, Benefits Management, Project Management, Project Success, Maturity Models, IS/IT Investment Management.

Arturo Luque Gonzalez is full professor at the Technical University of Manabí, Ecuador, and member of Euro-Mediterranean Observatory on Public Policies and Democratic Quality at the Universidad Rey Juan Carlos (Spain) and visiting Professor at the University of Rosario, Colombia. He holds a Ph.D. in Social Sciences and Law and a Master of two years about Labor Relations. He supervises several doctoral theses (Ph.D.) in Córdoba (Spain) and in the Basque Country (GEZKI Institute) like a director and co-director. It has 81 indexed articles and his latest publications includes topics about social economy Market Economy and Good Living: Obstacles to Its Achievement in Orellana; Importance and Implications of Influential, Powerful, and Remarkable Economic Policy Mix: Pre-Pandemic and Post-Pandemic Challenges in Building Inclusive Global Knowledge Societies or Analysis of Labor Reform During COVID-19: The Case of Ecuador; digitalization (Practicality, support or premeditated calculation in the digital age: the case of Ecuador), Globalization (Analysis of the concept of informal economy through 102 definitions: legality or necessity), corporate social (Ir)responsibility (How corporate social (ir)responsibility in the textile sector is defined, and its impact on ethical sustainability: An analysis of 133 concepts), transnational companies (The transnational textile companies relationship with environment: a Delphi analysis approach) and their relations with ethics (Corruption in the transnational textile industry: an exception or the rule?), social economy and cooperative system like economic alternative (Socially responsible public management: case spinning development in Ecuador), media analysis and social conflicts (Analysis of the indigenous uprising of Ecuador, 2019: between a measured legal response and lawfare, 2019) and sustainability (Public Strategy and Eco-Social Engagement in Latin American States: An Analysis of Complex Networks Arising from Their Constitutions). Arturo Luque, Technical University of Manabí, Portoviejo, (Ecuador) and Euro-Mediterranean Observatory on Public Policies and Democratic Quality, Rey Juan Carlos University (Spain). https://orcid.org/0000-0002-4872-891X.7b207062-c912-4aa7-b74e-e73866e43138

Yash Khattar, currently a sophomore in the Information Communication program at the University School of Information Communication and Technology, has a strong passion for App Development. He has been dedicatedly learning Flutter for app development and has also shown a keen interest in the field of research.

Jayalakshmi M. is currently pursuing MCom degree at Christ University, Bangalore. She is a BCom graduate from Christ University, with a specialization in Accounting and Finance. Her exceptional research skills were recognized at the International Conference on AI in Fintech held in Coimbatore, Tamil Nadu and her paper was awarded the best paper in the conference.

Bartolomé Marco-Lajara is Professor of Business Organization at the University of Alicante (Spain). He holds a PhD in Economics and his doctoral dissertation focused in strategic alliances management. His research interests are on Strategic Management and Tourism Management. He is author of several books, book chapters and international articles related to teaching methodology and the areas above mentioned. On the other hand, he is member of the Tourism Research Institute at the University of Alicante since its foundation. He has participated in many public- and private-funded projects, being the main researcher in many of them. He was assistant dean of the Economics Faculty at the University of Alicante during eight years, holding now the position of Head of the Department of Business Organization at this University.

Javier Martínez Falcó is Assistant Professor in the Department of Management at the University of Alicante. In the field of research, he focuses his interest on issues related to the Strategic Management of the Company, specifically in the areas of Knowledge Management and Corporate Sustainability of wine companies, on which he has written several publications in the form of articles, book chapters and contributions to conferences. He has also participated in several national research projects and teaches Strategic Management on the ADE, TADE and DADE degree courses.

Luis Antonio Millán Tudela is Assistant Professor in the Department of Management at University of Alicante. MBA and Bachelor of Mechanical Engineering, his research focuses on business longevity, and more specifically on the factors that influence the survival of companies. This activity is developed within the research group "Dirección Estratégica, conocimiento e innovación en una economía global (DECI-GLOBAL)". He also teaches strategic management in the Degree of Business Administration.

Nitish Kumar Minz, an exemplary Bachelor of Commerce student specializing in Business Administration and Management at K.R. Mangalam University, has made significant contributions to several research papers and book chapters currently in the final stages of publication. Holding the esteemed position of Secretary of Extension and Outreach Activity in the Student Council of K.R. Mangalam University, Mr. Minz has showcased a remarkable work ethic, unwavering commitment to excellence, and honed skills in project management and strategic planning through his internship at KEIC (KRMU Entrepreneurship & Incubation Center). He has also been chosen as NEP SAARTHI- Student Ambassador for Academic Reforms in Transforming Higher Education at K.R. Mangalam University and recently achieved the Chancellor's Excellence Award.

Mário José Batista Romão is an Associate Professor of Information Systems at ISEG – University of Lisbon. He is Director of the Master's program in Computer Science and Management. He holds a PhD in Management Sciences by ISCTE-IUL and by Computer Integrated Manufacturing at Cranfiel University (UK). He also holds a MsC in Telecommunications and Computer Science, at IST - Instituto Superior Técnico, University of Lisbon. He is Pos-Graduated in Project Management and holds the international certification Project Management Professional (PMP), by PMI – Project Management International. He has a degree in Electronic Engineering from IST.

Girish S. is an Associate Professor at Christ University, where he has been a dedicated member of the faculty since 2009. His impressive academic career is marked by his educational background that includes MCom, MPhil, MBA, and PhD. With a commitment to advancing knowledge, Dr. Girish S has authored 20 journal articles, 2 books, 3 book chapters and contributed to 15 conference proceedings which reflect his expertise in his chosen field. These books are a testament to his commitment to knowledge dissemination and academic excellence. His contributions have undoubtedly had a profound impact on his field and continue to inspire and inform the next generation of academics and researchers.

Eduardo Sánchez García (PhD) is an Assistant Professor in the Department of Management at the University of Alicante (Spain). He specializes in the study of industrial agglomeration, knowledge management, entrepreneurship, and innovation, focusing on the energy sector and the wine industry.. He is co-author of several papers presented at conferences, both national and international, as well as several articles and book chapters related to his field of research.

Index

www.ingramcontent.com/pod-product-compliance
Lightning Source LLC
LaVergne TN
LVHW080340011026
849161LV00009B/2141